a horrible experience of
unbearable length

a horrible experience of unbearable length: more movies that **SUCK**

roger ebert

Andrews McMeel
Publishing, LLC
Kansas City • Sydney • London

Andrews McMeel Publishing, LLC
an Andrews McMeel Universal company
1130 Walnut Street, Kansas City, Missouri 64106

www.andrewsmcmeel.com

12 13 14 15 16 MLY 10 9 8 7 6 5 4 3 2 1

ISBN: 978-1-4494-1025-4

Library of Congress Control Number: 2011932653

All the reviews in this book originally appeared in the *Chicago Sun-Times*.

dedication

● ● ● ● ● ● ● ● ●

This book is dedicated to Peter Sobczynski and his merry band of wise-crackers at the Lake Street Screening Room.

introduction

● ● ● ● ● ● ● ● ●

I received several messages from readers asking me why I felt it was even necessary for me to review *The Human Centipede II (Full Sequence)*. (There was also one telling me it should have been titled *Human Centipede Number Two*, but never mind that one.) My reply was that it was my duty. I feared it would attract large crowds to the box office, and as it turned out I was right. I did what I could to warn people away. Certain colleagues of mine discussed it as a work of art (however "flawed"). I would beg them to think really, really hard of another movie opening the same weekend that might possibly be better for the mental health of their readers.

It was not my duty to review many of the other movies in this book. I review most of the major releases during the year, but I also make it a point to review lots of indie films, documentaries, foreign films, and what we used to call "art movies" and might now call "movies for grown-ups." If I had skipped a few of these titles, I don't believe my job would have been threatened. But I might have enjoyed it less.

After reviewing a truly good movie, the second most fun is viewing a truly bad one. It's the in-between movies that can begin to feel routine. Consider, for example, the truly bad *Transformers: Revenge of the Fallen* (2009), the movie that provided the title for this book. I saw the movie, returned home, sat down at the computer keyboard, and the opening words of my review fairly flew from my fingertips: "*Transformers: Revenge of the Fallen* is a horrible experience of unbearable length, briefly punctuated by three or four amusing moments."

Where did those words come from? They were the simple truth. Gene Siskel always argued that he was a newspaperman first and a film critic second: "I cover the movie beat." What that meant for him is that his first paragraph should be the kind of "lead" they teach you to write in journalism school. Before you get to your opinion about a new movie, you should begin with the news. We could have an interesting discussion about whether the opening of my *TROF* review was news or opinion. To me, it was completely factual. To many readers who posted comments on my blog, it was completely inaccurate. It was opinion, and my opinion was wrong.

Yes, there are people who like the Transformers movies. I sorta liked the first one myself, in 2007. The charm wore off. The third in the series, *Transformers: Dark of the Moon* (2011), was no better. Predictably, some critics were inspired by *TDOM* to analyze the visual style of Michael Bay. Finding success in a Michael Bay film is like finding the Virgin on a slice of toast, but less rewarding.

Sometimes in my negative reviews I have weaknesses. I'm aware of them, and yet I indulge them all the same. Show me a bad movie about zombies or vampires, for example, and I will inevitably go into speculation about the reality that underlies their conditions. A few days ago, I was rewatching Murnau's original *Nosferatu* (1922), and something struck me for the first time. As you may recall, Graf Oriok, a character inspired by Count Dracula, encloses himself in a coffin and ships himself, along with a group of similar coffins, on a freighter bound for Wisborg. He carries with him the plague, which will kill everyone on board.

It struck me that this was an extraordinary leap of faith on his part. Inside the coffin he is presumably in the trancelike state of all vampires. He certainly must anticipate that everyone on board will soon be dead. The ship will be at the mercy of the winds and tides. If by good chance it drifts to Wisborg (which it does), what can the good people of Wisborg be expected to do? Prudently throw the coffins overboard or sink the ship to protect themselves from the black death, I imagine. But if they happen to open his coffin in sunlight, Graf Oriok will be destroyed. Luckily, he releases himself from the coffin at night, sitting bolt upright in a famous scene. But think of the things that could have gone wrong.

That's how my mind works. We are now far away from the topic of Nosferatu. I am also fascinated by how Darwin's theory of evolution applies to zombies. Since Dawkins teaches us that the only concern of a selfish gene is to survive until the next generation of the organism that carries it, what are the prospects of zombie genes, which can presumably be transmitted only by the dead? And how do zombies reproduce, or spread? Oh, I could go on. Why must they eat flesh? Why not a whole-foods diet of fruits, vegetables, and grains? Maybe a little fish?

I know this has nothing to do with film criticism. I am blown along by the winds of my own zeal. If a good vampire or zombie movie comes along, I do my best to play fair with it. With a bad one, I am merciless and irresponsible. That's why I like the bad ones best.

Perhaps my reasoning goes like this: Few people buying the newspaper are likely to require a serious analysis of, for example, James Raynor's *Angry and Moist: An Undead Chronicle* (2004). (This is a zombie movie I haven't seen, so it will work well as an example.) Therefore, it is my task to write a review that will be enjoyable to read, even if the reader has no interest in the film and no plans to ever see it.

I suppose that explains a good many of the reviews in this book. Some of the films herein are only fairly bad. Some are not bad so much as evil and reprehensible. Others, let's face it, have no importance at all other than in inspiring movie reviews. Of all the films in this book, it is for those I am most grateful.

Roger Ebert

A

Alien Trespass

(DIRECTED BY R. W. GOODWIN; STARRING ERIC MCCORMACK, JENNI BAIRD; 2009)

Alien Trespass is a sincere attempt to make a film that looks like one of those 1950s B movies where a monster from outer space terrorized a small town, which was almost always in the desert. Small, to save on extras and travel. In the desert, because if you headed east from Hollywood that's where you were, and if you headed west you were making a pirate picture.

The movie is in color, which in the 1950s was uncommon, but otherwise it's a knowing replication of the look and feel of those pictures, about things with jaws, tentacles, claws, weapons that shot sparks, and eyes that shot laser beams at people, only they weren't known as laser beams but as Deadly Rays. Facing them are plucky locals, dressed in work clothes from Sears, standing behind their open car doors and looking up to watch awkward special effects that are coming—coming!—this way!

The movie doesn't bend over backward to be "bad." It tries to be the best bad movie that it can be. A lot of its deliberate badness involves effects some viewers might not notice. For example: bad back projection in shots looking back from the dashboard at people in the front seat. In the 1950s, before CGI, the car never left the sound stage, and in the rear window they projected footage of what it was allegedly driving past. Since people were presumed not to study the rear window intently, they got away with murder. In *Casablanca*, Rick and Ilsa drove from the Champs-Elysées to the countryside instantly.

The plot: Astronomer Ted Lewis (Eric McCormack) and his sexpot wife, Lana (Jody Thompson), are grilling cow-sized steaks in the backyard when something shoots overhead and crashes in the mountains. The sexpot wife is an accurate touch: The monster genre cast pinups like Mamie Van Doren and Cleo Moore, who were featured on the posters with Deadly Rays shooting down their cleavage.

Ted goes to investigate. When he returns, his body has been usurped by Urp, an alien. Urp means well. He needs help to track down another alien who arrived on the same flying saucer, named the Ghota, which has one eye, enough to qualify it as a BEM, or a Bug-Eyed Monster. The Ghota consumes people in order to grow, divide, and conquer. Sort of like B.O.B. in *Monsters vs. Aliens*, which is *also* a send-up of 1950s BEM movies. So far, Todd Haynes's *Far from Heaven* (2002) is the only movie ever made in tribute to a *great* movie of the 1950s.

The Ghota is battled by Urp and his plucky new buddy Tammy (Jenni Baird), a local waitress who is a lot more game than Lana. As nearly as I can recall, in the 1950s good girls were never named Lana and bad ones were never named Tammy. There are also hapless but earnest local cops (Robert Patrick and Dan Lauria) and an assortment of Threatened Townspeople. Also great shots of the Lewis family home, separated from the desert by a white picket fence, surrounded by the age-old story of the shifting, whispering sands.

Alien Trespass, directed by R. W. Goodwin (*The X Files* on TV) from a screenplay by Steven P. Fisher, is obviously a labor of love. But why? Is there a demand for cheesy 1950s sci-fi movies not met by the existing supply? Will younger audiences consider it to be merely inept, and not inept with an artistic intention? Here is a movie more suited to Comic-Con or the World Science Fiction Convention than to your neighborhood multiplex.

If you must see a science fiction movie about a threat from beyond Earth, there's one right now that I think is great: *Knowing*. If you're looking for a *bad* sci-fi movie about a threat, etc., most of the nation's critics mistakenly believe it qualifies. How can you lose? "From beyond the stars—a mysterious force strikes terror into the hearts of men!"

All About Steve

(DIRECTED BY PHIL TRAILL; STARRING SANDRA BULLOCK, BRADLEY COOPER; 2009)

It is not much fun to laugh at a crazy person. None, I would say. Sandra Bullock plays a character who is bonkers in *All About Steve,* which is billed as a comedy but more resembles a perplexing public display of irrational behavior. Seeing her run around as a basket case makes you appreciate Lucille Ball, who could play a dizzy dame and make you like her. Overacting is risky even in a screwball comedy. Perhaps especially.

Bullock plays Mary Horowitz, a crossword puzzle constructor who knows a vast number of words and how they're spelled, but not much about how they might enlighten her. Because her apartment has to be fumigated, she moves back home with her parents. The headline here is how she earned enough to move out in the first place. I may be mistaken, but I think of crossword puzzle construction as more of a second job for smart people.

Anyway, Mary is fortyish and still single, perhaps in part because she wears extraordinarily clumpy shiny red disco boots everywhere, all the time—even on a 5K charity hike, I can only assume. Her parents arrange a blind date with Steve (Bradley Cooper of *The Hangover*), a television cameraman for a cable news network. The network must not be as big as CNN because there's only evidence of one crew: Steve and his on-air talent Hartman Hughes (Thomas Haden Church).

Mary lays her eyes on Steve and wants to lay everything else. This isn't love at first sight; it's erotomania. On their first date, she gives his tonsils a tongue massage. Soon he's fleeing from sightings of her, and she's in hot pursuit. Her desperation extends to a scene where she runs in her disco boots beside the TV news van, breathlessly small-talking to Steve through the window. If Steve had mercy, he would stop or speed up—anything would be better than playing her along.

The crew is assigned to the site of a big breaking story. A group of small deaf children has fallen into a well. Why deaf? Diversity in casting, I guess. It's not like they have to do anything other than be rescued. Mary pursues them to the accident scene, and in a shot destined to go viral on YouTube, she runs across the field behind Steve, waving wildly, and falls into the hole herself.

You see what I mean. The point comes when we're rolling our eyes right along with Mary. But don't get me wrong. I am fond of Sandra Bullock. I've given her some good reviews, as recently as this summer (*The Proposal*). But how does she choose her material? If she does it herself, she needs an agent. If it's done by an agent, she needs to do it herself. The screenplay by Kim Barker requires her to behave in an essentially disturbing way that began to wear on me. It begins as merely peculiar, moves on to miscalculation, and becomes seriously annoying. One of its most unfortunate elements is seeing Bullock so stranded and helpless in a would-be comic frenzy. An actress should never, ever be asked to run beside a van in red disco boots for more than about half a block, and then only if her child is being kidnapped.

Alvin and the Chipmunks

(DIRECTED BY TIM HILL; STARRING JASON LEE, DAVID CROSS; 2007)

The most astonishing sight in *Alvin and the Chipmunks* is not three singing chipmunks. No, it's a surprise saved for the closing titles, where we see the covers of all the Alvin & C albums and CDs. I lost track after ten. It is inconceivable to me that anyone would want to listen to one whole album of those squeaky little voices, let alone ten. "The Chipmunk Song," maybe, for its fleeting novelty. But "Only You"?

There are, however, Alvin and the Chipmunks fans. Their latest album rates 4.5/5 at the iTunes store, where I sampled their version of "Only You" and the original by the Platters, and immediately downloaded *The Platters' Greatest Hits*. I imagine people even impatiently preorder the Chipmunks, however, which speaks highly for the drawing power of electronically altered voices by interchangeable singers. This film is dedicated to Ross Bagdasarian Sr., "who was crazy enough" to dream them up. I think the wording is about right.

Despite the fact that the film is set in the present, when the real (or "real") Chipmunks already have a back catalog bigger than Kimya Dawson's, the movie tells the story of how they become rock stars and almost get burned out on the rock circuit. Jason Lee stars as Dave Seville, who accidentally brings them home in a basket of muffins, discovers they can talk, and is soon shouting "Alvin!" at the top of his lungs, as Chipmunk lore requires that he must.

David Cross plays Ian, the hustling tour promoter who signs them up and takes them on the road, where they burn out and he suggests they start lip-synching with dubbed voices. Now we're getting into Alice in Wonderland territory, because of course they *are* dubbed voices in the first place. Indeed the metaphysics of dubbing dubbed chipmunks who exist in the real world as animated representations of real chipmunks is . . . how did this sentence begin?

That said, whatever it was, *Alvin and the Chipmunks* is about as good as a movie with these characters can probably be, and I am well aware that I am the wrong audience for this movie. I am even sure some readers will throw it up to me that I liked the Garfield movie better.

Yes, but Garfield didn't sing, and he was dubbed by Bill Murray. My duty as a reporter is to inform you that the chipmunks are sorta cute, that Jason Lee and David Cross manfully play roles that require them, as actors, to relate with empty space that would later be filled with CGI, and that at some level the movie may even be doing something satirical about rock stars and the hype machine.

I was also grateful that Alvin wears a red sweater with a big "A" on it as an aid to identification, since otherwise all the chipmunks seem to be identical, like mutant turtles or Spice Girls. It doesn't much matter which one is Theodore and which one is Simon, although Simon is always the one who seems a day late and a walnut short.

The Answer Man

(DIRECTED BY JOHN HINDMAN; STARRING JEFF DANIELS, LAUREN GRAHAM; 2009)

Anyone writing a book titled *Me & God* has a big idea of himself or a small idea of God. Yet Arlen Faber's best-seller has captured 10 percent of the "God market" and held that position for twenty years. During those two decades his idea of himself has grown smaller. He tries to do his daily meditation, he really tries, but when the doorbell interrupts, he instinctively reacts with a string of fairly impressive swear words, strung together as if he's had practice. Here is a man in deep spiritual doo-doo. One day he throws out his back and is in such pain he must crawl on his hands and knees to the new local chiropractor. She pushes here and probes there and soon he's back on his feet. He was in such pain when he crawled in that he gave his real name, having long been under deep cover and avoiding his fellow man. Elizabeth the doctor (Lauren Graham) has never heard of him, but her receptionist Anne (Olivia Thirlby) certainly has, and this is the start of his gradual recovery as a social being.

Arlen (Jeff Daniels) does an excellent job of portraying a misanthrope with back pain, but not so much as a man on a first-pronoun basis with God. Everything we see of him leads us to suspect that readers whose lives were changed by his book did the heavy lifting themselves. What's amazing is that his book is still read after twenty years and yet no one in the film, no one, repeats a single thing to be learned from it. Inquiring minds need to know: "What did he tell God?"

This is not a movie about spirituality, however, but a romantic comedy, with a clunky subplot involving a book seller (Lou Taylor Pucci) who has just graduated from rehab and needs advice only this shambling, foul-mouthed wreck Arlen can give. Arlen is thus reluctantly hauled into the problems of another human being, while meanwhile gradually becoming involved in the life of Elizabeth and her young son, Alex (Max Antisell).

Early sequences in the film seem inspired by outtakes from a manic Jim Carrey comedy. That's not such a bad thing. Later the movie follows the timeworn pathways of countless romcoms before it. How much more interesting is a film like *500 Days of Summer*, which is about the complexities of life, in comparison with this one, which cheerfully cycles through the clichés?

Now about that God business. It is necessary for me to share one of my favorite journalism stories. It's said that Richard Harding Davis was dispatched by William Randolph Hearst to cover the Johnstown flood. Here was his lead: "God stood on a mountaintop here and looked at what his waters had wrought." Hearst cabled back: "Forget flood. Interview God."

A wonderful story. Checking out the quote online, I found a blog entry by Dennis G. Jerz of Seton Hill University, reporting that I have related this same story four times in print since 1993, sometimes changing it slightly. Good gravy! My only defense for using it once again is that it's more interesting than anything else I could write about *The Answer Man*.

The A-Team

(DIRECTED BY JOE CARNAHAN; STARRING LIAM NEESON, JESSICA BIEL; 2010)

The A-Team is an incomprehensible mess with the 1980s TV show embedded inside. The characters have the same names, they play the same types, they have the same traits, and they're easily as shallow. That was OK for a TV sitcom, which is what the show really was, but at over two hours of queasy-cam anarchy it's punishment.

The movie uses the new style of violent action, which fragments sequences into so many bits and pieces that it's impossible to form any sense of what's happening, or where, or to whom. The actors appear in flash-frames, intercut with shards of CGI and accompanied by loud noises, urgent music, and many explosions. This continues for the required length, and then there's some dialogue. Not a lot. A few words, a sentence, sometimes a statement that crosses the finish line at paragraph length.

The plot: Wrongly framed for counterfeiting, the team members, all Iraq veterans, bust out of various prisons and go after the engraving plates, which would be pretty much worn out while printing enough $100 bills to pay for the millions in property damage they cause in the process.

Bored out of my mind during this spectacle, I found my attention wandering to the subject of physics. *The A-Team* has an action scene that admirably demonstrates Newton's Third Law, which instructs us that for every action there is always an equal and opposite reaction.

The movie illustrates this as the heroes fall from an exploding airplane while inside an armored tank. As the tank hurtles to the ground (cf. Newton's Law of Gravity), the team leader, Hannibal Smith (Liam Neeson), looks out an opening and barks out commands for the tank's gun. I am paraphrasing:

"Turn forty-five degrees to the left! Fire! Twenty-five degrees to the right! Fire!" etc. In this way he is able to direct the fall of the tank and save their lives. This is very funny.

The action scenes also benefit from everyone having had a glance at the choreography beforehand. Consider a scene when a team member is confronted by a Talking Killer. This is, of course, a killer who only has to pull the trigger but pauses to sneer and boast. He and his target are standing in the middle of a jumble of dozens of freight shipping containers that have been spilled onto a dock. He talks just a little too long, and B. A. Baracus ("Rampage" Jackson) comes roaring to the rescue through the air on his motorcycle and wipes him out.

I know there are Harley lovers among my devoted readers. Am I right in assuming that it is difficult to get enough speed for a good aerial jump while biking across a crooked heap of freight containers? I ask because, as I hinted above, no action in this movie necessarily has any relationship to the actions surrounding it.

The characters here have that annoying ability to precisely predict what will happen and coordinate their response to it. An example. A slimy double-dealer is about to kill another team member, never mind who, when suddenly behind him a container is lifted into the air, and behind it are revealed all of the other team members lined up in a row, with choice words and brief phrases to say.

I don't want to be tiresome, but (1) how did they know the two guys were behind precisely that container; (2) how did they line up a crane and hook up the container without being heard or noticed; (3) how were they able to gather the members so quickly after the chaos of the preceding action; and (4) was someone eavesdropping to give the cue at the right moment to lift the container? Ten seconds later, and it might have been too late. Ten seconds earlier, and dialogue would have been stepped on.

Are my objections ridiculous? Why? How is it interesting to watch a movie in which the "action" is essentially colorful abstractions? Isn't it more satisfying if you know where everyone is and what they're doing and how they're doing it in real time? In other words, isn't *The Hurt Locker* more interesting than *The A-Team*?

To give it credit, the movie knows it is childish. The PG-13 is appropriate. There's little actual gore, no sex beyond a chaste kiss, no R-rated language, but—ohmigod—there's smoking! Alert to preteens: Try one of those fat cigars Hannibal smokes and you won't feel like dinner.

Atlas Shrugged: Part 1
(DIRECTED BY PAUL JOHANSSON; STARRING TAYLOR SCHILLING, GRANT BOWLER; 2011)

I feel like my arm is all warmed up and I don't have a game to pitch. I was primed to review *Atlas Shrugged*. I figured it might provide a parable of Ayn Rand's philosophy that I could discuss. For me, that philosophy reduces itself to: "I'm on board; pull up the lifeline." There are, however, people who take Ayn Rand even more seriously than comic book fans take *Watchmen*. I expected to receive learned and sarcastic lectures on the pathetic failings of my review.

And now I am faced with this movie, the most anticlimactic non-event since Geraldo Rivera broke into Al Capone's vault. I suspect only someone very familiar with Rand's 1957 novel could understand the film at all, and I doubt they will be happy with it. For the rest of us, it involves a series of business meetings in luxurious retro leather-and-brass boardrooms and offices, and restaurants and bedrooms that look borrowed from a hotel no doubt known as the Robber Baron Arms.

During these meetings, everybody drinks. More wine is poured and sipped in this film than at a convention of oenophiles. There are conversations in the English language after which I sometimes found myself asking, "What did they just say?" The dialogue seems to have been ripped throbbing with passion from the pages of *Investor's Business Daily*. Much of the excitement centers on the tensile strength of steel.

The story involves Dagny Taggart (Taylor Schilling), a young woman who controls a railroad company named Taggart Transcontinental (its motto: "Ocean to Ocean"). She is a fearless and visionary entrepreneur, who is determined to use a revolutionary new steel to repair her train tracks. Vast forces seem to conspire against her.

It's a few years in the future. America has become a state in which mediocrity is the goal and high-achieving individuals the enemy. Laws have been passed prohibiting companies from owning other companies. Dagny's new steel, which is produced by her sometimes lover Hank Rearden (Grant Bowler), has been legislated against because it's better than other steels. The Union of Railroad Engineers has decided it will not operate Dagny's trains. Just to show you how bad things have become, a government minister announces "a tax will be applied to the state of Colorado in order to equalize our national economy." So you see how governments and unions are the enemies of visionary entrepreneurs.

But you're thinking, railroads? Yes, although airplanes exist in this future, trains are where it's at. When I was six, my Aunt Martha brought me to Chicago to attend the great Railroad Fair of 1948, at which the nation's rail companies celebrated the wonders that were on the way. They didn't quite foresee mass air transportation. *Atlas Shrugged* seems to buy into the fair's glowing vision of the future of trains. Rarely, perhaps never, has television news covered the laying of new railroad track with the breathless urgency of the news channels shown in this movie.

So OK. Let's say you know the novel, you agree with Ayn Rand, you're an objectivist or a Libertarian, and you've been waiting eagerly for this movie. Man, are you going to get a letdown. It's not enough that a movie agree with you, in however an incoherent and murky fashion. It would help if it were, like, you know, entertaining?

The movie is constructed of a few kinds of scenes. (1) People sipping their drinks in clubby surroundings and exchanging dialogue that sounds like assorted corporate lingo; (2) railroads, and lots of 'em; (3) limousines driving through cities in ruin and arriving in front of vast, ornate buildings; (4) city skylines; (5) the beauties of Colorado. There is also a love scene, which is shown not merely from the waist up but from the ears up. The man keeps his shirt on. This may be disappointing for libertarians, who I believe enjoy rumpy-pumpy as much as anyone.

Oh, and there is Wisconsin. Dagny and Hank ride blissfully in Taggart's new high-speed train, and then Hank suggests they take a trip to Wisconsin, where the state's policies caused the suppression of an engine that runs on the ozone in the air, or something (the film's detailed explanation won't clear this up). They decide to drive there. That's when you'll enjoy the beautiful landscape photography of the deserts of Wisconsin. My free advice to the filmmakers: If you want to use a desert, why not just refer to Wisconsin as "New Mexico"?

Atlas Shrugged closes with a title card saying, "End of Part One." Frequently throughout the film, characters repeat the phrase, "Who is John Galt?" Well they might ask. A man in black, always shot in shadow, is apparently John Galt. If you want to get a good look at him and find out why everybody is asking, I hope you can find out in Part Two. I don't think you can hold out for Part Three.

The Back-Up Plan

(DIRECTED BY ALAN POUL; STARRING JENNIFER LOPEZ, ALEX O'LOUGHLIN; 2010)

Some movies are no better than second-rate sitcoms. Other movies are no better than third-rate sitcoms. *The Back-Up Plan* doesn't deserve comparison with sitcoms. It plays like an unendurable TV commercial about beautiful people with great lifestyles and not a thought in their empty little heads. So timid is this film that when it finally arrives at its inevitable childbirth scene, it bails out after two "pushes"!

Jennifer Lopez has never looked better. That's about all she does here, is look better. She is talented and deserves more than this bird-brained plot about characters who have no relationship to life as it is lived by, you know, actual people. The movie deals with artificial insemination, romance, sex, and organic goat cheese, which are promising areas for investigation, but it's so watered down it approaches homeopathy.

Lopez plays Zoe, a Manhattan pet shop owner who despairs of finding the perfect inseminator and decides to become artificially impregnated. Leaving the doctor's office, she is so happy she finds herself singin' in the rain. Then she hails a cab and a strange man pops into the backseat the same moment she does. As a Meet Cute, this ranks right down there with two characters bending over to pick up the same thing and bumping heads, which is what Tony Randall is always doing whenever I think of Meet Cutes.

This stranger is Stan (Alex O'Loughlin). We know, according to the Law of Conservation of Dramatic Resources, that (a) Zoe will become pregnant, and (b) she and Stan will fall in love. Consider the alternatives: (a1) she doesn't become pregnant, and (b2) they never see each other again. Anyway, fate brings them together, and then again, and soon they're falling for each other.

This Stan is a prime catch. Not only does he personally sell organic goat cheese in a ridiculously upscale farmers' market, but he produces it himself, on his own upstate farm. I am at a loss to explain why the movie squandered an opportunity to show Lopez milking a goat. Or having a goat eat her shoes, or whatever goats usually do in movies of this sort.

Obviously, the only way to make this feature-length is for Zoe and Stan to break up and get back together again, which they do, I think, three times. Their breakups tend toward communications difficulties, as one or the other idiotically misunderstands dialogue that is crystal clear to everyone in the audience. In Little Movie Glossary lore this is Damon Knight's famous Idiot Plot, in which all difficulties could be resolved by the uttering of one or two words.

I don't believe *The Back-Up Plan* is intended to be set in the real Manhattan. Take a close look at the farmers' market. It's more of a Farmer's Faire at a church benefit in a rich suburb. Farmer Stan and his goats, indeed. But consider the scene where Zoe is a bridesmaid at a wedding, and her water breaks. What does she do? Rush to the hospital? No, she commandeers the wedding's rented white Bentley and is driven to the market, where the auto shoulders its way right down the middle of the street and halts before the organic goat cheese stall, where Zoe can leap out and make up with Stan right there in public, while onlookers all smile and listen like benevolent insiders, instead of New Yorkers wondering who the hell these jerks are. Does Stan happen to have one of those little boxes with a ring in it handy? What does a goat do in the woods? I have neglected poor little Nuts, Zoe's Boston terrier. Nuts follows her everywhere, and whenever he gets a close-up, he barks appropriately, as if he understands what is said. When was the last time in a movie where somebody said something, and there was a cut to a dog who barked, and you thought, "That's so funny!" Nuts is paralyzed from the waist down and pulls himself everywhere on his little cart, without the benefit of much loving and cooing from his mistress, who relates to him as exactly what he is, a prop. But the little tyke can really wheel around and is always there when he's needed on camera.

This movie is desperately boring. No one says much of anything interesting. They have extremely limited ranges of interest. There are older characters: Zoe's Nana (Linda Lavin) and grandpa (Tom Bosley) and gynecologist (Robert Klein). They seem human, so the camera cuts away lest they get started on something. At the playground where Stan hangs out (allegedly fascinated by the prospect of fatherhood), there's "Playground Dad" (Anthony Anderson), a proud black father who gives Stan pep talks on the joys of parenting. African-Americans are so wise in movies like this, always playing proud dads and wise advisers and God and so forth, it's a wonder the movies are about anyone else.

Bad Teacher

(DIRECTED BY JAKE KASDAN; STARRING CAMERON DIAZ, JUSTIN TIMBERLAKE; 2011)

Jake Kasdan's *Bad Teacher* immediately brings *Bad Santa* to mind, and suffers by the comparison. Its bad teacher is neither bad enough nor likable enough. The transgressions of Elizabeth Halsey (Cameron Diaz) are more or less what you'd expect, but what's surprising is that she's so nasty and unpleasant. Billy Bob Thornton, as the bad Santa, was more outrageously offensive and yet more redeemed by his desperation. He was bad for urgent reasons. Elizabeth seems bad merely as a greedy lifestyle choice.

As the film opens, the Diaz character is engaged to a rich guy she leeches on but doesn't love. She's dumped and has to return to middle school teaching, an occupation she has no talent for or interest in, and passes the time showing DVDs to her students and napping, drinking, and doing drugs at her desk. This creates astonishment and indignation in the charmingly named Amy Squirrel (Lucy Punch), whose classroom is right across the hall.

The school characters also include the backup teacher Scott Delacorte (Justin Timberlake), amiable but juiceless; the veteran teacher Ms. Pavicic (Jillian Armenante), a sweet dumpling; the hunky gym teacher Russell Gettis (Jason Segel); and the dolphin-obsessed Principal Wally Snur (John Michael Higgins).

Of these characters, the rival played by Lucy Punch is the most colorful because she's the most driven and obsessed. The others seem curiously inconsequential, content to materialize in a scene, perform a necessary function, and vaporize. There's no urgency, and that was the one quality *Bad Santa* dripped with.

None of the film's major characters is a student, which seems odd. Yes, there's a kid who writes bad poetry and has a crush on the class sexpot, but his desperation seems well within comic bounds. There are no vindictive students, none with aggressive behavior, no little Omens in training. The casting of the children seems lacking in imagination, but then what does the screenplay give them to do?

Cameron Diaz has proven that she is gifted with comedy. But here her Elizabeth is a mean, antagonistic money-grubber on autopilot. Where did she come from? Why did she get into teaching in the first place? Has she no heart? There are times in *Bad Santa* when we feel sorry for the poor SOB, but nothing in *Bad Teacher* inspires more than distaste for the character.

Other problems: There is no chemistry, or indeed even much mutual awareness, between Diaz and Timberlake. You know those annual Bad Sex Awards for the worst sex scene in a movie? Their dry-humping scene deserves an award for the decade. The scene itself is pathetic. The shot it ends on—the wet spot on Timberlake's blue jeans—had the audience recoiling.

Whole chunks of the plot seem to have gone missing. And how, oh how, can we possibly understand the eventual development between

Elizabeth and Russell the gym teacher? You know what that feels like? It feels like they called Diaz and Jason Segel in for one additional day of shooting to provide a preposterous happy ending. Jolly music keeps elbowing its way onto the sound track in an unconvincing attempt to cue us that we've seen a good comedy.

Baghead

(DIRECTED BY MARK DUPLASS AND JAY DUPLASS; STARRING ROSS PARTRIDGE, STEVE ZISSIS; 2008)

The modestly named "mumblecore" movement in new American indies is not an earthquake like the French New Wave, more of a trembling in the shrubbery. *Baghead*, by the Duplass brothers, Mark and Jay, is an example. Mumblecore movies are very low budget, shot on video, in love with handheld QueasyCam effects, and more often than not shot in the woods, where locations and extras are not a problem. *The Blair Witch Project* was not really a mumblecore movie, according to Peter Debruge, whose *Variety* article was definitive in defining the genre, but it's an early example of a Do It Yourself in the Woods genre that doesn't really cry out for more titles. On the other hand, I am informed by Jim Emerson, editor of rogerebert.com, a mumblecore shot in the woods is a bonus: "Actually, they're more likely to be shot in the filmmakers' apartments."

If you walk out after ten or fifteen minutes, you will have seen the best parts of the film. It opens at an underground film festival, where the director of a $1,000 epic (*We Came Naked*) takes questions after his premiere. Knowledgeable festival veterans will smile at the questions: "What was your budget?" of course, and "Did you use improvisation?" Why the budget is such a matter of concern puzzles me, but the people who ask that obligatory question always nod gratefully for the answer.

Anyway, our heroes attend the screening and attempt to crash the after-party without invitations. Walking past the security guard while carrying on an animated cell phone conversation seems to work, but not when you lack a cell phone and try to fake it with your wallet. At their own after-after-party, the four protagonists decide, the hell with it—they'll make their own movie.

The heroes are Matt (Ross Partridge), leader of the pack; his long-time on-again, off-again girlfriend, Catherine (Elise Muller); his buddy Chad (Steve Zissis); and Chad's date, Michelle (Greta Gerwig), who seems more attracted to Matt than Chad. This generates what can be generously described as sexual tension in the woods, although not by me.

Their location is a cabin eleven miles up a country road (this distance later becomes important). They settle down to write a screenplay about four people in a cabin in the woods (that is, themselves), who are threatened by a guy with a bag over his head. I guess it's a guy. Girls aren't that stupid. During the course of their creativity session, one of them is indeed frightened by a guy with a bag over his head, and it apparently couldn't be one of the other three. This baghead appears again at such perfectly timed moments that he must have a copy of the (unwritten) screenplay.

Here's where I have my problem. How is an uninformed total outsider going to *happen* to be eleven miles out in the woods with a bag over his head, and just *happen* to stumble upon these four people who *happen* to be writing exactly such a story? I weary, yes, I weary. He is obviously simply a device to make the movie long enough to qualify as a feature, and the denouement will be one of stunning underwhelmingness.

The dialogue contains way too many cries of "Matt!" and "Catherine!" and "Chad!" and "Michelle!" and "Matt! Where are you, Matt?" and so forth. There are better movies to be seen. Thousands. Their budget was low. Yes, I think I sensed they used improvisation. The film had its premiere at Sundance 2008, where I assume they were all invited to their after-party. I hope someone slipped in making a cell phone call on his wallet.

Basic Instinct 2

(DIRECTED BY MICHAEL CATON-JONES; STARRING SHARON STONE, DAVID MORRISSEY; 2006)
Basic Instinct 2 resembles its heroine: It gets off by living dangerously. Here is a movie so outrageous and preposterous it is either (a) suicidal or

(b) throbbing with a horrible fascination. I lean toward (b). It's a lot of things, but boring is not one of them. I cannot recommend the movie, but . . . why the hell can't I? Just because it's godawful? What kind of reason is that for staying away from a movie? Godawful and boring, *that* would be a reason.

I have here an e-mail from Adam Burke, a reader who says: "I'm tired of reading your reviews where you give a movie three stars but make sure we know it isn't a great movie. You always seem to want to cover your ass, making sure we know you're smarter than the movie." He has a point. Of course, I am smarter than most movies, but so are you. That doesn't always prevent us from enjoying them. What Burke doesn't mention is my other maddening tendency, which is to give a movie 1½ stars and then hint that it's really better than that.

Which brings us full circle to *Basic Instinct 2*. It has an audacious plot, which depends on (a) a psychopathic serial killer being able to manipulate everyone in her life, or (b) a woman who uncannily seems to be a psychopathic serial killer, while there is (c) an alternative explanation for everything. True, (a), (b), and (c) are equally impossible, but they're the only possibilities, I think. That leaves us feeling screwed at the end, which is how everyone in the film feels, so we cross the finish line together.

So much for the plot. Now for Sharon Stone. She may get some of the worst reviews in years, but she delivers the goods. Playing Catherine Tramell, a trashy novelist who toys with life, death, and sex while doing "research" for her next best-seller, Stone brings a hypnotic fascination to her performance. You don't believe it, but you can't tear your eyes away. She talks dirty better than anyone in the movies. She can spend hours working her way through "every position in Masters and Johnson," she sighs wistfully, and forget all about it in a week, "but I'd remember it if a man died while having sex with me."

She says this, and lots of other things, to a shrink named Dr. Michael Glass (David Morrissey). He's appointed by the courts to evaluate her sanity after the car she is driving goes off a bridge at 110 mph and her passenger, a soccer star, drowns. In court we learn she has a "risk addiction" so severe that "the only limit for her would be her own death."

They say that with any addiction you have to hit bottom. Death may be taking it too far.

Back on the street after unlikely legal technicalities, she comes salivating after Dr. Glass, who insanely accepts her as a client. Also involved in the tangled web are his ex-wife (Indira Varma); a gossip writer (Hugh Dancy) the ex-wife is currently bonking; a Freudian in a fright wig (Heathcote Williams); a fellow shrink (Charlotte Rampling) who warns Glass he is playing with fire; and a cop (David Thewlis) who sniffs around the case like a dog convinced that if liverwurst is not in the room at this moment, it was here not very long ago.

Some of these people die unpleasantly during the course of the film, possibly giving Tramell something to remember. Some of them are suspected of the murders. The details are not very important. What matters are the long scenes of dialogue in which Tramell mind-whacks Dr. Glass with speculations so detailed they rival the limerick about who did what, and with which, and to whom.

The Catherine Tramell role cannot be played well, but Sharon Stone can play it badly better than any other actress alive. The director, Michael Caton-Jones, alternates smoldering close-ups with towering dominatrix poses, and there's an extended Jacuzzi sequence in which we get the much-advertised full frontal nudity—which does not, somehow, manage to be full, frontal, and nude all at the same time. First a little nude, then a little full, then a little frontal, driving us crazy trying to load her simultaneously onto our hard drive.

Dr. Glass is played by Morrissey as a subdued, repressed basket case who listens to Tramell with a stony expression on his face. This is because he is either (a) suppressing his desire to ravage her in lustful abandon, or (b) suppressing delirious laughter. I'll bet there are outtakes of Stone and Morrissey cracking up. How else to respond to dialogue such as, "Don't take it so hard—even Oedipus didn't see his mother coming."

Basic Instinct 2 is not good in any rational or defensible way, but not bad in irrational and indefensible ways. I savored the icy abstraction of the modern architecture, which made the people look like they came with the building. I grinned at that absurd phallic skyscraper that really does exist in London. I liked the recklessness of the sex-and-speed sequence that opens the movie (and, curiously, looks to have been shot in Chicago). I could appreciate the plot once I accepted that it was simply jerking my chain. You can wallow in it.

Speaking of wallowing in the plot, I am reminded of another of today's e-mails, from Coralyn Sheridan, who tells me that in Parma they say, "The music of Verdi is like a pig: Nothing goes to waste." Those Parmesans.

Of Sharon Stone, what can I say except that there is within most men a private place that responds to an aggressive sexual challenge, especially when it's delivered like a lurid torch song, and Stone plays those notes like she worked out her own fingering.

Note No. 1: The last shot in the film is wrong. It should show only the eyes.

Note No. 2: My 1½ star rating is like a cold shower, designed to take my mind away from giving it four stars. I expect to hear from Adam Burke about this.

Battle: Los Angeles

(DIRECTED BY JONATHAN LIEBESMAN; STARRING AARON ECKHART, MICHELLE RODRIGUEZ; 2011)

Battle: Los Angeles is noisy, violent, ugly, and stupid. Its manufacture is a reflection of appalling cynicism on the part of its makers, who don't even try to make it more than senseless chaos. Here's a science-fiction film that's an insult to the words "science" and "fiction," and the hyphen in between them.

Meteors fall to Earth near the coasts of the world's major cities (and in Ireland's Dingle Bay—that meteor must have strayed off course). They contain alien troops, which march up from the beach with their weapons of war and attack mankind. No reason is given for this, although it's mentioned they may want our water. We meet the members of a U.S. Marine platoon and its battle-scarred staff sergeant. They're helicoptered into Santa Monica and apparently defeat the aliens. Since all of Los Angeles is frequently seen in flames, it's not entirely clear how the Santa Monica action is crucial, but apparently it is.

The aliens are hilarious. Do they give Razzies for special effects? They seem to be animal/machine hybrids with automatic weapons growing from their arms, which must make it hard to change the baby. As the marines use their combat knives to carve into an alien, they find one layer after another of icky, gelatinous, pus-filled goo. Luckily, the other aliens are mostly seen in long shot, where they look like stick figures whipped up by apprentice animators.

Aaron Eckhart stars as Staff Sergeant Nantz, a twenty-year veteran who has something shady in his record that people keep referring to, although the screenwriter, Christopher Bertolini, is too cagey to come right out and describe it. Never mind. Eckhart is perfectly cast, and let the word go forth that he makes one hell of a great-looking action hero. He is also a fine actor, but acting skills are not required from anyone in this movie.

The dialogue consists almost entirely of terse screams: "Watch it! Incoming! Move! Look out! Fire! Move!" The only characters I remember having four sentences in a row are the anchors on cable news. Although the platoon includes the usual buffet of ethnicities, including Hispanics, Asians, and a Nigerian surgeon, none of them get much more than a word or two in a row, so as characters they're all placeholders.

You gotta see the alien battleships in this movie. They seem to have been assembled by the proverbial tornado blowing through a junkyard. They're aggressively ugly and cluttered, the product of a planet where design has not been discovered and even the Coke bottles must look like pin cushions. Although these ships presumably arrived inside the meteors, one in particular exhibits uncanny versatility, by rising up from the earth before the very eyes of the startled marines. How, you may ask, did it burrow for ten or twelve blocks under Santa Monica to the battle lines at Lincoln Boulevard? And well you may ask.

There is a lazy editing style in action movies these days that assumes nothing need make any sense visually. In a good movie, we understand where the heroes are and where their opponents are and why, and when they fire on one another we understand the geometry. In a mess like this, the frame is filled with flashes and explosion and shots so brief that nothing makes sense. From time to time there'll be a close-up of Aaron Eckhart screaming something, for example, and on either side of that shot there will be unrelated shots of incomprehensible action. When I think of the elegant construction of something like *Gunfight at the OK Corral*, I want to rend the hair from my head and weep bitter tears of despair. Generations of filmmakers devoted their lives to perfecting techniques that a director like Jonathan Liebesman is either ignorant of or indifferent to. Yet he is given millions of dollars to produce this assault on the attention span of a generation.

Young men: If you attend this crap with friends who admire it, tactfully inform them they are idiots. Young women: If your date likes this movie, tell him you've been thinking it over and you think you should consider spending some time apart.

Bee Movie

(DIRECTED BY STEVE HICKNER AND SIMON J. SMITH; STARRING JERRY SEINFELD, RENEE ZELLWEGER; 2007)

From each according to his ability, to each according to his need.

—Karl Marx

Applied with strict rigor, that's how bee society works in Jerry Seinfeld's *Bee Movie*, and apparently in real life. Doesn't seem like much fun. You are born, grow a little, attend school for three days, and then go to work for the rest of your life. "Are you going to work us to death?" a young bee asks during a briefing. "We certainly hope so!" says the smiling lecturer to appreciative chuckles all around.

One bee, however, is not so thrilled with the system. His name is Barry B. Benson, and he is voiced by Seinfeld as a rebel who wants to experience the world before settling down to a lifetime job as, for example, a crud remover. He sneaks into a formation of ace pollinators, flies out of the hive, has a dizzying flight through Central Park, and ends up (never mind how) making a friend of a human named Vanessa (voice by Renee

Zellweger). Then their relationship blossoms into something more, although not very much more, given the physical differences. Compared to them, a Chihuahua and a Great Dane would have it easy. This friendship is against all the rules. Bees are forbidden to speak to humans. And humans tend to swat bees (there's a good laugh when Barry explains how a friend was offed by a rolled-up copy of *French Vogue*). What Barry mostly discovers from human society is *gasp!* that humans rob the bees of all their honey and eat it. He and his best pal, Adam (Matthew Broderick), even visit a bee farm, which looks like forced labor of the worst sort. Their instant analysis of the human-bee economic relationship is pure Marxism, if only they knew it.

Barry and Adam end up bringing a lawsuit against the human race for its exploitation of all bees everywhere, and this court case (with a judge voiced by Oprah Winfrey) is enlivened by the rotund, syrupy-voiced Layton T. Montgomery (John Goodman), attorney for the human race, who talks like a cross between Fred Thompson and Foghorn Leghorn. If the bees win their case, Montgomery jokes, he'd have to negotiate with silkworms for the stuff that holds up his britches.

All of this material, written by Seinfeld and writers associated with his TV show, tries hard, but never really takes off. We learn at the outset of the movie that bees theoretically cannot fly. Unfortunately, in the movie, that applies only to the screenplay. It is really, really, really hard to care much about a platonic romantic relationship between Renee Zellweger and a bee, although if anyone could pull if off, she could. Barry and Adam come across as earnest, articulate young bees who pursue logic into the realm of the bizarre, as sometimes happened on *Seinfeld*. Most of the humor is verbal and tends toward the gently ironic rather than the hilarious. Chris Rock scores best, as a mosquito named Mooseblood, but his biggest laugh comes from a recycled lawyer joke.

In the tradition of many recent animated films, several famous people turn up playing themselves, including Sting (how did he earn that name?) and Ray Liotta, who is called as a witness because his brand of Ray Liotta Honey profiteers from the labors of bees. Liotta's character and voice work are actually kind of inspired, leaving me to regret the absence of

B. B. King, Burt's Bees, Johnny B. Goode, and the evil Canadian bee slave-master Norman Jewison, who—oh, I forgot, he exploits maple trees.

The Big Uneasy

(DIRECTED BY HARRY SHEARER; STARRING HARRY SHEARER, MARIA GARZINO; 2011)
What Hurricane Katrina did to New Orleans was not an act of God, a "natural disaster," or a failure by FEMA. It was the almost inevitable result of years of incompetent and dangerous work by the Army Corps of Engineers, which then used its power to cover its ass. That is the message, much repeated, in Harry Shearer's documentary *The Big Uneasy*.

Using soil and flood-control experts, Google maps, new footage, and damning video, Shearer builds a compelling case against the corps's flawed planning and leaky levees. I was convinced. Unfortunately, I was also convinced that trapped within this ninety-eight-minute film is a good thirty-minute news report struggling to get out. Shearer, who is a bright and funny man, comes across here as a solemn lecturer.

His facts are depressing. The Army Corps constructed levees on sand that was water permeable and unable to hold concrete walls in place under the pressure of flood waters. He shows large sections of levees not "breeched," as we were told, but actually pushed aside by the flooding. He documents—with the aid of a corpswoman whose whistle-blowing was disregarded at the time—that pumps installed to handle flood waters were inadequate and malfunctioning. He shows that the lovely city was set up for destruction, and that with wiser planning it might have suffered no worse than "wet ankles." Incredibly, we learn that one of the contractors whose company was constructing the levees even went into court to argue the corps's plans were flawed—and lost.

His view of the army engineers is thoroughly depressing. Far from welcoming advice and analysis from academic experts, they installed barbed-wire fences to block their access to crucial areas. They spent more than $1 million on a public relations campaign to repair their image. They were responsible directly or indirectly for the firing, demotion, or silencing of many of their critics. They stand indicted—and, Shearer says, their similar mistakes may mean the city of Sacramento is vulnerable to flood damage on a similar scale. This is important and needs to be made known. Unfortunately, Shearer as a documentarian is not the right man for the job. *The Big Uneasy* lacks the dramatic impact and artistic imagination of many recent docs about environmental issues. An attempt to liven things up by shoehorning John Goodman into the action fails, when he appears out of any context to introduce awkward segments in which Shearer and other New Orleans residents answer criticisms of their city. *The Big Uneasy* plays way too much like an educational film.

Blindness

(DIRECTED BY FERNANDO MEIRELLES; STARRING JULIANNE MOORE, MARK RUFFALO; 2008)

Blindness is one of the most unpleasant, not to say unendurable, films I've ever seen. It is a metaphor about a group of people who survive under great stress, but frankly, I would rather have seen them perish than sit through the final three-quarters of the film. Not only is it despairing and sickening, it's ugly. Denatured, sometimes overexposed, sometimes too shadowy to see, it is an experiment to determine how much you can fool with a print before ending up with mud, intercut with brightly lit milk.

In an unspecified city (Toronto, mostly), an unspecified cause spreads blindness through the population. First a driver goes blind at a traffic light. Then his eye doctor goes blind. And so on, until just about the entire population is blind, except for the doctor's wife. Three wards in a prison are filled with people who are quarantined; armed guards watch them. Then I guess the guards go blind. I am reminded of my Latin teacher, Mrs. Link, making us memorize a phrase every day: *Pone seram, prohibe. Sed quis custodiet ipsos custodes?* *

Many of the imprisoned survivors soon descend into desperation and hunger. The big problem is with Ward Three and its savage leader

(Gael Garcia Bernal). Finding a gun, he confiscates all the food and sells it to Ward One in return for jewelry and sexual favors. Oddly enough, I don't recall Ward Two, unless Ward Three was Ward Two and I missed Ward Three, and who cares?

Oh, what an ordeal. Clothes falling off. Nude in the cold. People fighting, dying, and raping. Blundering around and tripping over things. Hitting their heads. Being struck by pipes they don't see coming, swung by people who don't know what they're swinging at. In the midst of the hellhole is the doctor's wife (Julianne Moore), who doesn't know why she can still see, but loyally stays with her husband.

Is she a symbol of a person with sight leading the blind against the evildoers? Ouch, I stumbled! Who put that there? Maybe that's what she is. In a film that doesn't even try to explain the blindness (not that it could), there's room for nothing but symbols and metaphors and the well-diversified group we identify with, which includes an Asian couple (Yusuke Iseya and Yoshino Kimura), the doctor and his wife (Mark Ruffalo and Moore), a wise old black man (Danny Glover), a single woman (Alice Braga), a boy (Mitchell Nye), and a dog (uncredited).

And the noise. Lordy! This is a sound track so aggressive I was cringing in my seat. No merciful slumber during this film. Metal clangs, glass shatters, bullets are fired, people scream, and the volume of these sounds seems cranked up compared to the surrounding dialogue, like they do with TV commercials. My eyes, ears, and patience were assaulted. My hands and feet, OK.

What a pedigree this film has. Directed by Fernando Meirelles. Based on the novel by Portugal's Jose Saramago, winner of the 1998 Nobel Prize. I learn he long resisted offers to make his book into a movie. Not long enough. It is my good fortune to be attending a screening tonight of the newly restored print of *The Godfather.* I'm looking forward to the peace and quiet.

Lock her up; put away the key. But who will guard the guards?

—Juvenal

Mrs. Link told me that someday, and that day may never come, I'd call upon that phrase to do a service for me.

The Boondock Saints II: All Saints Day

(DIRECTED BY TROY DUFFY; STARRING SEAN PATRICK FLANERY, NORMAN REEDUS; 2009) *The Boondock Saints II: All Saints Day* is an idiotic ode to macho horseshite (to employ an ancient Irish word). It is, however, distinguished by superb cinematography. It's the first film in ten years from Troy Duffy, whose original *Boondock Saints* (1999) has become a cult fetish. It's such a legendary cult film, a documentary was even released about it.

No, not one of those "the making of" jobs. One made by two of Duffy's former pals who got pissed off during the filming. They show him as a possibly alcoholic egomaniac. You know you're in trouble when your movie scores 16 percent on the Tomatometer, and the documentary about it scores 79 percent.

To quote from my review of the 2004 doc: "*Overnight* tells a riches-to-rags story, like *Project Greenlight* played in reverse. *Greenlight,* you will recall, is the Miramax contest to choose and produce one screenplay every year by a hopeful first-time filmmaker. In *Overnight,* the director starts out with a contract and money from Miramax, and works his way back to no contract, no film, and no money. Call it *Project Red Light.*"

The documentary validates Gene Siskel's favorite verdict on a film: "I'd rather see a documentary of the same people having lunch." In this case, you see the same people getting drunk. After Duffy signs with the William Morris Agency, he brags to his pals, "I get drunk at night, wake up the next morning hungover, go into those meetings in my overalls, and they're all wearing suits." Being Hollywood agents, they were probably more familiar with the danger signals of alcoholism than Duffy was.

The Boondock Saints cost $7 million and grossed $25,000 in two weeks in five theaters. Then a miracle occurred. It became a big hit on DVD—so big, this sequel was justified. It's a well-photographed picture with extensive special effects and good actors (Sean Patrick Flanery, Norman Reedus, Billy Connolly, Clifton Collins Jr., Julie Benz, Judd Nelson, and an unrecognizable Peter Fonda).

Flanery and Reedus are back from the original, as Connor and Murphy MacManus, two Irish Catholic brothers who executed countless Boston villains with bullets through the head and pennies on their eyes. Brothers?

To me they look like twins. They now lead a quiet life in Ireland, herding sheep and smoking. Brokeback bachelors. After ten years, still unmarried, they live at home with old Poppy MacManus (Billy Connolly) in a cottage perhaps once inhabited by Ryan's Daughter's great-grandmother. Word comes that a beloved Irish-American priest has been executed back in Boston, with pennies on his eyes. This calls for revenge: Someone is imitating their style! Electrified, the lads rush back to the States on a freight ship and go into action killing, oh, I'd say, hundreds of people, easily. This is done very well, in the way of stunts, f/x, and heavy metal cranked up to twelve.

The lads borrow a page from their old Poppy and don leather vests with built-in holsters for either four or six handguns, I forget. These they typically use while leaping in slo-mo off concealed trampolines while firing two guns each at the camera. If they always jump side by side, does that make it harder for their enemies to miss at least one? Can you fly forward through the air while firing two heavy-duty handguns without your arms jerking back and smacking you in the chin? Would that violate one of Newton's laws? Just askin'.

There's a lot of pious Roman Catholic iconography in the movie, although no one except the beloved executed priest ever goes into a church for purposes other than being murdered. The lads are loyal to the church in the same way fans are loyal to Da Bears. They aren't players themselves, but it's their team and don't mess with it. They do hold a quasi-religious ceremony, however, standing in a circle with a pal and vowing to never, ever stop smoking or drinking or attend an AA meeting. Drinking doesn't bother them anyway. They chug Irish whiskey like Gatorade. The only thing that bothers them, and they're super sensitive about this, is the slightest suggestion that they're gay.

The Bounty Hunter

(DIRECTED BY ANDY TENNANT; STARRING JENNIFER ANISTON, GERARD BUTLER; 2010)
I'm on the brink of declaring a new entry for Ebert's Little Movie Glossary: No comedy not titled *Caddyshack* has ever created a funny joke involving a

golf cart. The only thing preventing me is that I can't remember if *Caddyshack* had golf cart jokes. In any event, if there is a golf cart, it will sooner or later drive into a water hazard. The funny angle here is that the filmmakers went to all that trouble because they trusted the audience to laugh.

I stared with glazed eyes at *The Bounty Hunter.* Here is a film with no need to exist. Among its sins is the misuse of Jennifer Aniston, who can be and has been very funny, but not in dreck like this. Lacking any degree of character development, it handcuffs her to a plot of exhausted action comedy clichés—and also to a car door and a bed.

The handcuffer is her former husband, Milo (Gerard Butler), a former cop who is now a bounty hunter and draws the assignment of tracking down his ex-wife, who has skipped bail. Have I lost touch here, or are bounty hunters routinely deployed to track down criminals accused of no more than a nonfatal traffic violation? Never mind.

Let's do a little mental exercise here, the same sort that the screenplay writer, Sarah Thorp, must have done. Remember the ground rules: The movie must contain only clichés. I used to test this exercise on my film class. I'd give them the genre, and begin sentences ending with an ellipsis. They'd compete to be first to shout out the answer.

1. The story involves a formerly married couple. He is a bounty hunter tracking her down for . . .
2. They dislike one another. Therefore by the end of the movie . . .
3. He drives a . . .
4. Because . . .
5. And his beloved . . .
6. He loves to gamble. Their road trip takes them to . . .
7. Where he . . .
8. And gets into trouble with . . .
9. Inspiring . . .
10. In a golf cart, they . . .
11. During the movie, he gets kicked . . .
12. She wears clothes so we can . . .

Well, I already gave you number ten. To the others, clever students would answer: (1) a nonserious crime, since this is a comedy; (2) they will fall back in love; (3) vintage convertible; (4) movies like them because older cars look like real cars, and with a convertible you can more easily light the characters and show the landscape at the same time; (5) gets damaged; (6) you can be excused for guessing Las Vegas, but it's Atlantic City; (7) wins big or loses big, but either way . . . ; (8) gangsters; (9) chase scenes, CGI sequences, impossible action, and lots of shots of her running in high heels; (10) you know; (11) in the crotch; (12) peek down her neckline.

Why, oh why, was this movie necessary? Could it have been redeemed by witty dialogue? Perhaps, but neither character is allowed to speak more than efficient sentences serving to further the plot. Hollywood movies started to simplify the dialogue when half the gross started to roll in from overseas. Has anyone noticed the great majority of nations dub foreign movies, so that subtitles aren't a problem?

Gerard Butler is a handsome hunk who can also act; he's currently starring in Ralph Fiennes's *Coriolanus*. Jennifer Aniston is a gifted comedienne. If you could pay their salaries, wouldn't you try to put them in a better movie than this? I saw the poster and had a sinking feeling the title gave away the whole story.

Bride Wars

(DIRECTED BY GARY WINICK; STARRING KATE HUDSON, ANNE HATHAWAY; 2009)

Is there anyone old enough to care about weddings and naive enough to believe *Bride Wars*? Here is a sitcom about consumerism, centering on two bubble-brained women and their vacuous fiancés, and providing them with not a single line that is smart or witty. The dialogue is fiercely on-topic, dictated by the needs of the plot, pounding down the home stretch in clichés, obligatory truisms, and shrieks.

Kate Hudson and Anne Hathaway, who play the would-be brides, are good actors and quick-witted women, here playing characters at a level of intelligence approximating HAL 9000 after he has had his chips pulled. No one can be this superficial and survive without professional care. Compare this film with the wonderful *Rachel Getting Married,* for which

Hathaway won an Oscar nomination as Rachel's sister, and now see how she plays a prenuptial Stepford Wife.

I am sure there are women who will enjoy *Bride Wars,* as a man might enjoy a film about cars and Hooters girls. It's like a moving, talking version of *Brides* magazine. Hudson and Hathaway play Liv and Emma, girlhood friends who made a vow to realize their dreams of both getting married at the Plaza. They're serious. They've been saving up the money for their big days for more than ten years. No daddies are around to fork over.

Liv is a lawyer and has perhaps made some money. Emma, without parents, is a schoolteacher. They both go to the most famous wedding planner in Manhattan (Candice Bergen) and, with *three months' notice,* are able to nail down dates at the Plaza for a June wedding. This is before Madoff forced the wholesale cancellation of reservations.

Do you have any idea what such weddings would cost, after flowers and table decorations, invitations, gowns, limos, a reception, dinner, music, the sweets table, the planner, the event room at the Plaza, and rooms for the wedding parties to get dressed? Plus tips? For enough room to get the bride and her bridesmaids whipped into shape, I think you could all squeeze into an Edwardian Park suite, 1,000 square feet with a king-size bed, which next June 7 will go for $2,195. Family of the bride? Impecunious out-of-town relatives? Groom and his best men? Have them wait in the hallway.

At least there will be no expenses for a honeymoon, since neither couple ever discusses one. The movie is about the brides and their weddings, and that's that. The grooms are, in fact, remarkably inconsequential, spending a lot of time sitting on couches and watching their brides act out romantic and revenge fantasies. That's because after both weddings are scheduled for the same time, Emma and Liv forget their lifelong bonds of friendship, start feuding, and play practical jokes involving a deep orange suntan, blue-dyed hair, and a projected video from their bachelorette party. They end up in a cat fight in the aisle. Fortunately neither one thinks of introducing E. coli into the punch bowl.

Women and men have different visions of wedding ceremonies. This I know from *Father of the Bride* (1991), with Steve Martin and Diane Keaton as the parents. Martin envisions the swell ceremony he will provide for his daughter: lots of balloons in the backyard and him manning the barbecue grill. Keaton gently corrects him. Even at the time I reviewed the movie, there was a newspaper story about a father who offered his daughter the choice of a nice ceremony or a condo.

Bride Wars is pretty thin soup. The characters have no depth or personality, no quirks or complications, no conversation. The story twist is so obvious from the first shot of two characters talking that they might have well been waving handkerchiefs over their heads and signaling: "Watch this space for further developments." The whole story is narrated by Candice Bergen as the wedding coordinator, who might as well have been instructing us how to carve bars of Ivory Soap into little ducks.

The Bucket List

(DIRECTED BY ROB REINER; STARRING JACK NICHOLSON, MORGAN FREEMAN; 2008)

The Bucket List is a movie about two old codgers who are nothing like people, both suffering from cancer that is nothing like cancer, and setting off on adventures that are nothing like possible. I urgently advise hospitals: Do not make the DVD available to your patients; there may be an outbreak of bedpans thrown at TV screens.

The film opens with yet another voice-over narration by Morgan Freeman, extolling the saintly virtues of a white person who deserves our reverence. His voice takes on a sort of wonderment as he speaks of the man's greatness; it was a note that worked in *The Shawshank Redemption* and *Million Dollar Baby,* but not here, not when he is talking of a character played by Jack Nicholson, for whom lovability is not a strong suit.

Nicholson plays Edward, an enormously rich man of about seventy, who has been diagnosed with cancer, given a year to live, and is sharing a room with Carter (Freeman), about the same age, same prognosis. Why does a billionaire not have a private room? Why, because Edward owns the hospital, and he has a policy that all patients must double up, so it would look bad if he didn't.

This is only one among countless details the movie gets wrong.

Doesn't Edward know that hospitals make lotsa profits by offering private rooms, "concierge service," etc.? The fact is, Edward and Carter must be roommates to set up their Meet Cute, during which they first rub each other the wrong way, and then have an orgy of male bonding. Turns out Carter has a "bucket list" of things he should do before he kicks the bucket. Edward embraces this idea, announces, "Hell, all I have is money," and treats Carter to an around-the-world trip in his private airplane, during which they will, let's see, I have the itinerary right here, visit the pyramids, the Taj Mahal, Hong Kong, the French Riviera, and the Himalayas.

Carter is faithfully married to his loving wife, Virginia (Beverly Todd), who is remarkably restrained about seeing her dying husband off on this madcap folly. She doesn't take it well, but I know wives who would call for the boys with butterfly nets. Edward, after four divorces, has no restraints, plenty of regrets, and uses his generosity to mask egotism, selfishness, and the imposition of his goofy whim on poor Carter. That his behavior is seen as somehow redemptive is perhaps the movie's weirdest fantasy. Meanwhile, the codgers have pseudo-profound conversations about the Meaning of It All, and Carter's superior humanity begins to soak in for the irascible Edward.

The movie, directed by Rob Reiner, is written by Justin Zackham, who must be very optimistic indeed if he doesn't know that there is nothing like a serious illness to bring you to the end of sitcom clichés. I've never had chemo, as Edward and Carter must endure, but I have had cancer, and believe me, during convalescence after surgery the *last* item on your bucket list is climbing a Himalaya. It's more likely to be topped by keeping down a full meal, having a triumphant bowel movement, keeping your energy up in the afternoon, letting your loved ones know you love them, and convincing the doc your reports of pain are real and not merely disguising your desire to become a drug addict. To be sure, the movie includes plenty of details about discomfort in the toilet, but they're put on hold once the trots are replaced by the globe-trotting.

Edward and Carter fly off on their odyssey, during which the only realistic detail is the interior of Edward's private jet. Other locations are created, all too obviously, by special effects; the boys in front of the pyramids look about as convincing as Abbot and Costello wearing pith helmets in front of a painted backdrop. Meanwhile, we wait patiently for Edward to realize his inner humanity, reach out to his estranged daughter, and learn all the other life lessons Carter has to bestow. All Carter gets out of it is months away from his beloved family, and the opportunity to be a moral cheering section for Edward's conversion.

I'm thinking, just once, couldn't a movie open with the voice-over telling us what a great guy the Morgan Freeman character was? Nicholson could say, "I was a rich, unpleasant, selfish jerk, and this wise, nice man taught me to feel hope and love." Yeah, that would be nice. Because what's so great about Edward, anyway? He throws his money around like a pig and makes Carter come along for the ride. So what?

There are movies that find humor, albeit perhaps of a bitter, sardonic nature, in cancer. Some of them show incredible bravery, as in Mike Nichols's *Wit*, with its great performance by Emma Thompson. *The Bucket List* thinks dying of cancer is a laff riot, followed by a dime-store epiphany. The sole redeeming merit of the film is the steady work by Morgan Freeman, who has appeared in more than one embarrassing movie but never embarrassed himself. Maybe it's not Jack Nicholson's fault that his role cries out to be overplayed, but it's his fate, and ours.

Burlesque

(DIRECTED BY STEVEN ANTIN; STARRING CHER, CHRISTINA AGUILERA; 2010)

The burlesque shows in *Burlesque* feature no nudity, no striptease, no baggy-pants comedians, and no performers with names like Porsche Galore. Other than that, the shows are identical to the offerings at the Rialto and Follies burlesque houses that flourished on South State Street when I first visited Chicago as a sin-seeking teenager.

This is burlesque if it died and went to heaven. Behind a tawdry side entrance on Sunset Strip, a club exists that would make a Vegas casino proud. It has the eerie expanding and contracting dimensions of fantasy. At first, the stage is the right size for an intimate cabaret; later, there's enough space to present a production number with dozens of (unaccounted for) dancers descending a staircase worthy of Busby Berkeley. The audience is all shadowy extras, whose friends will have to look real hard to spot them. The Burlesque Lounge attracts the attention of Ali (Christina Aguilera), the proverbial small-town girl just off the bus from Iowa. She walks in just in time to see Tess (Cher) conveniently performing the number "Welcome to Burlesque." In this scene and throughout the movie, Cher looks exactly as she always does. Other people age. Cher has become a logo.

The movie has a limited cast of broadly drawn characters, used to separate song and dance numbers. Tess co-owns the club with her ex-husband, Vince (Peter Gallagher). As a couple, they inspire games of What Is Wrong with This Picture? His function is to eagerly hope they can sell out to Marcus (Eric Dane), the real-estate developer who wants to tear down the club and put up condos. The club bartender is Jack (Cam Gigandet), who wears eyeliner but turns out to be straight. He allows Ali to crash on his sofa, but there's no sex because he has a fiancée in New York and also because the film has a PG-13 rating. The stage manager is Sean (Stanley Tucci). He's gay, except for one unforgettable night with Tess in Reno. Or Lake Tahoe. She forgets.

The star dancer is Nikki (Kristen Bell), who grows instantly angry with Ali after the farm girl tells her she looks like a drag queen. They must not see many drag queens in Iowa. There is also the nice girl named Georgia (Julianne Hough), who . . . well, a plot like this only leaves one thing for her, doesn't it?

Sorry, I got distracted again, thinking of the condo tower Marcus wants to build. How big a footprint will it need? We get repeated shots of the exterior of the lounge, which consists of an arch of lightbulbs next to what looks like the side of a modest frame building with outside steps to a second floor that doesn't seem to exist inside.

On the landing of those steps on that first night, Ali sees a black girl standing, who smiles nicely to her. We see this same girl repeatedly during the film, but she never gets a name or any dialogue. She has the role of the Black Girl Who Is Seen but Not Heard as a Member of the Club Family. She shouldn't complain. No other dancer gets to be anything at all.

In the film, both Cher and Christina Aguilera are showcased in big song numbers, which I enjoyed on a music video level. Aguilera has an unforced charm in her early scenes, but as she morphs into a glamorous star, she becomes increasingly less interesting. We learn she is an orphan. That simplifies the backstory.

You know how in Bollywood musicals the star actress will be all by her lonely self on a mountaintop, and when she starts to sing and dance, a dozen male singer-dancers materialize out of thin air? That happens here in the big final number. The girls form a perfect chorus line, a stairway to the stars appears, and a dozen male dancers descend. Where did they come from? Where will they go? Remember, this club is so small there is only one clothing rack backstage for all the costumes.

Is this the movie for you? It may very well be. You've read my review, and you think I'm just making snarky comments and indulging in cheap sarcasm. Well, all right, I am. *Burlesque* shows Cher and Christina Aguilera being all that they can be, and that's more than enough.

Cassandra's Dream
(DIRECTED BY WOODY ALLEN; STARRING EWAN MCGREGOR, COLIN FARRELL; 2008)
Woody Allen's *Cassandra's Dream* is about two brothers, one single and modestly successful, one struggling but in a happy relationship, who are both desperate to raise money and agree to commit a crime together. The identical premise is used in Sidney Lumet's *Before the Devil Knows You're Dead*, which is like a master class in how Allen goes wrong.

The Lumet film uses actors (Ethan Hawke and Philip Seymour Hoffman) who don't look like brothers but feel like brothers. Allen's actors

(Ewan McGregor and Colin Farrell) look like brothers but don't really feel related. Lumet's film involves family members in a crime that seems reasonable but goes spectacularly wrong. Allen has a family member propose a crime that seems spectacularly unreasonable and goes right, with, however, unforeseen consequences. One of the brothers in both movies is consumed with guilt. And so on.

Lumet seems comfortable with his milieu, middle-class affluence in a New York suburb. Allen's milieu is not and perhaps never will be the Cockney working class of London, and his actors seem as much tourists as he is. Nevertheless, they plug away, in a plot that is intrinsically absorbing at times even with so much going against it.

McGregor and Farrell play Ian and Terry Blaine, Ian a partner in his dad's restaurant, Terry a hard-drinking, chain-smoking garage mechanic. Terry at least seems comfortable with his life and his supportive girlfriend (Sally Hawkins), although he dreams of getting rich quick; he gambles unwisely at the dog tracks. Ian also wants cash, and not only for a fishy-sounding opportunity to invest in California hotels. While driving a classic Jaguar borrowed from the garage where his brother works, he meets a high-maintenance sexpot actress (Hayley Atwell) and presents himself as a "property speculator" far richer than he is.

The brothers share a dream to own a boat. Terry wins big at the track, enough to buy a rusty bilge bucket, fix it up, and have a great day sailing with their two girls. But then Terry loses big-time, owes ninety thousand pounds, and discovers that guys are after him to break his legs. That's when rich Uncle Howard (Tom Wilkinson) returns from China (or somewhere) to make a proposition. His business empire is built on fraud, a colleague is about to squeal, and Howard wants the boys to do him a favor and murder the man.

Wilkinson, always a cool persuader, couches this in terms of family loyalty. That convinces the boys not nearly as much as does their own desperation. What happens I will not detail. This stretch of the movie does work and involves us, but then the lads run smack into an ending that was, to me, completely possible but highly unsatisfactory. Its problem is its sheer blundering plausibility. Allen's great *Match Point* (2005), on the other hand, also about crime and social con games, had an ending that was completely implausible and sublimely satisfactory. Remember how that ring falls at the end? What is fiction for, if not to manipulate the possible?

Certifiably Jonathan

(DIRECTED BY JIM PASTERNAK; STARRING JONATHAN WINTERS, JEFFREY TAMBOR; 2011)

Jonathan Winters is a fine and funny fellow, and deserves better than this. Out of the goodness of his heart, he agreed to be at the center of a mockumentary directed by Jim Pasternak. The result is not merely a bad film, but a waste of an opportunity. As he approaches eighty-six, Winters is still active, still funny, enthusiastically involved in painting, and could have been the subject of a good film. This isn't it.

The mockumentary form has many possibilities. They usually depend on satirizing the tone and feeling of a genre. The simple fact that it's fake doesn't make one successful. This one purports to show Winters at a crucial moment in his late flowering as an artist, during which he gets a gallery opening, is championed by a famous art critic, and promised a show at the Museum of Modern Art. None of these nonevents is staged with style or conviction. They are simply walked through as if really happening.

At the gallery, one of his paintings is stolen from a wall and Winters goes into a depression, finding himself unable to paint. It was, you see, his favorite painting. Pasternak leads a team that includes Winters himself to go to the house of the alleged thief. The house is unlocked, they walk in and find the painting, and Winters can paint again. Is there anyone reading this who can't think of an approach that isn't so lame?

Consider, too, the "curator" at the Museum of Modern Art. She is a pleasant woman who looks at negatives of Winters's sub-Dali paintings through a little magnifier and declares him worthy of a show. No effort is made to make her character or her process funny.

It appears one reason for this film was for Pasternak to gain access to Jonathan Winters, spend an excess amount of time personally on camera, and use Winters as bait to lure his famous friends into the film. These include Robin Williams, Howie Mandel, Nora Dunn, Jim Carrey, Sarah

Silverman, Tim Conway, Jeffrey Tambor, Jimmy Kimmel, Robert Klein, Ryan Stiles, Rob Reiner, Kevin Dunn, David Arquette, Patricia Arquette, and Rosanna Arquette.

All of these friends are seen briefly and forgettably. Only Robin Williams is funny. The others seem to be paying courtesy calls. With that much talent on the screen, it's significant that the funniest moments belong to Winters, seen on old TV shows.

Much is made, in the title and by Winters himself, of his history of bipolar disorder. It's assumed that today's audiences will know what's being referred to. In general, they won't. It's sad but true that many younger viewers won't quite know the range of Winters's brilliance. What would have been more appropriate: a tour through film and TV archives, memories of friends rather than testimonials, a real documentary instead of a fake one, and Jim Pasternak nowhere to be seen.

Chandni Chowk to China

(DIRECTED BY NIKHIL ADVANI; STARRING AKSHAY KUMAR, DEEPIKA PADUKONE; 2009)
Chandni Chowk is a historic marketplace in the walled city of old Delhi, so now you understand the title of *Chandni Chowk to China,* and because the plot is simplicity itself there is nothing else to understand but its origins. This is the first Bollywood movie to get a North American release from a major studio, and was chosen, I suspect, because it is a slapstick comedy containing a lot of kung fu. That, and maybe because it stars Akshay Kumar, described in the publicity as "the heartthrob of Indian cinema and current reigning king of Bollywood."

I would need to see Kumar in something other than this to understand his fame. He comes across here as a cross between Jerry Lewis and Adam Sandler, but less manic than Jerry and not as affable as Sandler. What I can understand is that his costar, Deepika Padukone, abandoned a promising start as a badminton champion to become a model and actress. She is breathtaking, which of course is standard in Bollywood, where all the actresses are either breathtaking or playing mothers.

The story plays as though it could be remade as a Sandler comedy with no changes except for length. When you go to a movie in India, you get your money's worth, in what takes the time of a double feature. As my Mumbai friend Uma da Cunha told me, big Bollywood movies give you everything: adventure, thrills, romance, song, dance, stunts, the works. In India, when you go to the movies, you go to *the movies*. *Chandni Chowk to China* plays at 168 minutes, having been shortened, I learn, for the American release. It would be safe to say few viewers will complain of its brevity.

Kumar stars as Sidhu, a lowly potato and onion chopper in his father's potato pancake stand. He adores his Dada (Mithun Chakraborty), despite the old man's propensity for kicking him so high over Delhi that he's a hazard to low-flying aircraft. As eager to please as a puppy, he has a gift for getting into trouble, but all that changes the day he finds the image of a god on one of his potatoes. This image, to my eye, makes the eBay portraits on grilled cheese sandwiches look like Norman Rockwells.

No matter. He exhibits the potato and collects donations, which are stolen by the nefarious Chopstick (Ranvir Shorey), while meanwhile, in China, a village is menaced by an evil hoodlum named Hojo (Gordon Liu), no relation to the U.S. pancake vendor. Two villagers happen upon Sidhu in Chandni Chowk and are convinced he is the reincarnation of the mighty kung fu warrior who saved them from bandits in times long past. Sidhu is soon lured to their village, being promised wealth and voluptuous pleasures, but is now expected to defeat Hojo, who uses his bowler hat as a flying guillotine and may plausibly be related to Odd Job.

Enter the ravishing Deepika Padukone, in a dual role of Sakhi and Meow Meow, an Indian home shopping network hostess and Chinese tigress. As you see the film, you may reflect that the opportunities of an Indian actress to achieve dramatic greatness are limited by the industry's practice in filming them only as spectacular beauties, preferably with the wind rippling their hair. Kissing in public is severely frowned upon in India, so that the greatest tension in all romances comes as a heroine is maybe, just maybe, *about* to kiss someone. This is always spellbinding and illustrates my maxim that it is less erotic to snoggle for sixty minutes than spend sixty seconds wondering if you are almost about to be snoggled.

I gather that Akshay Kumar usually plays more stalwart heroes, with the obligatory unshaven look, wearing his testosterone on his face. It's unlikely he could have become the heartthrob of Indian cinema playing doofuses like this. He becomes involved with both Sakhi and Meow Meow, whose surprise relationship might have been more surprising had they not been played by the same actress. There are lots of martial arts sequences, and of course several song-and-dance numbers, including an Indian rap performance. It's done with great energy but with a certain detachment, as if nothing really matters *but* the energy.

My guess is that *Chandni Chowk to China* won't attract many fans of kung fu—or Adam Sandler, for that matter. The title and the ads will cause them to think for a second, an unacceptable delay for fanboys. The movie will appeal to the large Indian audiences in North America and to Bollywood fans in general, who will come out wondering why this movie of all movies was chosen as Hollywood's first foray into commercial Indian cinema. I don't know a whole lot about Bollywood, and even I could name some better possibilities.

The Change-Up

(DIRECTED BY DAVID DOBKIN; STARRING RYAN REYNOLDS, JASON BATEMAN; 2011)
The Change-Up is one of the dirtiest-minded mainstream releases in history. It has a low opinion of men, a lower opinion of women, and the lowest opinion of the intelligence of its audience. It is obscene, foulmouthed, scatological, creepy, and perverted. As a bonus, it has the shabbiest low-rent main titles I've seen this side of YouTube.

It is a body-switch comedy. You remember those. There must have been dozens. Through some sort of magic, two characters find themselves occupying each other's bodies, or their own bodies at different ages. This can be charming, as when Tom Hanks did it in *Big*, or Jodie Foster in *Freaky Friday*. And remember Francis Ford Coppola's *Peggy Sue Got Married*, with Kathleen Turner becoming herself as a teenager.

To mention such movies in connection with this one is a sacrilege.

Setting aside considerations of the story, *The Change-Up* sets out to violate and transgress as many standards of civilized conduct as it can. Don't get me wrong. Faithful readers know I treasure cheerful vulgarity. But readers, I've seen *The Hangover*, and this is no *Hangover.*

Here you will see projectile pooping into faces. Two men exposing themselves and urinating in a "magic fountain" in a shopping mall in the presence of small children. Three tattoo artists closely scrutinizing a woman's vagina. Women systematically required to bare their breasts. Language in which nonobscene words provide an oasis. Best buddies essentially sharing the same wife.

OK, OK. In the context of a different movie, I can imagine all of those things working in a comedy. Except the public pissing. I think we can all agree that's problematical. So let's get back to the bare breasts. There are a great many of them, frequently and roughly fondled, for one reason only, and it isn't eroticism. If it were, I would sympathize. It has to do with the systematic exploitation of every actress in a film where God forbid an actor would be asked to display his penis. (We don't see penises in the urination scene. Only the kids can.)

Now consider the leading characters. They are Mitch (Ryan Reynolds), a pothead layabout, and Dave (Jason Bateman), an attorney and father of three. They've been best friends since grade school. They envy each other's lives. Through pissing in the fountain, they switch bodies and find out what that would be like.

This involves Mitch, in Dave's body, moving in with Dave's wife, Jamie (Leslie Mann), and Dave involved in Mitch's budding career as a porn actor. There is also a key role for Sabrina (Olivia Wilde), a legal aide at the law firm, who seduces Dave in the body of Mitch.

Never mind who does what and with which and to whom. The problem is that the movie requires us to accept this premise by making the characters aggressively stupid. Assume for the moment you are Jamie. Two men appearing to be your husband and his buddy Mitch claim their minds are in each other's bodies. They tell you to ask them something the other guy wouldn't know. She asks "Mitch" what "his" wedding anniversary is. Of course he doesn't remember. But asking some men for their wedding anniversary is almost a gotcha! question. For women, a wedding anniversary is as ingrained as New Year's Day. For men, it is more like Easter, and you can never remember what day it falls on this year.

A few more questions, and the testing ends. Mitch and Dave give up and reconcile themselves to their fates. Dave moves into Mitch's bachelor pad. Mitch moves into Dave's suburban home. Say what? If you found your mind in another body, wouldn't that be profoundly disturbing? Would it leave you capable of performing the duties in a movie comedy?

One problem with the movie is that it requires us to constantly remind ourselves which of these two pleasant-looking thirty-somethings is which. Another problem is that no matter which, they are both low and crude beings with no respect for decency, and their language is foul beyond the call of fictional necessity. The film, in fact, seems to go out of its way to be vulgar and offensive, as if *adult* audiences crave such an assault. Anyone who enjoys this film cannot fairly be considered an adult. Pity about the R rating. It will keep out those callow enough to enjoy it.

Cirque du Freak: The Vampire's Assistant

(DIRECTED BY PAUL WEITZ; STARRING JOHN C. REILLY, KEN WATANABE; 2009)

Cirque du Freak: The Vampire's Assistant includes good vampires, evil Vampaneze, a wolf-man, a bearded lady, a monkey girl with a long tail, a snake boy, a dwarf with a four-foot forehead, and a spider the size of your shoe, and they're all boring as hell. The movie has good special effects and suitably gruesome characters, but it's bloodless.

It's also a mess. The movie is shot through with curious disconnects. Often within a single sequence of events, we won't know where we are or how they're related in space or time. Characters like the bearded lady (Salma Hayek) drop in and out at random. Willem Dafoe plays a man who keeps intensely bursting in, but I didn't know who he was or where he went when he wasn't on the job. His name, I learn, is Gavner Purl, which doesn't ring a bell.

There is a mannered giant named Mr. Tiny (Michael Cerveris), who has flaming gay affectations for no purpose, since anyone who can evoke purple gas to shrink humans into living mummies already has, you would think, sufficient interest. Cerveris gives the only really interesting performance in the movie. And there's a paternal vampire named Larten Crepsley (John C. Reilly), who is proud of having developed a system of feeding off humans without killing them or turning them into vampires (i.e., "blooding them").

All of these characters travel with the Cirque du Freak, which comes to town for a one-night stand in an abandoned and shuttered theater. You slide your money into a slot at the bottom and something tries to bite you. Inexplicably, there is a small audience of normal customers who apparently don't object to this treatment.

Oh, and I almost forgot the two high school kids (Josh Hutcherson and Chris Massoglia) who are allegedly the hero and the antihero. They're equally bland, for my money. Turns out there are warring vampire factions: the followers of Larten Crepsley, who don't kill when they dine, and the evil Vampanese, who don't need to kill but do anyway, apparently because the habits of centuries are hard to break. The lads end up on opposing teams.

All of this gruesome grotesquerie is incredibly wrapped up into a story that grunts and groans and laboriously offers up a moral at the end, which is, and I quote: "It's not about what you are, it's about who you are." I could have told you that.

Conan the Barbarian

(DIRECTED BY MARCUS NISPEL; STARRING JASON MOMOA, STEPHEN LANG; 2011)

Conan the Barbarian involves the clash of civilizations whose vocabularies are limited to screams, oaths, grunts, howls, ejaculations, exclamations, vulgarities, screeches, wails, bellows, yelps, and woofs. I'd love to get my hands on the paycheck for subtitling this movie.

The plot involves—oh, never mind. You have your Barbarians and they kill one another in an unending series of battle scenes. I guess Conan is the good guy, but what difference does it make? He has no cause or belief. He's driven by revenge against the sadistic Khalar Zym (Stephen Lang), who trapped Conan's father under a vat of molten iron, assigned young Conan to exert his little muscles to try to keep it from tipping, and screamed at the old man: "You will watch your child die trying to save you!"

Luckily, Conan (the muscular Jason Momoa) survives and grows up with no worse than a photogenic scar on his face, where some wayward molten iron dripped. He and his father, Corin (Ron Perlman), had earlier forged his sword at the steel moltery; earlier still, the infant Conan was delivered on a battlefield by an emergency cesarean performed by Corin's own sword on his mother, who survives long enough to say, "He shall be named Conan." She was so weak she lacked the breath to say, "Conan the Barbarian."

The movie is a series of violent conflicts. People who despair of convincing me to play video games tell me, "Maybe if you could just watch someone else playing one!" I feel as if I now have. Conan carves, beheads, disembowels, and otherwise inconveniences the citizens of several improbable cities, each time in a different fanciful situation. The evil Khalar Zym and his girlfriend, Marique, (Rose McGowan), turn up regularly, uttering imprecations, with Marique especially focused on Conan's warrior gal pal, Tamara (Rachel Nichols).

This Marique, she's a piece of work. She has white pancake makeup, blood red lips, cute little facial tattoos, and wickedly sharp metal talons on her fingers. At one point she blows some magic dust at Conan, and the dust turns into a team of warriors made of sand. This is a neat special effect, although it raises the question: If you turn back to sand when Conan slices you, what kind of a life is that?

The film ends with a very long battle involving Conan, Khalar Zym, Tamara, and Marique, a sentence I never thought I'd write. It takes place largely with Tamara strapped to a revolving wheel above a vertiginous drop to flames far below. Mention is made of a volcano, but never further explained. The entire cavern crumbles around them, big chunks of rock falling everywhere except, luckily, upon them.

Conan the Barbarian is a brutal, crude, witless high-tech CGI contrivance, in which no artificial technique has been overlooked, including 3-D. The third dimension once again illustrates the principle that when a movie largely takes place indoors in dimly lit spaces, the last thing you need is a pair of dark glasses.

Cop Out

(DIRECTED BY KEVIN SMITH; STARRING BRUCE WILLIS, TRACY MORGAN; 2010)
Jimmy and Paul are cops hunkered down across the street from a stakeout when they see a mysterious figure run across rooftops and break into a house. Seconds later, he can clearly be seen in an upper window, sitting on a toilet and reading a magazine. "What kindofa guy breaks into a house and takes a crap?" asks Paul, or words to that effect.

Paul explains he always delays this elementary function until he gets home. He's not relaxed until then. But once he's home—ooohhh boy! Then he lets loose. He describes the results in great detail. The walls, the ceilings. All right! I'm thinking, all right, already! I got it! Mudslide! Paul isn't finished. Now he's talking about the reaction of the neighbors.

How do you know this is a scene from a Kevin Smith film? The imitation of a nine-year-old describing bodily functions might be a clue. But the clincher is when that mysterious guy runs across the rooftops. Paul (Tracy Morgan) explains to his partner Jimmy (Bruce Willis): "That's known as 'parkour.' It's a new martial art." Well, thanks, Paul. I didn't know that until yesterday, when it was explained in *District 13: Ultimatum*. What synchronicity. That other movie costars the man who gave "parkour" its name. The movie is filled with it. I suspect its presence as a brief walk-on in *Cop Out* can be explained this way: Kevin found out about it, thought it was cool, and slipped in a little quick "parkour" for fun.

If you combine the enthusiasms of a geek with the toilet humor of a third-grader, you'll be pretty close to defining the art of Kevin Smith. Hey, I'm not complaining. If we lose our inner third-grader, we begin to die. When the muse visits him, Smith gets inspired and makes fun movies like *Zack and Miri Make a Porno*. Alas, *Cop Out* is not one of those movies. Tracy Morgan is forced to go way over the top; Bruce Willis seems eager to have a long, sad talk with his agent; and Kevin Pollak, who gets costar billing, does at least appear for longer than a quark at Fermilab.

Cop Out tells your standard idiotic story about buddy cops who screw up, get suspended by the captain, and redeem themselves by overthrowing a drug operation while searching for the valuable baseball card Jimmy wants to sell to pay for his daughter's wedding. Paul spends an unreasonable amount of time dressed as a cell phone, considering there is nothing to prevent him from taking it off.

A lot of the dialogue is intended to be funny, but man, is it lame. Many of the gags possibly looked good on paper, but watching Willis and Morgan struggle with them is like watching third-graders do Noel Coward, if Noel Coward had been rewritten by Kevin Smith. At St. Joseph's Boys' Camp there was this Chicago kid named Bob Calvano who was naturally hilarious around the campfire every night. Then I'd get up and flop with my memorized bits from Buddy Hackett records. "Ebert," he advised me kindly, "it isn't funny if you act like it's supposed to be funny. Act like you don't know." All I can do is pass along Calvano's advice.

Couples Retreat

(DIRECTED BY PETER BILLINGSLEY; STARRING VINCE VAUGHN, JASON BATEMAN; 2009)

Couples Retreat tells the story of four troubled couples and how they're healed by sitcom formulas. Why are they troubled? Because the screenplay says so. It contains little comedy except for freestanding one-liners, and no suspense except for the timing of the obligatory reconciliation. It doesn't even make you think you'd like to visit its island paradise.

The couples are apparently all from Buffalo Grove, which supplies nothing visual except for a T-shirt. Three of them think they're reasonably happy, but their friends Jason (Jason Bateman) and Cynthia (Kristen Bell) beg them to join them for a week at a resort devoted to healing relationships (if four couples go, it's half price).

Jason and Cynthia are anguished because they haven't had a child. The other couples are Dave (Vince Vaughn) and Ronnie (Malin Akerman); Joey (Jon Favreau) and Lucy (Kristin Davis); and Shane (Faizon Love) and Trudy (Kali Hawk). Their troubles: (1) Parenting duties distract from romance; (2) Joey's wandering eye; (3) Shane has split from his wife and is dating a twenty-year-old bimbo.

They fly to the Eden resort, which uses locations on Bora Bora, a truly enchanted place that's reduced to the beach party level. Eden is run by Monsieur Marcel (Jean Reno), a martial arts mystic, and managed by Sctanley (Peter Serafinowicz), who explains his name is spelled with a "C." Other staff include Salvadore (Carlos Ponce), doubling for a model on the cover of a lesser romance novel.

The formula itself might have supported hilarity, but the story lacks character specifics. Each couple behaves relentlessly as an illustration of their problem. The movie depends for excitement on a shark attack during a scuba-diving exercise, featuring clueless sharks and an enormous pool of blood apparently leaked from a tiny superficial scratch. Salvadore charms the wives somewhat ambiguously with his oiled pecs and bottles of pineapple-rum drinks. The men don't bond so much as stand together on-screen and exchange bonding dialogue.

There is a twin resort named East Eden, which has all swinging singles as opposed to troubled couples. It's a party scene every night; as nearly as I could tell, our four couples are the only clients on West Eden, so no wonder there was a 50 percent off deal, despite Sctanley's talk of the long waiting list.

Among the better things in the movie, I count Vaughn's well-timed and smart dialogue; the eccentricity of Love and Hawk in contrast to the cookie-cutter couples; and Serafinowicz's meticulous affectations, which suggest psychotropic medication.

The concluding scenes are agonizing in the way they march through the stages dictated by an ages-old formula. We know all four couples must arrive at a crisis. We know their situations must appear dire. We expect a transitional event during which they realize the true nature of their feelings. This is a wild party night at East Eden. We expect sincere confessions of deep feelings. And we know there must be a jolly conclusion that wraps everything up.

In the context of the film, the jolly conclusion must be seen to be believed. Were all the transitional events anticipated, even planned, by the

all-seeing Monsieur Marcel? Marcel hands each couple an animal representing their true inner animal spirits. These are carved from a dark wood,
which I deduced after seeing the second, third, and fourth animals. The
first was a rabbit, which looked like nothing else than a chocolate bunny.
That would have been strange.

● ● ● ● ● ● ● ● ●

Dark Streets

(DIRECTED BY RACHEL SAMUELS; STARRING GABRIEL MANN, BIJOU PHILLIPS; 2008)
Dark Streets is the kind of film you can appreciate as an object, but not as
a story. It's a lovingly souped-up incarnation of the film noir look, contains
well-staged and performed musical numbers, and has a lot of cigarettes,
tough tootsies, bad guys, and shadows. What it doesn't have is a story that
pulls us along or a hero that seems as compelling as some of the supporting characters.

The hero is Chaz (Gabriel Mann), who has inherited a nightclub from
his secretive father, who was a power magnate. Night after night, he sits in the
club, smoking and regarding his stage shows. Too many nights after nights.
The most noticeable thing about Chaz is his pencil-thin mustache. OK, so it's
the 1930s, and actors like William Powell and Clark Gable had mustaches like
that and played good guys, but somehow don't you associate the style more
with snaky villains and riverboat gamblers? A very young man wearing such
a mustache is trying to tell us something we don't want to know.

His club feels more like a set than a business. The whole film feels
that way: as if the sets, actors, and dialogue are self-consciously posing as
classic film noir instead of sinking into the element. Look at a film like
Dark City, which is obviously made of sets but feels like noir to its very

bones. Here, the moment Bijou Phillips and Izabella Miko appear on the screen, they exude: *I'm the dame in a movie nightclub!* That's not to say they're not good. In fact, they're surprisingly good, especially in the club's jazz-based production numbers, where they sing and dance and are sultry and entertaining. It's wrong of me, but I'm always a little startled when someone like Bijou or Paris Hilton turns out to be talented, because it's wrong that's not what they're famous for.

It's difficult to imagine how Chaz's smallish club, even though it does good business, can afford to stage those production numbers, which, although not Vegas in scope, are at least comparable to those on a big-time cruise ship. I'm reminded of Broadway musicals where six extras play the audience in *42nd Street*. Other details seem out of scale. If Chaz's dad really was a power tycoon, shouldn't the offices of this vast monopoly be more impressive than some gold stenciling on the glass of an office door? I think the power blackouts that keep shutting down the city may be intended to remind us of Enron's deliberate California blackouts, but that plot thread leads nowhere.

The movie is directed by Rachel Samuels, with a screenplay by Wallace King, based on Glenn Stewart's play *City Club*. Since it plays more like the book for a musical, maybe she should have just gone ahead and made it a musical. That would have forgiven the lapses in logic, explained the sets and production numbers, and shrugged off problems of scale. And it would have built on the movie's strength (not just the performances but a nice sound track presence by Etta James, B. B. King, Natalie Cole, and others). You'd still need to make Chaz more formidable. At least in a musical, he doesn't need to be Robert De Niro.

The Day the Earth Stood Still

(DIRECTED BY SCOTT DERRICKSON; STARRING KEANU REEVES, JENNIFER CONNELLY; 2008)
SPOILER WARNING: *The Day the Earth Stood Still* need not have taken its title so seriously that the plot stands still along with it. There isn't much here you won't remember from the 1951 classic, even if you haven't seen

it. What everyone knows is that a spaceship lands on Earth, a passenger named Klaatu steps out and is shot, and then a big metal man named Gort walks out and has rays shooting from its eyes, and the army opens fire. That movie is at No. 202 in IMDb's top 250. Its message, timely for the nuclear age, was that mankind would be exterminated if we didn't stop killing one another. The message of the 2008 version is that we should have voted for Al Gore. This didn't require Klaatu and Gort. That's what I'm here for. Actually, Klaatu is nonpartisan and doesn't name names, but his message is clear: Planets that can sustain life are so rare that the aliens cannot allow us to destroy life on this one. So they'll have to kill us.

The aliens are advanced enough to zip through the galaxy yet have never discovered evolution, which should have reassured them life on Earth would survive the death of mankind. Their space spheres have landed all over the planet, and a multitude of species have raced up and thrown themselves inside, and a Department of Defense expert intuits: "They're arks! What comes next?" The defense secretary (Kathy Bates) intones: "A flood." So this is the first sci-fi movie based on intelligent design, except the aliens plan to save all forms of life *except* the intelligent one.

All this is presented in an expensive, good-looking film that is well made by Scott Derrickson, but to no avail. As is conventional in such films, the fate of the planet narrows down to a woman, a child, and Klaatu. Jennifer Connelly plays Helen Benson, a Harvard scientist who is summoned by the government to advise it on the glowing sphere in Central Park. She has to leave behind her beloved little Jacob (Jaden Smith), her late husband's son by his first wife (more detail than we require, I think; just "her son" would have been fine). She meets Klaatu (Keanu Reeves), who looks human (and we already know why), but is a representative, or negotiator, or human-looking spokesthing, or something, for the aliens.

She discovers his purpose, takes him with her in her car, flees a federal dragnet, walks in the woods, introduces him to her brilliant scientist friend (John Cleese), lets him listen to a little Bach, tells him we can *change* if we're only given the chance, and expresses such love for Jacob that Klaatu is so moved he looks on dispassionately.

That's no big deal, because Klaatu looks on everything dispassionately. Maybe he has no passions. He becomes the first costar in movie history to elude falling in love with Jennifer Connelly. Keanu Reeves is often low-key in his roles, but in this movie, his piano has no keys at all. He is so solemn, detached, and uninvolved he makes Mr. Spock look like Hunter S. Thompson at closing time. When he arrives at a momentous decision, he announces it as if he has been rehearsing to say: "Yes, one plus one equals two. Always has, always will."

Jennifer Connelly and Kathy Bates essentially keep the human interest afloat. Young Jaden Smith is an appealing actor, but his character Jacob could use a good spanking, what with endangering the human race with a snit fit. Nobody is better than Connelly at looking really soulful, and I am not being sarcastic—I am sincere. There are scenes here requiring both actors to be soulful, and she takes up the extra burden effortlessly.

As for Bates, she's your go-to actress for pluck and plainspoken common sense. She announces at the outset that the president and vice president have been evacuated to an undisclosed location (not spelling out whether undisclosed to her or by her), and they stay there for the rest of the movie, not even calling her, although the president does make an unwise call to a military man. Make of this what you will. I suspect a political undertow.

One more detail. I will not disclose how the aliens plan to exterminate human life, because it's a neat visual. Let me just observe that the destruction of human life involves the annihilation of Shea Stadium, which doesn't even have any humans in it at the time. And that since the destruction begins in the mountains of the Southwest, yet approaches Shea from the East, the task must be pretty well completed by the time Jennifer Connelly needs to look soulful. And that Klaatu is a cockeyed optimist if he thinks they can hide out in an underpass in the park.

Dear John

(DIRECTED BY LASSE HALLSTROM; STARRING CHANNING TATUM, AMANDA SEYFRIED; 2010)

Lasse Hallstrom's *Dear John* tells the heartbreaking story of two lovely young people who fail to find happiness together because they're trapped in an adaptation of a Nicholas Sparks novel. Their romance leads to bittersweet loss that's so softened by the sweet characters that it feels like triumph. If a Sparks story ended in happiness, the characters might be disappointed. They seem to have their noble, resigned dialogue already written. Hemingway wrote one line that could substitute for the third act of every Sparks story: "Isn't it pretty to think so?"

Channing Tatum stars as John Tyree, a handsome Army Special Forces specialist home on two weeks' leave at the South Carolina shore. Amanda Seyfried plays Savannah, an ethereal beauty whose purse falls off a pier. John dives in and retrieves it, and we guess it could have been worse. He could have gotten her kitten down from a tree. In the few precious days they share, they fall deeply into PG-13 love.

John was raised by his father (Richard Jenkins), a quiet man who wears white gloves while admiring his coin collection, and cooks chicken every Saturday and lasagna every Sunday. Savannah meets him and casually observes to John that he is autistic—a mild case, she gently suggests. John is angered by this insult. Did he never, by the age of twenty-two, observe that his father was strangely mannered? Did no one else? What was his (now absent) mother's thinking? Did the movie mention any employment history for Mr. Tyree? I could have missed it.

In a Sparks story, as we know from *The Notebook*, problems like autism and Alzheimer's are never seen in their tragic stages, but always allow the good souls of their victims to visibly glow. Diseases don't destroy and kill, but exist primarily to inspire admirable conduct by nexts of kin. John and Savannah get over his unhappiness, and he pledges that he'll be back at the end of twelve months so they can wed.

But then 9/11 happens, and like every man in his group he re-enlists. And continues to re-enlist until the movie's title hints at what he receives in the mail. Because Savannah is a true-blue heroine, her new love is of course a nice and decent man, someone John can accept, so that we can smile sadly and not get all messy and depressed. That's the note Sparks aims for: the sad smile. First love is not to be, but the moon still looks so large when it rises, and people treat each other gently, and if someone should die, that is very sad, but perhaps it will provide an opportunity for someone else to live a little longer before they, too, must travel to that undiscovered country from whose bourne no traveler ever returns.

John and Savannah are awfully nice. She comes from a rich family who have a mansion, and John and his dad live in a humble but cozy frame house that in its South Carolina island location might easily be purchased for less than $500,000. That would leave a portion of Mr. Tyree's unspecified income free to invest in rare coins and amass a collection worth a fortune. I am just enough of a numismatist to know that you need to invest money to collect rare coins. You don't just find them in your spare change.

I know I'm being snarky. I don't get much pleasure from it. *Dear John* exists only to coddle the sentiments of undemanding dreamers, and plunge us into a world where the only evil is the interruption of the good. Of course John is overseas on a series of missions so secret that Savannah cannot be told where, exactly, he is. In the years after 9/11, where, oh where, could he be? Apparently not in Iraq or Afghanistan, because it can hardly be a military secret that the men of Special Forces are deployed there. But somewhere, anyway, and he re-enlists for a good chunk of her early childbearing years, perhaps because, as *The Hurt Locker* informs us, "war is a drug."

It matters not. In this movie, war is a plot device. It loosens its grip on John only long enough to sporadically renew his romance, before claiming him again so that we finally consider Savannah's Dear John letter just good common sense. And now that I've brought that up: Considering that the term "Dear John Letter" has been in constant use since World War II, and that the hero of this movie is inevitably destined to receive such a letter, is it a little precious of Sparks to name him "John"? I was taught in Dan Curley's fiction class that when the title of a story is repeated in the story itself, the story's spell is broken. But then Sparks never took Curley's class.

Death Race

(DIRECTED BY PAUL W. S. ANDERSON; STARRING JASON STATHAM, TYRESE GIBSON; 2008)
Hitchcock said a movie should play the audience like a piano. *Death Race* played me like a drum. It is an assault on all the senses, including common.

Walking out, I had the impression I had just seen the video game and was still waiting for the movie. The time is the near future, not that it matters. Times are bad. Unemployment is growing. A steelworker named Jensen Ames (Jason Statham) loses his job when the mill closes. He comes home to his loving wife and baby daughter, a masked man breaks in, the wife is killed, he is wounded, he is found guilty of his wife's murder and sentenced to the dreaded Terminal Island prison.

Treasure those opening scenes of drama, however brief they may be. The movie will rarely pause again. Prisons, we learn, are now private corporations, and Terminal raises money by pay-for-view Internet races. Its Death Race involves prisoners driving heavily armored cars bearing weapons such as machine guns, rocket launchers, and other inconveniences. If a prisoner wins five races, he gets his freedom.

But why, oh why, must I describe the rules of a Death Race? They hardly matter, nor will I take your time to tell you why Jensen Ames is enlisted to drive as the superstar Frankenstein, who wears a mask, so he could be anybody, which is the point. All of that is simply babble to set up the races.

In a coordinated visual and sound attack, mighty cars roar around the prison grounds, through warehouses, down docks, and so on, while blasting at each other, trying to avoid booby traps, and frequently exploding. Each car is assigned gimmicks like oil slicks and napalm, which can be used only once. Did I say this played like a video game? Jensen's archenemy is Machine Gun Joe (Tyrese Gibson), who is gay, which the plot informs us and thereafter forgets. Jensen's chief mechanic is Coach (Ian McShane), whose oily voice provides one of the film's best qualities. Natalie Martinez plays Case, Jensen's copilot, who screams, "Left turn! Left turn! NOW!"

And the warden of the prison is Hennessey, played by Joan Allen. Yes, that ethereal beauty, that sublime actress, that limitless talent, reduced to standing in an observation post and ordering her underlings to "activate weapons." She has a line of dialogue that employs both the f-word and the s-word and describes a possible activity that utterly baffles me. It is a threat, shall we say, that has never been uttered before and will never be uttered again. She plays her scenes with an icy venom that I imagine she is rehearsing to use in a chat with her agent.

Roger Corman is one of this film's producers, but *Death Race* is not a remake of his *Death Race 2000* (1975). That was a film about a cross-country race in which competitors were scored by how many people they ran over (one hundred points for someone in a wheelchair, seventy points for the aged, fifty points for kids, and so on). Sylvester Stallone played Machine Gun Joe. David Carradine played Frankenstein, but here he only plays the voice of one of the earlier (doomed) Frankensteins. Let us conclude that *Death Race* is not a brand that guarantees quality. That it will no doubt do great at the box office is yet another sign of the decline of the national fanboy mentality.

December Boys

(Directed by Rod Hardy; starring Daniel Radcliffe, Christian Byers; 2007)

In Australia, the height of summer arrives, of course, in December, which is not how *December Boys* gets its name. The title comes because four boys at the height of adolescence all have December birthdays, and so the nuns at their orphanage have arranged a special treat: a holiday at the seaside. After that summer, nothing will ever be the same again, an observation the movie should use on its posters. Hang on; it is on the posters.

The lads go to stay with a salty old sea dog named Bandy McAnsh (Jack Thompson) and his sickly wife, Mrs. McAnsh (Kris McQuade). He has retired from the navy and they have settled here, their eyes to the sea, their backs to the barren landscape. This is in about 1960, years and years before anyone will think of soaking T-shirts in a soup of red dirt and selling them as Red Dirt Shirts.

The boys are Misty, the narrator (Lee Cormie), Spark (Christian Byers), Spit (James Fraser), and Maps (Daniel Radcliffe, in his first major post-Potter role). *Variety*, the showbiz bible, cuts to the chase in the opening words of its review: "Destined to be forever known as 'Harry Potter Gets Laid.'" As orphans, the boys (all except for Maps) are as eager to be adopted as puppies in an animal shelter. They meet a circus couple and decide they would make ideal parents. Fearless (Sullivan Stapleton) is a daredevil motorcycle rider, and his girlfriend, Teresa (Victoria Hill), is a French babe who has brought topless sunbathing to Australia years ahead of schedule.

The other three boys all wag their tails and try to seem adoptable. But Maps has his eye on another prize, a girl named Lucy (Teresa Palmer). As they have a flirtation and qualify the movie for *Variety*'s rewrite of the title, I was so forcibly reminded of another one that I wished I were seeing it instead. That would be *Flirting* (1991), where Thandie Newton and Noah Taylor play students at nearby Australian single-sex boarding schools and create the most tender and realistic love (not sex) scene I can remember. They set a high mark, which I'm afraid Maps and Lucy do not approach in a seduction that is by the numbers, only Lucy counts by twos.

She also gives Maps his first puff on a cigarette. The sight of Harry Potter smoking is a little like Mickey Mouse lighting up, but the period detail is accurate, and Radcliffe is convincing as the young man; he proves he can move beyond the Harry role, which I guess is the objective of this movie, but I am not sure that it proves he has star power—not yet, anyway, unless his costar, so to speak, is Harry Potter.

There are some elements in the film that baffle me, one of them being an underwater appearance by the Virgin Mary. I guess we might expect such a manifestation in some movies about Catholic orphans, but not in one so chockablock with mortal sins. To balance her, there is the earthy wisdom of Father Scully (Frank Gallacher), who escorts the lads on their holiday and gives them sales talks on being adopted, as if they were opposed to the idea. He knows the good Catholic couple, the McAnshes, and is their friend in need.

The movie is based on a novel by Michael Noonan, unread by me, which is described as "young adult fiction" by Amazon. Its young and adult elements fit together awkwardly, however, and it is hard to reconcile the storybook qualities of the first sequences with what the MPAA catalogues as PG-13-rated "sexual content, nudity, underage drinking, and smoking," and parents of younger Radcliffe fans will describe as "ohmigod." There seem to be two movies going on here at the same time, and *December Boys* would have been better off going all the way with one of them.

Dedication

(DIRECTED BY JUSTIN THEROUX; STARRING BILLY CRUDUP, MANDY MOORE; 2007)
Henry Roth, the hero of *Dedication*, is a writer who does one thing correctly: He talks like he's taking dictation from himself. "Life is nothing but the occasional burst of laughter rising above the interminable wail of grief," he informs us, which may be true enough, but does little to set the mood for a romantic comedy.

Henry (Billy Crudup), possibly named after the author of *Call It Sleep,* threatens, like the real Roth, to become a one-book wonder. He writes children's books, which it is not in his nature to do because he hates children along with the rest of the human race. What kind of man goes out of his way to tell children that there is no Santa Claus?

He has written a best-seller, *Marty the Beaver,* with his collaborator, Rudy (Tom Wilkinson), an illustrator. Then Rudy dies, which is not a spoiler, but it might be a spoiler to reveal that he stays around for the rest of the movie in the form of a ghost. This strands Henry without his only friend. Henry, you understand, is a very odd man with a lot of problems, which seem less like a consistent syndrome than a collection of random neurotic tics.

For example, he is as attached to an old towel as Linus is to his security blanket. When he is having anxiety attacks, which are frequent, nothing will calm him but to put weights on his chest. And he manifests various forms of obsessive-compulsive behavior.

We meet his editor, Planck (Bob Balaban), who sits behind his desk looking mournful at the prospect of there being no further adventures of Marty the Beaver. He orders Henry to team up with another illustrator, Lucy (Mandy Moore), this despite Henry's inability to allow anyone into his life for purposes of collaboration on Marty the Beaver or anything else. And it's at about that point that *Dedication* jumps *onto* the rails and follows a familiar romcom pathway: Will these two completely incompatible people work out their differences and eventually fall in love? What are the odds, considering they have the lead roles in the movie? Have we spent all that money only to see Mandy Moore's occasional laughter fading off into an interminable wail of grief? I think not.

The movie is a first-time directorial effort by Justin Theroux, a splendid actor, son of the writer Phyllis, nephew of the novelist Paul. He might have done better to have adapted something by them. My candidate for a novel begging to be filmed: Paul's *Chicago Loop*, about a respectable businessman who leads a macabre secret life. Instead, he began with a first screenplay by David Bromberg, which plays like a serve-yourself buffet of bits and pieces cobbled from other movies.

Billy Crudup and Mandy Moore are immensely likable actors. We like them so much we regret having to see them in this story, even though occasionally they slip into a cranny of it and seem to create their own private outtakes. Consider, for example, Crudup's explanation of why any woman should be overjoyed to share life with such a basket case as he. True, such a life wouldn't be boring, but remember the ancient Chinese curse (are there no modern Chinese curses?), "May you live in interesting times."

Maybe I would like *Dedication* more if I had not seen its separate elements time and again. Once Henry and Lucy have been handcuffed together by the plot, for example, I know with a certainty that they will end up in love. But I also know the screenplay structure requires a false dawn before the real dawn. There must be an element that threatens their obligatory happiness. And there is, in the person of Jeremy (Martin Freeman), her former lover, now back in the picture. And there must be a private problem of her own to balance Henry's peculiarities. And there is, in the person of her mother (Dianne Wiest), who wants to evict her, raising the specter that she will move in with the Wrong Person.

In a movie of unlikelihoods, the most problematical is Balaban, as the publisher, offering Lucy $200,000 on the side as a bonus to do all she can to make Henry function again. If there was money like that in children's books, Marty the Beaver would have a lot of new little friends.

The Devil Wears Prada

(DIRECTED BY DAVID FRANKEL; STARRING MERYL STREEP, ANNE HATHAWAY; 2006)
When I was young there was a series of books about boys and girls dreaming of the careers they'd have as grown-ups. I can't remember what the titles were, but let's say one was *Don Brown, Boy Announcer*. Don dreams of being a radio announcer, and one day, when an announcer falls ill at the scene of a big story, he grabs the mike and gets his chance: *The engineer nodded urgently to me and I began to describe the fire, remembering to speak clearly. I was nervous at first, but soon the words flowed smoothly.*

There were books about future coaches, nurses, doctors, pilots, senators, inventors, and so on. I also read the *Childhood of Famous Americans* series, but the "boy announcer" books were far superior, because they were about the childhood of me. *I took a deep breath and began. This was the chance I had been waiting for!*

The Devil Wears Prada is being positioned as a movie for grown-ups and others who know what, or who, or when, or where, Prada is. But while watching it I had the uncanny notion that, at last, one of those books from my childhood had been filmed. Call it *Andy Sachs, Girl Editor.* Anne Hathaway stars as a fresh-faced Midwesterner who comes to New York seeking her first job. "I just graduated from Northwestern," she explains. "I was editor of the *Daily Northwestern!*" Yes! *It had been a thrill to edit the student newspaper, but now, as I walked down Madison Avenue, I realized I was headed for the big time!*

Andy still dresses like an undergraduate, which offends Miranda Priestly (Meryl Streep), the powerful editor of *Runway,* the famous fashion magazine. Miranda, who is a cross between Anna Wintour, Graydon Carter, and a dominatrix, stands astride the world of fashion in very expensive boots. She throws things (her coat, her purse) at her assistants, rattles off tasks to be done immediately, and demands "the new Harry Potter" in "three hours." No, not the new book in the stores. The unpublished manuscript of the next book. Her twins want to read it. So get two copies.

Young Andy Sachs gets a job as the assistant to Miranda's assistant. That's Emily (Emily Blunt), who is terrified of Miranda. She is blunt to Andy: She'll need to get rid of that wardrobe, devote twenty-four hours a

day to the job, and hope to God she remembers all of Miranda's commands. *I was impressed when I first saw the famous Miranda Priestly. She had the poise of Meryl Streep, the authority of Condoleezza Rice, and was better-dressed than anyone I'd ever met, except the Northwestern dean of women. And now she was calling my name! Gulp!*
Young Andy has a live-in boyfriend, which wasn't allowed in those old books. He is Nate (Adrian Grenier), who has a permanent three-day beard and loves her but wonders what has happened to "the old Andy I used to know." *I was heartbroken when I had to work late on Nate's birthday, but Miranda swamped me with last-minute demands.* Emily, the first assistant, lives for the day when she will travel to Paris with Miranda for Spring Fashion Week. But then Emily gets a cold or, as Miranda puts it, becomes "an incubus of viral plague." By this time Young Andy has impressed Miranda by getting the Harry Potter manuscript, and she's dressing better, too. *Nigel took me into the storage rooms, where I found myself surrounded by the latest and most luxurious fashion samples!* So Andy replaces Emily on the Paris trip.
"You are the one who has to tell Emily," Miranda kindly explains. *Ohmigod! I was dreaming! Paris, France! And as Miranda Priestly's assistant! But how would I break the news to Emily, who had dreamed of this day? And how could I tell Nate, whose own plans would have to be changed?* Actually, by this time Young Andy has a lot of things to discuss with Nate, including her friendship with Christian (Simon Baker), a famous writer for *New York* magazine. *Ohmigod! Christian said he would read my clippings!*
The Devil Wears Prada is based on the best-selling novel by Lauren Weisberger, which oddly enough captures the exact tone, language, and sophistication of the books of my childhood: *There was nowhere to wipe my sweaty palms except for the suede Gucci pants that hugged my thighs and hips so tightly they'd both begun to tingle within minutes of my securing the final button.* This novel was on the *New York Times* best-seller list for six months and has been published in twenty-seven countries. I hope some of the translators left the word "both" out of that sentence.
Streep is indeed poised and imperious as Miranda, and Hathaway is a great beauty (*Ella Enchanted, Brokeback Mountain*) who makes a convincing career girl. I liked Stanley Tucci, too, as Nigel, the magazine's fash-

ion director, who is kind and observant despite being a careerist slave. But I thought the movie should have reversed the roles played by Grenier and Baker. Grenier comes across not like the old boyfriend but like the slick New York writer, and Baker seems the embodiment of Midwestern sincerity, which makes sense, because he is from Australia, the Midwest of the Southern Hemisphere.

Did You Hear About the Morgans?

(DIRECTED BY MARC LAWRENCE; STARRING HUGH GRANT, SARAH JESSICA PARKER; 2009) What possible reason was there for anyone to make *Did You Hear About the Morgans?* Or should I say "remake," because this movie has been made over and over again, and oh, so much better. Feuding couple from Manhattan forced to flee town, find themselves Fish Out of Water in Strange New World, meet Colorful Characters, survive Slapstick Adventures, end up Together at the End. The only part of that formula that still works is The End.

I grant you Hugh Grant and Sarah Jessica Parker evoke charm in the right screenplay. This is the wrong screenplay. I concede that Sam Elliott is always welcome, except in that one eerie role he played without his mustache. I agree Mary Steenburgen is a merry and fetching lass. I realize yet once again the durable validity of Siskel's Question: Is this movie more entertaining than a documentary of the same actors having lunch?

Grant and Parker play Paul and Meryl Morgan, a wealthy Manhattan couple, childless, but they hope to adopt. This virtually guarantees a cute little orphan in the final reel. She is Manhattan's number-one "boutique Realtor." One night they're going together to show one of her multimillion-dollar properties when they witness her client being pushed from its balcony by a mean-looking villain.

He gets a good look at them. It was an important murder. Of course they must be sealed inside the Witness Protection Program and shipped out west, to where the men are men and the women are happy of it. In this strange new world where the men wear cowboy hats and the women wear cowboy hats and bake, will they find themselves in a rodeo? Let's put it this way: The close-up of a local rodeo poster and the matching shot of Hugh Grant squinting at it virtually guarantee that.

Saints preserve us! Not another one of those movies where Hugh Grant and Sarah Jessica Parker end up as the front and back halves of the rodeo clowns' cow suit! What's that you say? This is the first one where they've been inside the cow? Does it feel that way to you? What's that you say? You bet they'll be chased by a bear? Come on, now: Surely only one of them!

Paul and Meryl (unusual name, that; where did they find it?) end up as the houseguests of Clay and Emma Wheeler (Elliott and Steenburgen), the local sheriff and his deputy. Now that's clever thinking! Where better to hide Protected Witnesses than as the guests of the local law enforcement couple. Of course, Clay and Emma are hard to spot as they patrol on their horses with rifles and cowboy hats and mustaches and whatnot.

Paul and Meryl are dudes without a ranch. The small town embraces them. It's in Wyoming, I think someone said, and of course it has all of Wyoming's friendliness: The locals turn out with open arms, as they always do when two East Coast elites hit town and start asking people in the local cafe to refrain from smoking. Why, look! There, at the next table! It's Wilford Brimley! Smoking! It's not every day one movie offers the two most famous mustaches in Hollywood.

Well, you'll never be able to guess what happens then. And whether the villain turns up. And whether anyone is chased by a bear. And whether Paul and Meryl go to the rodeo. And what kind of an animal they wind up playing the front and back halves of. And whether they adopt a cute little orphan. And whether that mean old Wilford Brimley ends up grudgingly liking them after all. And whether he ever stops smoking. But one thing's for sure. You'll feel like you've already heard about the Morgans.

Diminished Capacity

(DIRECTED BY TERRY KINNEY; STARRING MATTHEW BRODERICK, ALAN ALDA; 2008)

Diminished Capacity is a mild pleasure from one end to the other, but not much more. Maybe that's enough, serving as a reminder that movie comedies can still be about ordinary people and do not necessarily have to feature vulgarity as their centerpiece. Yes, I'm still hurting from the *The Love Guru* nightmare.

Dim Cap, as Uncle Rollie shortens the phrase, is about Cooper, a Chicago political columnist (Matthew Broderick), and his Uncle Rollie (Alan Alda), who are both suffering from memory loss. With Cooper, who was banged against a wall in somebody else's bar fight, the impairment is temporary. With Uncle Rollie, it may be progressing; his sister, Belle (Lois Smith), who is Cooper's mother, asks Cooper to come home and help her talk Rollie into a mental health facility. It's easy for Cooper to get away since he's just been fired from his newspaper job (at the *Tribune,* as you can tell from countless hints, although the paper is mysteriously never mentioned).

Cooper drives to his small hometown to find his mother overseeing Rollie, who has a big new project: He has attached fishing lines to an old-fashioned typewriter, so that every time he gets a bite, a letter gets typed. He searches the resulting manuscripts for actual words and combines them into poetry. Well, if monkeys can do it, why not fish?

The plot deepens. Uncle Rollie treasures a baseball card given him by his grandfather. The card features Frank Schulte, who played right field for the 1908 Chicago Cubs, and I don't need to tell you what the Cubs did in 1908. It may be the only card of its kind in existence, and Cooper and his mom realize that if Rollie sold it, all of his unpaid bills would be behind him. Meanwhile, Cooper has run into his old girlfriend Charlotte (Virginia Madsen), who has split with her husband; they slowly rekindle their romance. And what with one thing and another Charlotte and her son drive with Cooper and Rollie back to Chicago for a big sports memorabilia convention. They're trailed by the fiendish, rifle-toting hometown drunk Donny Prine (Jim True-Frost), who wants to steal the card.

Matthew Broderick has two light comedies in release this summer; the other is *Finding Amanda,* where he goes to Vegas to try to rescue his niece from a life of sin. In both films he reminded me of his amiability and quietly meticulous comic timing. He and Madsen find the right note for two old lovers who are casually renewing their romance.

The convention provides the movie's big set piece, as our heroes meet a nice baseball card dealer named Mad Dog McClure (Dylan Baker) and a crooked one named Lee Vivyan (Bobby Cannavale). It is Mad Dog who levels Lee with a withering curse: "You're bad for the hobby!" Baker and Cannavale more or less walk away with the scenes at the sports convention.

There is, of course, a duel over the invaluable card, and a fight, and a highly improbable showdown on a catwalk far above the convention arena, and a bit part for Ernie Banks, and a big kiss between Cooper and Charlotte, and it's all very nice, but not a whole lot more. The film is a coproduction of Chicago's Steppenwolf Theater, directed by veteran actor Terry Kinney, and inspired by Sherwood Kiraly's novel. Kinney shows himself a capable director, but isn't the material a little lightweight for Steppenwolf?

Drive Angry 3-D

(DIRECTED BY PATRICK LUSSIER; STARRING NICOLAS CAGE, AMBER HEARD; 2011)

Drive Angry 3-D opens with a muscle car racing across a burning bridge out of hell, while we hear a famous twelve-letter word used three or four times. So right away we know where we're at. Here is an exercise in deliberate vulgarity, gross excess, and the pornography of violence, not to forget garden variety pornography. You get your money's worth.

A movie review should determine what a movie hoped to achieve and whether it succeeded. The ambition of *Drive Angry 3-D* is to make a grind house B movie so jaw-droppingly excessive that even Quentin Tarantino might send flowers. It succeeds. I can't say I enjoyed it. But I can appreciate it. It offends every standard of taste except bad. But it is well made.

Of course it stars Nicolas Cage. Is there another actor who could or would have dared to sign on? Cage is a good actor in good movies, and an almost indispensable actor in bad ones. He can go over the top so effortlessly he rests up and makes lemonade for everybody. Here he plays a man named John Milton, a reference I fear will be lost on the film's target audience. Milton is hell-bent to rescue his baby granddaughter. A satanic cult enslaved and murdered his daughter, and now plans to sacrifice the infant by the light of the full moon. This Milton cannot abide.

The cult is led by Jonah (Billy Burke), who is obeyed by slavish followers he seems to have recruited from porn movies and guests on Jerry Springer shows about redneck incest. Their idea of partying is a topless orgy around a fire in an abandoned prison yard, while swigging Jack Daniels and warming up for a midnight infanticide. Their ranks are swelled by the usual shaved-headed and tattooed fatsos. There must be a pool of Hollywood extras who play big bald guys who can take three steps forward and glower into the camera.

Anyway, Milton's quest begins in a bar named Bull by the Balls, where he meets a barmaid named Piper (Amber Heard). After inconceivable violence, they link destinies. You've heard of girls attracted to the wrong kinds of guys? Piper inexplicably stays with Milton, despite many questions, which are even better than she thinks. Heard makes a plucky heroine who, although Piper's sexy and Milton likes the ladies, doesn't fall into the usual abyss of "love interest," but slugs it out like a cage fighter.

On their trail is the enigmatic Accountant (William Fichtner). This seemingly (spoiler alert) supernatural figure is relentless in pursuit, yet moves with the speed of a plodding gumshoe when he's not at the wheel of a muscle car or, oh, say, a tanker truck filled with liquid hydrogen. (The movie, of course, contains the official quota of walking-away-from-fiery-explosions-in-slo-mo shots.) As Milton chases Jonah and the Accountant chases Milton, Jonah's followers chase Milton, which is a great convenience, allowing Drive Angry 3-D to be more or less nothing but chase scenes, except for some interior gun battles and much portentous dialogue. (Cage brings an inimitable personal touch to, "The bullet is still in there." Pause. "I can feel it.")

Gene Siskel drew the line at children in danger. As a father, he disapproved of thrillers that exploited violent scenes involving kids. What would he have made of an extended sequence here where Jonah commands one of his followers to sacrifice an infant? He would have despised it, I believe. The only justification for it is that this entire movie is so broadly, grotesquely over the top that the baby is more of a prop than a human child. And Drive Angry 3-D trusts its audience to put every principle of Western civilization on hold.

So my review is a compromise. I'm giving it two stars. That's halfway between three stars (well made) and one star (loathesome). Nic Cage once again provides the zeal and energy to wade through a violent morass. William Fichtner makes the Accountant so intriguing that, although all CPAs aren't from hell, we know this one is. He has a nice twitchy reserve. Amber Heard and Billy Burke do everything that can possibly be done with their characters, and don't stop there.

Oh, and the 3-D? For an extra charge you get to wear glasses that make it look like it was shot where the sun don't shine.

Eagle Eye

(DIRECTED BY D. J. CARUSO; STARRING SHIA LABEOUF, MICHELLE MONAGHAN; 2008)
SPOILER WARNING: The word "preposterous" is too moderate to describe *Eagle Eye*. This film contains not a single plausible moment after the opening sequence, and that's borderline. It's not an assault on intelligence. It's an assault on consciousness. I know, I know. I liked *The Mummy: Tomb of the Dragon Emperor,* but that film intended to be absurd. *Eagle Eye* has real cars and buildings and trains and CNN and stuff, and purports to take place in the real world.

You might like it, actually. Lots of people will. It involves relentless action: chases involving planes, trains, automobiles, buses. Hundreds of dead. Enough crashes to stock a junkyard. Lots of stuff being blowed up real good. Two heroes who lack any experience with violence, but somehow manage to stick up an armored car at gunpoint, walk on board an unguarded military transport plane, and penetrate the ultrasecret twenty-ninth-floor basement of the Pentagon.

They are Jerry and Rachel (Shia LaBeouf and Michelle Monaghan).

Both are ordinary Chicagoans until they start getting commands from a mysterious female voice on their cell phones. Now try to follow this: Whatever force is behind the voice has control of every cell phone and security camera in the nation. "They" can control every elevated train and every stoplight. Can observe the traffic and give precise driving instructions. Can control the movements of cranes in junkyards, the locations of garbage barges, and arrange for a rendezvous on a dirt road in an Indiana country field. Oh, and when a guy drives down the road to meet them in a van, They can instruct them to warn the guy that if he walks away he will be killed. If They don't want him dead, then why do They kill him— since the situation clearly reflects Their power?

We haven't even arrived at the Pentagon yet, and already the audience is chuckling at the impossibilities. I won't even get started on the air cargo container, the syringes inside, and the on-time recovery of the heroes after they give themselves shots. Turns out the syringes were in a briefcase that the heroes survived incredible death and destruction to pick up, and it isn't even needed after the plane takes off. I won't give it away, but the only thing They really need is an attribute of Jerry's. So here's an idea that would save billions of dollars and hundreds of lives: Why not get a couple of no-neck guys from the West Side to kidnap Jerry, haul him on board a private jet, and transport him to Them?

OK, OK. Enough with the implausibilities. This whole movie is a feature-length deus ex machina, and if you don't know what that is, look it up, because you're going to need it to discuss *Eagle Eye*. And yet, I think I'll use the tricky star-rating system to give it two stars. Now why would I give it two instead of, oh, say, one star? Both *because* of the elements I've complained about, and *in spite* of the elements I've complained about.

Let me explain. If you're looking for a narrative that makes much sense, *Eagle Eye* lacks one. It's essentially a lot of CGI and stunt work, all stuck together in a row. Shia LaBeouf is a good young actor, but you wouldn't discover that here. I barely had time to observe that he resembles an underweight John Cusack when he was off and running, as Jerry and Rachel became elements in effects scenes. The movie obviously intends to resemble and inspire a video game, and at that it is slick. I look forward to professor David Bordwell's students using their clickers to work out the average shot length. I'm predicting less than three seconds. So to summarize, *Eagle Eye* is great at all the things I object to, and I admit it. But I didn't enjoy it.

Eat Pray Love

(DIRECTED BY RYAN MURPHY; STARRING JULIA ROBERTS, JAMES FRANCO; 2010)

Elizabeth Gilbert's book *Eat Pray Love*, unread by me, spent 150 weeks on the *New York Times* best-seller list and is by some accounts a good one. It is also movie material, concerning as it does a tall blonde (Gilbert) who ditches a failing marriage and a disastrous love affair to spend a year living in Italy, India, and Bali, seeking to find the balance of body, mind, and spirit. During this journey, great-looking men are platooned at her, and a wise man, who has to be reminded who she is, remembers instantly, although what he remembers is only what she's just told him.

I gather Gilbert's "prose is fueled by a mix of intelligence, wit and colloquial exuberance that is close to irresistible" (*New York Times Book Review*), and if intelligence, wit, and exuberance are what you're looking for, Julia Roberts is an excellent choice as the movie's star. You can see how it would be fun to spend a year traveling with Gilbert. A lot more fun than spending nearly two and a half hours watching a movie about it. I guess you have to belong to the narcissistic subculture of Woo-Woo.

Here is a movie about Liz Gilbert. About her quest, her ambition, her good luck in finding only nice men, including the ones she dumps. She funds her entire trip, including scenic accommodations, ashram, medicine man, guru, spa fees, and wardrobe, with her advance to write this book. Well, the publisher obviously made a wise investment. It's all about her, and a lot of readers can really identify with that. Her first marriage apparently broke down primarily because she tired of it, although Roberts at (a sexy and attractive) forty-three makes an actor's brave stab at explaining they were "young and immature." She walks out on the guy (Billy Crudup), and he still likes her and reads her on the Web.

In Italy, she eats such Pavarottian plates of pasta that I hope one of the things she prayed for in India was deliverance from the sin of gluttony. At one trattoria she apparently orders the entire menu, and I am not making this up. She meets a man played by James Franco, about whom, enough said. She shows moral fiber by leaving such a dreamboat for India, where her quest involves discipline in meditation, for which she allots three months rather than the recommended lifetime. There she meets a tall, bearded, bespectacled older Texan (Richard Jenkins) who is without question the most interesting and attractive man in the movie, and like all of the others seems innocent of lust.

In Bali she revisits her beloved adviser Ketut Liyer (Hadi Subiyanto), who is a master of truisms known to us all. Although he connects her with a healer who can mend a nasty cut with a leaf applied for a few hours, his own skills seem limited to the divinations anyone could make after looking at her, and telling her things about herself after she has already told him.

Now she has found Balance and begins to dance on the high-wire of her life. She meets Felipe (Javier Bardem), another divorced exile, who is handsome, charming, tactful, forgiving, and a good kisser. He explains that he lives in Bali because his business is import-export, "which you can do anywhere"—although later, he explains, "I live in Bali because my business is here." They've both forgotten what he said earlier. Unless perhaps you can do import-export anywhere, but you can only import and export from Bali when you live there. That would certainly be my alibi.

The audience I joined was perhaps 80 percent female. I heard some sniffles and glimpsed some tears, and no wonder. *Eat Pray Love* is shameless wish fulfillment, a Harlequin novel crossed with a mystic travelogue, and it mercifully reverses the life chronology of many people, which is Love Pray Eat.

El Cantante

(Directed by Leon Ichaso; starring Marc Anthony, Jennifer Lopez; 2007)

This bulletin just in: If you use cocaine or heroin, you are very likely to become addicted, and if you become addicted, there are usually two choices:

(1) get clean, or (2) die. The math is clear and has been proven in countless biopics about addicted musicians. The presumption in many of the pictures is that artists somehow need drugs because they are so talented they just can't stand it, or because of the "pressure" they're under, or because they need to be high all the time and not just on the stage, or because people won't leave them alone, or because they feel insecure or unworthy.

All lies. They are addicted because they are addicted. They got addicted by starting to take the stuff in the first place. It's chemistry. At some point, they don't use to get high, but to stop feeling sick. It is a sad, degrading existence, interrupted by flashes of feeling "OK." George Carlin once asked, "How does cocaine make you feel?" And he answered: "It makes you feel like having some more cocaine."

El Cantante, the life and death story of Hector Lavoe (Marc Anthony), the godfather of salsa, retraces the same tired footsteps of many another movie druggie before him. He lies, cheats, disappoints those who love him, and finally dies, although even the movie loses patience with the dying process and cuts out before getting to his years with AIDS (from an infected needle). All along the way, he is enabled and berated in equal measure by his wife and sometime manager, Puchi (Jennifer Lopez), who is our guide to his story in black-and-white flashbacks.

The end of the movie is a foregone conclusion, and Hector's inexorable descent is depressing, although interrupted by many upbeat musical numbers. Indeed, there seem to be two films here: a musical, with Anthony doing a terrific job of covering Lavoe's music, and a drugalogue. The sound track would be worth having. But there is nothing special about Lavoe's progress toward the grave: just the same old same old.

Lavoe was a gifted musician in Puerto Rico who moved to New York, changed his name from Perez, partnered with the great trombonist Willie Colon (who could have borrowed the leftover Perez), and began to blend Latin genres, jazz, and a dash of rock into something that was known as salsa and became very big. We sense the excitement of the new music in Anthony's stage performances, where he is backed by orchestras full of gifted musicians (Colon is played by John Ortiz), and where his moves project the joy of the music.

But always in the wings, looking worried, is Puchi. She loves the guy and his music, but not his drugs, and they have ceaseless arguments about his drug use, sometimes punctuated by her own. These period sequences are intercut with a modern-day Puchi, looking not a day older, remembering her life with Hector and reciting the litany of his fall from life. Since Puchi lived until 2002, she must have learned something about drugs, if only to stop, but her memories mostly take the form of puzzled complaints: That was a great night, but then . . . he went out and scored, used, passed out, etc., etc. They have a child, who functions as an afterthought in a few scenes, but mostly they roast in their private hell.

If you're a fan of Lavoe and salsa, or Lopez and Anthony, you'll want to see the movie for what's good in it. Otherwise, you may be disappointed. The director (Leon Ichaso) and his cowriters haven't licked a crucial question: Why do we need to see this movie and not just listen to the music?

The 11th Hour

(Directed by Leila Conners Petersen and Nadia Conners; 2007)

I agree with every word in this tedious documentary. As you can guess from the title, *The 11th Hour* sounds a warning that we have pretty much depleted the woodpile of planet Earth and, to keep things running, have been reduced to throwing our furniture on the fire. It is a devastating message.

Once there was a time when Earth existed on current energy. This year's sunlight fell on this year's crops, feeding and warming this year's human beings. With the exploitation of coal and oil, however, we have set fire to millions of years of stored energy as fast as we can, and the result is poisonous pollution, global warming, and planetary imbalance. What lies at the end of this suicidal spending spree? Stephen Hawking paints a future in which Earth resembles Venus, with a temperature of 482 degrees Fahrenheit. There would still be rain, however, although unfortunately of sulfuric acid.

Earth is cartwheeling out of balance. Did you know, as I learned in the new issue of *Discover,* that while fish stocks disappear from the oceans, their place is being taken by an unimaginably huge explosion of jellyfish—literally brainless creatures with a lifestyle consisting of eating? Sounds like us.

The 11th Hour gathers a group of respected experts to speak from their areas of knowledge about how we are despoiling our planet and what we might possibly do to turn things around. We don't have much time. The architects John Todd and Bruce Mau explain how we could build "green" buildings that would use solar energy, consume their own waste, and function much like a tree. There is no reason why every home (every newly built one, for sure) could not have solar panels on the roof to help heat, light, and cool itself. Well, one reason actually: The energy companies would resist any effort to redirect their own gargantuan subsidies toward eco-friendly homeowners.

We hear of the destruction of the forests, the death of the seas, the melting of the poles, the trapping of greenhouse gases. And in another forthcoming documentary, *In the Shadow of the Moon,* about the surviving astronauts who walked on the moon, we see their view of Earth from 250,000 miles away; it strikes us what an awfully large planet this is to be wrapped in such a thin and vulnerable atmosphere.

All of this is necessary to know. But are we too selfish to do anything about it? Why isn't everybody buying a hybrid car? They can get up to a third more fuel mileage. They are getting cheaper as gas grows more expensive. And here's the kicker: *They can go faster* because they have two engines. So you ask people if they're getting a hybrid, and they squirm and say, gee, they dunno, they'd rather stick to the old way of going slower, spending more on gas, and destroying the atmosphere. If booze companies advertise for responsible drinking and tobacco companies warn of health hazards, why don't gas companies ask you to buy a hybrid?

Some of these facts are in *The 11th Hour,* others are offered by me, and the point is: We more or less know all this stuff anyway. So does the movie motivate us to act on it? Not really. After I saw Al Gore's *An Inconvenient Truth,* my next car was a hybrid. After seeing *The 11th Hour,* I'd be thinking more about my next movie.

The film sidesteps one of the oldest laws of television news and documentaries: *Write to the picture!* When Gore's film tells you something, it shows you what it's talking about. Too much of the footage of *The 11th Hour* is just standard nature photography, as helicopter-cams swoop over hill and dale and birds look unhappy and ice melts. This is intercut with fifty experts, more or less, who talk and talk and talk. The narrator and coproducer is Leonardo DiCaprio, who sounds like he's presenting a class project. Everyone is seen as talking heads, so we see them talk, then get some nature footage, then see them talk some more, until finally we're thinking, enough already; I get it. "A bore," Meyer the hairy economist once told the private eye Travis McGee, "is anyone who deprives you of solitude without providing you with companionship." This movie, for all its noble intentions, is a bore. Rent *An Inconvenient Truth* instead. Even if you've already seen it.

Evening

(DIRECTED BY LAJOS KOLTAI; STARRING CLAIRE DANES, TONI COLLETTE; 2007)
There are few things more depressing than a weeper that doesn't make you weep. *Evening* creeps through its dolorous paces as prudently as an undertaker. Upstairs, in the big Newport mansion, a woman is dying in a Martha Stewart bedroom. She takes a very long time to die, because the whole movie is flashbacks from her reveries. This gives us time to reflect on deep issues, such as, who is this woman?

Everybody in the film knows her, and eventually we figure out that she is Ann (Vanessa Redgrave), once the young sprite played in the flashbacks by Claire Danes. I know I must be abnormally obtuse to be confused on this question, but I persisted in thinking she might be the aged form of Lila, who as a young girl (Mamie Gummer) is getting married as the movie opens (it opens in a flashback, then flashes forward to the bed where it is flashing back from). How could I make such a stupid error? Because the mansion she is dying in looks like the same mansion Lila was married from, so I assumed old Lila was still living there. Maybe it's a different mansion. Real estate confuses me.

There are two grown daughters hanging around at the bedside: Constance (Natasha Richardson) and Nina (Toni Collette). But you can't figure out who they are from the flashbacks, because neither has been born yet. However, the flashbacks devote a great deal of time to examining how Lila has had a crush on Harris (Patrick Wilson), a young doctor and wedding guest whose mother was the family's housekeeper. Lila's brother Buddy (Hugh Dancy) has also had a lifelong crush on Harris, but his love dare not speak its name. Ann is Lila's best friend and maid of honor, and she also falls in love with Harris.

Lila is scheduled to be married on the morrow to the kind of a bore who (I'm only guessing) would be happy as the corresponding secretary of his fraternity. She does not love him. She loves Harris. I already said that. But what makes this Harris so electrifying? Search me. If he is warm, witty, and wonderful on the inside, those qualities are well concealed by his exterior, which resembles a good job of aluminum siding: It is unbending and resists the elements.

Oh, but I forgot: Harris has one ability defined in my *Little Movie Glossary*. He is a Seeing-Eye Man. Such men are gifted at pointing out things to women. Man sees, points, woman turns, and *now* she sees, too, and smiles gratefully.

Harris is a very highly evolved Seeing-Eye Man. Not once but twice he looks at the heavens and sees a twinkling star. "That's our star," he says, or words to that effect. "See it there?" He points. Young Ann looks up at the billions and billions of stars, sees their star, and nods gratefully. Director Lajos Koltai cuts to the sky, and we see it, too. Or one just like it.

In the upstairs bedroom, old Ann dies very slowly, remembering the events of the long-ago wedding night and the next morning. Out of consideration for us, her reveries are in chronological order, even including events at which she was not present, like before she arrived at the house. She is attended by a nurse with an Irish accent (Eileen Atkins), who sometimes prompts her: "Remember a happy time!" Dissolve to Ann's memory of a happy time. It is so mundane that if it qualifies as a high point in her life, it compares with Paris Hilton remembering a good stick of gum.

What horrors have I overlooked? Oh, the Plunge. Family tradition at weddings requires all male guests to plunge from a high rock into the sea. This inevitably leads to shots of the barren ocean, and cries of, "Buddy? Buddy?" But I'm not giving anything away because Buddy is good for no end of cries of "Buddy?" in this movie. At one point, he needs a doctor, and they remember that Harris is a doctor, and start shouting "Harris! Harris!" in the forest, having absolutely no reason to suppose Harris is within earshot. Buddy inevitably is an alcoholic whose family members are forever moving the wine bottle out of his reach. He has to get drunk as an excuse to kiss Harris. This is pathetic. Buddy should grow up, bite the bullet, and learn that it takes no excuse to get drunk.

Later on, women in the flashbacks get pregnant and deliver the children who will puzzle us in the flash forwards, and there is one of those poignant chance encounters in Manhattan in the rain, where two old lovers meet after many years and have hardly anything to say. You know the kind of poignant encounter I'm thinking of. All too well, I imagine.

Extraordinary Measures

(DIRECTED BY TOM VAUGHN; STARRING BRENDAN FRASER, HARRISON FORD; 2010)

Extraordinary Measures is an ordinary film with ordinary characters in a story too big for it. Life has been reduced to a Lifetime movie. The story, based on fact, is compelling: Two sick children have no more than a year to live when their father determines to seek out a maverick scientist who may have a cure. This is *Lorenzo's Oil* with a different disease, Pompe disease, although it fudges the facts to create a better story. The film centers on two dying children, nine and seven. In life, most children with Pompe die before age two, and those in the real story were fifteen months and seven days old when they got sick, and five and three when they were treated.

With children that young, the drama would have focused on the parents. By making Megan Crowley (Meredith Droeger) a wise and cheerful nine-year-old, *Extraordinary Measures* improves her as a story element. Her father is John Crowley (Brendan Fraser), an executive at Bristol-Myers. Her mother is Aileen (Keri Russell). Neither is developed any more deeply than the story requires. Their personal relationship is defined by their desperation as the deadlines for their children grow nearer.

Crowley discovers on the Internet a professor at the University of

Nebraska named Dr. Robert Stonehill (Harrison Ford). He's working on a controversial cure for Pompe that the medical establishment rejects, and when he won't return messages, Crowley impulsively flies to Nebraska to confront him.

Dr. Robert Stonehill doesn't exist in life. The Pompe cure was developed by Dr. Yuan-Tsong Chen and his colleagues while he was at Duke University. He is now director of the Institute of Biomedical Science in Taiwan. Harrison Ford, as this film's executive producer, perhaps saw Stonehill as a plum role for himself; a rewrite was necessary because he couldn't very well play Dr. Chen. The real Chen, a Taiwan University graduate, worked his way up at Duke from a residency to professor and chief of medical genetics at the Duke University Medical Center. He has been mentioned as a Nobel candidate.

I suspect Dr. Chen might have inspired a more interesting character than "Dr. Stonehill." The Nebraskan seems inspired more by Harrison Ford's image and range. He plays the doctor using only a few spare parts off the shelf. (1) He likes to crank up rock music while he works. (2) He doesn't return messages. (3) He's so feckless he accidentally hangs up on Crowley by pulling the phone off his desk. (4) He likes to drink beer from longneck bottles in a honky-tonk bar and flirt with the waitress. (5) "I'm a scientist, not a doctor." He's not interested in Pompe patients, only the chemistry of the disease.

This becomes tiresome. Later he becomes invested in the Crowleys, but of course he does. They hope to fund a high-tech startup and deal with venture capitalists whose scenes are more interesting than many of the medical ones. Contrast this with the character of Augusto Odone, played by Nick Nolte in *Lorenzo's Oil*—a self-taught parent who discovers his own cure for a rare nerve disease. Ford is given no lines that suggest depth of character, only gruffness that gradually mellows.

The film also fails to explain that the cost of the medication is $300,000 a year for life, which limits its impact in the United States because many American insurance companies refuse to pay for it. According to Wikipedia: "The vast majority of developed countries are providing access to therapy for all diagnosed Pompe patients."

Make no mistake. The Crowleys were brave and resourceful, and their proactive measures saved the lives of their children—and many more with Pompe. This is a remarkable story. I think the film lets them down. It finds the shortest possible route between beginning and end. And it sidesteps the point that the U.S. health care system makes it unavailable to many dying children; they are being saved in nations with universal health coverage.

● ● ● ● ● ● ● ● ●

Fame

(DIRECTED BY KEVIN TANCHAROEN; STARRING NATURI NAUGHTON, KAY PANABAKER; 2009)

Why bother to remake *Fame* if you don't have a clue about why the 1980 movie was special? Why take a touching experience and make it into a shallow exercise? Why begin with an R-rated look at plausible kids with real problems and tame it into a PG-rated after-school special? Why cast actors who are sometimes too old and experienced to play seniors, let alone freshmen?

The new *Fame* is a sad reflection of the new Hollywood, where material is sanitized and dumbed down for a hypothetical teen market that is way too sophisticated for it. It plays like a dinner theater version of the original. That there are some genuinely talented actors in the film doesn't help, because they're given little to build on or work with.

Do we, at this point, need another version of the creaky scene where a boyfriend misunderstands the way his girl smiles at another guy, and gets mad? Do we require parents who want their daughter to be a classical pianist and don't understand the need in her soul to perform hip-hop? Above all, do we need a big finale so elaborate and overproduced it looks like a musical number on the Oscars and could not possibly be staged in any high school?

As an admirer of Alan Parker's 1980 film, I was interested to see what would be done with this one. I suspect its director, Kevin Tancharoen

(*Britney Spears Live from Miami*), didn't understand the Parker film. It was not an excuse for a musical. It was a film with great musical performances growing out of tangible dramatic situations.

The new screenplay by Allison Burnett is shallow and facile. No personal or family relationships are dealt with in other but clichés. Some of the student-teacher scenes are expected, but effective, because such adult actors as Charles S. Dutton, Bebe Neuwirth, Megan Mullally, and Debbie Allen (from the original film and TV series) speak from conviction and not plot contrivance.

The film, like the original, is broken into segments: "Freshman Year," and so on. In 1980 we got a sense of time passing and characters changing. In the new film these years relentlessly follow the standard screenplay formula: Introduction, Development, Problems, Resolution, Happy Ending. As "Junior Year" started, I looked at my watch to confirm how little time had passed. The film feels hurried. It is perhaps evidence of postproduction cutting that the fourth-billed Kelsey Grammer, playing a teacher, is on screen so rarely (his first dialogue is nice, however).

I got little sense of who these kids were. Some of them I liked a lot. They don't parallel the original characters or use their names, but I gather that Naturi Naughton, as Denise, is intended to function like Irene Cara, as Coco. Naughton is touching and talented, but the scenes involving her controlling father are written on autopilot. And is it plausible that such a gifted classical pianist would have so little feeling for her art?

Kay Panabaker, as Jenny, makes a sort of Molly Ringwald impression, but her character isn't gifted enough to convince us she'd make it through auditions. Anna Maria Perez de Tagle, as Joy, looks so fetching we wish she had been given more substantial scenes. Collins Pennie, as Malik, has the thankless role of the kid angry about childhood memories; that he is twenty-five makes his adolescent angst less convincing.

The filmmakers have stacked the deck, with several experienced actors in their twenties looking very little like fourteen-year-old freshmen and dancing like Broadway veterans. Their inexperience is acted, not felt. The irony is that Dutton's character in the film provides advice the film should have taken to heart.

Fanboys

(DIRECTED BY KYLE NEWMAN; STARRING SAM HUNTINGTON, CHRISTOPHER MARQUETTE; 2009)

A lot of fans are basically fans of fandom itself. It's all about them. They have mastered the *Star Wars* or *Star Trek* universes or whatever, but their objects of veneration are useful mainly as a backdrop to their own devotion. Anyone who would camp out in a tent on the sidewalk for weeks in order to be first in line for a movie is more into camping on the sidewalk than movies.

Extreme fandom may serve as a security blanket for the socially inept, who use its extreme structure as a substitute for social skills. If you are Luke Skywalker and she is Princess Leia, you already know what to say to each other, which is so much safer than having to ad lib it. Your fannish obsession is your beard. If you know absolutely all the trivia about your cubbyhole of pop culture, it saves you from having to know anything about anything else. That's why it's excruciatingly boring to talk to such people: They're always asking you questions they know the answer to.

But enough about my opinions; what about *Fanboys*? Its primary flaw is that it's not critical. It is a celebration of an idiotic lifestyle, and I don't think it knows it. If you want to get in a car and drive to California, fine. So do I. So did Jack Kerouac. But if your first stop involves a rumble at a *Star Trek* convention in Iowa, dude, beam your ass down to Route 66.

The movie, set in 1999, involves four *Star Wars* fanatics and, eventually, their gal pal, who have the notion of driving to Marin County, breaking into the Skywalker Ranch, and stealing a copy of a print of *Star Wars Episode 1: The Phantom Menace* so they can see it before anyone else. This is about as plausible as breaking into the U.S. Mint and stealing some money so you can spend it before anyone else.

Fanboys follows in the footsteps of *Sex Drive* by allowing one of its heroes to plan a rendezvous with an Internet sex goddess. To avoid revealing any plot secrets in this movie, I will recycle my earlier warning: In a chat room, don't be too hasty to believe Ms. Tasty.

This plot is given gravitas because one of the friends, Linus (Christopher Marquette), is dying of cancer. His buddy Eric (Sam Huntington) is in favor of the trip because, I dunno, it will give Linus something to live for, I guess. The other fanboys are Hutch (Dan Fogler), who lives in his mother's garage/coach house, and Windows (Jay Baruchel), who changed his name from MacOS. Just kidding. Windows, Hutch, and Linus work in a comic book store, where their favorite customer is Zoe (Kristen Bell). She's sexy *and* a *Star Wars* fan. How cool is that? She's almost better than the date who turns into a pizza and a six-pack when the deed is done.

The question of Linus's cancer became the subject of a celebrated Internet flame war last summer, with supporters of *Fanboys* director Kyle Newman running Anti-Harvey Web sites opposing Harvey Weinstein's alleged scheme to cut the subplot out of the movie. The subplot survived, but it's one of those movie diseases that is mentioned occasionally so everyone can look solemn, and then dropped when the ailing Linus dons a matching black camouflage outfit and scales the Skywalker Ranch walls with a grappling hook.

Fanboys is an amiable but disjointed movie that identifies too closely with its heroes. Poking a little more fun at them would have been a great idea. They are tragically hurtling into a cultural dead end, mastering knowledge that has no purpose other than being mastered, and too smart to be wasting their time. When a movie's opening day finally comes and fanboys leave their sidewalk tents for a mad dash into the theater, I wonder who retrieves their tents, sleeping bags, portable heaters, and iPod speakers. Warning: Mom isn't always going to be there to clean up after you.

Fast and Furious

(DIRECTED BY JUSTIN LIN; STARRING VIN DIESEL, PAUL WALKER; 2009)

Fast and Furious is exactly and precisely what you'd expect. Nothing more, unfortunately. You get your cars that are fast and your characters that are furious. You should. They know how to make these movies by now. Producer Neil Moritz is on his fourth, and director Justin Lin on his second in a row. Vin Diesel and other major actors are back from *The Fast and the Furious* (2001). All they left behind were two definite articles.

This is an expertly made action film, by which I mean the special effects are good and the acting is extremely basic. The screenplay rotates these nouns through various assortments of dialogue: Race. Driver(s). Nitro. Meth. Sister. FBI. Border. Dead. Mexico. Murder. Prison. Traffic violations. Tunnel. Muscle car. Import. Plymouth. Funeral. Helicopter(s). Toretto. Ten seconds. Corona. Cocaine.

The plot. Dom Toretto (Vin Diesel) has been in the Dominican Republic for the last six years but now returns to America, where he is a wanted man. Probable charges: vehicular homicide, murder, smuggling, dating an FBI agent's sister. Reason for return: Letty (Michelle Rodriguez), the girl he loved, has been killed.

After Toretto's arrest all those years ago, he was allowed to escape by FBI agent Brian O'Conner (Paul Walker), for reasons explained in this film. Now Brian is back, on a task force to track down Toretto and the leader of a drug cartel.

This provides a scaffolding on which to hang the body of the movie, which involves a series of chase scenes, fights, explosions, and sexy women who would like to make themselves available to Toretto, to no avail. He is single-minded.

The pre-title chase scene is pretty amazing. Toretto and his group team up in four racing vehicles to pursue a truck hauling not one, not two, not three, but *four* enormous tanks of gasoline. Their method: Toretto drives close behind fourth tank, girl climbs out of sun roof, stands on hood, leaps to ladder on back of tank, climbs on top, runs to front of tank, leaps down, uncouples tank from third one. The reason the girl does this while Toretto drives is, I guess, well, you know what they say about women drivers.

Ever seen a truck hauling four enormous gas containers? I haven't. On a narrow mountain road? With a sudden, steep incline around a curve, when it narrows to one lane? Not me. Why are they going to this trouble? So their buddies can have free gas for a street race that night in L.A. I say let them buy their own damn gas. The race is down city streets with ordinary traffic on them. Then the wrong way on an expressway. Not a cop in sight. Where are the TV news choppers when you want them? This would get huge ratings.

I dunno. I admire the craft involved, but the movie leaves me profoundly indifferent. After three earlier movies in the series, which have been transmuted into video games, why do we need a fourth one? Oh. I just answered my own question.

Fay Grim

(DIRECTED BY HAL HARTLEY; STARRING PARKER POSEY, JEFF GOLDBLUM; 2007)

Hal Hartley's *Fay Grim* stars Parker Posey and Jeff Goldblum in a search for a mysterious terrorist named Henry Fool. This man, we learn, has been part of intrigues involving Chile, Iraq, Israel, France, Germany, Russia, England, China, and the Vatican (where the pope *threw a chair at him*). All in the last seven years.

Posey plays the title character, a mom from Queens whose son gets in trouble at school for showing around a hand-cranked toy movieola with pornographic images. Who mailed him the device? Could it have something to do with her brother Simon (James Urbaniak), a Nobel Prize–winning poet who has been jailed for helping Henry Fool escape the United States? Or with Henry Fool (Thomas Jay Ryan) himself? Enter Fulbright (Goldblum) and Fogg (Leo Fitzpatrick), CIA agents searching for Henry's missing confessions. Soon Fay is caught up in an international intrigue.

But a peculiar intrigue it is, because Hartley's style seems determined to dampen our interest in the plot. Working with a usually tilting camera, he photographs his characters taking part in lugubrious and maddening dialogue of bewildering complexity. And he minimizes the action, which mostly takes place offscreen.

When a man leaps from a hotel roof, for example, we don't see what happens, but we hear a crash. When a man is hit by a car, we don't see it happen, but Hartley cuts to a staged and unconvincing shot of him rolling off the car's hood. Shoot-outs are handled with montages of still images.

The result is that we feel deliberately distanced from the film. It is not so much an exercise in style as an exercise in search of a style. The story doesn't involve us because we can't follow it, and we doubt if the characters can either. But am I criticizing Hartley, a leading indie filmmaker, for not making a more conventional thriller, with more chases and action scenes? Not at all. I am criticizing him for failing to figure out what he wanted to do instead, and delivering a film that is tortured in its attempt at cleverness and plays endlessly.

Parker Posey and Jeff Goldblum labor at their characters, and are often fun to watch. But in the absence of a screenplay that engages them, they have to fall back on their familiar personalities and quirks. They bring more to the movie than it brings to them.

Fay Grim is the sequel to *Henry Fool*, Hartley's 1998 film, which won the screenwriting prize at Cannes. In that one, Henry first motivated Simon to become a poet and didn't seem involved in intrigues. He was an enigma with no purpose other than being enigmatic. Now we find out much more about Henry, but it all seems arbitrary and made up on the spot.

As for Hartley's tilted camera, tilt shots have traditionally been used to create a heightened sense of danger; the characters can hardly hold onto the screen. Here they're used for scenes of stultifying dialogue and seem more like a desperate attempt to add interest to flat material. I like it better when style seems to emerge from a story (as in *The Third Man*) than when it feels trucked in from the outside.

Note: Much is made of the fact that Henry's confessions may be encrypted. It is ironic, therefore, that the key encryption simply involves initials that are seen upside down and need to be turned over? But see if you can figure out how Fay finds the blind antiques dealer who can explain it all to her. Kind of a coincidence?

Feast of Love

(DIRECTED BY ROBERT BENTON; STARRING MORGAN FREEMAN, GREG KINNEAR; 2007)

Morgan Freeman returns in *Feast of Love* as a wise counselor of the troubled and heartsick. Apart from his great films, of which there are many, this is almost his standard role, although he also seems to spend a lot of time playing God. Most of his insights seem not merely handed down the mountain, but arriving as a successful forward pass. At the beginning of the film, he gives us the ground rules: "They say that when the Greek gods were bored, they invented humans. Still bored, they invented love. That wasn't boring, so they tried it themselves. And then they invented laughter—so they could stand it."

The Greek gods had one thing going for them. They were immutable. Zeus was always Zeus and Hera was always Hera, and they were always in character, always Zeuslike and Heraesque. In *Feast of Love*, however, Freeman plays a professor named Harry who is forced to contend with confused lovers who don't know, or can't reveal, their own hearts.

He lives in Portland, Oregon, in a long and happy marriage with Esther (Jane Alexander). Spare hours are spent in Jitters coffee shop, where his coffee cup is an omnipresent prop and useful timing device; sips punctuate his wisdom. The shop is owned by Bradley (Greg Kinnear), who thinks he is in love with his wife, Kathryn (Selma Blair). But he is living in a fool's paradise, as Harry easily sees one evening when they all go to a bar after a women's softball game.

"I saw two women fall in love with one another tonight," he tells Esther when he gets home. Yes, he watched as Jenny (Stana Katic), a shortstop on the opposing team, put a quarter in the jukebox, a hand on Kathryn's leg, and whispered, "From now on, that will be our song." Harry is bemused: "Bradley was sitting right there, and he didn't see a thing."

Bradley has blindness when it comes to women. He brings home a dog for Kathryn's birthday present, although she has told him time and again that she hates and fears dogs. Maybe there is a clue to their incompatibility when, during a forced visit to the animal shelter, she named this particular dog "Bradley."

This Bradley, he's a pushover. Next he falls in love with a Realtor named Diana (Radha Mitchell), who walks into his shop on a rainy day. She smokes organic cigarettes. Those are the ones that kill you but don't support Big Tobacco. She's having a heartless, purely physical affair with the studly David (Billy Burke), whom she has not quite broken up with. Bradley doesn't see this.

Meanwhile, Oscar (Toby Hemingway), the counterman in the coffee shop, falls in love with a girl who walks in one day and makes her love for him clear. This is Chloe (Alexa Davalos), who is good and true, but Oscar has problems of his own. He lives with his father, Bat (Fred Ward), a drunk who staggers around so comically he looks like he thinks he's in a silent comedy and lurks in the bushes brandishing a knife. No movie can be very good that contains Fred Ward's worst performance (it's the fault of the character, to be sure).

Have I left out any combinations? Only the doctor (Sherilyn Lawson) who bandages Bradley's finger after he cuts himself as punishment for losing Diana. All of these scenarios unwind under the thoughtful gaze of Harry, who returns with his nightly reports to Esther. They have had a wounding personal loss—an esteemed son, dead of an overdose. But Esther seems content to sit at home alone until such intervals as Harry can free himself from his coffee shop, park bench, and other counseling stations.

There are some good things in the movie. Some scenes play well as self-contained episodes. The city of Portland is beautifully evoked. Jane Alexander and Morgan Freeman make a couple we love. Greg Kinnear raises fecklessness to an art. And there is a lot more nudity than you'd expect, if you like that sort of thing.

All of these stories are woven into a tapestry by director Robert Benton, working from a screenplay by Allison Burnett, which is based on the novel by Charles Baxter. Benton has made better movies about doomed marriages (*Kramer vs. Kramer*), but this one has no organic reality because it depends on three artifices: (1) the clockwork success and failure of relationships, (2) the need for Harry as a witness, (3) the lickety-split time span that compresses the action so much it loses emotional weight. Harry is always looking on as if he already knows how every story will turn out. We're looking on in exactly the same way.

Film Socialisme

(DIRECTED BY JEAN-LUC GODARD; STARRING CATHERINE TANVIER, CHRISTIAN SINNIGER; 2011)

One sunny day at Cannes, I sat at lunch with the British director Ken Russell, who had been well served and was feeling relaxed. As far as he was concerned, he said, he was pleased home video had been invented because now films could be watched on fast-forward, saving everyone's time. There was a quiet smile on Russell's face as he dozed off. "You're kidding!" I said. He awoke with a start. "Certainly not!" he said, and pushed back from the table.

I suppose it was only a matter of time until Russell's insight reached Jean-Luc Godard. The great director began with films that we would all agree fit the definition of "movie," and has relentlessly been putting more and more distance between himself and that form. With *Film Socialisme,* made in his seventy-ninth year, the pioneer of the French New Wave has been swept out to sea.

This film is an affront. It is incoherent, maddening, deliberately opaque, and heedless of the ways in which people watch movies. All of that is part of the Godardian method, I am aware, but I feel a bargain of some sort must be struck. We enter the cinema with open minds and good will, expecting Godard to engage us in at least a vaguely penetrable way. But in *Film Socialisme* he expects us to do all the heavy lifting.

When the film premiered at Cannes 2010, it was received with the usual bouquet of cheers, hoots, and catcalls. Defenders of Godard wrote at length about his content and purpose, while many others frankly felt insulted. In the spirit of Ken Russell, Godard actually posted an online video that used fast-forward to show his entire film in about four minutes. That, I concede, showed wit. You can see it here: http://bit.ly/lznp1u.

In the film, he shows us fragmented scenes on a cruise ship traveling the Mediterranean, and also shots which travel through human history, which for the film's purposes involve Egypt, Greece, Palestine, Odessa (notably its steps), Naples, Barcelona, Tunisia, and other ports. Then we see fragments of a story involving two women (one a TV camerawoman) and a family living at a roadside garage. A mule and a llama also live at the garage. There are shots of kittens, obscurely linked to the Egyptians, as well as parrots. The cruise ship is perhaps a metaphor for our human voyage through time. The garage is anybody's guess.

There is also much topical footage, both moving and still. Words are spoken, some of them bits of language from eminent authors. These words appear in uppercase subtitles, and are mostly nouns. These subtitles,

Godard explained, are what he calls Navajo English. I guess he learned it from old Westerns.

His Navajo speakers touch on socialism, gambling, nationalism, Hitler, Stalin, art, Islam, women, Jews, Hollywood, Palestine, war, and other large topics. It all seems terrifically political, but there is nothing in the film to offend the most devout Tea Party communicant, and I can't say what, if anything, the film has to say about socialism.

Godard has sent my mind scurrying between ancient history and modern television, via Marxism and Nazism, to ponder—well, what? In addition to standard digital video, Godard uses a state-of-the-art iteration of high-def video; some shots, especially aboard the cruise ship, are so beautiful and glossy they could be an advertisement for something, perhaps a cruise ship. Other shots seem taken with cell phones, and there are bits and pieces from old movies.

The film closes with large block letters: NO COMMENT. I would have looked forward to attending Godard's press conference, but of course he didn't attend it. Once, at Montreal, I sat next to him at a little dinner for film critics, at which he arranged his garden peas into geometric forms on his plate and told us, "Cinema is the train. It is not the station." Or perhaps my memory has tricked me, and he said, "Cinema is the station. It is not the train." Both are equally true. Or not.

Filth and Wisdom
(DIRECTED BY MADONNA; STARRING EUGENE HUTZ, HOLLY WESTON; 2008)

Aren't we all way beyond being shocked by sexual fetishes simply because they exist? Haven't we all stopped thinking, "Ohmigod! That's a guy in drag!" or "Ohmigod! That's a dominatrix!" or "Ohmigod! She's tattooed!" or having any kind of reaction to body piercing, which no longer even qualifies as a fetish, except when practiced on body areas we are unlikely to see anyway?

We live in a time, a sad time, I think, when some fetishes are even marketed to children. Consider the dominatrix Barbie doll. Of course, films that are *about* sexual fetishes can be fascinating. Remember *Secretary*, about

S&M, or *The Crying Game,* about transvestism, or *Kissed,* about necrophilia. All very good films. But in simply observing the fact of a fetish, the old frisson is gone. I mention this because Madonna still gets intrigued, I guess, simply by regarding a stripper sliding down a pole.

Filth and Wisdom, Madonna's directing debut, is a pointless exercise in "shocking" behavior, involving characters in London so shallow that the most sympathetic is the lecherous Indian dentist (Inder Manocha) who is supposed to be a villain, maybe. The central character is A.K. (Eugene Hutz), a rock singer who moonlights as a male dominator and will dress up like a ringmaster and whip you if you pay the big bucks. He is a fountain of wise little axioms, of which one is actually profound: "The problem with treating your body like a cash register is that you always feel empty."

A.K. is the landlord for flatmates Holly (Holly Weston) and Juliette (Vicky McClure), and also their unpaid adviser, who steers Holly into stripping at a lap-dance sleaze pit. Madonna thinks it's funny, or sad, or something, that Holly is not too good at hanging upside-down from the pole and erotically sliding down it.

I saw my first strip show at the old Follies Burlesque on South State Street one day after I moved to Chicago, and I interviewed the immortal Tempest Storm when she appeared here. The strippers at that time performed slowly and seductively, and it was a "tease." Today's strippers leap on stage already almost naked and perform contortions that gotta hurt. Some are so gifted they can get one boob going clockwise and the other counterclockwise.

Ugh. They're erotic only to men who enjoy seeing women humiliate themselves. I was but a callow youth from a small town amid the soy fields, but, reader, I confess I idealized some of them. I haven't attended a strip show in years and years, and for that I am grateful. Oh, there was that time we were in Bangkok and saw the show with the Ping Pong balls. Who could think of sex during such a skillful display?

But I wander. *Filth and Wisdom* also places a blot on the record of Richard E. Grant, who brought snarkiness to perfection in *Withnail and I* and *How to Get Ahead in Advertising.* Here he's made to play an elderly, blind, gay, depressed poet who is smiling on the outside, and you know the rest.

For what purpose? To help Madonna fill the endless eighty-one-minute running time with characters we don't care about, who don't care about one another except when dictated to by the screenplay, in a story nobody cares about. This is a very deeply noncaring movie. I liked Hutz when he sang. I imagine Gene Shalit ate his heart out when he saw Hutz's moustache.

Fired Up

(DIRECTED BY WILL GLUCK; STARRING NICHOLAS D'AGOSTO, ERIC CHRISTIAN OLSEN; 2009)

After the screening of *Fired Up*, one of my colleagues grimly observed that *Dead Man* was a better cheerleader movie. That was, you will recall, the 1995 Western starring Johnny Depp, Robert Mitchum, Billy Bob Thornton, and Iggy Pop. I would give almost anything to see them on a cheerleading squad. Here is a movie that will do for cheerleading what *Friday the 13th* did for summer camp.

The story involves two callow and witless high school football players, Shawn and Nick, who don't want to attend summer football training camp in the desert. They also want to seduce the school cheerleaders, so they decide to attend cheerleading camp, ha ha. Their high school is in Hinsdale, Illinois, whose taxpayers will be surprised to learn the school team trains in the desert just like the Cubs, but will be even more surprised to learn the entire film was shot in California. And they will be puzzled about why many of the cheers involve chants of the letters *F!U!*—which stand for *Fired Up*, you see.

Oh, is this movie bad. The characters relentlessly attack one another with the forced jollity of minimum-wage workers pressing you with free cheese samples at the supermarket. Every conversation involves a combination of romantic misunderstandings, double entendres, and flirtation that is just sad. No one in the movie has an idea in their bubbly little brains. No, not even Philip Baker Hall, who plays the football coach in an eruption of obligatory threats.

The plot involves a cheerleading competition along the lines of the one in *Bring It On* (2000), the *Citizen Kane* of cheerleader movies. That movie involved genuinely talented cheerleaders. This one involves ungainly human pyramids and a lot of uncoordinated jumping up and down. Faithful readers will recall that I often ask why the bad guys in movies wear matching black uniforms. They do in this one, too. The villains here are the Panther cheerleading squad. How many teams play in all black?

I could tell you about Carly, Bianca, Gwyneth, Poppy, and the other sexy cheerleaders, but I couldn't stir myself to care. There is an old rule in the theater: If the heroine coughs in the first act, she has to die in the third. In this movie, the cutest member of the squad is Angela (Hayley Marie Norman). She also has the nicest smile and the best personality and is on screen early and often, so I kept expecting her big scene, but no: She seems destined to be the cheerleader's cheerleader, pepping them up, cheering them on, smiling, applauding, holding up the bottom of the pyramid, laughing at funny lines, encouraging, bouncing in sync, and projecting with every atom of her being the attitude *You go, girls!* You've got a problem when you allow the most intriguing member of the cast to appear in that many scenes and never deal with her. That is not the movie's fatal flaw, however. Its flaw is that I was thinking about things like that.

5 Days of War

(DIRECTED BY RENNY HARLIN; STARRING RUPERT FRIEND, EMMANUELLE CHRIQUI; 2011)

At the end of this film there is a montage of sad people holding photographs of their grandparents, parents, husbands, wives, or children who were killed during the 5 *Days of War* between Russia and Georgia. It is unforgivable to borrow human grief and evoke it to lend weight to an action movie scarcely deeper than a Michael Bay extravaganza. Here you will hear a great deal about the war but learn not so very much, and all from the Georgian point of view. Mind you, I'm not saying its POV is wrong—only that a cheesy war thriller financed with Georgian funds seems an odd way to publicize it.

The heroes of the film are war correspondents. The film opens with the fact that five hundred reporters have been killed in war in the last decade. That is a tragedy, but one must reflect that countless more soldiers and civilians have been killed during the same period, and so the focus seems a little misguided—especially since some of these reporters are less than noble. Consider Dutchman (Val Kilmer), an enigmatic journalist apparently in search of a good time. The hero is Thomas Anders (Rupert Friend), a reporter who free-lances for cable. His cameraman is Sebastian Ganz (Richard Coyle). In a prologue set in Iraq, they're teamed with Miriam (Heather Graham), his girlfriend, who is killed—sending him back to Los Angeles (so informs the subtitle), until Dutchman Skypes him from the bathtub with the joyous news: "This place is about to blow!" He's right, and Anders will go through most of the movie with an open wound on his nose, perhaps fearing that a Band-Aid would remind moviegoers of Jack Nicholson in *Chinatown*.

How, you may wonder, do actual Georgians figure in this film, except in the coda? Well, the reporters get invited to a wedding, which is attacked by Russian helicopters. Anders has become friendly with Tatia (Emmanuelle Chriqui), who is to be his translator, and after many deaths at the wedding, Anders and Sebastian end up fleeing with Tatia and family members. This consists of them running hunched over and ducking behind fences while accounting for the points of view of many unrelated action scenes.

None of the action is coherent; shots and shells are fired, people are killed or not, explosions rend the air, SUVs spin aloft (the same one more than once, I think), and there is no sense of strategy. Occasionally we cut to the state offices of Mikheil Saakashvili, the Georgian president, who is played by Andy Garcia, it being his misfortune to resemble Saakashvili. There are also vignettes involving a sadistic mercenary (Mikko Nousi-ainen) and a ruthless Russian (Rade Serbedzija), both of whom commit the Fallacy of the Talking Killer.

Renny Harlin is known for his action pictures (*Die Hard 2*, *Cliffhanger*) and not for his geopolitical insights. If the purpose of this film is to whip up sympathy for the Georgians, I doubt if few moviegoers not from that area will care. It's a lot of tough guys running around blowing up stuff real good, and getting so many good peeks at crucial action that we wonder why neither the Georgians nor the Russians can see people hiding behind a fence even when we can see them.

The Foot Fist Way

(DIRECTED BY JODY HILL; STARRING DANNY MCBRIDE, MARY JANE BOSTIC; 2008)

The hero of *The Foot Fist Way* is loathsome and reprehensible and isn't a villain in any traditional sense. Five minutes spent in his company, and my jaw was dropping. Ten minutes, and I realized he existed outside any conventional notion of proper behavior. Children should not be allowed within a mile of this film, but it will appeal to *Jackass* fans and other devotees of the joyously ignorant.

The hero is named Fred Simmons. He's played by Danny McBride with a cool confidence in the character's ability to transgress all ordinary rules of behavior. Fred runs a Tae Kwan Do studio. He has the instincts of a fascist. His clients are drilled to obey him without question, to always call him "sir," to respect him above all others. Some of his clients are four years old. He uses profanity around them (and to them) with cheerful oblivion.

To a boy about nine years old, named Julio, he explains, "People are shit. The only person that you can trust is me, your Tae Kwan Do instructor." Julio needs consoling after he's disrespected by little Stevie, who is maybe a year younger. To teach Stevie respect, Fred beats him up. Yes. There are several times in the movie when Fred pounds on kids. He doesn't pull his punches. Most people in the audience will wince and recoil. I did. Others will deal with that material by reasoning that the fight stunts are faked and staged, their purpose is to underline Fred's insectoid personality, and "it's only a movie."

Which side of that fence you come down on will have a lot to do with your reaction. A zero-star rating for this movie could easily (in my case, even rapturously) be justified, and some fanboys will give it four. In all fairness it belongs in the middle. Certainly *The Foot Fist Way* doesn't like Fred; it regards him as a man who has absorbed the lingo of the martial arts but doesn't have a clue about its codes of behavior. He's as close to a martial arts practitioner as Father Guido Sarducci is to a Catholic priest. And the movie is often funny; I laughed in spite of myself.

Fred's offensiveness applies across a wide range of behavior. He is insulting to his wife's dinner guests, tries to kiss and maul students in his office, and asks one young woman who studies yoga: "Have you ever heard of it saving anyone from a gang-rape type of situation?" He has found very few friends. He introduces his students to his buddy from high school, Mike McAllister (Jody Hill, the director), who has a fifth-degree black belt and a penetrating stare that seems rehearsed in front of a mirror.

Fred and Mike worship above all others Chuck "The Truck" Wallace (Ben Best, the cowriter), a movie star whose credits include the intriguingly titled 7 *Rings of Pain 2*. When Chuck appears at a nearby martial arts expo, Fred asks him to visit his studio's "testing day," and then invites him home and shows him the master bedroom ("the wife and I will bunk on the couch"). That he assumes a movie star will want to spend the night is surprising, although perhaps less so when The Truck gets a look at Fred's wife, Suzie (Mary Jane Bostic). Fred leaves the two of them together while he teaches a class and is appalled when he returns to find Suzie and The Truck bouncing on the couch. What does he expect? Suzie has photocopies of her boobs and butt in "work papers from the office," and excuses her behavior at a party by saying, "I got really drunk—Myrtle Beach drunk."

McBride's performance is appallingly convincing as Fred. Despite all I've written, Fred comes across as a person who might almost exist in these vulgar times. McBride never tries to put a spin on anything, never strains for laughs. He says outrageous things in a level, middle-American monotone. He seems convinced of his own greatness, has no idea of his effect on others, and seems oblivious to the manifest fact that he is very bad at Tae Kwan Do. He is a real piece of work.

I cannot recommend this movie, but I can describe it, and then it's up to you. If it sounds like a movie you would loathe, you are correct. If it doesn't, what can I tell you? What it does, it does well, even to its disgusting final scene.

Note: The title is a translation of Tae Kwan Do.

Footloose

(DIRECTED BY CRAIG BREWER; STARRING KENNY WORMALD, JULIANNE HOUGH; 2011)

There's one thing to be said for a remake of a 1984 movie that uses the original screenplay. This 2011 version is so similar—sometimes song for song and line for line—that I was wickedly tempted to reprint my 1984 review, word for word. But That Would Be Wrong. I think I could have gotten away with it, though. The movies differ in such tiny details (the hero now moves to Tennessee from Boston, not Chicago) that few would have noticed.

Was there then, or is there now, a town in Tennessee or any other state in which the city council has passed a law against dancing in public? There may have been a brief period, soon after Elvis first began grinding his pelvis and preachers denounced rock 'n' roll as "the devil's music." But for most young moviegoers this plot point is going to seem so unlikely as to be bizarre.

We again get a plot in which a high school beer party leads to a fatal crash, taking the lives of five teenagers. The city council bans the music, under the influence of Rev. Shaw Moore (Dennis Quaid). Rev. Moore, who seems to be the only preacher in town, acts as the de facto civic moral leader. He is paranoid about his daughter, Ariel (Julianne Hough), a free spirit who attracts the attention of a local bad kid, Chuck Cranston (Patrick John Flueger).

Ren MacCormack (Kenny Wormald) arrives in the hamlet of Bomont from Boston. He's got the Kevin Bacon role, but not the Kevin Bacon charisma; the Reverend Shaw Moore should be able to take one look at Ren and figure he's harmless. But Ren gets arrested for playing his car radio too loud, and soon is leading a movement of the town's kids to petition the council to allow dancing—in public, anyway. This is the setup for several dance scenes where those kids seem suspiciously well choreographed for a town where they have allegedly never danced.

Meanwhile, the loutish Chuck Cranston, who considers Ariel his girl, resents Ren because he's attracting Ariel's smiles. This Chuck is a knuckle-dragging bully who patrols in his pickup truck with a posse of sidekicks. Attention, Posse Members of Bullies: When the local bully tools around in his pickup, but makes you guys all ride back there in the truck bed, you are being disrespected. What, aren't you good enough to ride up front with Chuck?

The bad boys and girls in high school movies always have a posse, usually two or three members, who follow close behind their leader and look ominous and slack-jawed. Are they issued instructions? Are they told, "Walk a few steps behind me and look worshipful"?

This new *Footloose* is a film without wit, humor, or purpose. It sets up the town elders as old farts who hate rock 'n' roll. Does it have a clue that the Reverend Shaw Moore and all the other city council members are young enough that they grew up on rock 'n' roll? The film's message is this: A bad movie, if faithfully remade, will produce another bad movie.

Four Christmases

(DIRECTED BY SETH GORDON; STARRING VINCE VAUGHN, REESE WITHERSPOON; 2008)
So here's the pitch, boss. *Four Christmases.* We star Reese Witherspoon and Vince Vaughn as a happily unmarried couple whose parents are divorced and remarried, and since nobody is talking to one another, they have to visit all four households on Christmas.

Why don't they just invite everybody over to their house or rent a private room at Spago?

No, no. They usually don't go to Christmas with *anyone*. They usually tell their parents they're out of cell phone contact, breast-feeding orphans in Guatemala.

Both of them?

They're really in Fiji. But their flight is canceled because of heavy fog. They're interviewed on TV, and now everybody knows they're still in town, and they have to make the rounds.

How long will this take to establish?

We introduce them, they go to the airport, they're on TV, *ba-bing, ba-bing, ba-bing.*

Cut two ba-bings. What's next?

First stop, Vince's dad. We'll get Robert Duvall. Mean old snake. Both of Vince's brothers are like extreme duel-to-the-death cage fighters. They beat the crap out of Vince, while ol' dad sits in his easy chair and verbally humiliates him.

Who are the brothers?

Jon Favreau and Tim McGraw.

Jon Favreau as a cage fighter?

He got a trainer.

Does McGraw sing?
That would slow down the family fight.
What about Reese?
Wait until she gets to her mom. Wait until we get to both moms. Her mom is Mary Steenburgen. She's sex hungry. His mom is Sissy Spacek. She's in love with Vince's best friend.
Those are both good actresses.
Right, but they can handle this. Jon Voight for her dad. He lives on Lake Tahoe. Perfect for Christmas.
What's his problem?
He lends the picture gravitas.
The audience, does it laugh while his brothers beat the crap out of Vince?
That's what we're hoping.
Tell me something else that's funny.
Two babies that urp on everyone.
That's funny?
OK, they projectile vomit.
A little better.
Also, we have Dwight Yoakam as Pastor Phil.
Spare me the religious details. All I want to know is, does Yoakam sing?
Nope.
We got two gold-record singers and they don't sing?
So? We got five Oscar-winning actors and they don't need to act much. There *can't* be any singing, boss. If McGraw doesn't sing, then Yoakam doesn't sing. It's in the contract. A most-favored-nations clause.
Most-favored-nations would not even remotely apply here. That is insane.
There ain't no sanity clause.

The Fourth Kind

(DIRECTED BY OLATUNDE OSUNSANMI; STARRING MILLA JOVOVICH, ELIAS KOTEAS; 2009)
Boy, is the Nome, Alaska, chamber of commerce going to be pissed off when they see *The Fourth Kind*. You don't wanna go there. You can't drive

there, that's for sure. The only ways in are by sea, air, dogsled, or birth canal. Why the aliens chose this community of 9,261 to abduct so many people is a mystery, as is why owls stare into bedroom windows. Nome has been the center of an alarming series of strange disappearances, we learn. So many, the FBI has sent agents there ten times more than to big Anchorage. *The Fourth Kind* is based on the testimony of a psychologist who found, circa 2000, that many of her patients reported waking at 3 a.m. with the sense that something was wrong and seeing an owl with its eyes on them.

The film goes to great lengths to be realistic. "I am the actress Milla Jovovich," Jovovich tells us at the outset, explaining that in the film she plays the psychologist Abigail, whose testimony was videotaped. Other fact-based characters are her colleague (Elias Koteas), the local sheriff (Will Patton), and a professor who interviews her (Olatunde Osunsanmi). "Every scene in this movie is supported by archived footage," she says, and to prove it, Osunsanmi, who's also the director, uses split screen to show Jovovich and the *real* Abigail talking almost simultaneously. The real Abigail's name has been changed, but since she's right there on the screen, how much of a mystery can she be in Nome?

It was with crushing disappointment that my research discovered this is all made up out of whole cloth, including the real Abigail. It wasn't even shot in Nome, but mostly in Bulgaria. And Dallas Massie, a retired state trooper who's acting police chief, says he's heard nothing about aliens. I learn all this from the blog of an *Anchorage Daily News* reporter, Kyle Hopkins, who says about twenty people have indeed disappeared in the area since the 1960s, and writes: "The FBI stepped in, reviewing two dozen cases, eventually determining that excessive alcohol consumption and the winter climate were a common link in many of the cases. Some of the dead were killed by exposure or from falling off a jetty into the frigid Snake River."

All right then, *The Fourth Kind* is a pseudo-documentary like *Paranormal Activity* and *The Blair Witch Project*. But unlike those two, which just forge ahead with their home video cameras, this one encumbers the flow of the film with ceaseless reminders that it is a dramatization of real events.

When we see Will Patton, for example, there's a subtitle informing us: "Will Patton, actor." Oh! I already know well that Will Patton and Elias Koteas are actors, and Jovovich identifies herself at the start. I wish they'd had a really big-name star. It might have been funny to read "Bruce Willis: Actor."

Now here's a good question. In the film we see the "real" footage of the "actual" client interviews with "Abigail." Why would an actual psychologist release confidential videotapes to a horror film, especially tapes showing the clients having seizures? Who *are* those "actual clients," really? The end credits don't thank them, although the film claims to account for them. Remember, even in a movie "based on a true story" (like *Fargo*), nothing before the actual end credits needs to be true. You want to watch those like a hawk. My theory is, the "actual" clients are played by the actors playing their fictional versions. Of course, I can't be sure of that. Think about it.

Jovovich is good, actually. It's a broad, melodramatic role with lots of screaming, and after two *Resident Evil* movies, she's good at being an endangered heroine and makes a competent psychologist. And a successful one, too. Her log cabin arts and crafts office looks like it was surely subleased from a (Bulgarian) millionaire. We see there's a lot of business in Nome for a specialist in owl staring.

Fred Claus

(Directed by David Dobkin; starring Vince Vaughn, Paul Giamatti; 2007)

Know how a character in one movie can be so terrific another movie is spun off just to take advantage? That happened with Ma and Pa Kettle, who had small roles in *The Egg and I*, which led to their very own series. But enough of today's seminar on the history of cinema. What I'm wondering is whether a *scene* can inspire a spin-off.

I'm thinking of the best scene in *Fred Claus*, which takes place at a twelve-step support group for brothers of famous people. Maybe it's called Recovering Siblings Anonymous. Fred Claus (Vince Vaughn), who has suffered all of his life in the shadow of his beloved younger brother, Santa Claus, sits in the circle and shares. Also at the meeting are Roger Clinton,

Frank Stallone, and Stephen Baldwin, and I'm not spoiling a laugh, because it's what they say that is so funny. I'm thinking, too bad Billy Carter didn't live to steal this movie. But there are plenty more brothers to go around. Neil Bush comes to mind. How about Clint Howard, although he's been doing well lately? Or Jeffrey Skilling of Enron, now serving twenty-four years while his brother Tom is the popular and respected Chicago weatherman? This could be a movie like the Fantastic Four, where the brothers form a team. Tom Skilling screws up the weather forecast at the North Pole after Clint Howard feeds him bad info from a garbled headset at Santa's Mission Control, and Neil Bush saves the day by arranging for an executive pardon.

If you at least chuckled during my pathetic attempt at humor, that's more than may happen during long stretches of *Fred Claus*, which has apparently studied *Elf* and figured out everything that could have gone wrong with its fish-out-of-water Christmas fable. The movie begins centuries ago in the Black Forest, when Mr. and Mrs. Claus and their first son, Fred, welcome a new bundle of joy: Nicholas Claus. Fred vows that he will be the bestest big brother little Nicky could ever hope for, but alas, Nicholas is such a paragon that you can't get over him, you can't get around him, and all Fred can do is go under him, in a bitter and undistinguished life. Think about it. What does Santa (Paul Giamatti) need with a brother? He's one-stop shopping.

It gets worse. Nicholas Claus becomes a saint. And it turns out, in a development previously unreported by theologians, that if you're a saint, that means both you and your family live forever. Yes! So Fred has to be St. Nick's brother forever and ever after. And this sad old planet would benefit, according to the Catholic count, by at least ten thousand immortal saints, although the Church reassures us with some confidence that they are all in heaven.

Flash forward to, yes, Chicago. Vince Vaughn should earn some kind of grace just for bringing this production to his hometown. He is in love with a meter maid (Rachel Weisz), who has moved here from London, which explains her accent if not her job choice. Fred stays pretty much out of touch with his famous kid brother, until he gets in a financial squeeze and has to call Santa for a $50,000 loan to open an off-track betting parlor across from the Chicago Mercantile Exchange—not a bad idea, actually.

The action moves to the North Pole and involves the flint-hearted Clyde Northcutt (Kevin Spacey), who is cracking down on cost overruns at the Pole, for whom, I'm not sure. That leads to turmoil among the elves, and Fred at last finds his role in life, but see for yourself.

The movie wants to be good-hearted but is somehow sort of grudging. It should have gone all the way. I think Fred Claus should have been meaner if he was going to be funnier, and Santa should have been up to something nefarious, instead of the jolly old ho-ho-ho routine. Maybe Northcutt could catch Santa undercutting his own elves by importing toxic toys from China, and Fred could save the lives of millions of kids by teaming up with Shafeek Nader.

Free Style

(Directed by William Dear; starring Corbin Bleu, Madison Pettis; 2009)
There are some charming actors in this movie, all dressed up but with no place to go. *Free Style* is remorselessly formulaic, with every character and plot point playing its assigned role. That it works is primarily because of the charisma of Corbin Bleu (did his parents meet in a French restaurant?) and Sandra Echeverria, as a boy who likes to ride motorcycles and a girl who likes to ride horses.

Bleu plays Cale, a teenager who delivers pizza and races for a motocross team. His best friend runs off the track and crashes during a race, and he turns his bike around and drives upstream to the rescue. I am not a motocross expert, but doesn't this seem idiotic?

The sponsor of his bike withdraws his support, as indeed he should. One day Cale delivers a pizza to a farm and two things catch his eye: a beaten-up old motorcycle, and Alex (Sandra Echeverria), who is not old nor the least bit beaten-up. He's given the bike and goes to work fixing it up, and Alex becomes his girlfriend—although not without the exhausted scene where she sees him with his former girl and leaps to the wrong conclusion. This scene is so obligatory, I think sometimes they even create an old girlfriend just to make it possible.

Cale and his mom (Penelope Ann Miller) argue about his career track. He dreams of making the professional motocross tour. His mom thinks he should focus on school. I think she's right. But noooo—he has a Dream. When will there be a film about a motocross racer or skateboarder, say, who decides, the hell with it, I could break my neck. I think I'll just go to college.

You may know that Penelope Ann Miller is white, and that Corbin Bleu (star of all the *High School Musical* films) is biracial. Why do I mention this? Because the movie makes a big point of it, even providing an absent black father Cale seeks out, perhaps because then, God help us, the father can turn up at the end of the Big Race and nod approvingly. Why not simply provide the kid with two parents? Because the Single Mom is also a beloved cliché, you say? Two for the price of one.

Anyway, all leads up to the Big Race, etc., and the False Dawn, the Fake Crisis, and the Real Dawn, all following the recipe. My primary enjoyment was entertaining myself by mentally casting Corbin Bleu and Sandra Echeverria in other movies. Well, there's hope. Echeverria has the lead in three upcoming movies from Mexico. Bleu (who is handsome and not merely cute) works constantly. In later years people won't be wearing out their DVDs of a movie like this, but as a career step, it's a good one. Better than pro motocross.

Friday the 13th

(DIRECTED BY MARCUS NISPEL; STARRING JARED PADALECKI, AMANDA RIGHETTI; 2009)
Friday the 13th is about the best *Friday the 13th* movie you could hope for. Its technical credits are excellent. It has a lot of scary and gruesome killings. Not a whole lot of acting is required. If that's what you want to find out, you can stop reading now.

OK, it's just us in the room. You're not planning to see *Friday the 13th,* and you wonder why anyone else is. Since the original movie came out in 1980, there were ten more films—sequels, retreads, fresh starts, variations, whatever. Now we get the 2009 *Friday the 13th,* which is billed as a "remake" of the original.

That it is clearly not. Let me test you with a trick question: How many kids did Jason kill in the first movie? The answer is none, since Mrs. Voorhees, his mother, did all of the killings in revenge on the camp counselors who let her beloved son drown in Crystal Lake.

Mrs. Voorhees is decapitated at the end of number one and again in the new version, so the new movie is technically a remake up until that point—but the decapitation, although preceded by several murders, comes *before* this movie's title card, so everything after that point is new.

It will come as little surprise that Jason still lives in the woods around Crystal Lake and is still sore about the decapitation of his mom. Jason must be sore in general.

So far in the series, he has been drowned, sliced by a machete in the shoulder, hit with an ax in the head, supposedly cremated, aped by a copy-cat killer, buried, resurrected with a lightning bolt, chained to a boulder and thrown in the lake again, resurrected by telekinesis, drowned again, resurrected by an underwater electrical surge, melted by toxic waste, killed by the FBI, resurrected through the possession of another body, returned to his own body, thrown into hell, used for research, frozen cryogenically, thawed, blown into space, freed to continue his murder spree on Earth 2, returned to the present, faced off against Freddy Krueger of *A Nightmare on Elm Street,* drowned again with him, and made to emerge from Crystal Lake with Freddy's head, which winks.

I know what you're thinking. No, I haven't seen them all. Wikipedia saw them so I didn't have to. The question arises: Why does Jason continue his miserable existence, when his memoirs would command a seven-figure advance, easy? There is another question. In the 1980 movie, twenty years had already passed since Jason first went to sleep with the fishes. Assuming he was a camper aged twelve, he would have been thirty-two in 1980, and in 2009 he is sixty-one. That helps explain why one of my fellow critics at the screening was wearing an AARP T-shirt.

SPOILER WARNING: At the end of this film, Jason is whacked with an ax and a board, throttled with a chain, and dragged into a wood chipper, although we fade to black just before the chips start to fly, and we are reminded of Marge Gunderson's immortal words. The next day brings a dawn, as one so often does, and two survivors sit on the old pier with Jason's body wrapped and tied in canvas. Then they throw him into Crystal Lake. Anyone who thinks they can drown Jason Voorhees for the fifth time is a cockeyed optimist.

Note: In my research, I discovered that the scientific name for fear of Friday the 13th is "paraskavedekatriaphobia." I envision a new franchise: Paraskavedekatriaphobia: A New Beginning, Paraskavedekatriaphobia: Jason Lives, Paraskavedekatriaphobia: Freddy's Nightmare, *etc.*

From Paris with Love

(DIRECTED BY PIERRE MOREL; STARRING JOHN TRAVOLTA, JONATHAN RHYS MEYERS; 2010)

Pauline Kael has already reviewed this movie in her book *Kiss Kiss Bang Bang*, and it only took her the title. I could go through my usual vaudeville act about chase scenes and queasy-cams and Idiot Plots, but instead I'd like you to join me in the analysis of something that increasingly annoys me.

Imagine we are watching *From Paris with Love* on a DVD with a stop-action button. We look at an action scene all the way through. John Travolta stars as Charlie Wax, an American Mr. Fix-It with a shaved head and goatee, who has been sent to Paris on a mysterious assignment. Not mysterious to him, mysterious to us. It involves Asian drug dealers and/or terrorists from the Middle East. Doesn't matter who they are or what they do, because their only function here is to try to kill Charlie and his fall-guy partner James Reece (Jonathan Rhys Meyers).

OK. We're on the sofa. We look at the scene. We take a second look. We focus on Travolta. This is an athlete. His reflexes are on a hair-trigger. He can deal with several enemies at a time. He can duck, jump, hurdle, spin, and leap. One slight miscalculation, and he's dead. He doesn't miss a beat. He's in superb condition, especially for a guy whose favorite food is

Cheese Royales. That's a little joke reminding us of *Pulp Fiction,* and the *last* thing you should do is remind the audience of a movie they'd rather be watching.

Now we go through the scene a frame at a time. We don't miss much in the way of continuity because it's pretty much glued together a frame at a time. We see a dizzying cascade of images, but here's a funny thing: We don't see Travolta completing many extended physical movements, and none involving any danger. The shots of him involve movement, but in bursts of a few frames, intercut with similar bursts of action by his attackers. There is no sense of continuous physical movement taking place within a defined space. No overall sense of the choreography.

I hasten to say this is not criticism of John Travolta. He succeeds in this movie by essentially acting in a movie of his own. The fight construction is the same with most modern action movies. In past decades, studios went so far as to run fencing classes for swordfights. Stars like Buster Keaton, Douglas Fairbanks Sr., and Errol Flynn did their own stunts and made sure you could see them doing them. Most of the stunts in classic kung fu movies, starring actors such as Bruce Lee and Jackie Chan, were really happening. Sure, they used camera angles, trampolines, and wires, but you try it and see how easy it is.

CGI makes that unnecessary. The stunt work is done by computers and the editing process. I fear that classic action sequences would be too slow for today's impatient action fans, who have been schooled on impossibilities. The actual stunt driving done in such chase landmarks as *The French Connection* and *Bullitt,* where you could observe real cars in real space and time, has been replaced by what is essentially animation.

I mention this because last week I saw a good South Korean thriller named *The Chaser,* and its best scene involved a foot chase through the narrow streets of Seoul by two actors who, you could see, were actually running down streets. In modern actioners, the only people who work up a sweat are the editors.

Anyway, that's what I had on my mind. As for *From Paris with Love,* it's mostly bang bang and not kiss kiss, and as an actress once asked Russ Meyer, what's love got to do with it?

Gentlemen Broncos

(DIRECTED BY JARED HESS; STARRING MICHAEL ANGARANO, JENNIFER COOLIDGE; 2009)
As an amateur collector of the titles of fictional novels in movies, I propose that this one has the worst of all time: *Yeast Lords: The Bronco Years.* You say you smiled? Me, too, and there are precious few smiles and laughs in *Gentlemen Broncos,* which is not a very good movie title either, although it might work for an X-rated film. The author of *Yeast Lords* is a teenager named Benjamin who hopefully writes science fiction and idolizes a famous sci-fi novelist named Dr. Ronald Chevalier as much as I once, and still do, admire the good doctor Asimov.

Benjamin Purvis (Michael Angarano) lives in a Buckydome house with his mother, Judith (Jennifer Coolidge), and let's pause right here to observe that Jennifer Coolidge, here and in Werner Herzog's forthcoming *Bad Lieutenant,* possesses what I like to think of as the Walken Factor. That is, her appearance in any scene immediately inspires our particular interest because we sense something unexpected and amusing is about to happen. So it was with her iconic appearance as Stifler's mom in *American Pie* (1999), in which she had the rare honor of inspiring the Internet acronym *MILF.* If you doubt me, look it up in Wiktionary. Hard as it is to believe, *MILF* was not used until Stifler's mom appeared.

Here she is Purvis's mom, and she encourages his budding writing skills by allowing him to attend the Cletus Fest, a teenage authors' event that offers the awesome presence of Dr. Ronald Chevalier (Jemaine Clement). He's a science-fiction author with writer's block, and when Benjamin presses a copy of *Yeast Lords: The Bronco Years* into his hands, in a moment of desperation he snatches it up, makes some changes, and submits it as his own work.

That sounds, I suppose, as if *Gentlemen Broncos* might tell a good story. Perhaps the Hollywood gurus who advise, "story, story story" might add: "but don't stop there." The director, Jared Hess, who made *Napoleon Dynamite*, a film I admit I didn't get, has made a film I don't even begin to get. He invents good characters: Purvis, Purvis's mom, Dr. Ronald Chevalier, and Tabitha (Halley Feiffer, daughter of the immortal Jules), who is a wannabe romance novelist, as are we all. Mike White turns up toward the end, providing another Walken Factor moment. But then Hess loses them in a jumbled plot that sometimes seems to mystify the characters. A character-driven plot, if it isn't *The Big Lebowski,* involves people who know what they want and when they want it.

Benjamin sells the film rights to his work to Tabitha and her friend Lonnie (Hector Jimenez), who is the Masha to her Rupert Pupkin. They plan a production that promises to be a mumblecore version of *Star Wars,* and, of course, there are problems with Dr. Ronald Chevalier. This film, Benjamin's novel, and the doctor's rewrite inspire different versions of the fictional hero under various names, and these fantasy sequences are sometimes amusing, but they seem freestanding and a little forlorn. They do suggest that the worst movie title in history would be *Yeast Lords: The Bronco Years: The IMAX Experience.*

Ghosts of Girlfriends Past

(DIRECTED BY MARK WATERS; STARRING MATTHEW MCCONAUGHEY, JENNIFER GARNER; 2009)

Remember *Harry, the Rat with Women?* This time his name is Connor Mead, but he's still a rat. A modern Scrooge who believes marriage is humbug, he is taught otherwise by the ghosts of girlfriends past, present, and future, and one who spans all of those periods. Just like Scrooge, he's less interesting after he reforms.

Matthew McConaughey plays Connor as a rich and famous *Vanity Fair* photographer whose ambition is to have sex with every woman he meets, as soon as possible. Sometimes this leads to a logjam. Impatient to sleep with his latest quarry, a model who just allowed an apple to be shot off her head with an arrow, Connor actually arranges an online video chat session to break up with three current girlfriends simultaneously, but is big-hearted enough to allow them to chat with one another after he logs off.

Connor appears on the eve of the wedding of his younger brother Paul (Breckin Meyer), who lives in the mansion of their late Uncle Wayne (Michael Douglas), a structure designed roughly along the lines of Versailles. (Actually, it's Castle Hill, in Ipswich, Massachusetts, built by the Crane family of Chicago, whose toilets you may have admired.) Connor is attending the wedding only to warn against it; he has a horror of getting hitched and extols a lifetime of unrestrained promiscuity.

The movie is apparently set in the present. I mention that because every woman Connor meets knows all about his reputation for having countless conquests, and yet is nevertheless eager to service him. These days, I suspect a great many of those women, maybe all of them, would view him primarily as a likely carrier of sexually transmitted diseases. To be fair, in a fantasy scene, his used condoms rain from the heavens, an event not nearly as thought-provoking as the raining frogs in *Magnolia*.

Attending the wedding is Jenny (the lovely Jennifer Garner, from *Juno*), who was his first girlfriend and the one he should have married. The ghost of Uncle Wayne materializes as a spirit guide and takes Connor on a guided tour of his wretched excess, after which he bitterly regrets his loss of Jenny, leading to a development which I do not have enough shiny new dimes to award to everyone who can predict it.

Michael Douglas is widely said to have modeled his hair, glass frames, and general appearance on the noted womanizer Bob Evans, but actually he reminded me more of Kirk Douglas playing Bob Evans. It's an effective performance either way you look at it.

The potential is here for a comedy that could have been hilarious. But the screenplay spaces out some undeniably funny lines in too much plot business, and Matthew McConaughey, while admirably villainous as a lecher, is not convincing as a charmer. Just this weekend a new Michael Caine movie is opening, which makes me remember his Alfie, a performance that is to lechers as Brando is to godfathers.

Maybe the movie's problem runs a little deeper. It's not particularly funny to hear women described and valued exclusively in terms of their function as disposable sexual partners. A lot of Connor's dialogue is just plain sadistic and qualifies him as that part of an ass it shares with a doughnut.

G.I. Joe: The Rise of Cobra

(DIRECTED BY STEPHEN SOMMERS; STARRING ADEWALE AKINNUOYE-AGBAJE, CHRISTOPHER ECCLESTON; 2009)

G.I. Joe: The Rise of Cobra is a 118-minute animated film with sequences involving the faces and other body parts of human beings. It is sure to be enjoyed by those whose movie appreciation is defined by the ability to discern that moving pictures and sound are being employed to depict violence. Nevertheless, it is better than *Transformers: Revenge of the Fallen*.

The film is inspired by Hasbro's famous line of plastic action figures. The heroes are no longer exclusively Americans, but a multinational elite strike force from many nations, which provides Paramount the opportunity to give top billing to an actor named Adewale Akinnuoye-Agbaje. And to think there was a time when Maurice Micklewhite was not considered a good name for a star. At last Hollywood allows actors to possess their real names.

The Joes, as they are called, are needed to counter "nanomites," a secret weapon that eats up people and buildings and stuff. This weapon has been invented by the evil disfigured scientist named McCullen (Christopher Eccleston), who steals it *back* from the people he sold it to and plans to use it to conquer the world. Why is McCullen so pissed off? His Scottish clan was insulted centuries ago. Those Scots.

His conquest plans are not sophisticated. He launches four nano-missiles at world capitals. Two of them are Moscow and Washington. The third one is destroyed, and if I'm not mistaken the fourth one is forgotten by the plot and is still up there somewhere. But that's the kind of detail I tend to get wrong because that's more fun than getting it right.

How fast are these missiles? They rocket into space and zoom down to Earth. A Joe named Ripcord (Marlon Wayans) commandeers the enemy's rocket airplane, and even though he's never seen it before, flies it so well that he catches up to the Moscow missile and destroys it, and *then* he turns around and flies halfway around the globe to catch up with the missile headed for Washington. He uses verbal commands to fire his air-to-air weapons, after a fellow Joe named Scarlett (Rachel Nichols) intuits that McCullen would have programmed his plane to respond to Celtic, which, luckily, she happens to speak.

These plot details are not developed at great depth, because the movie is preoccupied with providing incomprehensible wall-to-wall computer-generated special effects. I should have been carrying a little clicker to keep count, but I believe that director Stephen Sommers has more explosions in his movie than Michael Bay had in *Transformers 2* only last month. World records don't last long these days.

What is Cobra? What nationality are its leaders, other than Scottish? What will it gain by destroying world capitals? Reader, I do not know. Even the U.S. president (Jonathan Pryce) asks incredulously, "Don't they have any demands?" His role is otherwise limited to being briefed about the Joes.

Cobra has a woman named the Baroness (Sienna Miller) to match Scarlett of the Joes. These women are interesting. They have leather fetish-wear and are seductively made up, but are otherwise honorary boys, because us Joe fans don't like to watch a lot of spit swapping. But because us fans liked the two jive-talkin' robots in *Transformers*, G.I. Joe gives us Ripcord, who is comic relief, says black stuff, and can't control his high-tech armored suit, so he runs into things. We guess he's a contrast to the calm, macho heroism of Adewale Akinnuoye-Agbaje.

The two teams also each have a skilled Ninja fighter from Japan. Why is this, you might ask? Because Japan is a huge market for CGI animation and video games, that's why. It also has a sequence set in the Egyptian desert, although there are no shots of dead robots or topless pyramids. And Cobra headquarters are buried within the miles-deep ice of the Arctic. You think construction costs are high here. At one point, the ice cap is exploded real good so it will sink and crush the G.I. Joes' submarine. We thought ice floated in water, but no, you can see big falling ice chunks real good here. It must be only in your Coke that it floats.

There is never any clear sense in the action of where anything is in relation to anything else. You get more of a binary action strategy. You see something, it fires. You see something else, it gets hit. Using the power of logic, you deduce that the first thing was aiming at the second thing.

Yet I say this movie is certainly better than *Transformers: Revenge of the Fallen.* How so? Admittedly, it doesn't have as much cleavage. But the high-tech hardware is more fun to look at than the transforming robots, the plot is as preposterous, and although the noise is just as loud, it's more the deep bass rumbles of explosions than the ear-piercing bang of steel robots pounding on each other.

I mentioned the lack of pyramids. We do, however, see the Eiffel Tower as it is eaten up by nano technology and topples over onto the Place de la Concorde. Missiles also strike Mount Rushmore. No, wait! That was during one of the Coming Attractions.

The Good Heart

(DIRECTED BY DAGUR KARI; STARRING BRIAN COX, PAUL DANO; 2010)

Every once in a while a movie comes along and you watch it and the credits come up and you sit there feeling a certain sadness. The actors are good ones and they work hard and the look and feel of the film are evocative—but good gravy! Where did that plot come from? The actors cast themselves adrift on the sinking vessel of this story and go down with the ship.

Few people know the name of Horatio Alger anymore. He was long outdated when I heard of him, but in those ancient times people still referred to "a Horatio Alger story." That would be a story sopping wet with cornball sentimentalism, wrapped up in absurd melodrama, and telling some version of the rags-to-riches story. Poor farm boy stops runaway carriage carrying banker's daughter, they fall in love, he inherits bank. I believe Alger used that actual plot.

The Good Heart isn't that obvious, but it's that corny. Poor homeless lad named Lucas (Paul Dano) lives in cardboard shack under the freeway, befriends forlorn kitten. Kitten is found hanged, lad attempts suicide, wakes up in intensive care next to nasty old banker. Sorry! Nasty old tavern owner. This barkeep, named Jacques (Brian Cox), has just had his fifth heart attack and is so foul-tempered even the nurses hate him. Jacques finds out the lad is homeless, brings him home, gives him a garret room above the bar, and tells him he can have the bar after he dies.

In my extensive research into the world of bars, I have observed that they survive by selling drinks at retail. The House of Oysters doesn't follow this time-tested model. Jacques has three business policies he drums into Lucas: (1) No walk-ins from the street. (2) No women allowed—and BTW it's not a gay bar. (3) No being nice to the customers.

Rule No. 1 seems paradoxical. If no walk-in customers are allowed, how does anybody ever get to be a regular? Presumably the regulars have all been there since Jacques got the place from a man who sold oysters. One of the oysters killed someone, the guy sold out, Jacques took over, discontinued food, and inherited the regulars.

They are a group who need fumigating. The bar itself is a skanky dump. Jacques throws customers out regularly, but they come back, maybe because they're barred everywhere else. One day the beautiful April (Isild Le Besco) walks in and orders champagne. She has a sad story. No, she's not a fallen woman with a heart of gold. She's a flight attendant from France, who can't go home again or find a job because, I kid you not, she's afraid to fly.

Lucas and April fall in love, Jacques hates her for violating all the rules, and now I am biting my hand hard enough to make it bleed in order to prevent myself from blurting out more plot details. No, I will not—I must not—tell you what happens at the end of this movie, except to say I was stupefied that anyone in modern times (i.e., since 1910) would have the gall to sell such cornball at retail.

So now my review must end. But wait. I haven't even mentioned the bar's pet goose. This goose is kept in a sturdy cage, but escapes from time to time and must be chased down by Lucas. The ending of *The Good Heart* is supposed to be sad, but for me the saddest thing in this movie is that Lucas didn't chop off the head of that goose when he had the chance. No animals are harmed during the filming of a picture, and look where it gets you.

Good Luck Chuck

(DIRECTED BY MARK HELFRICH; STARRING DANE COOK, JESSICA ALBA; 2007)

Here is the dirty movie of the year, slimy and scummy, and among its casualties is poor Jessica Alba, who is a cutie and shouldn't have been let out to play with these boys. *Good Luck Chuck* layers a creaky plot device on top of countless excuses to show breasts, sometimes three at a time, and is potty-mouthed and brain-damaged.

It stars the potentially likable Dane Cook as the lovelorn Charlie Logan, leading me to wonder why, in the same week when Michael Douglas plays a flywheel named Charlie, that name seems to fit so well with characters who are two slices short of a pizza. Young Charlie, who is not called "Chuck" except in the title, is hexed by an eleven-year-old goth girl at a spin-the-bottle party. Because he fights off her enthusiastic assault, she issues this curse: Every woman he falls in love with will leave him and immediately find the man of her dreams.

Charlie grows up to become a dentist. His best friend is still the short, chubby, curly-haired Stu (Dan Fogler). The naming rule here is, Charlie for hero, Stu for best friend, and if there's a villain, he should be referred to only by his last name, which must have a Z or W in it, or a hissing sound. Stu, obsessed by breasts, has grown up to become a plastic surgeon, and so loves his craft that he has purchased Pam Anderson's former breast implants and keeps them in an oak display case, where they look surprisingly small, more like ice packs for insignificant wounds. One peculiarity of the dentist and the plastic surgeon is that they have adjacent offices with an adjoining door, so that Charlie can pop over to Stu's and offer a layman's opinion on his latest boob job.

Anyway, Charlie, who has been unlucky in love, meets Cam (Jessica Alba), who works at a seaquarium and loves penguins so much she might herself be willing to sit on one of their eggs all winter. Apart from being beautiful and friendly, her character trait is that she's a klutz, so physically dangerous she might even step on her own toes. Whatever she touches, she breaks, knocks over, turns on, or damages.

Although he's in love with Cam, Charlie is distracted by the seduction attempts of dozens of beautiful women because a rumor has spread all over town that if they sleep with him, they'll find the husband of their dreams. Stu does some follow-through research and finds out the rumor is true. Funny thing is, the women who crowd Charlie's waiting room all look as if they have come through the connecting door after enhancement by Stu. Charlie connects with so many of them that at one point the screen splits into sixteen separate copulation scenes, just to keep up.

You see Charlie's problem. Cam, a nice girl, doesn't want to date him because he's such a "sport." And Charlie realizes that if he ever sleeps with her, she'll immediately leave him for the man of her dreams. How will this paradox be resolved? By putting us through the agony of an automatic plot device, that's how.

The startling thing about the movie is how juvenile it is. Stu, in particular, is a creepy case of arrested development. Consider the whole scenario he stages with a fat woman who might break Charlie's hex. She's not only fat, she has pimples all over, and yes, we get a close-up of them. There is a word for this movie, and that word is ick.

A Good Old Fashioned Orgy

(DIRECTED BY ALEX GREGORY; STARRING JASON SUDEIKIS, LESLIE BIBB; 2011)

An orgy provides an opportunity to perform in public what you cannot perform in private with sufficient satisfaction. To have an orgy with strangers is dangerous, and to have one with your best friends is unspeakably sad. My reactionary ideas make me unsuited as a grateful audience member for *A Good Old Fashioned Orgy*, which completes our long, hot summer of vulgar comedies.

This is a comedy without wit and soul. It strands fairly likable actors in a morass of the kind of dialogue only stupid characters ever say—and then only when reading stupid screenplays. No one in the movie has a morsel of intelligence. They all seem to be channeling more successful characters in better comedies. This would be touching if it were not so desperate.

To take off your clothing and engage randomly in sex with nine or ten other people reveals an appalling lack of self-respect. Is that all sex means to you, rummaging about in strange genitals? Masturbation seems healthier. It is performed with someone you admire. If a sexual orgy is as exciting as the people here pretend, why do they need to spice it up with costumes from fraternity toga parties, and sex toys from the remainder bins of adult stores across from truck stops on lonely interstate highways?

If the people in this movie had a plausible association with humanity, it would be painful and embarrassing. You don't want to witness the humiliation of people you believe in. I believed in none of these. They were a small step up from a porn movie starring Barbie and Ken, and, of course, their best friends, Midge and Allan, and Tanner the pooping dog. If Barbie had arrived in her pink Corvette convertible, I'd rather play with that.

There are actors here you have heard of and may like, such as Jason Sudeikis, Lucy Punch, Don Johnson, and David Koechner. The only one who will make an impression in this movie is Tyler Labine, who looks and behaves so much like Jack Black as makes no difference. The effect of a leopard-skin thong is wasted on him; it gets lost in the folds. He'd need a digital camera set on auto timer to admire the effect.

Lucy Punch plays Kate, who gets engaged to her one true love, Glenn (Will Forte). Of course they aren't invited to the orgy. There should be a sacred instant early in a romance when a couple's needs are fulfilled by each other, don't you agree? Yet Glenn and Kate turn up for it, anyway, and are mad because they weren't invited: "We thought you were our friends!" If we don't all agree that newlyweds should be virgins on their wedding nights, we might compromise by suggesting they haven't attended any orgies with Jack Black types. I'll bet even Jack himself would go along with that.

The orgy is planned on Labor Day for a summer home in the Hamptons owned by Eric (Jason Sudeikis). This will be a farewell wallow: Eric's dad (Johnson) is selling the house. Dad's real estate agent, Kelly, played by Leslie Bibb, is an attractive woman who appeals to Eric. He tries to keep the orgy a secret from her. You know you're in a limited crowd when the designated adult is a real estate agent.

The Greatest

(DIRECTED BY SHANA FESTE; STARRING PIERCE BROSNAN, SUSAN SARANDON; 2010)

The Greatest includes a great performance and a very good one at the center of vagueness and confusion. The film's people and situation are perfectly clear, and with this cast might have made a powerful film, but the screenplay contains baffling omissions, needless confusions, and questions we should not be thinking of.

The film opens with two teenagers deeply, joyously in love. It's the kind of love where they've flirted with their eyes and their hearts since they started school, and now, on the last day of their senior year, he finally finds the courage to speak to her, and her face lights up, and this is all they dreamed of, and they make love, and then he's killed when their car is hit by a truck.

Not a spoiler. It's the setup for the whole film. The girl is Rose (Carey Mulligan, the Oscar nominee from *An Education*). The boy is Bennett (Aaron Johnson, on screen briefly but with all the presence necessary to make their love significant). We cut to the funeral, and then to an extraordinary shot of three people in the backseat of a funeral limousine: Bennett's father, Allen (Pierce Brosnan), his mother, Grace (Susan Sarandon), and his kid brother, Ryan (Johnny Simmons).

They do not speak. They do not look at one another. They do not offer comfort. The shot lasts maybe a minute. It establishes that these people are grieving in their own private ways. Bennett was a wonderful boy, known as "the Greatest" since grade school because . . . well, he was. Grace is inconsolable. They all are, but she's the most intense, and Allen tries to hold the family together while Ryan disappears into his room and drugs and who knows.

Three months pass in this way. Rose appears at their door and tells Allen she is pregnant. It was the first time for both Rose and Bennett. She didn't even know you could get pregnant the first time. She moves in with them because—well, I don't know exactly. Apart from one enigmatic phone call late in the film, perhaps involving a mother, she seems to have no one. She attended high school in an affluent neighborhood for three years, she was a gifted pianist, she's in a fatal crash, and now she has no one? No family, no friends, not one single person, and this is never explained?

Maybe she comes from a troubled background? Hard to see. Carey Mulligan plays Rose as upbeat, cheerful, able to cope. Grace is cold and distant; Sarandon plays her as unforgiving. Rose overhears her saying she wishes it was Rose, and not Bennett, who had been killed. She doesn't give a damn about Bennett's child. She wants her own child back.

Allen tries to be friendly. There are a couple of scenes, indeed, that are oddly handled because there's no question of Allen and Rose growing intimate, but the film's staging allows such a question to occur. Meanwhile, Ryan starts attending a grief support group where the leader does what no support group leader should ever do, and offers a diagnosis and recommendation to members after one comment.

In this group, a young woman named Ashley (Zoe Kravitz) reaches out to Ryan, and he responds and improves emotionally, and they like each other, and a romance seems to be in the works, and then he knocks on her door and her sister (I guess) answers and says something (I'm not sure what) and he runs off, and Ashley runs after him but that's the end of that subplot. What's that about?

And what about the scene where Ryan consumes what may be Ecstasy and then smokes pot. OK . . . and then? Nothing. He gets high and comes down, I guess. Meanwhile, Grace sits at the bedside of Jordan (Michael Shannon), the truck driver who hit her son's car. She knows her son lived for seventeen minutes after the crash, and that Jordan spoke to him, and she's obsessed to know what he said. But after the conversation, Jordan went into a coma. Some months later, we see her at his bedside, hearing the story of the seventeen minutes.

I will omit certain additional details involving Allen and Rose (separately), and I suppose I shouldn't describe the melodrama of the closing scenes, except to say they're an anthology of clichés. And there's a car ride in which way too much communication takes place, at long last, in a much too facile fashion.

So the screenplay is a soap operatic mess, involving distractions, loose ends, and sheer carelessness. Yet Sarandon creates a wrenching performance of a woman torn apart by grief, and Brosnan is convincing as a man holding it together as long as he can. As for Mulligan and Simmons, what can I say? There is nothing they do wrong, but this film written and directed by Shana Feste leaves both characters deprived of explanation, development, and revelation. And you can't get me to believe that after you have sex one time and get pregnant, and your lover is killed, and you have absolutely *nobody* to turn to except his parents, and his mother hates you, a teenage girl can have this much self-confidence. Even Juno would have disintegrated under the pressure.

The Green Hornet
(DIRECTED BY MICHEL GONDRY; STARRING SETH ROGEN, JAY CHOU; 2011)
The Green Hornet is an almost unendurable demonstration of a movie with nothing to be about. Although it follows the rough story line of previous versions of the title, it neglects the construction of a plot engine to pull us through. There are pointless dialogue scenes going nowhere much too slowly, and then pointless action scenes going everywhere much too quickly.

Seth Rogen deserves much of the blame. He cowrote the screenplay giving himself way too many words, and then hurls them tirelessly at us at a modified shout. He plays Britt Reid, a spoiled little rich brat who grows up the same way, as the son of a millionaire newspaper publisher (Tom Wilkinson, who apparently remains the same age as his son ages from about ten to maybe thirty). After his father's death, he shows little interest in running a newspaper but bonds with Kato (Jay Chou), his father's auto mechanic and coffee maker. Yes.

Kato is the role Bruce Lee played on TV. Jay Chou is no Bruce Lee, but it's hard to judge him as an actor with Rogen hyperventilating through scene after scene. Together, they devise a damn fool plan to fight crime by impersonating criminals. This they do while wearing masks that serve no purpose as far as I could determine except to make them look suspicious. I mean, like, who wears a mask much these days?

The crime lord in the city is Chudnofsky (Christoph Waltz, the Oscar winner from *Inglourious Basterds*). That provides the movie with a villain but hardly with a character. The war between Chudnofsky and the

Hornet is played out in a great many vehicle stunts and explosions, which go on and on and on, maddeningly, as if screenwriter Rogen tired of his own dialogue (not as quickly as we, alas) and scribbled in: "Here second unit supplies nine minutes of CGI action."

There is a role in the film for Cameron Diaz as Lenore Case, would-be secretary for young Reid, but nothing for her to *do*. She functions primarily to allow us to cut to her from time to time, which is pleasant but unsatisfying. Diaz has a famously wonderful smile, and curiously in her first shot in the film she smiles for no reason all, maybe just to enter the smile in the record.

The director of this half-cooked mess is Michel Gondry, whose *Eternal Sunshine of the Spotless Mind* is as good as this one is bad. Casting about for something to praise, I recalled that I heard a strange and unique sound for the first time, a high-pitched whooshing scream, but I don't think Gondry can claim it because it came from the hand dryers in the men's room.

Grown Ups

(DIRECTED BY DENNIS DUGAN; STARRING ADAM SANDLER, KEVIN JAMES; 2010)

Grown Ups is a pleasant, genial, good-hearted, sometimes icky comedy that's like spending a weekend with well-meaning people you don't want to see again any time real soon. They're the kind of people where, in the car driving home, you ask, "What was that all about?" Try to imagine the Three Stooges slapping one another's faces with dehydrated reconstituted bananas. No, really.

The pretense for the story: Five kids were on a basketball team in middle school. Their beloved old coach has died. To mourn him they return to the lakeside cabin where they celebrated their victory all those years ago. Wouldn't you know, the five kids on the team they beat are at the same lake for the same weekend.

The five buddies are played by Adam Sandler, Rob Schneider, Kevin James, Chris Rock, and David Spade. Sandler's wife is a famous designer (Salma Hayek). Schneider's much older wife is Joyce Van Patten. Rock's pregnant wife is Maya Rudolph. His Madea-style mother is Ebony Jo-Ann. James's wife is Maria Bello, who is still breast-feeding their four-year-old at every opportunity. Spade is unmarried, which, given the size of the cast, is just as well, since the characters have five children (I think), and there are also roles for Steve Buscemi as a guy who ends up in a body cast, Di Quon as Sandler's Asian nanny, and, of course, Schneider's three daughters from two previous marriages, two of them towering models, the third short and stout. There are so many characters in the movie that some scenes look like everyone lined up for a group shot.

The physical humor is not sophisticated. One character ends up with her face in a cake, and another has his face pushed twice into doggy-doo. The nursing mother squirts milk here and there, and her son is warned that if he doesn't wean himself soon he'll have a "got milk?" mustache with real hair. The gang all goes to a water park. There's a basketball game to settle old scores. And so on.

What's strange is how laid-back it all is. The five old pals at times sound positively like they're idly remembering old times. Lots of stuff seems intended only to be pleasant. When it looks like Sandler and his wife will be given the bedroom with the water mattress, for example, he says, naw, let the kids all share it. Does that sound like the set-up for a joke? There isn't one.

Joyce Van Patten (who is seventy-five) and Rob Schneider (who is forty-six) play a married couple, which generates some laughs, mostly on the nice side, and no vulgarities. See, they really like each other. And during the obligatory scene where every character makes a confession or relates one of life's lessons, she makes a warm and genuine speech that is well delivered, but hardly seems to belong in this movie.

The comedy talent here is seen but not much heard, given the human traffic jam of the cast. Chris Rock and Kevin James are underutilized. Maria Bello is reduced to breast-feeding and milk-pumping scenes. The character of Ebony Jo-Ann, with her farts, bunions, and pratfalls, comes perilously close to an insulting caricature. Maya Rudolph spends much of her time reacting to others and caressing her pregnancy. Adam Sandler plays a good guy who never does much more than be a good guy.

The direction by Dennis Dugan never overcomes the ungainly size of the cast. It's such a challenge to keep all the characters alive that he sometimes does round-robins of reaction shots—a fatal strategy when it comes to timing. Some of the dialogue is broken down into one-shots; some of the characters spend stretches of merely responding. It's all, as I said, pleasant and good-natured, but it feels too much as if all these nice people are trying to keep the conversation going. A comedy it is, but *The Hangover* or *Death at a Funeral* it isn't.

The Hangover Part II

(Directed by Todd Phillips; starring Bradley Cooper, Ed Helms; 2011)

Is this some kind of a test? *The Hangover Part II* plays like a challenge to the audience's capacity for raunchiness. It gets laughs, but some of them are in disbelief. As if making sure no one was not offended, it has a montage of still photos in the closing titles that includes one cruel shot that director Todd Phillips should never, ever have used. The MPAA's elaboration of the R rating says the movie has "pervasive language, strong sexual content including graphic nudity, drug use, and brief violent images." Also other stuff. Maybe their space was limited.

It's not that I was shocked. This is a raunch-fest, yes, but not an offense against humanity (except for that final photo, which is a desecration of one of the two most famous photos to come out of Vietnam). The movie has its share of laughs. There's a wedding toast that deserves some sort of award for deliberate social embarrassment. And Alan (Zach Galifianakis), the character who stole much of the original 2009 film, walks off with a lot of this one, too.

If you saw that earlier film (which grossed $485 million, so you may have), there's not much need for me to describe the plot this time. It's the same story. Phillips seems to have taken the *Hangover* screenplay and moved it laterally from Las Vegas to Bangkok while retaining the same sequence of scenes: call to bewildered bride-to-be, flashback to wedding plans, ill-advised bachelor party, four friends waking up with terminal hangovers in unfamiliar hotel room, ominous signs of debauchery, desperate quest to discover what happened, etc.

As the picture opens, a few years have passed. The dentist, Stu (Ed Helms), is now the prospective groom. He's engaged to a beautiful Thai woman named Lauren (Jamie Chung). Her father (Nirut Sirichanya) is not happy. His son Teddy (Mason Lee) is a brilliant sixteen-year-old pre-med student at Stanford, and the father tells Stu: "In this country, we do not consider dentist a doctor." At a pre-wedding feast, he calmly and implacably offers a toast comparing Stu to a flavorless rice pudding.

Then the lads go down to the beach for one (1) beer, and the next thing they know, they're regaining consciousness in a sleazy Bangkok fleabag, Stu has a facial tattoo, and young Teddy is missing, except for a severed finger wearing a Stanford class ring. That sets off their search through the city's underbelly for people who might be able to help them reconstruct the missing hours? days? Let me just observe that no search of the Bangkok underbelly that involves Ping-Pong balls is going to be altogether reassuring.

Their adventures are punctuated by a series of behavioral eruptions by Alan (Galifianakis), who links passive aggression with clueless troublemaking. These interventions have a certain charm, but Alan's funniest scene takes place in his own bedroom before he ever gets to Thailand. Describing himself as a "stay-at-home son," he issues commands to his mother through a speaker system and seems determined to remain a fanboy for life. This character, as seen in this scene, could inspire a movie of its own that I would pay good money to see. (Galifianakis should regrow his hair, however; I like him looking like a shaggy bear more than like the bouncer in a biker bar.)

I'm no expert, but I've been to Bangkok, and while the city no doubt has a seamy side, let it be said that much of *The Hangover Part II* plays like an anti-travelogue paid for by a rival tourist destination—Singapore, maybe. Some of its surprises would shock only those who know little about the city's sex workers, but others are truly unexpected, including the appearance of Paul Giamatti as a crime boss, and Nick Cassavetes as a tattoo artist. The gangster Mr. Chow (Ken Jeong) is back for the second film, still in need of serious tranquilizing.

While many weekend comedies these days seem too timidly in search of the PG-13, *The Hangover* embraced its R, and *Part II* seems to be testing the MPAA's patience. I wonder if there will be an unrated director's cut. The sequel repeats the medical miracle of the first film, in that the characters are able to regain consciousness after horrifying debauches and quickly return to the land of the living. In real life, they'd check themselves into an emergency room.

Hatchet II

(DIRECTED BY ADAM GREEN; STARRING DANIELLE HARRIS, TONY TODD; 2010)

You want gore, you get gore. *Hatchet II* plays less like a slasher movie than like the highlights reel from a slasher movie. It comes billed as, I dunno, satire or homage. Homage it certainly is, to the tradition of movies where everyone starts out alive at the beginning and ends up pretty much dead at the end. If satire means doing what your target does but doing it twice as much, then it's satire, too.

This is the continuation of *Hatchet* (2006), by the same director, Adam Green. Having missed that film, incredibly enough, I learn it ended at the same moment this one begins, with a monstrous swamp creature savaging the heroine, Marybeth (Danielle Harris). Since Marybeth was played by Tamara Feldman in the earlier film, this may cause some confusion if the movies play as a double feature, but hey, if Luis Bunuel could make one movie with two women playing the lead, why can't Adam Green do it with two movies?

As an exercise, let's see how quickly I can summarize the plot.

Marybeth escapes from the swamp into the shack of a swamp fisherman (John Carl Beuchler), who offers her a drink from a plastic hospital urinal. He finds out who she is, and throws her out. She appeals to the Reverend Zombie (Tony Todd), who runs Zombie Shop in the French Quarter. He musters a posse of armed men to venture into the swamp, retrieve any left-over body parts of Marybeth's father and brother, and shotgun the Swamp Thing, named Crowley (Kane Hodder). The nonswamp dialogue scenes are dispatched as swiftly as possible, and then Crowley sets about slicing, dicing, slashing, disemboweling, chainsawing, and otherwise inconveniencing the men in the boat.

Man, Adam Green must have run up a bill at the local butcher. Hundreds of dollars' worth of sweetmeats, livers, gizzards, hearts, lungs, and other organs of animals (none of them human, I trust) are seemingly ripped out of Crowley's victims, while blood helpfully obscures our view of the details of these eviscerations.

There is an explanation for Crowley's behavior, a revelation about who he is, an occult connection with Reverend Zombie, and some business involving the bounty hunters, and this information is used by Adam Green as sort of an *amuse-bouche*—you know, the little serving of sorbet that French chefs offer to cleanse your palate between main courses.

There are a number of good movies opening this weekend. *Hatchet II* is not one of them. Tickets are not cheap and time is fleeting. Why would you choose this one? That's a good topic for a long, thoughtful talk with yourself in the mirror.

The Haunting in Connecticut

(DIRECTED BY PETER CORNWELL; STARRING VIRGINIA MADSEN, KYLE GALLNER; 2009)

The Haunting in Connecticut isn't based on just any old true story. No, it's based on *the* true story. That would be the case of the Snedeker family, who in the 1970s moved into a ghost-infested house in Southington, Connecticut, and had no end of distress. We know their story is true because it was vouched for by Ed and Lorraine Warren, the paranormal sleuths, who also backed up Bill Ramsey, a demonic werewolf who bit people, *The Amityville Horror,* and the story of Jack and Janet Smurl, who inspired the movie *The Haunted.*

Even so, I doubt it's "based on." More likely it was "loosely inspired by" a story. At the end of the movie, the Snedeker house is consumed by flames, and yet we're told before the credits that it was restored, rehabbed, and lived in happily ever after. So much for any hopes of a sequel. Of course, *Amityville* inspired a prequel, so I may not be safe. I don't believe a shred of this movie is true. Ray Garton, the author of *In a Dark Place,* a book including the case, observed that the Snedekers couldn't get their stories straight. When he reported this to the investigators, Wikipedia says, he was instructed to "make the story up" and "make it scary."

But what does that matter if all you're looking for is a ghost story? *The Haunting in Connecticut* is a technically proficient horror movie, well acted by good casting choices. We have here no stock characters, but Virginia Madsen and Martin Donovan in a troubled marriage, Kyle Gallner as their dying son, and Elias Koteas as a grim priest. They make the family, now known as the Campbells, about as real as they can be under the circumstances.

The movie has an alarming score and creepy photography, and a house that doesn't look like it has been occupied since the original inhabitants . . . died, let's say. So all the elements are there, and one of my fellow critics said he "screamed like a girl three times," although he is rather known for doing so. There are two scream-able elements: (1) surprises and (2) specters.

The surprises are those moments when a hand, a face, a body, a body part, or (usually) a cat leaps suddenly into the frame, and you jump in your seat and then say, "Aw, it was only a cat." Or a face, a body part, a vampire bat, etc. The specters involve some ghostly apparitions that may or may not be physical. There are so many of them that the movie, set in Connecticut but filmed in Canada, has credits for "ghost coordinators" in both Vancouver and Winnipeg. Having seen Guy Maddin's brilliant *My Winnipeg,* I believe the ghosts coordinate themselves there.

Matt, the Campbells' son, is dying of cancer and must be driven many miles for his radiation treatments. Madsen, playing his mother, makes an "executive decision" to buy a house in the distant town so Matt, with radiation burns and nausea, doesn't have to drive so far. She gets a really good deal. Let me ask you something. If you found a terrific price on a three-story Victorian mansion with sunporches, lots of bedrooms, original woodwork, and extensive grounds in Connecticut, and it hadn't been lived in since events in the 1920s, how willing would *you* be to laugh off those events?

If the movie has a flaw, and it does, it's too many surprises. Every door, window, bedroom, hallway, staircase, basement area, attic, and crawl space is packed with surprises, so that it is a rare event in the house that takes place normally. The Campbells are constantly being surprised, so often they must be tuckered out at day's end from all of that running, jumping, and standing real still.

But I must not be too harsh, because surprises are what a movie like this trades in. I also thought Elias Koteas did a great job as the priest, who was not a ghostbuster in a Roman collar but a fellow radiation patient who never looked like he was confident good would win out in the end. (It is noteworthy that the Catholic Church does what it can to discourage exorcism, even though it could have done a lot of business in the boom times after *The Exorcist*.)

So. A preposterous story, so many scares they threaten to grow monotonous, good acting and filmmaking credits, and what else? Oh, what's with the ectoplasm? Didn't Houdini unmask that as a fraud? And the Amazing Randi? And what's it doing still being treated as real in *the* true story?

The Heartbreak Kid
(DIRECTED BY BOBBY FARRELLY AND PETER FARRELLY; STARRING BEN STILLER, MALIN AKERMAN; 2007)

The premise of *The Heartbreak Kid* is that a man marries a woman who quickly becomes unbearable to him. The problem is that she just as quickly becomes unbearable to us. Perhaps it is a tribute to Malin Akerman, who plays the new bride, named Lila, that she gets the job done so well; after a point, we cringe when she appears on the screen.

Nor do we have much sympathy for her new husband, Eddie, played by Ben Stiller. Eddie is a shallow, desperate creature, driven by his hungers, always looking as if he'd like to gnash the flesh of those who oppose him. So here we have a marriage between two unpleasant people, and into these jaws of incompatibility is thrown the person of Miranda (Michelle Monaghan), a sweet girl who deserves better.

The movie is a remake of Elaine May's splendid 1972 comedy, written by Neil Simon, much revised by May. Her movie starred Charles Grodin as a passive-aggressive social climber, May's own daughter Jeannie Berlin as his alarming first wife, and Cybill Shepherd as the WASP goddess on a Florida beach whom he falls in love with on his honeymoon. That film was better in every way, not least because it did not require the Lila character to be revealed as a potty-mouthed sexual predator.

The plot outlines are the same. Man ends his prolonged bachelorhood with an unwise marriage, discovers on honeymoon (then to Florida, now to Mexico) that she has Big Problems. After she collapses with an ugly sunburn, he meets the real girl of his dreams on the beach, and they fall in love while he neglects to mention that he is married.

As Neil Simon and Elaine May knew, this is a good comic situation. As the Farrelly brothers do not know, there are certain kinds of scenes that are deal breakers, rupturing the fabric of comedy and becoming just simply, uncomfortably unpleasant. They have specialized in over-the-top transgressive comedy (*There's Something About Mary*), but always before with characters who could survive their sort of acid bath. Here the characters are made to do and say things that are outside their characters and maybe outside any characters.

Consider the question of the parents of the newlywed. Lila's mother (Kathy Lamkin) is revealed as a very overweight fatso, with the implication that Lila will eventually balloon to such a size. But what's so great about Eddie's father (Jerry Stiller), a vulgarian with an orange toupee, who sees women as throwaway commodities, advises his son to get all the sex he can, anywhere he can, and ends up in a Las Vegas hot tub with a blonde (Kayla Kleevage, yes, Kayla Kleevage) whose breasts are so big they bring the show to a halt the same way a three-legged woman might? There is also an example of a "Mexican Folklore Dance" that involves a donkey with unappetizing sexual equipment. The Farrellys' overkill breaks the fabric of their story.

There are small moments of real humor. The hair on the head of the first child of Eddie's best pal (Rob Corddry), for example. Lila's showdown between a deviated septum and a shrimp. The suspicions that Miranda's cousin (Danny McBride) has about Eddie. The way Eddie is vilified in the speeches after the wedding of a former girlfriend. More of that and less of peeing on poisonous jellyfish might have helped. But the film is a squirmy miscalculation of tone.

Hell Ride

(DIRECTED BY LARRY BISHOP; STARRING LARRY BISHOP, MICHAEL MADSEN; 2008)

I read an article the other day saying the average age of motorcyclists is going up. Judging by *Hell Ride,* the average age of motorcycle gang members is approaching the Medicare generation, not that many will survive to collect the benefits. Some of the "plot" involves revenge for the torching of the girlfriend of the gang president. That took place in the bicentennial year of 1976, which was, let's see, thirty-two years ago. By the time they kill the guy who did it, he's a geezer with so many chin whiskers they can barely cut his throat.

The movie was written and directed by Larry Bishop, who also stars as Pistolero, president of an outlaw club named the Victors. Bishop starred in a motorcycle movie named *The Savage Seven* in 1968, which was, let's see, forty years ago. He was also in *The Devil's 8, Angels Unchained,* and *Chrome and Hot Leather.* It's a wonder he doesn't have a handicapped placard for his hog.

In between searching for a killer, he leads a gang whose members are sort of hard to tell apart, except for The Gent (Michael Madsen), so called because instead of leathers he wears a ruffled formal shirt under a tux jacket with his gang colors stitched on the back. Why does he do that? The answer to that question would require character development, and none of the cast members develop at all. They spring into being fully created and never change, like Greek gods.

There are cameo roles for two icons of biker movies, Dennis Hopper and David Carradine, who play old-timers—that is, contemporaries of the other gang members. Madsen, at fifty, may be the youngest cast member, and also brings along expertise in doing The Walk. That would be the scene made famous from *Reservoir Dogs* and a zillion other movies where three or four tough guys lope along in unison away from something that is about to blow up and don't flinch when it does.

Wait a minute. Maybe the guy who gets blown up was the killer and not the grizzled old-timer. I dunno. The enemy gang of the Victors are the 666ers, but I couldn't tell them apart except for the close-ups of the colors on their backs, which had the disadvantage of not showing their faces. There is a character named Deuce, but I don't know why. Or maybe he is a gang.

The movie was executive-produced by Quentin Tarantino. Shame on him. He intends it no doubt as another homage to grindhouse pictures, but I've seen a lot of them, and they were nowhere near this bad. *Hell's Angels on Wheels,* for example: pretty good.

All these guys do is shoot one another and roll around in bars with naked girls with silicone breasts—who don't seem to object to the bikers' smelly grime. The girls look about twenty-five, tops, but the only reference to age in the movie is when a biker names his bike after the horse Trigger, and is asked, "How old is Trigger in horse-bike years?" Quick—whose horse was Trigger? Can anyone under twenty-five answer? OK, then: Silver? Champion? Topper?

Henry's Crime

(DIRECTED BY MALCOLM VENVILLE; STARRING KEANU REEVES, VERA FARMIGA; 2011)
Keanu Reeves seems on mild sedation during most of *Henry's Crime.* I think that's intentional. He plays the feckless Henry Torne, an overnight toll booth attendant in Buffalo, who agrees to play in a softball game,

drives a car filled with other players, and discovers that what they're actually planning is a bank robbery. Henry gets caught and thrown in the slammer, and takes it philosophically.

Our problem is finding a way to care about these events more than Henry apparently does. He seems to hover above his own life, detached, an observer. Into this life enter people who become more involved in it than he does. There's his conniving friend Eddie Vibes (Fisher Stevens), who tricked him into the bank robbery. His prison cell mate is Max Saltzman (James Caan), a wiseguy from way back who knows all the angles, except how to stay out of prison. Henry's wife, Debbie (Judy Greer), ends their marriage while he's behind bars, becoming preggers in a way that he should find particularly ironic, yet Henry remains calm.

Finally a woman discovers how to really get his attention. This is Julie Ivanova (Vera Farmiga), who hits him with her car. That'll do it. She's an actress rehearsing a production of Chekhov's *Cherry Orchard*, which is being directed by Darek Millodragovic (Peter Stormare—yes, who fed his friend into a wood chipper in *Fargo*). Henry begins to like Julie. Then he discovers that one of the dressing rooms in the theater is connected to an old tunnel that leads to the bank the softball team was trying to rob.

This is perhaps beginning to sound to you like a screwball comedy. Imagine such a comedy if it has gone forty-eight hours without sleep. All the elements are present: Henry needs to be cast in the play to gain access to the tunnel, Max and Eddie get involved, Julie is remarkably accepting, any romance between Julie and Henry hangs in the balance, split-second exits and entrances are called for, and so on. Now imagine everyone sprinting through quicksand.

Keanu Reeves has many strings in his bow, but screwball comedy isn't one of them. Vera Farmiga, James Caan, and Fisher Stevens can do it, but they often seem to be looking back, waiting for Reeves to pass the baton. What you need, I think, is someone nervous to play Henry. A Steve Buscemi, for example. Reeves maintains a sort of Zen detachment. Whatever happens is all right with him.

The film was directed by Malcolm Venville, who seems to muse when he should be fretting. How uninvolved is his direction? A friend of mine in Buffalo went to see the movie, at a premiere, I guess. He wrote me complaining a city block that supplies one of the locations "was shot from a boring angle." When a comedy inspires observations like that, you know you're in trouble.

He's Just Not That Into You
(DIRECTED BY KEN KWAPIS; STARRING BEN AFFLECK, JENNIFER ANISTON; 2009)

Ever noticed how many self-help books are limited to the insight expressed in their titles? You look at the cover, you know everything inside. The rest is just writing. I asked Amazon to "surprise me" with a page from inside the best-seller *He's Just Not That Into You,* and it jumped me to page 17, where I read: "My belief is that if you have to be the aggressor, if you have to pursue, if you have to do the asking out, nine times out of 10, he's just not that into you."

I personally would not be interested in a woman who needed to buy a book to find that out. Guys also figure out that when she never returns your calls and is inexplicably always busy, she's just not that into you. What is this, brain surgery? I have tried, but I cannot imagine what was covered in the previous sixteen pages of that book. I am reminded of the book review once written by Ambrose Bierce: "The covers of this book are too far apart."

The movie version of *He's Just Not That Into You* dramatizes this insight with comic vignettes played by actors who are really too good for this romcom. Jennifer Aniston in particular has a screen presence that makes me wonder why she rarely takes on the kinds of difficult roles her costars Jennifer Connelly, Scarlett Johansson, and Drew Barrymore have played. There are depths there. I know it.

The movie takes place in modern-day Baltimore, where those four, and Ginnifer Goodwin, play women who should ask themselves: Is he really that into me? Aniston, for example, plays Beth, who has been living for years with Neil (Ben Affleck), who is perfect in every respect except that he is disinclined to marry her. "We're happy just the way we are," he argues. The old "if it's not broke, don't fix it" routine. But if a woman knows her loved one won't ever want to marry her, it's her heart that's broke, and there is only one way to fix it. There are even evolutionary theories to explain this.

Gigi (Goodwin), on the other hand, doesn't have a perfect boyfriend, or any at all, and sits by her phone like a penguin waiting for the damn egg to hatch. Why hasn't that dreamy guy who asked for her number called back? Maybe, just maybe, it's because he doesn't want to. I haven't read the book, but I know that much. There was once a girl I didn't call, and she mailed me a book titled *The Dance-Away Lover.* How did I instinctively know the book was about me? Why did I know everything in it without having to read it? Because the book was intended for her, that's why.

Janine (Connelly) is married to Ben (Bradley Cooper), who doesn't share her ideas about home decoration, which are that you always make the more expensive choice. Not a lot of guys are into that. If you get one who is, he may make it a general policy and decide to trade you in for an advanced model. Look for a guy who treats you not as an acquisition but as an angel of mercy, the answer to the prayers of the rat he knows he is.

Mary (Barrymore) is surrounded by great guys, but they're all gay. They're from that subspecies of gay men who learned everything they know about life from Bette Davis. This is true even if they've never seen one of her movies. Then there's Anna (Johansson), who is courted fervently by Conor (Kevin Connolly), who would marry her in a second, except she's "committed" to a married man, who is committed to not marrying her, which is maybe what she likes about him, along with getting the right to constantly be the wronged one in a relationship she, after all, freely walked into.

The problem with most of the movie's women is that they are only interested in (a) the opposite sex, (b) dating, and (c) marriage. Maybe that's because the screenplay only has so much time. But a movie about one insecure woman talking to another can be monotonous, unless you're a masochist looking to share your pain. If you consider a partner who has no more compelling interests than a, b, or c, you're shopping for boredom.

There is one superb monologue in the movie, by Drew Barrymore, who complains that she is driven crazy by the way guys always seem to be communicating in another medium. She calls at home but he doesn't pick up. She calls on his cell, and he e-mails her. She texts him. He Twitters back and leaves coded hints on MySpace. She tries snail mail. He apparently never learned how to open one. She yearns for the days when people had one telephone and one answering machine, and a guy had either definitely called you, or he had not.

This is a very far from perfect movie, and it ends on an unsatisfactory note. Stop reading *now* because I am going to complain that most of the stories have happy endings. Not in the real world, they don't. In the real world, the happy endings come only with a guy who's really into you. I should write a self-help book: *If Some Guy Says He Loves You, Check It Out.*

Hidden Love

(DIRECTED BY ALESSANDRO CAPONE; STARRING ISABELLE HUPPERT, GRETA SCACCHI; 2010)
Hidden Love is a movie that knows exactly who it is about but doesn't know what it thinks of them. That leaves us four clearly seen characters and a story wandering in the murk of despair. Its principal casualty is Isabelle Huppert, who creates a flawless performance to no particular effect. She gives director Alessandro Capone what few actresses would be capable of, and he leaves her hanging.

Huppert plays Danielle, a woman who has been institutionalized after three suicide attempts. We meet her in therapy sessions with Dr. Nielsen (Greta Scacchi, focusing her attention with growing empathy). As Danielle speaks, it begins to appear she's in the twenty-third year of postpartum depression. All she wants to talk about is the indifference she felt toward her daughter, Sophie (Melanie Laurent), at the moment of giving birth and ever since.

Danielle looks ragged and depressed, makes obsessive hand movements, goes long periods without speaking, stares into space, and assures the psychiatrist that Sophie cannot be believed. Sophie, on the other hand, says her mother is playacting and is a selfish narcissist. What we see of Sophie suggests she is a loving mother to her own little girl. There's a scene where Sophie seems grateful to her mother while being taken to an abortion clinic but angry afterward. So eventually having her daughter was a form of revenge for Sophie, or what?

That and other events in the film go unexplained, or are seen in more than one version, and at the end all we can be sure of is that Danielle is depressed for reasons we can choose from cafeteria-style. The relationship between Dr. Nielsen and her husband (Olivier Gourmet) is, in contrast, briefly but well portrayed, especially during a scene where she confesses her despair over the case.

Isabelle Huppert makes one good film after another, most recently *Home* and *White Material*. She is fearless. Directors often depend on her gift for conveying depression, compulsion, egotism, and despair. She can be funny and charming, but then so can a lot of actors. She is in complete command of a face that regards the void with blankness. She gives her director a valuable asset. He doesn't know how to spend it.

So remorseless is this film that the ending comes like a slap in the face. Presumably it's the original ending, but it feels like nothing so much as one of those upbeat emergency rewrites slapped onto a Hollywood drama a mogul thought was too depressing. The happy nature of this ending is one of the most depressing elements of the film.

Holy Rollers

(DIRECTED BY KEVIN ASCH; STARRING JESSE EISENBERG, JUSTIN BARTHA; 2010)

One function of any traditional religious costume is to enforce the wearer's separation from the greater community. Those male Hasidic Jews who choose to dress in black and wear distinctive hats never seem to be anything else than Hasidic Jews. When they dress in the morning, they're making a decision to set themselves apart. This is not required in Jewish law, but is a sign of their devotion.

Apart from the hats, the side curls, and their religious beliefs, Hasidim are, well, a lot like everybody else. Sam Gold (Jesse Eisenberg) is a kid about twenty who is devout, naive, shy around women, loves his mom, respects his dad, and plans to go into the family business. Then his best friend's brother takes advantage of those qualities—and very specifically his dress style—to trick him into being a drug courier.

Holy Rollers is said to be based on a true story, circa 1990, of how Hasidic Jews from Brooklyn Heights were used to smuggle millions of Ecstasy pills from Amsterdam to New York. They weren't stopped by customs because they were so far from the profile of drug runners. In the movie, Sam is frustrated in his plans to build his father's business and accepts $1,000 from the brother to fly to Amsterdam and return with some "medicine."

Come on, you're thinking: How innocent can this kid possibly be? You should see him tongue-tied, sitting at the other end of a sofa from the girl he hopes to marry. Or even in Amsterdam, trying to avoid any body contact with women in a disco. Yes, the first trip he really does think the pills are medicine, and doesn't ask himself how what he's doing could possibly be legal.

He's a sweet kid as played by Eisenberg, who specializes in that line of work. The brother, Yosef (Justin Bartha), is persuasive, smooth, and hard to refuse. In Amsterdam, Sam meets a man named Jackie (Danny A. Abeckaser) and his girlfriend, Rachel (Ari Graynor), and is brought into their world of late-night clubs and loose living. On his second trip, things click into place, and he begins to put his good business sense to work.

It's that click that throws the movie off. Sam is moral and law-abiding, then changes seemingly overnight into a canny player in the drug trade. Before long he's instructing new Hasidim recruits on how to get past customs: "Act normal and look Jewish." It becomes apparent to his father and indeed his community what he's up to, but he's making good money and it seems so easy. For a long time he never even experiences Ecstasy.

The story may sound sensational, and you're possibly picturing traditional crime scenes: shoot-outs, chases, that sort of thing. But Holy Rollers is surprisingly matter-of-fact. Nobody gets shot, nobody gets chased, and Sam's anguish is internal.

The film's failure is to get from A to B. We buy both good Sam and bad Sam, but we don't see him making the transition. The film expects us to assume too much. Eisenberg is convincing as an essentially nice person who sounds confident but turns into a kid again when things start going wrong. But Kevin Asch, the director, keeps his distance from too many scenes; there's no particular suspense involved in getting past customs, for example. The movie relates to its story as Sam relates to women: look, talk, but don't get too close.

The Hottest State

(DIRECTED BY ETHAN HAWKE; STARRING MARK WEBBER, CATALINA SANDINO MORENO; 2007)

As a topic of fiction, the only things I have against young love are youth and romance. There has to be something more. Who would care about Romeo and Juliet if it hadn't been for their unfortunate misunderstanding? There has to be comedy, or tragedy, or suspense, or personality quirks, or *something* more than the fact that Young Person A loves Young Person B. This also applies to Old People A&B.

Ethan Hawke's *The Hottest State,* which he wrote, directed, and costars in, is based on his 1996 "semiautobiographical" novel, and therefore inspired in some way by his similarities to his hero: comes to New York from Texas, wants to be an actor, falls in love, etc. I would perhaps have enjoyed the movie more if it had been a "semibiographical" novel, based on *both* the boy and the girl. When his hero stands in the street reciting beneath her window from *Romeo and Juliet* (and he does), surely the point is not his gauche behavior but her failure to pour water on him.

The movie involves William (Mark Webber) and Sara Garcia (Catalina Sandino Moreno, from *Maria, Full of Grace*). She is a Latina from a wealthy background in Connecticut, cutting out any hope of culture clash, since Latinas will not have been unknown to him in Texas, although at least her background provides her with an interesting mother (Sonia Braga). William, we learn in flashbacks, is himself the product of young love that did not end well between a distant father (played by Hawke) and a mother (Laura Linney) whose realistic advice could be borrowed from Olympia Dukakis in *Moonstruck* (in place of sympathizing with William, she reminds him that in the long run he will be dead, and his heartbreak won't matter so much).

William and Sara meet in a bar, like each other, find out they're both in the arts, and play at boyfriend and girlfriend. Then they take a vacation to Mexico, seem to fall truly in love, finally have sex, and then when they meet next in New York she has decided she doesn't want him, or anyone, as a lover. Which breaks his heart and causes him to paste grieving messages on his windows, which she can see from hers. (Romantic tip: When a lover tells you they don't want to see you "or anyone," they already have someone else in mind.)

If the stakes were higher, all of this might matter more. But William and Sara have not interested us as themselves, and don't seem to interest each other as much as they like the romantic roles they're playing. Will the world be different, or their lives irrevocably changed, if they break up? I don't think so. Their tree falls in the forest, and nobody cares except the termites.

I admired Hawke's directorial debut, *Chelsea Walls* (2001), ever so much more than this movie because it was about more interesting people and more interesting love; it was set in the Chelsea Hotel, which, when people get beyond a certain threshold of "interesting," may be the only hotel in New York that will accept them. In *The Hottest State*, Hawke uses fairly standard childhood motivations for his unhappiness and reveals too little real interest in the Sara character. Why *did* she seem to fall in love and then announce she didn't want to see him anymore? From her point of view, I mean. In fact, the best angle on this whole story might be from her point of view.

Hounddog

(DIRECTED BY DEBORAH KAMPMEIER; STARRING DAKOTA FANNING, CODY HANFORD; 2007)

Dakota Fanning takes an impressive step forward in her career, but that's about the only good thing about *Hounddog*. The reigning child star, now fourteen, handles a painful and complex role with such assurance that she reminds me of Jodie Foster in *Taxi Driver*. But her character is surrounded by a swamp of worn-out backwoods Southern clichés that can't be rescued even by the other accomplished actors in the cast.

She plays Lewellen, a barefoot tomboy who lives in a shack with her father (David Morse), a slovenly drunk and self-pitying whiner. Next door is Grammie (Piper Laurie), who keeps house well but is a hard-drinking slattern. Lewellen prowls the woods and frequents the swimming hole with her best friend, Buddy (Cody Hanford), as they trade awkward kisses and examine each other's private parts with great curiosity. The poverty of her family is indicated by the usual marker: rusting trucks in the lawn. Her father operates a tractor, which during a rainstorm is struck by lightning. This hurls him to the ground and makes him even more dramatically loony. He is seized by anxiety that his daughter will abandon him, and one night he walks into the local tavern seeking her, having failed to notice that he is stark naked. The pool players prod him with their cues. Lewellen stalks in and drags him home.

Somehow amid this chaos the young girl succeeds in being playful and high-spirited, until she is raped by an older teenager. She grows silent and morose, even comatose, and one night is visited by dozens of (imaginary?) snakes, who crawl in through her bedroom window and perform a function, whether demonic or healing, that is understood by her friend and protector Charles (Afemo Omilami), a black man who works in the stables of the local gentry. He brings her back to health and lectures her about making people treat her with respect.

Moving around the edges of the story is a character known in the credits as Stranger Lady (Robin Wright Penn). Her identity and function are left unclear, except for the fact that it will be immediately obvious to any sentient viewer exactly who she is. It has been some time since I quoted from Ebert's Little Movie Glossary, but the Stranger Lady perfectly fits the Law of Economy of Characters, which teaches us that whenever an important star appears in a seemingly unexplained role, that character will represent the solution to a plot question.

Now about *Hounddog.* Lewellen is a passionate fan of Elvis and has some small local fame for her Elvis impersonations. Her life may be transformed when she hears Charles and his friends, including Jill Scott as Big

Mama Thornton, performing in the rhythm and blues tradition that inspired Elvis. Lewellen is obsessed with the news that Elvis will be performing in a local concert and is cruelly tricked when she thinks she can get a ticket. One moonlit night, Elvis himself drives past in a pink Cadillac and blows her a kiss. Yes. Elvis would have driven himself to the concert, alone, down back roads, of course.

Hounddog is assembled from the debris of countless worn-out images of the Deep South, and is indeed beautifully photographed. But the writer-director, Deborah Kampmeier, has become inflamed by the imagery and trusts it as the material for a story, which seems grotesque and lurid. David Morse's Daddy, well played as the character may be, is a particularly dreary presence, pitiful instead of sympathetic. Having seen so many of these fine actors in other roles, my heart goes out for them. Still, the discovery here is the remarkable Dakota Fanning, opening the next stage in her career and doing it bravely, with presence, confidence, and high spirits.

House of the Sleeping Beauties

(DIRECTED BY VADIM GLOWNA; STARRING VADIM GLOWNA, ANGELA WINKLER; 2009)
House of the Sleeping Beauties has missed its ideal release window by about forty years. It might—*might*—have found an audience in that transitional period between soft- and hard-core, when men would sit through anything to see a breast, but even then, I dunno. It's discouraging to see a movie where the women sleep through everything. They don't even have the courtesy to wake up and claim to have a headache.

I know I am being disrespectful to what is obviously intended to be a morose meditation about youth, age, men, women, children, mothers, hookers, johns, life, death, and the endless possibilities I thought of at sixteen when I heard that song "Behind the Green Door." The movie has been inspired by a 1961 novella by Yasunari Kawabata, who explores the now-obsolete Japanese theory that a woman should be seen but not heard. Even then, they were supposed to wake up sometimes and speak submissively.

The film centers on five scenes in which Edmond, a dying man in his sixties (Vadim Glowna, the director), lies in bed next to sleeping nude women of about twenty, all breathtakingly beautiful, and utters a mournful interior soliloquy about his age, their perfection, his mother, a childhood sexual experience, and his own misery. This is an intensely depressing experience for Edmond and for us, intensified by his robotic smoking habit. Sometimes he shakes a woman or slaps her on her butt, but if anything is going to wake her up, his breath will.

Surrounding these scenes is a plot more intriguing than they deserve, involving Edmond's old friend Kogi (Maximilian Schell), who advised him to visit the brothel in the first place. Kogi is concerned that Edmond is depressed by the death of his wife and young daughter in an auto accident. This happened fifteen years ago. I think the human ability to heal ourselves is such that, after fifteen years, you can expect to be sad and deeply regretful, but if you are still clinically depressed, you need medical attention.

It is also a wonder that this shambling sad sack and secret drinker is still apparently the head of a big corporation and has a full-time driver for his stretch BMW. Here is one tycoon who could definitely not be played by Michael Douglas. We've seen ultrarich Masters of the Universe before, but now we get the first Masturbator of the Universe.

The brothel is a one-bedroom operation supervised by Madame (Angela Winkler), a handsome woman of a certain age, who explains that the women have been "prepared" to sleep the whole night through, and the man is invited to sleep next to them (sleeping pills provided) and feast his eyes, or perhaps caress, but no funny business like sticking his finger in her mouth. Since Madame goes away all night, there's no telling what could happen to these helpless women, of course.

Do you find this premise anything but repugnant? It offends not only civilized members of both sexes, but even dirty old men, dramatizing as it does their dirtiness and oldness. Obvious questions arise, but, no, Madame will not explain why the women sleep so soundly, and the house rules strictly forbid any contact with the women outside the house. How does she find the women? Who are they? Why do they seem to sleep peacefully instead of as if they are drugged? How do they keep their hair and makeup impeccable? Why don't they snore?

Does Edmond get up to nastiness? There is a close-up of his tumescence, which looks younger and healthier than the rest of him, but no explicit sex. It hardly matters; the film is intended as allegory, although I am unsure what the allegory teaches us. Perhaps the message is: "You see what can happen to you if you direct and star yourself in a movie like this."

How Do You Know

(DIRECTED BY JAMES L. BROOKS; STARRING REESE WITHERSPOON, OWEN WILSON; 2010)
The one thing we don't see Reese Witherspoon doing in *How Do You Know* is playing softball. Considering that she portrays a softball player, this seems strange. To be sure, she's dropped from the team roster early in *How Do You Know*, so that's a reason. But there's something so deeply Witherspoonish about the idea of Reese stealing second that I am unconsoled.

It's established that she's a very good softball player indeed. Her teammates love her, her play is superb, she's a great role model, and her only problem is she's almost thirty. This is apparently past retirement age for women softball players. It's time for her to round third and collect a gold watch.

No sooner does she get some free time on her hands than two would-be lovers complicate her life. Matty (Owen Wilson) is a pro baseball pitcher with a multimillion-dollar contract, and George (Paul Rudd) is a big-time financial wheeler-dealer who works for the firm controlled by his father, Charles (Jack Nicholson). George is the nicer man. Matty is a two-timing, womanizing narcissist. But it looks as if George will be indicted and spend time in prison, and Lisa (Witherspoon) moves into Matty's penthouse, which is large enough for batting practice.

Lisa has sex with Matty and presumably with George, but it's that romcom kind of sex that remains, for an outsider, largely conceptual. Intimate personal behavior doesn't much enter in because all of the characters are limited to sitcom problems. Matty's troubles are shallowness and sex addiction. George is a nice man, ethical, who faces indictment on a technicality. In theory, he should have known every detail about the financial malfeasance of his father's company. It doesn't always work out that way.

I expected this movie to be better. The writer-director is James L. Brooks, and this is the fourth time he's worked with Jack Nicholson (including *Terms of Endearment* and *As Good as It Gets*, for both of which he won acting Oscars). So let's start with Nicholson. Brooks hasn't given him much to work with. He plays a conniving tycoon who doesn't deserve his son's loyalty. It's a heavy role, and there's little to lighten it. In his best roles Jack always seems to be getting away with something. He is here, too, but it's not funny. We like to identify with his onscreen sins, and this is a rare time when Nicholson is simply a creep.

The best-written and funniest role in the film is for Owen Wilson, as the pro pitcher. You know how his characters can have that ingratiating niceness, that solicitude for you while they're serving themselves? Here he plays a man tone-deaf to the feelings of women and clueless about his own behavior. But he's so nice about it that Lisa agrees to move in, and that provides an opening for what every actress should master, the scene where she repacks her bags and marches out.

Rudd's George is very likable. This is the wrong time for him to fall in love. His world is collapsing, and he finds himself in a cheap rented apartment surrounded by packing boxes. He has nothing to offer Lisa, and not enough trust in himself or her to realize she loves him, the big dummy.

All of this whizzes along a few feet off the ground, like most romcoms. Reese Witherspoon is always immensely cuddly, but it's not Lisa's heart that's involved here; it's her story line. Nothing heats up. The movie doesn't lead us; it simply stays in step. Jack Nicholson is one of the few actors who always inspires a quiet chuckle of anticipation when he first appears in a movie. This is a rare movie that doesn't give him a chance to deserve it.

The Human Centipede
(DIRECTED BY TOM SIX; STARRING DIETER LASER, ASHLEY C. WILLIAMS; 2010)

It's not death itself that's so bad. It's what you might have to go through to get there. No horror film I've seen inflicts more terrible things on its victims than *The Human Centipede*. You would have to be very brave to choose this ordeal over simply being murdered. Maybe you'd need to also be insane.

I'm about to describe what happens to the film's victims. This will be a spoiler. I don't care, because (1) the details are common knowledge in horror film circles, and (2) if you don't know, you may be grateful to be warned. This is a movie I don't think I should be coy about.

OK. Dr. Heiter is a mad scientist. He was once a respected surgeon, but has now retreated to his luxurious home in the forest, which contains an operating room in the basement. His skin has a sickly pallor, his hair is dyed black, his speech reminds us of a standard Nazi, and he gnashes his teeth. He is filled with hatred and vile perversion.

He drugs his victims and dumps them into his Mercedes. When they regain consciousness, they find themselves tied to hospital beds. He provides them with a little slide show to brief them on his plans. He will demonstrate his skills as a surgeon by—hey, listen, now you'd really better stop reading. What's coming next isn't so much a review as a public service announcement.

Heiter plans to surgically join his three victims by sewing together their mouths and anuses, all in a row, so the food goes in at the front and comes out at the rear, you see. They will move on their hands and knees like an insect with twelve limbs. You don't want to be part of the human centipede at all, but you most certainly don't want to be in the middle. Why does Dr. Heiter want to commit such an atrocity? He is insane, as I've already explained.

He also wants to do it because he is in a movie by Tom Six, a Dutch director whose previous two films average 4 out of 10 on the IMDb scale, which is a score so low very few directors attain it. Six has now made a film deliberately intended to inspire incredulity, nausea, and hopefully outrage. It's being booked as a midnight movie, and is it ever. Boozy fanboys will treat it like a thrill ride.

And yet within Six there stirs the soul of a dark artist. He treats his material with utter seriousness; there's none of the jokey undertone of a classic Hammer horror film like *Scream and Scream Again* (1970), in which every time the victim awoke, another limb had been amputated. That one starred the all-star trio of Vincent Price, Christopher Lee, and Peter Cushing, and you could see they were having fun. Dieter Laser, who plays

Dr. Heiter, takes the role with relentless sincerity. This is his sixty-third acting role, but, poor guy, this is seemingly the one he was born to play.

Tom Six is apparently the director's real name. I learn his favorite actor is Klaus Kinski, he is an AK-47 enthusiast, and wears RAF sunglasses and Panama hats. Not the kind of guy you want to share your seat on a Ferris wheel. He has said, "I get a rash from too much political correctness." I promise you that after this movie his skin was smooth as a Gerber baby's.

I have long attempted to take a generic approach. In other words, is a film true to its genre and does it deliver what its audiences presumably expect? *The Human Centipede* scores high on this scale. It is depraved and disgusting enough to satisfy the most demanding midnight movie fan. And it's not *simply* an exploitation film.

The director makes, for example, an effective use of the antiseptic interior of Heiter's labyrinthine home. Doors and corridors lead nowhere and anywhere. In a scene where the police come calling, he wisely has Heiter almost encourage their suspicions. And there is a scene toward the end, as the human centipede attempts escape, that's so piteous it transcends horror and approaches tragedy.

The members of the centipede are Ashley C. Williams, Ashlynn Yennie, and Akihiro Kitamura. The Japanese actor screams in subtitled Japanese, perhaps because he will broaden the film's appeal among Asian horror fans. In the last half of the film, the two American actresses don't scream at all, if you follow me.

I am required to award stars to movies I review. This time, I refuse to do it. The star rating system is unsuited to this film. Is the movie good? Is it bad? Does it matter? It is what it is, and occupies a world where the stars don't shine.

The Human Centipede 2 (Full Sequence)

(DIRECTED BY TOM SIX; STARRING LAURENCE R. HARVEY, DOMINIC BORRELLI; 2011)

In the first *Human Centipede* movie, a young woman found herself sewn mouth to anus by a sadistic surgeon with two other victims. Every cloud has a silver lining. In *The Human Centipede 2 (Full Sequence)* we meet the same actress (Ashlynn Yennie), and from what we can judge she survived that ordeal with little permanent facial damage.

Despite what must have been an unhappy professional experience, Miss Yennie is a trouper, and soon after the beginning of *Human Centipede 2*, she optimistically looks forward to what she thinks will be a meeting with Quentin Tarantino. I can imagine her letter home: "Hi Mom and Dad! Thanks for not seeing my first movie! I've got great news! Tarantino wants to consider me!"

Alas, this is not to be. She is met by the singularly disquieting Martin (Laurence R. Harvey), a pudgy, nearsighted, pear-headed, clammy-skinned, mentally disabled momma's boy who works as a security guard in a mostly deserted subterranean parking garage. Since Martin very rarely ever says anything in this movie, how, you may ask, have I made my diagnosis of his mental condition? I submit to you that if this man spends his waking moments looking at the first *Human Centipede* movie over and over and over again, and wants to make his own version by connecting as many as twelve people, he is four tires short of a car.

Laurence R. Harvey is described as "a British performance artist." I raced off to the always helpful Google and discovered that his artistic career to date hasn't generated a single link. It may be that his performance art consists entirely of walking down the street as himself. Gene Siskel liked to amuse himself by people watching and thinking, "When that person looked in the mirror before leaving the house, he thought he looked great."

Martin kills a lot of people in this movie, in addition to sewing others together. Perhaps the message is that the first movie influenced its viewers to do sadistic and cruel acts. Since both films were made by the same man, Tom Six, it is inarguable that the first film inspired him to make the second.

The film is reprehensible, dismaying, ugly, artless, and an affront to any notion, however remote, of human decency. It makes a point of Martin's lack of all surgical skills. He seems to have sewn his victims together with summer-camp skills, with which you stitch the parts of a billfold together with leather thread. I am left with this question: After Ashlynn Yennie's first movie role was in the first *Human Centipede* movie, and now her second is in *Human Centipede 2*, do you think she'll leave show business?

I

● ● ● ● ● ● ● ● ●

I Am

(DIRECTED BY TOM SHADYAC; STARRING DESMOND TUTU, HOWARD ZINN; 2011)
There is a scene in *I Am* where a laboratory technician embeds sensors in a puddle of yogurt and attaches them to a Bio-Response Meter. When Tom Shadyac directs his thoughts at the yogurt, the needle on the meter bounces back and forth. It is important for you to know that Shadyac is not physically attached to the meter—or to the yogurt, for that matter. When he thinks about his lawyer, the needle redlines.

It's obvious that the yogurt is reading his mind, right? Right? Hello? For Shadyac and the technician, this experiment demonstrates that our minds are wired to the organic world. For me, it raises the following questions: (1) Was the yogurt pasteurized? (2) How did the yogurt know to read Shadyac's mind and not the mind of the technician who was just as close? (3) How did it occur to anyone to devise an experiment testing whether yogurt can respond to human thoughts? (4) Did anyone check to see if the technician was connected to the meter? (5) Is this a case for the Amazing Randi?

You see I am a rationalist. That means I'm not an ideal viewer for a documentary like *I Am*, which involves the ingestion of woo-woo in industrial bulk. When I see a man whose mind is being read by yogurt, I expect to find that man in a comedy starring, oh, someone like Jim Carrey. Since we all understand There Are No Coincidences, it won't surprise you to learn that *I Am* was directed by Tom Shadyac, who earned untold millions by directing Jim Carrey in such films as *Ace Ventura: Pet Detective*.

This documentary is often absurd and never less than giddy with uplift, but that's not to say it's bad. I watched with an incredulous delight, and at the end I liked Tom Shadyac quite a lot. He's a goofball, yet his heart is in the right place. But don't get me started on hearts. Did you know that Shadyac's friend Rollin McCraty, Ph.D., the director of research for Heart-Math, has proven that the human heart controls the human brain via various types of biofeedback?

That's not all the heart can do. Try this on for size: When you are shown pleasant or frightening images on a computer screen, your brain (and heart) respond either positively or negatively. That makes sense. But wait. When the images are chosen at random from a big database, the heart sends positive or negative signals to the brain *two to three seconds in advance* of the image being chosen. In other words, the heart knows what the random image is going to be. Yes. Shadyac is grateful for this information. He doesn't ask any questions, like, for example, does the heart tell the brain what signal *would* have been displayed unless the power to the monitor went out in the milliseconds between when it was chosen and was to be displayed?

Dr. McCraty shares another piece of information that's interesting. There are random number generators distributed all over the world. Most of the time the numbers are truly random. But when a global catastrophe like 9/11 or the Japan calamity occurs, our collective minds send out such strong signals that the computers temporarily stop selecting random numbers. Yes. And the screen fills with lots of ones and zeroes to illustrate that.

So I'm thinking, not everybody found out about the Japan earthquake at once. Does McCraty have data showing if the globe's random number calculators failed simultaneously, or were timed to the spread of the news? (I can guess the answer: They all failed at once, because at a Gaia level we all sensed it simultaneously.)

What set Tom Shadyac to gather this information and make a film about it? In 2007 he was a multimillionaire living in a seventeen-thousand-square-foot mansion in Pasadena and flying in a private jet. Then he had a terrible bike accident, breaking bones and suffering a concussion. He became a victim of post-concussion syndrome, which meant the symptoms didn't clear up. He had blinding headaches and debilitating depressions, and contemplated suicide. Mercifully, the symptoms faded, leaving him sadder, wiser, and in search of truth.

He began with two questions: What's wrong with the world? What can we do about it? He traveled the world to pose these questions to many distinguished people, such as the linguist Noam Chomsky; Archbishop Desmond Tutu; Howard Zinn; Lynne McTaggart, an authority on consciousness and the new physics; people at the Institute of Noetic Sciences; his late father, Richard Shadyac, who was CEO of fundraising for St. Jude Hospital; and so on. None of these people necessarily agree with anything the others say. As for Shadyac, hey, he's just listening.

The thing is, he doesn't ask enough. He is not a skeptic. He asks his two questions and mashes together the answers with a lot of fancy editing of butterflies, sunsets, flocks of birds, schools of fish, herds of wild animals, and petri dishes filled with yogurt. From his tour emerges one conclusion: Everything is connected. Our minds, our bodies, our planet, our universe. This happens (you can see this coming) at the quantum level.

Another thing he learns is that money is the root of all evil. Like the fish, birds, animals, and untouched tribes, we have evolved to cooperate and arrive at consensus. By competing to enrich ourselves, we create bad vibes. Give Shadyac credit: He sells his Pasadena mansion, starts teaching college, and moves into a mobile home (in Malibu, it's true). Now he offers us this hopeful if somewhat undigested cut of his findings, in a film as watchable as a really good TV commercial, and as deep.

I leave you with a parting possibility raised by the film: What if your thoughts continue to affect the DNA you leave behind everywhere you go, all through life? At a quantum level, of course.

I Am Number Four

(DIRECTED BY D. J. CARUSO; STARRING ALEX PETTYFER, DIANNA AGRON; 2011)
I Am Number Four is shameless and unnecessary. That's sad, when a movie casts aside all shame, demonstrates itself willing to rip off anything that might attract audiences, and nevertheless fails. What we have here is a

witless attempt to merge the *Twilight* formula with the Michael Bay formula. It ends with sexy human teenagers involved in an endless special effects battle with sexy alien teenagers who look like humans, in a high school and on its football field.

Let's pause for a moment to consider this apocalyptic battle. It is all special effects. None of it is physically possible. It might as well be a cartoon; it's essentially CGI animation intercut with brief bursts of inane dialogue. Brief, because the global action market doesn't much care about dialogue, and besides, when people start talking about something, you could run into the hazard of having actual characters in a plot. Minute after relentless minute, creatures both human and alien, whom we care nothing about, wage war and occasionally disintegrate into clouds of tiny pixels for no particular reason.

I like science fiction. The opening shot of *I Am Number Four* holds promise, as John (Alex Pettyfer), the narrator, explains that he is a Mogadorian, no doubt from a planet named Mogador. Specifically, he is Mogadorian Number Four. Don't expect me to explain the Mogadorian numbering system. He is hiding out on planet Earth, and doing everything possible to disguise himself as a box office attraction like Edward Cullen. They have already killed Numbers One, Two, and Three.

Consider. The *Twilight* movies were about a handsome and sexy teenager who exerted a powerful attraction upon a virginal young girl, and yet held himself aloof because he was a vampire. Here John is a handsome and sexy teenager who is technically unavailable because he is an alien, although it appears that Mogador may luckily have evolved teenage boys indistinguishable from humans to such as Sarah (Dianna Agron). John has been on the lam around America to remain in hiding from those who would kill him, and is accompanied by his fellow Mogadorian Henri (Timothy Olyphant), who poses as his father and cautions him that his real father didn't die only to see John marry an Earth girl. Whether John has the option of returning to Mogador and settling down with a nice Mogadoress to raise Mogadorlings, I am not certain.

The high school elements in the plot revolve around John's popularity in some areas (he's an ace on a Jet Ski) and nonconformity in others (his palms function like high-powered searchlights). He is also free of the ordinary constraints of gravity, and can leap for dozens of yards and even fly. What this means is that the climactic battle scene can take place largely in the air, and Harry Potter's Quidditch games join the honor roll of the plundered.

There is, no doubt, a degree of identification available for the primary audience of *I Am Number Four*. Many teenage girls have perhaps imagined themselves in love with a handsome hunk with tousled blond hair, a three-day stubble, incredible athletic abilities, and hands that glow in the dark. That he is Not From Around Here makes him all the more attractive. In the film we see native Mogadorians, whose faces are deeply scarred with gill-like extrusions. I am not completely sure if this is how John really looks and he has somehow morphed into teenager form, or if he was forced to flee Mogador because he looked like an alien Edward Cullen. I'm sure this is all spelled out in the movie. Sometimes I find it so very, very hard to care.

Now imagine *I Am Number Four* as a "novelization." There would be the setup, a little dialogue, and then pages and pages of violent action: "John leaped one hundred yards into the air and struck him with a deadly ray! An enemy fighter disintegrated into an ashy gray cloud of pixels! Number Six, her hair flowing in slow motion, whirled around and kicked the Mogadorian commander! 'Look out!' John shouted. 'Behind you!' cried Sarah."

This would quickly grow old. Why audiences enjoy watching protracted sequences of senseless action mystifies me, but they do. There is no strategic or spatial way in which the battle in *I Am Number Four* makes any sense. It is movement and conflict edited together in incomprehensible chaos.

Where is Mogador? Why did nine of its citizens flee to Earth? How did they do so? How is it they breathe our air, eat our food, and make such expert use of our grooming products? Why didn't the other Mogadorians say to hell with it and leave them on Earth? What is a Mogadorian life span? Given what we know about the time and distance involved in space travel, are these the same nine individuals who fled Mogador or their descendants after many generations in an interstellar ark? What's the story on those spotlights in their hands? In all modesty, I think my questions are more entertaining than this movie.

I Hate Valentine's Day

(DIRECTED BY NIA VARDALOS; STARRING NIA VARDALOS, JOHN CORBETT; 2009)

I Hate Valentine's Day is a romantic comedy with one peculiarity: The heroine is stark staring mad. I will tell you how I arrived at this diagnosis. Genevieve has an unbreakable policy regarding men: Five dates, and she's out the door. She even specifies exactly what each of the dates must be like, leading up to number five, during which she doesn't say so, but going all the way is a possibility.

Why does she impose these draconian measures? Because she likes only the falling in love part of an affair and not the inevitable breaking up. She expects a guy to jump through the hoops and then disappear after number five, remaining, of course, a "friend." When a woman says, "We should stay friends," it translates as, "Take your genitals to a faraway place and limit our contact to sending me flowers on my birthday."

Let's assume conservatively that Genevieve started dating when she was twenty, and that she has met on average three men a year willing to accept her strictures. And that after completing all the requirements, half of them have triumphantly arrived at home plate. Given her age, which a gentlemen does not mention, that works out to thirty-nine sex partners. According to surveys reported by ABC News and the *New York Times,* which I don't necessarily believe, the average American woman has between four and seven sex partners in a lifetime. That means Genevieve is not only an obsessive-compulsive, but a nympho.

Yet she looks so sweet. And knows she does. Yes, this is the second movie in a month, after *My Life in Ruins,* in which Nia Vardalos goes through the entire film smiling brightly and almost continuously. Nobody smiles that much unless they suffer from the rare giocondaphobia, or Constantly Smiling Syndrome, a complaint more often seen among listeners of Bill O'Reilly and field hands in *Gone With the Wind.*

Genevieve is a woman beloved by all who encounter her, when in life I would be terrified of her. She is considered a source of great wisdom about romance, although Dr. Phil might advise protective custody. In *I Hate Valentine's Day,* she runs the cutest little florist's shop in Brooklyn and dispenses invaluable advice to men uncertain about a Valentine's Day gift ("flowers"). She has two gay assistants who think she is about the best thing since Maria Callas. And this cute guy opens a tapas bar next door, named Get on Tapas, ha ha.

The cute guy is played by John Corbett, her costar in *My Big Fat Greek Wedding*. He is way too desirable to have to settle for the five-date rule. The women from *Sex and the City* would be camped out in pup tents on his sidewalk. It should have occurred to someone, maybe Vardalos, the writer and director, that it would have been funnier and way more plausible to make the hero a needy schlub who is lovestruck by her and would agree to waterboarding for even one date. The movie is set up as a valentine to Vardalos. She should try sending herself flowers.

I Love You, Beth Cooper

(DIRECTED BY CHRIS COLUMBUS; STARRING HAYDEN PANETTIERE, PAUL RUST; 2009)

The writer of *I Love You, Beth Cooper* says the story is based on a dream. I believe him. This is one of the very few movies where I *wanted* the hero to wake up and discover it was only a dream. But it's a dream all the way through—a dream evoking just another teen romcom.

The situation is so universal. The high school nerd harbors a secret crush on the most popular girl in school. He chooses the occasion of his valedictory speech to publicly proclaim this love. We can believe that, all the way up to the valedictory speech. But, yes, this is another movie hailing a hero with the courage to say what he really believes and accept the consequences.

Sometimes, as in a dream, doing that will pay off abundantly by focusing the popular girl's attention on how unique and special you are. Sometimes the popular girl will reveal herself as actually a warm and cuddly human being. Sometimes. More often, the nerd will confirm everyone's belief in his nerdhood, humiliate himself, selfishly derail the whole graduation exercise, and discover that the most popular girl really *is* a bitch. Lots of wonderful girls fall in love with nerds. They may not become the most popular girl in school, but they don't care. That honor carries with it a terrible lifetime price tag.

So what I wish is that *I Love You, Beth Cooper* had awakened from its dream and been a smart high school comedy, even one subscribing to an alternate set of clichés in which the hero discovers he really loves the nerdy girl once she takes off her glasses.

I am also tiring of the way high school movies insist that all non-heroic characters travel in posses of three. All Most Popular Girls arrive flanked by two girlfriends who follow them by half a step. And all macho villains have two underlings who follow their orders. In *I Love You, Beth Cooper,* the girlfriends are nice enough, because the heroine is. But the villain, "Muncher" Munsch (Jack Carpenter), is a uniformed ROTC officer who, along with his sidekicks, is a muscular master of the martial arts, a skilled gymnast, and a vicious bully. When he whistles, his minions snap to attention. And they attack with coordination worthy of a dance troupe.

The movie also goes over the top with special effects, where the theory "less is more" must be in an incomprehensible language. I know that fierce struggles over romance can break out in high school, but with these kids, I doubt they would threaten to be lethal. Nor is driving an SUV into a house commonplace. Scene after scene is on autopilot.

I'm thinking of films that remember what it's like to be a teenager with a hopeless love. *Almost Famous, Lucas, Say Anything, The Man in the Moon.* If I were a filmmaker like Chris Columbus, who has directed two of the Harry Potter films, I don't know if I'd bother with this genre unless I felt I could make a film aspiring to that kind of stature.

Of the two costars, what I can say is that I'm looking forward to their next films. Hayden Panettiere (Beth) is professional and lovable and convincingly projects emotions and has a face the screen loves. Paul Rust (Denis the valedictorian) can be very earnest and sincere, and seems to actually take the plot seriously, which is more than I could do.

Inkheart

(DIRECTED BY IAIN SOFTLEY; STARRING BRENDAN FRASER, PAUL BETTANY; 2009)

I never knew reading was so dangerous. No child seeing *Inkheart* will ever want to be read to again, especially if that child loves its mother, as so many do. Here is a film about a man named Mo who, when he reads aloud, has the power of liberating fictional characters into the real world. The drawback is that real people are trapped within the same book. Tit for tat. A law of physics must apply.

The film opens with its best scene, for me, anyway: the professional book buyer Mo (Brendan Fraser) and his twelve-year-old daughter, Meggie (Eliza Hope Bennett), poking through an open-air book market. As always I was trying to read the titles on the spines. Not realizing that *Inkheart* is based on a famous fantasy novel, I had the foolish hope the movie might be about books. No luck. Wait till you hear what it's about.

At the edge of the market is a dark little bookstore presided over by a dark little man. As Mo prowls its aisles, he hears the faint chatter of fictional characters calling to him. (Dictionaries must be almost impossible to shut up.) Sixth sense leads him to discover, on an obscure shelf, the novel *Inkheart*, in the format of a Penguin mystery from the 1950s. He buys it, slips it into his pocket, and the two of them are followed by a mysterious skulking man.

We discover this is the very book Mo was reading when his wife, Meggie's mother (Sienna Guillory), was sucked into its pages, and that is the true story, Meggie, of how your mom suddenly disappeared when you were little. Yeah, right, Dad. At the same time, various demonic creatures were liberated from the book's pages. They have now set up shop in a mountaintop castle and are conspiring to command Mo's power now that he has discovered their book again. Do they want to return to its pages, or be reunited with old chums in the real world? And how do you get a mortgage to buy a castle when you're a demonic creature and your résumé mentions only fictional adventures in an out-of-print book? The banks must have been lending carelessly there awhile back.

Mo and Meggie take refuge in a cliffside mansion occupied by her great-aunt Elinor (Helen Mirren). Mansion? Looks to me like a dreamy tourist hotel from a Merchant-Ivory production. Elinor is a nasty scold who always wears a turban, the reliable standby of the actress tired of having her hair fussed over every second. I hope good Dame Helen passed this tip along to young Eliza Hope Bennett, who shows every sign of becoming an accomplished actress.

The movie now descends into the realm of your basic good guys vs.

wrathful wraiths formula, with pitched battles and skullduggery. The villains are Dustfinger (Paul Bettany) and the ambitious Capricorn (Andy Serkis), and there is always the threat of Mo and Meggie being transmogrified into the pages of the book. There they'd at least have the company of the missing mom and the shabby author Fenoglio (Jim Broadbent), who wrote the novel within *Inkheart*, and apparently was only set free to rise up one level, to the novel containing his novel. Thanks for nothing.

Lots of screams, horrible fates almost happening, close scrapes, cries for help, special effects, monomania, quick thinking, pluck, fear, and scrambling. You know the kinds of stuff. I learn there are two more novels in this series by Cornelia Funke, both of which will remain just as unread by me as the first. It is hard to guess what they will involve, however, because this one closes with a curiously cobbled-together ending that seems to solve everything, possibly as a talisman against a sequel.

The Invasion

(DIRECTED BY OLIVER HIRSCHBIEGEL; STARRING NICOLE KIDMAN, DANIEL CRAIG; 2007)
The Invasion is the fourth, and the least, of the movies made from Jack Finney's classic science-fiction novel *The Body Snatchers*. Here is a great story born to be creepy, and the movie churns through it like a road company production. If the first three movies served as parables for their times, this one keeps shooting off parable rockets that fizzle out. How many references in the same movie can you have to the war in Iraq and not say anything about it?

Don Siegel's classic *Invasion of the Body Snatchers* (1956) was about alien pods that arrived on Earth, sucked up the essence of human hosts, and became duplicates of them—exact copies, except for what made them human. It was widely decoded as an attack on McCarthyism. Phil Kaufman's *Invasion of the Body Snatchers* (1978), inexplicably described by Pauline Kael as "the American movie of the year," was said to have something to do with Watergate and keeping tabs on those who are not like you. Abel Ferrara's *Body Snatchers* (1994), by far the best of the films, might have been about the spread of AIDS.

And *The Invasion?* One of the alien beings argues persuasively that if everyone were like them, there'd be no war in Iraq, no genocide in Darfur—no conflict in general, I guess, although they don't seem to have much of a position on global warming. I don't have a clue what the movie thinks, if anything, about Iraq, which is mentioned so frequently, but it may be a veiled attack on cults that require unswerving conformity from their members. Which cults? I dunno.

In all four movies, alien spores arrive on Earth from space. In the early films they take the form of pods, which look like very large brown snow peas. Some viewers complained after Kaufman's movie that they couldn't believe aliens could truck those pods all over San Francisco, to which the obvious reply is: Do you expect a movie titled *Invasion of the Body Snatchers* to be plausible?

In Oliver Hirschbiegel's new version, the spores piggy-back on a returning space shuttle that crashes and scatters debris from Dallas to Washington. Anyone who touches the debris gets the infection, which is then spread by touch and the exchange of vomit (in more ways than you might imagine). In Washington, a psychiatrist named Carol (Nicole Kidman) has a patient who complains, "My husband just . . . isn't my husband anymore." Versions of this line do duty in all four films. The pod people look like the people they occupy and have the same memories ("Remember Colorado?"), but they walk like mannequins with arthritis, except when they're running like zombies.

Carol's estranged husband, Tucker (Jeremy Northam), is a disease control expert who becomes infected and after four years suddenly wants to start spending time with their child, Oliver (Jackson Bond). Little Oliver texts his mom that his dad is different. Carol's current good friend is a doctor named Ben (Daniel Craig), who is one of many to notice a new "flu virus" that is spreading through the land.

His colleague, a researcher named Dr. Galeano (Jeffrey Wright), gets a sample of the virus, and in a performance that would be the envy of every scientist since Newton, gazes at it through a microscope and almost immediately explains what it is, how it reproduces, how it takes over when we fall asleep, and (apparently only a day or two later) how to defeat it with an antibody that can seemingly be manufactured so quickly and in such quantities that it can be sprayed from crop dusters. By this point the movie has lost all coherence, not to mention flaunting a scene where a helicopter lands atop a towering skyscraper in Washington, where federal law decrees no building can be taller than the Capitol.

This may not be entirely Hirschbiegel's fault. Warner Bros. didn't approve of his original version and brought in the Wachowskis to rewrite it and James McTeigue (*V for Vendetta*) to direct their revisions. All three served time on the *Matrix* movies: just the team you'd want to add a little incomprehensible chaos.

The genius of the Ferrara version was to make his very sympathetic heroine a young girl on an Army base who can't get anyone to listen to her. You know how adults can be when kids claim they've seen aliens. The problem with this new version is that it caves in and goes for your basic car chase scenes (spinning tires, multiple crashes, car in flames, dozens of pod people hanging onto it, etc). If aliens are among us, we will not be saved by stunt driving.

Nicole Kidman, Daniel Craig, Jeremy Northam, little Jackson Bond, Jeffrey Wright, and other cast members do what they can with dialogue that can hardly be spoken, and a plot that we concede must be implausible but does not necessarily have to upstage the *Mad* magazine version. And the aliens themselves are a flop. Just like zombies, they're pushovers: easy to spot, slow-moving, not too bright, can be shot dead or otherwise disposed of. OK. Now we've had *Invasion of the Body Snatchers* twice, *Body Snatchers,* once and *Invasion* once. Somebody should register the title *Of The.*

Irene in Time

(DIRECTED BY HENRY JAGLOM; STARRING TANNA FREDERICK, ANDREA MARCOVICCI; 2009)

Henry Jaglom's new film, *Irene in Time,* is dedicated to "my daughter." A curious note to end on, since it is about a woman whose personality and selfhood have been destroyed by an absent, unreliable father. So much is she obsessed by this long-gone parent that her life is consumed by talking about her father, relating her childhood memories, hanging around with his old friends, and dating men she hopes will fill the gap in her life.

Irene's dating strategy is so inept and needy, however, it's a wonder one guy lasted for what she says is three months but he precisely times at two and a half months. Another poor guy, an architect, doesn't last through their first dinner together. She asks if he uses a protractor and compass in his drawing, and he says he does. And pencils and erasers? Yes, he says, all the tools. "And what is your favorite tool?" He doesn't have one. "Come on," she says, "close your eyes and concentrate! Name your favorite tool!" By now he's looking desperate, and asks: "What is your problem?"

Her Daddy's Little Girl act isn't helped by the books she studies about how to behave on dates, attract men, and so forth. If any of you, my dear readers, are women studying such books as *The Rules,* I offer this free advice: A wise man will stay far away from a woman playing him like a fish, and only a needy one will respond well if you are coy about returning his calls.

Irene (Tanna Frederick) is such an insecure flywheel that any man (repeat, any man) should know enough to start edging away after two minutes of conversation. A woman's stock of small talk shouldn't center on how magical her father was, especially when she's in her thirties and hasn't seen him since she was young.

Irene in Time follows Jaglom's "women's trilogy" of films about women's issues such as childbearing, weight, and compulsive shopping. I guess it's the women's quartet now. Irene hangs around with a posse of female friends who gossip, offer sometimes heartfelt advice, receive massages, have lunch, and attend parties. They're all apparently independently wealthy, well divorced, or kept women, since work never seems to interrupt their busy schedules. True, Irene has a job of sorts, making a recording with a band, but their woeful material seems well suited for the lounge of a cruise ship.

There's a dramatic revelation in the film, inspired by a trail of clues in the form of messages that Irene's father apparently left behind years ago for her to discover only now. Good thing she finds them. Note to disappearing fathers: If you want to communicate in twenty years with a daughter, write it down in a letter and leave it with your lawyer.

The revelation does, however, lead to two of the better scenes in the movie, involving older women played by Victoria Tennant and Andrea Marcovicci. Tennant plays her mother, and I must not tell you whom Marcovicci plays.

Jaglom has been producing his own films since 1971 and has made some good ones, notably *Deja Vu* (1997). This is not a good one. It offers certain pleasures, but suffers from an inability to structure events or know when to end a shot. And it has an ending that is simply, perhaps ridiculously, incomprehensible. That's if it means what I think it means, and I fear it does.

Note: Strolling around the Internet, I found a review of Irene *in* Time *by Tommy Garrett of the* Canyon News. *He compares Jaglom with Wilder and Hitchcock, then writes: "In Frederick's case, he has given her a vehicle which has propelled her into a category that no actress in the past 50 years could be placed. Frederick makes the list of very talented women in Hollywood: Garbo, Davis, Crawford and Hepburn."*

(I'm grateful to Tommy Garrett, who has achieved the feat of writing praise so astonishing we at last have someone to compare to the critic who said I Am Legend *was one of the greatest movies ever made.)*

I Spit on Your Grave

(DIRECTED BY STEVEN R. MONROE; STARRING SARAH BUTLER, JEFF BRANSON; 2010)

This despicable remake of the despicable 1978 film *I Spit on Your Grave* adds yet another offense: a phony moral equivalency. In the original, a woman foolishly thought to go on holiday by herself in a secluded cabin. She attracted the attention of depraved local men, who raped her, one after the other. Then the film ended with her fatal revenge. In this film, less time is devoted to the revenge and more time to verbal, psychological, and physical violence against her. Thus it works even better as vicarious cruelty against women.

First let's dispatch with the fiction that the film is about "getting even." If I rape you, I have committed a crime. If you kill me, you have committed another one. The ideal outcome would be two people unharmed in the first place. The necessity of revenge is embedded in the darker places of our minds, and most hate speech is driven by "wrongs" invented in unbalanced minds. No one who commits a hate crime ever thinks his victim is innocent.

That set aside, let's see what this movie does. The woman, Jennifer (Sarah Butler), is a writer who rents a cabin in the woods where she plans to stay by herself. Once we know this, we start waiting for the gas station occupied by demented rednecks. There's always one. Of course that's where Jennifer stupidly asks directions and reveals where she's going to ignorant, leering phallus carriers.

There are four. One is their "ringleader." One is his sidekick. One compulsively makes video recordings. The fourth is mentally handicapped and they treat him as their pet "retard." After many scenes involving alarming noises in the night and the usual Woman in Fear sequences, the men enter her cabin and terrorize her.

They use words and guns. They insinuate. They toy with her answers. They enjoy her terror. This is rape foreplay, and they stretch it out as long as they can. There is a reason for this. Rape is a crime of violence, not sex, and the male rapist typically savors the fear he causes more than the sex. Indeed, if he enjoyed sex more, he might not be a rapist. The true pornography in this film involves the dialogue and situation in the cabin *before* the physical assault. It is well done. This is a professionally made film. The audience is very, very quiet. Some share Jennifer's terror. Some, I am afraid, may be aroused or entertained by it.

When the rape inevitably arrives, it is the hapless mental deficient, Matthew (Chad Lindberg), who is forced by the others to go first. Otherwise he crouches whimpering in a corner. The movie's exploitation of his handicap is on a par with the cruel sadism of the film. Eventually Jennifer is thoroughly raped and runs away into the woods barefoot and almost naked and, when they approach with a shotgun to eliminate her as a witness, jumps from a high bridge and disappears.

We will slip past the movie's nonexplanation for her survival and reappearance to consider her revenge. I choose not to describe her methods. Let me suggest that if you recall any of the torture scenes described in the novels of Cormac McCarthy or Larry McMurtry, I suspect the director and writer of this film remember them as well. Jennifer's methods are elaborate, bizarre, and cruel.

Oh, sure, they have it coming to them—except for the pathetic Matthew, who has been a victim all his life and is now punished by Jennifer even though she witnessed his grief and innocence. He is a man and must die. A couple of tortures here inspired groans from the audience, but this stuff isn't a novelty for connoisseurs of horror movies. Consider *Saw* and anything with *chainsaw* in its title.

No, it's the first half of the movie that's offensive. It implicitly assigns us the POV of the men as they taunt and terrorize Jennifer in plausible ways—which are different from her killing methods, which are implausible, probably impossible, and offered and received as entertainment.

Now here's an interesting thing: There were walkouts from the packed screening I attended. Not many, maybe eight or nine. Nobody walked out in the second half; they all left in the first half. And . . . they were all men. Most of the audience looked like they were on dates. For conversation afterward, if you see this loathsome film, here are some suggestions:

Men, ask your dates: What bothered you more, the first or second half? Would you recommend this movie to your girlfriends? Did you enjoy it? (It's OK; you can be honest.)

Women, ask your dates: What part did you like the most, the first or second half? Would you recommend this movie to your sister? Why did we go to this particular film? Did you know there were two new four-star films playing in the same multiplex?

Both men and women may find some food for thought in the answers. Certain answers may cause you to ask yourself if you have any future with this other person.

Jonah Hex

(DIRECTED BY JIMMY HAYWARD; STARRING JOSH BROLIN, JOHN MALKOVICH; 2010)

Jonah Hex is a Western set around the town of Stunk Crick, although that doesn't entirely explain why the climactic scene involves an attack on the U.S. Capitol building in Washington. Using my powers of logic, I deduce that the characters traveled there from Stunk Crick. The movie is not precise in its geography. Most of the location filming was in Louisiana, which is not named, perhaps because that might make it hard to explain its vast deserts and dusty frontier town.

The thriller involves a man named Jonah Hex (Josh Brolin), who is bent on vengeance. During the Civil War, the evil Quentin Turnbull (John Malkovich) strapped him to a cross and made him watch as a house containing his family was set afire. Then Turnbull branded Jonah's face with a hot iron, causing difficulties with leaks when he tries to throw back a shot of whiskey. You can see why Jonah would want his revenge. To be sure, Turnbull mutters something about Jonah having previously murdered *his* family, meaning he isn't entirely without motive.

Stunk Crick is your standard frontier town with a wide Main Street, a saloon, and a room over the saloon occupied by Lilah, a sexy hooker. The presence of Lilah in the film is easily explained: She is played by Megan Fox. If you want a woman in an old western town, there are only three occupations open to her, hooking, schoolmarming, and anyone called Ma.

Lilah and Jonah are in love, for reasons unexplained. It certainly isn't because of the quality of their conversation. The only hooker in a Western I've ever believed in was in *Lonesome Dove,* but I've seen *Lonesome Dove,* and *Jonah Hex* is no *Lonesome Dove.*

It's based on some DC Comics characters, which may explain the way the plot jumps around. We hear a lot about graphic novels, but this is more of a graphic anthology of strange occult ideas. Consider, for example, that Jonah was once so close to death that he wandered around on the Other Side and made valuable contacts there. He can even talk to the dead, and one corpse revives long enough to tell him precisely where Quentin Turnbull can be found.

In what is possibly a confused stab at allegory, Jonah finds himself trying to prevent Turnbull from blowing up the Capitol building with a terrorist super weapon. In scenes set in the Oval Office, the U.S. president is concerned about this threat by Turnbull, who is an embittered Confederate general, and decides that the wanted outlaw Hex is the only man who can prevent the plot from being carried out.

A climactic battle scene takes place in the Potomac River between two ironclad ships. In U.S. history, you will recall, there was such a battle between the USS *Monitor* and the Confederate ship *Virginia*. One of these ships looks like the *Monitor*, but I'm unclear. Anyway, Turnbull is onboard, directing the Weapon, which is a big cannon. He's previously tested it by blowing up a Western town. Now he trains it on the Capitol, depicted in special effects that suggest the Capitol and the Washington Monument were the only two structures in Washington at that time, at least for purposes of being fired on.

After Hex saves the day, he's invited into the Oval Office, thanked, and then presented with a big badge. What is this badge? The president tells Hex: "America needs a sheriff." This provided the audience with a big laugh, which sounded like it might have been bottled up for a while.

The Joneses

(DIRECTED BY DERRICK BORTE; STARRING DEMI MOORE, DAVID DUCHOVNY; 2010)
Everyone wants to keep up with the Joneses. They're good-looking, friendly, popular, affluent, and they always seem ahead of the curve when it comes to what they drive, wear, play, and consume. They never boast. They never

have to. People just plain want to be just like them. And you had better stop reading now, because it's impossible to say more without a spoiler.

OK, for those still in the room, I wonder how many will really be surprised by the big plot "reveal." From the first moments of dialogue, there seems to be something off about the Joneses. Nothing is made explicit for a time, but they don't seem to relate to one another as family members. There's something they understand and we don't.

The fact is, they aren't a family; they're a marketing unit. Marketing people talk about "early adopters": People who influence a peer group by being the first to know about, use, wear, or attend something. At a conference I attended in Boulder, Colorado, total strangers followed Andy Ihnatko and his iPad around like a man with a T-bone at a dog pound. The Joneses are professional early adopters, paid to impersonate a family unit and consume the sponsor's products.

Among other advantages to this story idea, it makes product placement necessary, not merely venal. If you don't leave this movie more aware of the new Audi models, you slept through it. The Joneses never make a point of anything. It's just that Steve Jones (David Duchovny) makes great shots with his new golf clubs. Kate Jones (Demi Moore) entertains so brilliantly. Their teenagers, Jennifer (Amber Heard) and Mick (Ben Hollingsworth), wear such cool stuff. If the Joneses don't have a dog, maybe that's because there's not enough money in dog retailing.

It would seem to be a comfortable existence, consuming the best products ahead of the market and never having to pay for them. It's not that easy. It means denying your own impulses to be honest and confiding. Suppressing your own tastes. Not feeling genuine. Ask yourself who in your crowd insisted you had to see *How to Train Your Dragon* in 3-D, when you wanted to see it in 2-D, and what you *really* wanted to see was *My Son, My Son, What Have Ye Done*. That person is a Jones.

You, on the other hand, are a Larry or Summer (Gary Cole and Glenne Headly), the next-door neighbors who are always playing catch-up. You have ceded control of your taste to someone you admire for superficial reasons. This is a doomed enterprise, for you will never, ever catch up, and by definition you can never take the lead because the Joneses define the race.

The Joneses not surprisingly finds troubling flaws in the lives of this professional family. Try as they will to be disciplined and on message, they have emotions of their own. Some of them involve sex. Others involve a feeling of inner worthlessness. The strongest is Kate, played by the great-looking Demi Moore as a capable team leader aiming for a promotion. Steve is a former golf pro, so no stranger to the challenge of playing a role model, but his decency runs deeper than Kate's.

As for the kids, Jennifer and Mick, well, even their names are popular; Jennifer is the sixty-seventh most popular name in the nation and Michael is the third. But they're teenagers, and you know how that goes. So many raging hormones, either to follow or suppress. That Jennifer and Mick are so attractive, and so . . . advanced . . . for their age complicates their inner lives. At that age, you haven't been completely tamed by the corporate mind-set.

The Joneses was directed and cowritten by Derrick Borte, an advertising man, and contains a good deal of dark cynicism. It also hopes to entertain, and those two goals don't fit together easily. Either this is a tragic family or a satirical one, and the film seems uncertain which way to jump. In a perfect film, the noose of their inauthentic lives would draw more tightly, more swiftly, around the Joneses, and the movie might be angrier.

Still, Demi Moore is good as a corporate team player with no conscience (she could have played the George Clooney role in *Up in the Air*), and the others adequately act around the problems of the screenplay. It's just that somehow this movie should acknowledge how very close to life it is, and how in our society you don't have to pay the Joneses. They learn their roles from television and work for free.

Journey to the Center of the Earth

(DIRECTED BY ERIC BREVIG; STARRING BRENDAN FRASER, JOSH HUTCHERSON; 2008)
There is a part of me that will always have affection for a movie like *Journey to the Center of the Earth*. It is a small part and steadily shrinking, but once I put on the 3-D glasses and settled into my seat, it started perking

up. This is a fairly bad movie, and yet at the same time maybe about as good as it could be. There may not be an eight-year-old alive who would not love it. If I had seen it when I was eight, I would have remembered it with deep affection for all these years, until I saw it again and realized how little I really knew at that age.

You are already familiar with the premise, that there is another land inside of our globe. You are familiar because the Jules Verne novel has inspired more than a dozen movies and countless TV productions, including a series, and has been ripped off by such as Edgar Rice Burroughs, who called it Pellucidar and imagined that the Earth was hollow and there was another world on the inside surface. (You didn't ask, but yes, I own a copy of *Tarzan at the Earth's Core* with the original dust jacket.)

In this version, Brendan Fraser stars as a geologist named Trevor, who defends the memory of his late brother, Max, who believed the center of the earth could be reached through "volcanic tubes." Max disappeared on a mysterious expedition, which, if it involved volcanic tubes, should have been no surprise to him. Now Trevor has been asked to spend some time with his nephew, Max's son, who is named Sean (Josh Hutcherson). What with one thing and another, wouldn't you know they find themselves in Iceland, and peering down a volcanic tube. They are joined in this enterprise by Hannah (Anita Briem), whom they find living in Max's former research headquarters near the volcano he was investigating.

Now begins a series of adventures, in which the operative principle is: No matter how frequently or how far they fall, they will land without injury. They fall very frequently and very far. The first drop lands them at the bottom of a deep cave, from which they cannot possibly climb, but they remain remarkably optimistic: "There must be a way out of here!" Sure enough, they find an abandoned mine shaft and climb aboard three cars of its miniature railway for a scene that will make you swear the filmmakers must have seen *Indiana Jones and the Temple of Doom*. Just like in that movie, they hurtle down the tracks at breakneck speeds; they're in three cars, on three more or less parallel tracks, leading you to wonder why three parallel tracks were constructed at great expense and bother, but just when such questions are forming, they have to (1) leap a chasm, (2) jump from one car to another, and (3) crash. It's a funny thing about that little railway: After all these years, it still has lamps hanging over the rails, and the electricity is still on.

The problem of lighting an unlit world is solved in the next cave they enter, which is inhabited by cute little birds that glow in the dark. One of them makes friends with Sean and leads them on to the big attraction—a world bounded by a great interior sea. This world must be a terrible place to inhabit; it has man-eating and man-strangling plants, its waters harbor giant-fanged fish and fearsome sea snakes that eat them, and on the farther shore is a Tyrannosaurus rex.

So do the characters despair? Would you despair if you were trapped miles below the surface in a cave and being chased by its hungry inhabitants? Of course not. There isn't a moment in the movie when anyone seems frightened, not even during a fall straight down for thousands of feet, during which they link hands like skydivers and carry on a conversation. Trevor gets the ball rolling: "We're still falling!"

I mentioned 3-D glasses earlier in the review. Yes, the movie is available in 3-D in "selected theaters." Select those theaters to avoid. With a few exceptions (such as the authentic IMAX process), 3-D remains underwhelming to me—a distraction, a disappointment, and more often than not offering a dingy picture. I guess setting your story inside the earth is one way to explain why it always seems to need more lighting.

The movie is being shown in 2-D in a majority of theaters, and that's how I wish I had seen it. Since there's that part of me with a certain weakness for movies like this, it's possible I would have liked it more. It would have looked brighter and clearer, and the photography wouldn't have been cluttered up with all the leaping and gnashing of teeth. Then I could have appreciated the work of the plucky actors, who do a lot of things right in this movie, of which the most heroic is keeping a straight face.

Judy Moody and the NOT Bummer Summer
(Directed by John Schultz; starring Jordana Beatty, Heather Graham; 2011)

Judy Moody and the NOT Bummer Summer is a film that little kids might find perfectly acceptable. Little, little, little kids. My best guess is above fourth-grade level you'd be pushing it. The kids, on the other hand, might enjoy its zany adaptation of Megan McDonald's best-seller. That makes this a good candidate for watching on video. I doubt many parents would enjoy it much, and I can't see grown-ups attending unless they're on duty.

The movie tells the story of red-headed Judy Moody (Jordana Beatty), who learns in disbelief that while all her friends will be spending the summer doing neat things, her own parents will be away from home on an important trip. They plan to abandon Judy and her kid brother, Stink (Parris Mosteller), to the care of her dreaded Aunt Opal (Heather Graham). That information immediately reminded me that one of my mother's best friends was named Opal Hollingsworth. I heard the name "Opal Hollingsworth" so often that it's difficult for me to think of an Opal not named Hollingsworth.

What, you may ask, does that possibly have to do with *Judy Moody and the NOT Bummer Summer*? I must be honest. Both while watching the movie and again while writing this review, when I got to the name "Aunt Opal," my mind veered off on a tangent. There was little in the film to draw it back on course. It may seem unfair of me to change the subject so arbitrarily, but I am trying to signal my grown-up readers that they may find themselves looking for stuff to think about while watching this film.

Anyway, Aunt Opal turns up and is not nearly so bad as Judy Moody fears. She draws up a Thrill Chart, a weirdly unconnected checklist of things to keep Judy and Stink occupied during the summer, and the film works its way through some of these topics with lots of bright colors and jolly music. There are also some jokes about those basic bodily functions that little kids seem to find hilarious.

Jordana Beatty is capable here, sweet and spirited, and my wish for her is that life brings her screenplays that I will find more interesting. She might excel in *The Life of Opal Hollingsworth*, who was quite a character.

Just Go with It

(DIRECTED BY DENNIS DUGAN; STARRING ADAM SANDLER, JENNIFER ANISTON; 2011)

The people in this movie are dumber than a box of Tinkertoys. One fears they're so unfortunate it's not politically correct to laugh at them. That's not a problem because *Just Go with It* is so rarely funny. Here is a story that began as a French farce. Then it was adapted into a Broadway play named *Cactus Flower.* Then the play was made into a movie. Now it has been made into another movie. This process has diluted it like a homeopathic medicine, so that not an atom of the original formula can be found.

Consider. Danny (Adam Sandler) broke off his wedding at the last minute, but continues to wear the wedding ring. Women find the ring seductive and cannot resist having sex with a married man. Therefore, most (not all) of the women in his life are stupid. This works for him for approximately twenty-five years. In the meantime, he becomes a famous plastic surgeon in Beverly Hills. He is assisted by Nurse Katherine (Jennifer Aniston), who has two kids.

On the one day he isn't wearing his ring, he spends an idyllic night at the beach with the delicious twenty-three-year-old Palmer (Brooklyn Decker). Then she finds the ring in his pocket and thinks he is married, and he lies and says yes, but his divorce is almost final. She insists on meeting his wife. He makes Nurse Katherine pretend to be his wife. He buys her several thousand dollars' worth of clothes for her one (1) meeting with Palmer.

For reasons having to do with Palmer's love of children, they all fly to Hawaii together with Nurse Katherine's two kids and Danny's high school buddy Eddie (Nick Swardson), who pretends to be the nurse's fiancé. Eddie disguises himself with thick glasses and the worst German accent since the guy who worshipped Hitler in *The Producers.* He also brandishes a meerschaum pipe because everyone who has seen *Inglourious Basterds* knows all Germans smoke meerschaum pipes.

This might work as a farce. Maybe it did, in France. It worked as a Broadway play by Abe Burrows. It worked as a 1969 movie with Walter Matthau, Ingrid Bergman as the nurse, and Goldie Hawn as the young girl. It doesn't work now. The problem is the almost paralytic sweetness of the characters. Nobody is really trying to get away with anything. They're just trying to do the right thing in an underhanded way. Walter Matthau was crafty in the cradle. Goldie Hawn was the definitive ditz. Ingrid Bergman was *sigh*. The 1969 screenplay was by I. A. L. Diamond, who knew a thing or two about farce when he wrote *Some Like It Hot*. They made a good movie.

So nice is everyone here that even the completely surplus character played by Nicole Kidman is undermined. She plays the old standby, the popular girl who was mean to Nurse Katherine in high school. We know the cliché. Kidman could have done something with it, but the screenplay gives her nowhere to go. It's painful to endure the cloying scene where they kiss and make up.

Just Go with It is like a performance of the old material by actors who don't get the joke. The movie doesn't even have the nerve to caricature the Kidman character, who is presented as a true-blue, sincere Bo Derek clone. Adam Sandler stays well within the range of polite, ingratiating small-talk artists he unnecessarily limits himself to. Jennifer Aniston is alert and amused, but by giving her the fake boyfriend with the meerschaum the film indicates that she, too, is one tinker short of a toy.

There is one funny scene in the movie. It involves a plastic surgery victim with a roaming right eyebrow. You know the movie is in trouble when you find yourself missing the eyebrow.

Kick-Ass

(DIRECTED BY MATTHEW VAUGHN; STARRING AARON JOHNSON, CHRISTOPHER MINTZ-PLASSE; 2010)

Shall I have feelings, or should I pretend to be cool? Will I seem hopelessly square if I find *Kick-Ass* morally reprehensible, and will I appear to have missed the point? Let's say you're a big fan of the original comic book, and you think the movie does it justice. You know what? You inhabit a world I am so very not interested in. A motion picture camera makes a record of whatever is placed in front of it, and in this case it shows deadly carnage dished out by an eleven-year-old girl, after which an adult man brutally hammers her to within an inch of her life. Blood everywhere. Now tell me all about the context.

The movie's premise is that ordinary people, including a high school kid, the eleven-year-old, and her father, try to become superheroes in order to punish evil men. The flaw in this premise is that the little girl *does* become a superhero. In one scene, she faces a hallway jammed with heavily armed gangsters and shoots, stabs, and kicks them all to death, while flying through the air with such power it's enough to make Jackie Chan take out an AARP membership.

This isn't comic violence. These men, and many others in the film, are really stone-cold dead. And the eleven-year-old apparently experiences no emotions about this. Many children that age would be, I dunno, *affected* somehow, don't you think, after killing eight or twelve men who were trying to kill them?

I know, I know. This is a satire. But a satire of what? The movie's rated R, which means in this case that it's doubly attractive to anyone under seventeen. I'm not too worried about sixteen-year-olds here. I'm thinking of six-year-olds. There are characters here with walls covered in carefully mounted firearms, ranging from handguns through automatic weapons to bazookas. At the end, when the villain deliciously anticipates blowing a bullet hole in the child's head, he is prevented only because her friend, in the nick of time, shoots him with a bazooka shell at ten-foot range and blows him through a skyscraper window and across several city blocks of sky in a projectile of blood, flame, and smoke. As I often read on the Internet: Hahahahaha.

The little girl is named Mindy (Chloe Grace Moretz). She adopts the persona of Hit Girl. She has been trained by her father, Big Daddy (Nicolas Cage), to join him in the battle against a crime boss (Mark Strong). Her training includes being shot at point-blank range while wearing a bulletproof vest. She also masters the martial arts—more, I would say, than any other movie martial artist of any age I can recall. And she's gifted with deadly knife-throwing skill; a foot-long knife was presented to her by her dad as, I guess, a graduation present.

Big Daddy and Mindy never have a chat about, you know, stuff like how when you kill people they are really dead. This movie regards human beings like video game targets. Kill one, and you score. They're dead, you win. When kids in the age range of this movie's home video audience are shooting each other every day in America, that kind of stops being funny.

Hit Girl teams up with Kick-Ass (Aaron Johnson), the narrator of the film, a lackluster high school kid who lives vicariously through comic books. For reasons tedious to explain, he orders a masked costume by mail order and sets about trying to behave as a superhero, which doesn't work out well. He lacks the training of a Big Daddy. But as he and Hit Girl find themselves fighting side by side, he turns into a quick learner. Also, you don't need to be great at hand-to-hand combat if you can just shoot people dead.

The early scenes give promise of an entirely different comedy. Aaron Johnson has a certain anti-charm, his problems in high school are engaging, and so on. A little later, I reflected that possibly only Nic Cage could seem to shoot a small girl point-blank and make it, well, funny. Say what you will about her character, but Chloe Grace Moretz has presence and appeal. Then the movie moved into dark, dark territory, and I grew sad.

Lady Chatterley

(DIRECTED BY PASCALE FERRAN; STARRING MARINA HANDS, JEAN-LOUIS COULLOC'H; 2007)

Lady Chatterley is a kinder, gentler version of the story most people know as *Lady Chatterley's Lover.* It's based on an earlier version of D. H. Lawrence's once-scandalous novel that had the too-perfect title *John Thomas and Lady Jane*. While involving Lawrence's approval of transcendent lust, the film also has a great deal of time for flowers, running water, close-ups of hands, and long shots of trees. Also, of course, for the class struggle, lustful sex, and close attention to the genitals.

Let's begin with the genitals, or, as Groucho Marx called them, the netherlands. The story involves the young and fragrant Lady Connie Chatterley (Marina Hands) and her husband, Sir Clifford (Hippolyte Girardot), a wealthy mine owner who was paralyzed from the waist down in World War I. The movie's opening shot shows Connie waving good-bye from their country house as Clifford walks to his car and drives away, so we must assume they were married before the war. But Connie remains childless, and there is no heir to their estate.

Which leads us to questions involving the netherlands. Wandering the grounds lonely as a cloud, Connie comes upon the gamekeeper, Parkin (Jean-Louis Coulloc'h). He is sponging himself bare-chested, which inspires her (and us) to inspect her own naked body in a mirror. Life creeps along quietly at the country house, where Sir Clifford seems to observe a daily word limit, and the housekeeper, Mrs. Bolton (Helene Alexandridis), says little, wrings her hands, and has a look fraught with worry about, at a guess, everything.

But back to the netherlands. Connie and Parkin begin a love affair. Day after day she goes flower collecting in the woods, and they meet in his hut to make love on the floor. One day, as he is undressing, she says, "Turn around," and she (and we) gets a close-up of the netherlands flagpole. Later, after sex, she views him again and observes, "It's so funny, how now it's only a little bud." Which leads to the conclusion that her sex education with Sir Clifford must have been sadly limited, even before the war.

That may help explain why Clifford is satisfied to do without her all day every day and be content when she returns late with a handful of daffodils. She is a kind and dutiful wife, to be sure, and they spend quiet time reading, apparently always the same books. In other versions of the story, Clifford is enraged that Connie has been bagged by the gamekeeper, but here he seems almost willfully determined not to know. He would even understand if Connie were to become pregnant by another man (an Englishman, of "decent stock") to provide him with an heir, and she goes off with her sister for a month at the seaside, presumably to arrange this, although at the time she is already two months pregnant. Maybe three. Since Parkin is a strong, muscular man, Sir Clifford is about to be presented with the world's largest short-term baby.

All of this is shown with admittedly gorgeous photography, lyrical montages, and sylvan melodies. The film is spoken in French, directed by Pascale Ferran, although we are to understand that the characters are English. It won six Cesar awards, the French Oscars, including best film, best actress, most-promising actress, and best screenplay, and was nominated for four more. But not for best actor! Since Jean-Louis Coulloc'h takes the thankless role of Parkin and distinguishes it, that seems unfair.

I must also report that on www.rottentomatoes.com, the film is scoring an astonishing 100 percent favorable rating on the Tomatometer from those major critics the site deems "cream of the crop." Alas, my vote will spoil the perfect game, unless I am demoted to skim. Why do they love it so? They admire the way sex grows into true love, the gentleness and sweetness of the relationship, and that the film does not rush into sex but moseys there, in 168 minutes heavy with pastoral lyricism, and that Connie and Parkin learn to see, really see, the other person across the class divide.

So I am almost alone in my lack of enchantment, and yet even I feel some affection. Jean-Louis Coulloc'h is a fascinating Parkin. He's not a rough-hewn macho man, but a man who prefers to be left alone, a man whose mother said he was as much girl as boy, a tender lover, a brave partner, a tactful friend. And he seems real, not like a male model ready for underwear ads. He "looks a bit like Oliver Stone with a sleeker nose," writes my friend Lisa Nesselson, *Variety*'s Paris correspondent. Marina Hands is quiet, serene, daring, and beautiful, although David Noh, a good critic banished from the cream of the crop, not unfairly observes "one barely believes a single thought ever clouds Hands' porcelain brow."

All of the qualities its admirers see in the film are indeed there and visible, but I was not much moved. Lawrence wrote much better novels that inspired much better movies (*Sons and Lovers, Women in Love, The*

Rainbow, The Fox). Most of them include some version of the full monty, which in a Lawrence film is like the toy in a box of Cracker Jack. Watching this film, I reflected that there are only so many boxes of Cracker Jack you can eat before you decide to hell with the toy.

Larry Crowne

(DIRECTED BY TOM HANKS; STARRING TOM HANKS, JULIA ROBERTS; 2011)

Larry Crowne has Tom Hanks and Julia Roberts and a good premise and a colorful supporting cast, but what it doesn't have is a reason for existing. The screenplay carries blandness to a point beyond tedium. At some point the sinking realization sets in that Larry Crowne was born a nice guy, will always be a nice guy, will find few bumps in his road, and is destined for a happy ending. We watch not in suspense but in envy.

Hanks produced and directed the film, and cowrote the screenplay with Nia Vardalos, his pal since the days when Hanks's wife, Rita Wilson, produced Vardalos's *My Big Fat Greek Wedding* (2002). That was a good movie. Since then Vardalos wrote and starred in the awful *Connie and Carla* (2004), starred in the dismal *My Life in Ruins* (2009), and wrote and directed the train wreck *I Hate Valentine's Day* (2009). As a writer she seems drawn toward banality.

In *Larry Crowne*, Hanks plays a nice guy who gets fired from his retail job because he lacks the education to qualify him for a management position. This happens despite his countless awards for employee of the month. Larry cashes in his possessions, trades his car for a scooter, and decides to enroll in a local community college. As his economics teacher, he draws Dr. Matsutani (George Takei), the only character in the film interesting enough to have a movie made about him. As his public speaking teacher, he gets Mercedes Tainot (Julia Roberts), a character who seems to have drifted over from the auditions for *Bad Teacher.*

The story arc is simplicity itself: Larry Crowne is a nice man who becomes nicer with the encouragement of other nice people. He eventually inspires the bad teacher to become a good teacher, abandon her porn-surfing loser of a husband, cure herself of alcoholism, and fall in love with him. More than this a nice guy cannot be expected to do.

I watched the movie with all the pleasure I bring to watching bread rise. Don't get me wrong. I enjoy watching bread rise, but it lacks a certain degree of interest. You look forward to it being finished.

Larry is assisted in his lifestyle transition by the fetching Talia (Gugu Mbatha-Raw), who supervises a makeover; he ditches the regular-guy duds for basic black and gets a cool haircut. There is also character interest from his neighbors, Lamar (Cedric the Entertainer) and B'Ella (Taraji P. Henson), but that's what they're in the movie for: character interest. They don't seem essential. At the neighbor's garage sale, Larry buys a motor scooter and ends up as a member of a scooter club, which is like a motorcycle gang of environmentalists. How many scooter clubs are there in Los Angeles? Don't tell me. I don't want to know.

What we have here is a screenplay lacking in conflict. I often complain about screenwriters who slavishly follow the story arcs taught in screenwriting classes. Nia Vardalos might benefit from one of those classes. In place of conflict, the story substitutes cutesy whims. Tom Hanks on a motor scooter! Neat!

Julia Roberts is fine here, to the degree that the film permits it. She's pretty and has that warm smile and is transformed under the gentle pressure of Larry's sunny influence. Surely her marriage must be more deeply troubled than we ever see, but the movie's still waters don't run deep.

The Last Airbender

(Directed by M. Night Shyamalan; starring Noah Ringer, Nicola Peltz; 2010)
The Last Airbender is an agonizing experience in every category I can think of and others still waiting to be invented. The laws of chance suggest that *something* should have gone right. Not here. It puts a nail in the coffin of low-rent 3-D, but it will need a lot more coffins than that.

Let's start with the 3-D, which was added as an afterthought to a 2-D movie. Not only is it unexploited and unnecessary, but it's a disaster even if you like 3-D. M. Night Shyamalan's retrofit produces the drabbest, darkest, dingiest movie of any sort I've seen in years. You know something is wrong when the screen is filled with flames that have the vibrancy of faded Polaroids. It's a known fact that 3-D causes a measurable decrease in perceived brightness, but *Airbender* looks like it was filmed with a dirty sheet over the lens.

Now for the movie itself. The first fatal decision was to make a live-action film out of material that was born to be anime. The animation of the Nickelodeon TV series drew on the bright colors and clear-line style of such masters as Miyazaki, and was a visual pleasure to observe. It's in the very nature of animation to make absurd visual sights more plausible.

Since *Airbender* involves the human manipulation of the forces of air, earth, water, and fire, there is hardly an event that can be rendered plausibly in live action. That said, its special effects are atrocious. The first time the Waterbender Katara summons a globe of water, which then splashes (offscreen) on her brother Sokka, he doesn't even get wet. The Firebenders' flames don't seem to really burn, and so on.

The story takes place in the future, after man has devastated the planet and survives in the form of beings with magical powers allowing them to influence earth, water, and fire. These warring factions are held in uneasy harmony by the Avatar, but the Avatar has disappeared, and Earth lives in a state of constant turmoil caused by the warlike Firebenders.

Our teenage heroes Katara and Sokka discover a child frozen in the ice. This is Aang (Noah Ringer), and they come to suspect he may be the Avatar, or last Airbender. Perhaps he can bring harmony and quell the violent Firebenders. This plot is incomprehensible, apart from the helpful orientation that we like Katara, Sokka, and Aang, and are therefore against their enemies.

The dialogue is couched in unspeakable quasi-medieval formalities; the characters are so portentous they seem to have been trained for grade-school historical pageants. Their dialogue is functional and action driven. There is little conviction that any of this might be real even in their minds. All of the benders in the movie appear only in terms of their attributes and functions, and contain no personality.

Potentially interesting details are botched. Consider the great iron ships of the Firebenders. These show potential as steampunk, but are never caressed for their intricacies. Consider the detail Miyazaki lavished on *Howl's Moving Castle.* Try sampling a Nickelodeon clip from the original show to glimpse the look that might have been.

After the miscalculation of making the movie as live action, there remained the challenge of casting it. Shyamalan has failed. His first inexplicable mistake was to change the races of the leading characters; on television Aang was clearly Asian, and so were Katara and Sokka, with perhaps Mongolian and Inuit genes. Here they're all whites. This casting makes no sense because (1) it's a distraction for fans of the hugely popular TV series, and (2) all three actors are pretty bad. I don't say they're untalented; I say they've been poorly served by Shyamalan and the script. They are bland, stiff, awkward, and unconvincing. Little Aang reminds me of Wallace Shawn as a child. This is not a bad thing (he should only grow into Shawn's shoes), but doesn't the role require little Andre, not little Wally?

As the villain, Shyamalan has cast Cliff Curtis as Fire Lord Ozai and Dev Patel (the hero of *Slumdog Millionaire*) as his son, Prince Zuko. This is all wrong. In material at this melodramatic level, you need teeth-gnashers, not leading men. Indeed, all of the acting seems inexplicably muted. I've been an admirer of many of Shyamalan's films, but action and liveliness are not his strong points. I fear he takes the theology of the bending universe seriously.

As *The Last Airbender* bores and alienates its audiences, consider the opportunities missed here. (1) This material should have become an A-list animated film. (2) It was a blunder jumping aboard the 3-D bandwagon with phony 3-D retrofitted to a 2-D film. (3) If it had to be live action, better special-effects artists should have been found. It's not as if films like *2012* and *Knowing* didn't contain "real-life" illusions as spectacular as anything called for in *The Last Airbender.*

I close with the hope that the title proves prophetic.

Leaving

(DIRECTED BY CATHERINE CORSINI; STARRING KRISTIN SCOTT THOMAS, SERGI LOPEZ; 2010)

The French are considered, especially by themselves, to be expert in the arts of romance. Their films about love are often adult, thoughtful, perceptive, and observant. In order to preserve that reputation, they should have refused an export license to *Leaving*. Here we have characters who couldn't figure their way out of a Dr. Phil show.

We begin with the premise that sexual passion is sufficient to compel a French woman in her forties to abandon her husband and two children, her home, her profession, her reputation, and her credit cards in order to recline in the arms of a Spanish handyman who is an ex-con with no funds. He must be very handy indeed. She experiences love at first sight, a *coup de foudre*.

Suzanne (Kristin Scott Thomas) is in a loveless marriage with Samuel (Yvan Attal), a doctor. He is proper and polite, expects his meals on time, takes pride in his possessions, and agrees to remodel a room in one of their outbuildings so she can resume her practice of reflexology. Ivan (Sergi Lopez) turns up to perform this task, and soon they are reflexing to the same drummer.

Oh, it is love. Mad, heedless love. She can hardly wait to confess to her husband, because she cannot lie. Perhaps this compulsion can be understood because Suzanne is British. It explains something about the two nations that in the United Kingdom people sometimes have tea between five and seven, and in France they sometimes have *cinq à sept,* which you're going to have to look up for yourself. Suzanne could have avoided much unhappiness if she had only been able to keep a secret.

Suzanne is not only impetuous, but doesn't seem to know her husband very well. Samuel isn't a good sport. He demands his wife back. She should get out in that kitchen and rattle those pots and pans. He cuts off her allowance, freezes the bank account, cancels the credit cards, pulls strings to make both Ivan and Suzanne unemployable, and otherwise inconveniences them.

This makes no difference. In Ivan's arms she's like a teenager with her first boyfriend. He takes her to visit a ruined stone cottage on a remote hillside, and she dreams that they'll build a little love nest. Ivan keeps a cool head. He usually has good advice. He's in love, but he's not nuts. Now with Suzanne: I knew you could get galloping pneumonia, but I hadn't heard about galloping erotomania.

Still, I want to say a word in praise of Kristin Scott Thomas. She is a splendid actress. Because she's perfectly bilingual, she finds challenging roles in France while Hollywood would reduce her to playing Magical Women. (These are like Spike Lee's Magical Negroes—wise and kind characters who have nothing to do in the plot but stand around being wise and kind.) Sometimes in the past Thomas has seemed to be, well, a little brittle. Here she is warm, soft, and lovable. When she cuddles Ivan he purrs. Thomas walks around in jeans and a T-shirt and has that Isabelle Huppert lifelong little girl look. She's good. Pity about the movie.

Life As We Know It

(DIRECTED BY GREG BERLANTI; STARRING KATHERINE HEIGL; JOSH DUHAMEL; 2010)

Awww. Their best friends are killed in an auto accident, leaving behind their cute little one-year-old daughter, Sophie. Holly and Messer are appointed in the will as Sophie's joint custodians. Alas, Holly and Messer (Katherine Heigl and Josh Duhamel) can't stand each other. But the will specifies they should move into their friends' home, so Sophie won't miss her own room.

Awww. Sophie is just as cute as most one-year-old babies. She's always ready to roll, maybe because she's got backup; the character is played by triplets (Alexis, Brynn, and Brooke Clagett). Holly and Messer know nothing 'bout raisin' no babies. The first emergency comes when Sophie does do-do in her diaper.

Awww. This is really sad. Holly and Messer have to share the same enormous Atlanta mansion. I think it has room for an indoor one-hundred-yard dash. Although their friends Peter and Alison (Hayes MacArthur and Christina Hendricks) were young, they must have been loaded. "The mortgage is prepaid for a year," the lawyer tells Holly and Messer. How many people can say that?

Awww, this is never gonna work out. Messer is a tomcat on the prowl. Hell, that first night he met Holly on a blind date set up by Peter and Alison, he had another date lined up for later. And Holly—well, she's one of your organized types, spic and span, not a mess like Messer. Plus, she maybe has a crush on Sam (Josh Lucas), the handsome pediatrician.

Awww, I gotta admit, I liked the actors. Katherine Heigl and Josh Duhamel do what they can with this off-season TV material, and Josh Lucas is awfully nice, which of course a kindly young pediatrician would have to be to almost win the heart of Katherine Heigl. But the film is so clunky. It's not every romcom that starts out with the tragic deaths of the parents of a one-year-old and moves right on to the poop jokes.

So anyway, what happens in the movie? You'll never guess in a million years. Never. You might just as well give up. I don't like spoilers, so just let me say Holly and Sam adopt Sophie and live happily in the mansion forever after. Awww.

The Limits of Control

(DIRECTED BY JIM JARMUSCH; STARRING ISAACH DE BANKOLE, ALEX DESCAS; 2009)

I am the man in *The Limits of Control.* I cannot tell you my name because the screenplay has not given me one. There's only room for so many details in 116 minutes. Call me The Man With No Name. I wander through Spain saying as little as possible, as Clint Eastwood did in films I enjoyed as a boy. Now I am a man, handsome, exotic, cool, impenetrable, hip, mysterious, quiet, coiled, enigmatic, passive, stoic, and hungry.

On my journey, I enter cafés and always specify the same order: "Two espressos, in two separate cups." In each café, I am met by a contact. I exchange matchboxes. The one I hand over is filled with diamonds. The one I am given contains a note on a small piece of paper, which I eat. I meet strange people. I do not know them. They know me. I am the one with two espressos in two separate cups. One is a beautiful young woman, always nude, whom I would like to get to know better, but not in this movie.

The writer and director of the film is Jim Jarmusch. I've seen several of his movies and even appeared in a couple. This one takes the cake. He is making some kind of a point. I think the point is that if you strip a story down to its bare essentials, you will have very little left. I wonder how he pitched this idea to his investors.

As an actor, my name is Isaach De Bankole. I have the opportunity to appear in scenes with actors who are known for the chances they take. Sometimes an actor like that will prove nothing except that he is loyal to his friends or a good sport. Bill Murray is appearing so frequently in such films I think it is time for him to star in a smutty action comedy. The other good sports include Tilda Swinton, Gael Garcia Bernal, John Hurt, and Paz de la Huerta, who is nude all the time. That's a good sport and a half.

My acting assignment was not so hard. I costarred with Mathieu Amalric in *The Diving Bell and the Butterfly*. He played a man whose movement was restricted to one eye. Now there was a tough assignment. I acted in Lars von Trier's *Manderlay*, where the locations were suggested by chalk lines on the floor of a sound stage. Not as much fun as Spanish cafés. I starred in the Quebec film *How to Make Love to a Negro Without Getting Tired*, and I played the Negro, but I was the one who got tired.

So I'm not complaining. We actors enjoyed Spain. Often we would gather for a dinner of paella and sangria. One night Bill Murray quoted Gene Siskel: "I ask myself if I would enjoy myself more watching a documentary of the same actors having dinner." We all sat and thought about that, as the night breeze blew warm through the town and a faraway mandolin told its tale.

We were pretty sure it would be a good-looking movie. Jarmusch was working with the cameraman Christopher Doyle, and they spent a lot of time discussing their palette, figuring their exposure, and framing their compositions. That reminded me of a silent film named *Man with a Movie Camera*, which some people think is the best film ever made. It shows a man with a movie camera, photographing things. Was Jarmusch remaking it without the man and the camera?

Looking for Eric

(DIRECTED BY KEN LOACH; STARRING STEVE EVETS, ERIC CANTONA; 2010)

Looking for Eric is the last film I would have expected from Ken Loach, the great British director of films about working-class lives. His strength is social realism and a critique of the limited options within a class system. He works close to the earth and to his characters.

Here now is a most unexpected comedy, appealing to world soccer fans and based on a common enough daydream: A man's sports hero appears in his life and carries on friendly conversations with him. I call it a fantasy, but Loach approaches it as if it were quite real. He uses Eric Cantona, a famed star of Manchester United, and places him right there in the room with Eric Bishop (Steve Evets), a Manchester postal worker badly in need of encouragement.

The outlines of Eric's life are grim. The film begins after he survives a car crash and involves his two worthless grown sons, Ryan and Jess, and his lingering feelings for his estranged wife, Lily (Stephanie Bishop), who has refused to speak to him in seven years.

Into this sad man's life steps Cantona, a superstar in all the soccer-playing world, who becomes his confidant and confessor. Cantona, it must be said, is quite successful in his role: warm, persuasive, a source of common sense. He diagnoses Eric's problem: He should get back together with Lily. This is also the plan of Sam (Lucy-Jo Hudson), Eric and Lily's grown daughter.

This counsel provides a reason for flashbacks showing Eric and Lily's romance in earlier years, very touching, causing us to hope they'll fall in love all over again. But, excuse me, why does this require brokering by an imaginary sports star? Cantona himself produced the film and may have been involved in the financing, which could explain how it came to be made. What I can't explain is why Loach chose to make it. Maybe after so many great films he simply wanted to relax with a genre comedy. It has charm and Loach's fine eye and an expected generic payoff. But it doesn't make any sense.

I had another problem I'm almost ashamed to admit. Loach has always made it a point to use actors employing working-class accents, reflecting the fact that accent is a class marker. I've usually been able to understand the characters in his movies; it's the music as much as the words to begin with, and then I start to hear the words. This time his star, Steve Evets, uses a Manchester accent so thick many of the English themselves might not be able to understand it. Ironically Eric Cantona, who is French, is easier to understand.

Looking for Eric is inexplicable. It has elements of a Loach social drama, which might have been better used as the entire story. Cantona is nice enough, but so what? If there seem to be any comic possibilities in the story, Loach doesn't find them. If your world doesn't revolve around Eric Cantona, he'll come over as just a nice enough guy, no big deal. And can the great Ken Loach actually have fallen prey to the Obligatory Action in the Third Act virus?

A Love Affair of Sorts

(DIRECTED BY DAVID GUY LEVY; STARRING LILI BORDAN, DAVID GUY LEVY; 2011)

A Love Affair of Sorts answers the question of whether you can make a feature film with a Flip camera, and leaves open the question of whether you can make a good one. It's a "shakycam" meander through an unconvincing relationship, with detours considering the process of making the film. At 91 minutes it seems very long.

The stars are David Guy Levy, the director, and Lili Bordan. They share writing credits, although much of the film seems unwritten. He plays "David Guy" and she plays "Enci," so it's not a documentary, but I imagine these characters are not a million miles apart from the actors in real life. He is a pudgy geek, likable and low key, with an almost hostile taste in T-shirts. She is an attractive Hungarian-American. They live in places their characters don't seem able to afford.

They meet when he Flipcams her shoplifting. He persuades her to take another Flip so they can collaborate on a film. It's a good question whether he intends this as a project or a pickup technique. She agrees, and the film is edited from their separate footage. There is much talk about where the camera is, who is on cam, what they film when apart, and so on.

There is also the snaky "love affair of sorts." She kinda likes David, but we meet Boris (Ivan Kamaras), the testosterone engine she's sleeping with. A woman like her should have better taste than to date a man who wears a gigantic watch on one arm and a studded wristband on the other. The movie's dramatic highlight is when she discovers he left the camera pointed at the bed while they were preparing to make love. Yes, but after all, it's her camera.

David takes her to lunch and dinner; he has excellent taste in Formica diners. They go for walks. They talk a lot. They grow fond. He entertains either illusions or delusions of romance. She smokes all the time, with a certain style, and decides to stop smoking. That is the other dramatic high point. If Boris is the "wham, bam, thank you ma'am" type, David is more like wh . . . wh . . . wh. . . .

And that's it. The movie lacks a purpose other than its own existence. It is largely about filming itself. David's friend named Jonathan Beckerman appears and apparently doesn't know he is in a movie. So what difference does that make? There could possibly be an interesting story here about David and Enci, but that would involve imposing narrative and stylistic discipline. It could be filmed with a Flip, but why? Better cameras are also cheap. The movie's lasting contribution is to serve as an illustration of sub-mumblecore.

The Love Guru

(Directed by Marco Schnabel; starring Mike Myers, Jessica Alba; 2008)
What is it with Mike Myers and penis jokes? Having created a classic funny scene with his not-quite-visible penis sketch in the first Austin Powers movie, he now assembles, in *The Love Guru,* as many more penis jokes as he can think of, none of them funny except for one based on an off-screen *thump.* He supplements this subject with countless other awful moments involving defecation and the deafening passing of gas. Oh, and elephant sex.

The plot involves an American child who is raised in an Indian ashram (never mind why) and becomes the childhood friend of Deepak

Chopra. Both come to America, where Chopra becomes a celebrity, but Guru Pitka (Myers) seems doomed to anonymity. That's until Jane Bullard (Jessica Alba), owner of the Toronto Maple Leafs, hires him to reconcile her star player, Darren Roanoke (Romany Malco), with his estranged wife, Prudence (Meagan Good). Just at the time of the Stanley Cup play-offs, Prudence has left her husband for the arms and other attributes of star Los Angeles player Jacques "Le Coq" Grande (Justin Timberlake), said to have the largest whatjamacallit in existence.

And what *don't* they call it in *The Love Guru*? The movie not only violates the Law of Funny Names (usually not funny), but rips it from the Little Movie Glossary and tramples it into the ice. Yes, many scenes are filmed at the Stanley Cup finals, where we see much of the Maple Leafs' dwarf coach (Verne Troyer), also the butt of size jokes (you will remember him as Mini-Me in the Powers films). There is also a running gag involving the play-by-play commentators and occasional flashbacks to the guru's childhood in India, where he studied under Guru Tugginmypuddha (Ben Kingsley). One of the guru's martial arts involves fencing with urine-soaked mops. Uh-huh.

Myers, a Canadian, incorporates some Canadian in-jokes; the team owner's name, Bullard, evokes the Ballard family of Maple Leaf fame. At the center of all of this is Guru Pitka, desperately trying to get himself on *Oprah* and finding acronyms in some of the most unlikely words. He has a strange manner of delivering punch lines directly into the camera and then laughing at them—usually, I must report, alone.

Myers is a nice man and has made some funny movies, but this film could have been written on toilet walls by callow adolescents. Every reference to a human sex organ or process of defecation is not automatically funny simply because it is naughty, but Myers seems to labor under that delusion. He acts as if he's getting away with something, but in fact all he's getting away with is selling tickets to a dreary experience. There's a moment of invention near the beginning of the film (his flying cushion has a back-up beeper), and then it's all into the Dumpster. Even his fellow actors seem to realize no one is laughing. That's impossible because they can't hear the audience, but it looks uncannily like they can, and do.

Love in the Time of Cholera

(DIRECTED BY MIKE NEWELL; STARRING JAVIER BARDEM, GIOVANNA MEZZOGIORNO; 2007)

Small wonder that *One Hundred Years of Solitude,* Gabriel García Márquez's best novel, has never been filmed. Watching *Love in the Time of Cholera,* based on another of his great works, made me wonder if he is even translatable into cinema. Gabo's work may really live only there on the page, with his lighthearted badinage between the erotic and the absurd, the tragic and the magical. If you extract the story without the language, you are left with dust and bones but no beating heart.

Consider the story of *Love in the Time of Cholera.* A young man named Florentino (Javier Bardem) is struck by the thunderbolt of love when he first regards Fermina (Giovanna Mezzogiorno). Guarded by her fiercely watchful father (John Leguizamo), she finds ways to accept Florentino's love letters and his love, but when her father discovers what is going on, he ships her far away. Young love cannot survive forever at a distance, and Fermina, half-convinced by her father's ferocity that Florentino is beneath her, marries a successful man, a doctor named Juvenal Urbino (Benjamin Bratt). He is not a bad man, this doctor, and their marriage is not unhappy, and if Juvenal has a wandering eye, well, so did many men in South America of 150 years ago.

Florentino remains faithful to his first love, in spirit, if not in flesh. He makes love with many women, but he never loves them. That part of his heart is reserved forever for Fermina. Fifty years pass, the doctor dies, Florentino reappears to announce that his love is strong as ever, she wallops him, then she accepts him, and the decades are erased in their eyes, although not from their faces.

This is, perhaps, not a profound or classic story. Is it tragedy or soap opera? Ah, that's where Gabriel García Márquez has us. It is both, at the same time, and sad and funny, and there is foolishness in it, and drollery, and his prose dances over the contradictions. The British scandal rag *News of the World* (fondly known as *Screws of the World*) used to have a motto, "All human life is here," but it better applies to Gabo. He is said to have popularized the uniquely South American style of magic realism, but when I read him I feel no realism, only magic.

Now his delicate fantasy has been made concrete in this film. Characters who live in our imaginations have been assigned to actors, and places that exist in dreams have been assigned to locations. Yes, I know that's what all movies do with all stories, and most of the time it works. But not this time. I don't know when, watching a movie, I have been more constantly aware of the actors who were playing the roles. That's not a criticism but an observation.

Take, for example, Javier Bardem, because he is such a good actor. In *No Country for Old Men,* I completely lost sight of him in the character of the murderous Anton Chigurh. Now Chigurh is an absurd monstrosity, not really believable in any sense, but he *works* in the movie. Florentino Ariza is supposed to be believable, and in the book we care for him, but in the movie, why, that's Javier Bardem! And when he is an old man, why, that's Javier Bardem with all that makeup! Gene Siskel used to describe old-age makeup as making young actors look like turtles. The problem is not with bad old-age makeup, but with the impossibility of old-age makeup. Twenty or thirty years, yes, and then you're pushing it. Better take the solution of *The Notebook* and have two characters played by Rachel McAdams and Ryan Gosling when young, Gena Rowlands and James Garner when old. That way everyone can relax.

There is another problem with the movie, and it has to do with Mike Newell's direction. He is too bread-and-butter here. The story requires light footwork, a kind of dancing over the ice before it cracks, and Newell strides steadily onward. It does not matter much that the events all unfold right on time; they should seem to unfold themselves and be surprised that they have. Nothing should seem preordained, not even when Gabo uses leaps back and forth through time to let you know perfectly well what is coming. Good lord, you should think, it came to pass exactly as he said it would! Instead, you think, now her husband is going to die, and Florentino will reappear, and . . .

I'm wondering, as I started by saying, if what makes García Márquez so great a writer is his work's insistence on being read, not seen. The last internationally released film adaptation of his work, Arturo Ripstein's *No One Writes to the Colonel* (1999), played at Sundance and folded; the only country where it opened theatrically was Spain. Ruy Guerra's *Erendira* (1983) also barely opened. For an author whose *Solitude* has sold more than sixty million copies, that's not much of a record; some short stories have also been filmed, to little notice. I am told by the critic Jeff Schwager that Gabo himself has written the stories and screenplays for many Spanish-language films (IMDb lists thirty-eight!), but as none of them have leaped the language barrier with much ease, I wonder how successful they were.

Is there another great modern writer so hard to translate successfully into cinema? Saul Bellow? Again, it's all in the language. The only thing Saul and Gabo have in common is the Nobel Prize. Now that's interesting.

The Lovely Bones

(DIRECTED BY PETER JACKSON; STARRING MARK WAHLBERG, RACHEL WEISZ; 2010)

The Lovely Bones is a deplorable film with this message: If you're a fourteen-year-old girl who has been brutally raped and murdered by a serial killer, you have a lot to look forward to. You can get together in heaven with the other teenage victims of the same killer and gaze down in benevolence upon your family members as they mourn you and realize what a wonderful person you were. Sure, you miss your friends, but your fellow fatalities come dancing to greet you in a meadow of wildflowers, and how cool is that?

The makers of this film seem to have given slight thought to the psychology of teenage girls, less to the possibility that there is no heaven, and none at all to the likelihood that if there is one, it will not resemble a happy gathering of new Facebook friends. In its version of the events, the serial killer can almost be seen as a hero for liberating these girls from the tiresome ordeal of growing up and dispatching them directly to the Elysian Fields. The film's primary effect was to make me squirmy.

It's based on the best-seller by Alice Sebold that everybody seemed to be reading a couple of years ago. I hope it's not faithful to the book; if it is, millions of Americans are scary. The murder of a young person is a tragedy, the murderer is a monster, and making the victim a sweet, poetic narrator is creepy. This movie sells the philosophy that even evil things are God's will and their victims are happier now. Isn't it nice to think so. I think it's best if they don't happen at all. But if they do, why pretend they don't hurt? Those girls are dead.

I'm assured, however, that Sebold's novel is well written and sensitive. I presume the director, Peter Jackson, has distorted elements to fit his own "vision," which involves nearly as many special effects in some sequences as his *Lord of the Rings* trilogy. A more useful way to deal with this material would be with observant, subtle performances in a thoughtful screenplay. It's not a feel-good story. Perhaps Jackson's team made the mistake of fearing the novel was too dark. But its millions of readers must know it's not like this. The target audience may be doom-besotted teenage girls—the *Twilight* crowd.

The owner of the lovely bones is named Susie Salmon (Saoirse Ronan, a very good young actress, who cannot be faulted here). The heaven Susie occupies looks a little like a Flower Power world in the kind of fantasy that, murdered in 1973, she might have imagined. Seems to me that heaven, by definition outside time and space, would have neither colors nor a lack of colors—would be a state with no sensations. Nor would there be thinking there, let alone narration. In an eternity spent in the presence of infinite goodness, you don't go around thinking, "Man! Is this great!" You simply *are*. I have a lot of theologians on my side here.

But no. From her movie-set Valhalla, Susie gazes down as her mother (Rachel Weisz) grieves and her father (Mark Wahlberg) tries to solve the case himself. There's not much of a case to solve; we know who the killer is almost from the get-go, and, under the Law of Economy of Characters, that's who he has to be because (a) he's played by an otherwise unnecessary movie star, and (b) there's no one else in the movie he *could* be.

Here's something bittersweet. Weisz and Wahlberg are effective as the parents. Because the pyrotechnics are mostly upstairs with the special effects, all they need to be are convincing parents who have lost their daughter. This they do with touching subtlety. We also meet one of Susie's grandmothers (Susan Sarandon), an unwise drinker who comes on to provide hard-boiled comic relief, in the Shakespearean tradition that every tragedy needs its clown. Well, she's good, too. This whole film is Jackson's fault.

It doesn't fail simply because I suspect its message. It fails on its own terms. It isn't emotionally convincing that this girl, having had these experiences and destined apparently to be fourteen forever (although cleaned up and with a new wardrobe), would produce this heavenly creature. What's left for us to pity? We should all end up like her, and the sooner the better; preferably not after being raped and murdered.

Machine Gun Preacher

(DIRECTED BY MARC FORSTER; STARRING GERARD BUTLER, MICHELLE MONAGHAN; 2011)
If the Lord moves in mysterious ways his wonders to unfold, rarely can he have worked more mysteriously than in the case of Sam Childers, a real-life Pennsylvania ex-con, drug addict, and thief who was born again, and since 1998 has been leading a crusade on behalf of the wretched orphans of South Sudan. *Machine Gun Preacher* is a combination of uplift and gritty violence, and the parts don't fit.

We hear about Sudan all the time. There is little ambiguity there. A warlord named Joseph Kony runs something called the Lord's Resistance Army, which has murdered hundreds of thousands, burned villages, and kidnapped as many as fifty thousand children, forcing the boys to become soldiers and making the girls sex slaves. He is an evil man, and while we're occupied in trying to bomb Gadhafi, we might profitably drop a few on him.

In Pennsylvania, we meet Childers (Gerard Butler), who with his buddy Donnie (the always effective Michael Shannon), drinks, drugs, raises hell, and makes things hard on his wife, Lynn (Michelle Monaghan), and daughter. While he was in the pen, Lynn found God. One Sunday morning, after a bloody night of violence, Sam allows himself to be dragged along to a church service, where he confesses himself a sinner and undergoes a baptism of full immersion.

It takes. One day he hears a sermon from a missionary from Sudan, describing the plight of the orphans. Sam knows the construction business and informs his astonished wife that he feels called to go to Africa and see what he can do to help. There is a lot. Faced by the specter of overwhelming suffering, he builds an orphanage, raises money from home to help out, and becomes a driven man.

Eventually, so dire is the situation, Sam Childers returns to the instincts of his violent past and finds himself fighting against the Lord's Resistance Army as a commander in the Sudan People's Liberation Army. Thus the movie's title. Well, Childers isn't the first to go to war in the name of the Lord.

The enigma at the heart of the film is the quality of his actual spirituality. He's born again, yes, but he seems otherwise relatively unchanged. He still gives full vent to his drives and instincts, and still, if you get down to it, gives himself license to break the laws, such as they are, in Sudan. I learn from an article by Brett Keller in *Foreign Policy* magazine that, as Childers was fund-raising in the United States, the Sudan People's Liberation Army issued a statement saying, "The SPLA does not know Sam Childers. . . . We are appealing to those concerned to take legal measures against him for misusing the name of an organization which is not associated with him."

There's more, about "his narcissistic model of armed humanitarianism." That's what bothered me. He seems fueled more by anger and ego than spirituality, and essentially abandons his family to play with his guns. It's intriguing, however, how well Gerard Butler enlists our sympathy for the character. The film has been directed by Marc Forster (*Monster's Ball*), from a screenplay by Jason Keller that's efficient scene by scene, but seems uncertain where it's going or what it's saying. Since much of the killing in northern Uganda and South Sudan is driven by sectarian and tribal prejudice, I'm not sure that shooting back is a solution—particularly when it's done by a self-anointed white savior from the West.

The sight of Sam Childers with his machine gun and his ammo belt reminds me of the night at O'Rourke's when a guy flashed a handgun for my friend McHugh. "Why are you sportin' that pistol?" he asked. "John," the guy said, "I live in a dangerous neighborhood." McHugh replied: "It would be safer if you moved."

Mad Money

(DIRECTED BY CALLIE KHOURI; STARRING DIANE KEATON, QUEEN LATIFAH; 2008)

There is something called "found poetry." The term refers to anything that was not written as poetry but reads as if it was. I would like to suggest a new category: found reviews. These are not really reviews but serve the same function. I found one just now, and after a struggle with myself, I have decided to share it with you. It is about *Mad Money,* a movie in which Diane Keaton, Queen Latifah, and Katie Holmes are lowly workers who team up to rob a Federal Reserve Bank.

I was noodling around Rotten Tomatoes, trying to determine who played the bank's security chief, and noticed the movie had not yet been reviewed by anybody. Hold on! In the "Forum" section for this movie, "islandhome" wrote at 7:58 a.m. January 8: "review of this movie . . . tonight i'll post." At 11:19 a.m. January 10, "islandhome" was finally back with the promised review. It is written without capital letters, flush-left like a poem, and I quote it spelling and all:

hello sorry i slept when i got back
well it was kinda fun
it could never happen in the way it was portraid
but what ever its a movie
for the girls most will like it
and the men will not mind it much
i thought it was going to be kinda like how tobeat the high cost of living
kinda the same them but not as much fun
ill give it a 4 Out of 10

I read this twice, three times. I had been testing out various first sentences for my own review, but somehow the purity and directness of islandhome's review undercut me. It is so final. "for the girls most will like it / and the men will not mind it much." How can you improve on that? It's worthy of Charles Bukowski.

Anyway, here's how I was going to start out:

Mad Money is astonishingly casual for a movie about three service workers who steal millions from a Federal Reserve Bank. There is little suspense, no true danger, their plan is simple, the complications are few, and they don't get excited much beyond some high-fives and hugs and giggles. If there was ever a movie where Diane Keaton would be justified in bringing back "la-di-da," this is that movie.

Keaton costars with Queen Latifah and Katie Holmes. She's set up as a rich wife whose husband (Ted Danson) gets downsized. They owe a mountain of debt, their house is being repossessed, and she thinks she might as well (gulp) get a job. The best she can do is emptying the garbage at the Federal Reserve.

That's when she spots a loophole in the bank's famous security system. She figures out a way to steal used bills on the way to the shredder and smuggle them out of the building stuffed into her bra and panties, and those of her partners in crime, Katie and the Queen. This system works. And the beauty is, the money isn't missed because it has supposedly already been destroyed. All they're doing is spending it one more time on its way to the shredder. A victimless crime, unless it brings down the economy, of course.

I would have gone on to observe that the movie makes it all look so easy and painless that it's a good thing it opens with a flash-forward showing them in a panic mode, so we know that sooner or later something exciting will happen. In the meantime, we get more scenes starring Ted Danson, with a hairstyle that makes him look alarmingly like a cross between David Cronenberg and Frankenstein's monster. And there's of course a chief of security who is constantly being outwitted. And so on.

Mad Money is actually a remake of a 2001 TV movie, I discovered on IMDb. Britain's Granada made it about a team of cleaners who pull the same scam on the Bank of England. Two character first names are the same

(Bridget and Jackie), but the last name of the Keaton and Danson characters is changed from Watmore to Cardigan. Go figure. Or don't. The bottom line is, some girls will like it, the men not so much, and I give it 1½ stars out of 4.

Mamma Mia!

(Directed by Phyllida Lloyd; starring Meryl Streep, Pierce Brosnan; 2008)

I saw the stage version of *Mamma Mia!* in London, where for all I know it is now entering the second century of its run, and I was underwhelmed. The film version has the advantage of possessing Meryl Streep, Pierce Brosnan, Amanda Seyfried, Colin Firth, and Julie Walters—but they are assets stretched fairly thin. And there are the wall-to-wall songs by ABBA, if you like that sort of thing. I don't, not much, with a few exceptions.

But here's the fact of the matter. This movie wasn't made for me. It was made for the people who will love it, of which there may be a multitude. The stage musical has sold thirty million tickets, and I feel like the grouch at the party. So let me make that clear and proceed with my minority opinion.

The action is set on a Greek isle, where the characters are made to slide down rooftops, dangle from ladders, enter and exit by trapdoors, and frolic among the colorful local folk. The choreography at times resembles calisthenics, particularly in a scene where the young male population, all wearing scuba flippers, dance on the pier to "Dancing Queen" (one of the ABBA songs I do like).

It would be charity to call the plot contrived. Meryl Streep plays Donna, who runs a tourist villa on the island, where she has raised her daughter, Sophie (Seyfried), to the age of twenty. Sophie, engaged to Sky (Dominic Cooper), has never known who her father is. But now she's found an old diary and invited the three possible candidates to her forthcoming wedding. She'll know the right one at first sight, she's convinced. They are Sam (Pierce Brosnan), Bill (Stellan Skarsgard), and Harry (Colin Firth), and if you know the first thing about camera angles, shot choice, and screen time, you will quickly be able to pick out the likely candidate—if not for sperm source, then for the one most likely to succeed in one way or another.

Meryl Streep's character of course knows nothing of her daughter's invitations, but even so, it must be said she takes a long time to figure out why these particular men were invited. Wouldn't it be, like, obvious? She has earnest conversations with all three, two of whom seem to have been one-night stands; for them to drop everything and fly to Greece for her after twenty years speaks highly of her charms.

The plot is a clothesline on which to hang the songs; the movie doesn't much sparkle when nobody is singing or dancing, but that's rarely. The stars all seem to be singing their own songs, aided by an off-screen chorus of, oh, several dozen, plus full orchestration. Meryl Streep might seem to be an unlikely choice to play Donna, but you know what? She can play anybody. And she can survive even the singing of a song like "Money, Money, Money." She has such a merry smile, and seems to be actually having a good time.

Her two best friends have flown in for the occasion: Tanya (Christine Baranski, an often-married plastic surgery subject) and Rosie (Julie Walters, plainer and pluckier). With three hunks their age like Brosnan, Firth, and Skarsgard on hand, do they divvy up? Not exactly. But a lot of big romantic decisions do take place in just a few days.

The island is beautiful. Moviegoers will no doubt be booking vacations there. The energy is unflagging. The local color feels a little overlooked in the background; nobody seems to speak much Greek. And then there are the songs. You know them. You may feel you know them too well. Or maybe you can never get enough of them. Streep's sunshine carries a lot of charm, although I will never be able to understand her final decision in the movie—not coming from such a sensible woman. Never mind. Love has its way.

Man in the Chair

(DIRECTED BY MICHAEL SCHROEDER; STARRING CHRISTOPHER PLUMMER, MICHAEL ANGARANO; 2007)

Man in the Chair is a movie about a high school student who enlists two movie industry veterans from old-folks' homes to help him with his project. And I mean old folks. Flash Madden (Christopher Plummer) claims to have been given his nickname by Orson Welles on the set of *Citizen Kane,* which means, if he was twenty-five at the time, he is ninety-one now. And Mickey Hopkins (M. Emmet Walsh), a writer, claims to have written *Queen Christina,* which, if he was twenty-five at the time, would make him ninety-nine.

Of course we know Mickey didn't write *Queen Christina* (or *Gone With the Wind,* another one of his "credits"), and the odds are against Flash's story, too. The chances are they are both lying, but the kid, Cameron (Michael Angarano), doesn't think of that, and neither does the writer-director, Michael Schroeder, although it might have made this a better movie.

What it is, instead, is a half-baked idea for a movie with way too many characters and subplots. Do we really need another lovable cheering section of characters (and character actors) who live at the Motion Picture Home and have individual headlined character traits? Do we need animal haters who catch and kill dogs as a business? Do we need the kid to have a mean father? Do we need him to have a competitor who bullies him at school? Do we need for old Flash to be such an alcoholic that to still be drinking like that at ninety-one must mean he only started at ninety?

The movie works so hard at juggling its clichés that it fails to generate interest in its story—which turns out to be not the skateboarding drama the kid had in mind, but a docudrama Flash sells him on about the mistreatment of old folks like Mickey. Then the animal subplot takes over as the old folks and the kid attack the cruel dog pound, uh-huh. And there is a stunt involving gasoline that is way too far over the top.

Christopher Plummer is a superb actor. I applauded him off-Broadway as the best Iago I have ever seen. No doubt there were aspects of the *idea* of this character that appealed to him, but did he measure its probability? And as for Mickey, M. Emmet Walsh, also a great character actor, has made a living looking moth-eaten and ramshackle, but good Lord, what they do to Mickey in this picture, it's a mercy his poor mother isn't alive to see it (if she were 25 when she had Mickey, she'd be 124 now).

I know an old writer. His name is William Froug, he lives in Florida, and if you look him up on Amazon you will see he is still writing brilliant and useful books about screenwriting and teleplays. He is not merely as sharp as a tack, he is the standard by which they *sharpen* tacks. If he had been advising the kid, the kid would have made a better movie, and if he had been advising the director of *Man in the Chair,* we would have been spared the current experience. Just because you're old doesn't mean you have to be a decrepit caricature. One thing that keeps Froug young is that, unlike Flash Madden, he almost certainly does not sit on an expressway overpass guzzling Jack Daniel's from a pint bottle.

Note: If flashbacks are meant to recall reality, it is unlikely that the slate on Citizen Kane *would have misspelled the name of Orson Welles.*

The Marc Pease Experience
(DIRECTED BY TODD LOUISO; STARRING BEN STILLER, JASON SCHWARTZMAN; 2009)

The Marc Pease Experience is a cheerless and almost sullen experience. Not even its staging of a high school production of *The Wiz* can pep it up. It's badly written and inertly directed, with actors who don't have a clue about what drives their characters. This is one of those rare films that contains no chemistry at all. None. The actors scarcely seem to be in the same scenes together.

For that matter, I can't think of many titles that are worse. "Marc Pease" is a name that looks like a typo, and Marc has no "experience" other than allegedly existing during the events of this film. Oh, at the end he becomes more philosophical and human, but that's just the screenplay jerking his chain. There is no sense that a human is involved.

The movie involves two unpleasant men. There is a young woman who is intended as pleasant but lacks all dimension on the screen, so she is simply filling a blank space labeled "pleasant character." Both unpleasant men are attracted to this young woman, but there is not a single scene between her and either of them that has the slightest joy, playfulness, affection, credibility, or humanity. All three are like bad witnesses who have been coached.

Eight years ago, when he was in high school, Marc Pease (Jason Schwartzman) panicked on stage while playing the Tin Man, and ran off stage and out of the school screaming. His drama coach, who has the Dickensian name of Mr. Gribble (Ben Stiller), has never forgiven him. Both have designs on Meg Brickman (Anna Kendrick), who is a little young for Marc and inappropriately young for Mr. Gribble. She has a nice singing voice and is coached by Gribble, the letch.

Marc Pease, now a limo driver, lives with the dream that his eight-member a cappella singing group, now reduced to four members, will cut a demo tape and become famous. He believes Mr. Gribble will produce this demo. He sells his condo to finance the recording session. The people who made this movie presumably know someone in the recording business, who could have advised them that even in this housing market, you don't have to sell a condo to pay for a demo. Don't you kind of guess every member of the audience can figure that out?

This year Mr. Gribble is producing *The Wiz* again. Same costumes, etc. There is a crisis on opening night, involving behavior bordering on lunacy by Marc Pease and on the malevolent by Mr. Gribble. Nevertheless, Marc Pease saves the production, in a way I will not spoil for you in case someone kidnaps you, takes you to a theater, straps you to a seat, props your eyes open with toothpicks, and forces you to watch this film.

I learn that Ben Stiller had another job coming up and shot all of his scenes in two weeks. Perhaps he suspected this film was not his shot at an Academy nomination. Stiller, Schwartzman, and Anna Kendrick will all work again. My advice: as soon as possible.

Marmaduke

(Directed by Tom Dey; starring Lee Pace, Judy Greer; 2010)

Dogs cannot talk. This we know. Dogs can talk in the movies. This we also know. But when we see them lip-synching with their dialogue, it's just plain grotesque. The best approach is the one used by *Garfield* in which we saw the cat and heard Bill Murray, but there was no nonsense about Garfield's mouth moving.

The moment I saw Marmaduke's big drooling lips moving, I knew

I was in trouble. There is nothing discreet about a Great Dane with a lot on his mind, especially when he's the narrator of the film and never shuts up. And when his master, Phil, moves the Winslow family from Kansas to Orange County and he joins the crowd at the dog park of a vegetarian pet food company, well, what can I say about a movie that has more speaking parts for dogs (and a cat) than for humans?

This is a congenial PG-rated animal comedy. If you like the comic strip, now in its fifty-sixth year, maybe you'll like it, maybe not. Marmaduke's personality isn't nearly as engaging as Garfield's. Then again, if personality is what you're in the market for, maybe you shouldn't be considering a lip-synched talking-animal comedy in the first place.

The plot. In California, Marmaduke likes his new backyard, but gets in hot water with his family for a dumb reason and runs away. Mazie, the collie he's been romancing at the park, goes searching for him, and it rains, and Marmaduke gets lost, and his family piles in the station wagon and searches, and—long story made short—they all end up where a burst sewer has caused a big sink hole (although not as big as the one in Guatemala). Mazie falls in, Marmaduke leaps in after her, they're swept into a sewer, they come out in an aqueduct, Phil Winslow (Lee Pace) leaps in, and so on and so forth.

Great Danes can be your best friends, but they are not gifted comedians. Mazie is typecast as a sexy collie; just once couldn't a pug play the female lead, in a little nontraditional casting? And speaking of that, what's with William H. Macy as the owner of the pet food company? If you admire Macy as I do, you can imagine dozens of ways he could be funny as a pet food tycoon. The movie sidesteps all of them and has him play the role right down the middle as a businessman. Then why hire Macy in the first place?

And then . . . but enough. Why am I writing, and why are you reading, a review of a talking-animal movie? Little kids may like it. It's not offensive. I don't find Marmaduke particularly photogenic, but that's just me. Great Danes look like they have extra elbows. The movie gets two stars. It could have done a little better if Marmaduke had kept his mouth shut.

Martian Child

(DIRECTED BY MENNO MEYJES; STARRING JOHN CUSACK, JOAN CUSACK; 2007)

"I'm not human," little Dennis says at one point in *Martian Child*. So he believes. The lonely orphan has convinced himself that he was not abandoned by his parents but arrived here from Mars. To protect himself against the sun, he walks around inside a cardboard box with a slit cut for his eyes and wears a weight belt around his waist to keep himself from drifting up into the sky. At no point during the film does anyone take mercy on the kid and explain that the sun is much more pitiless on Mars and the gravity much lower.

Still, this isn't a film about planetary science but about love. Dennis attracts the attention of a lonely science fiction writer named David (John Cusack), a widower who can't get the cardboard box out of his mind and goes back to the orphanage one day with some suntan cream. Eventually, almost against his own will, he asks Dennis to come home with him for a test run and decides to adopt him. The movie is the sentimental, very sentimental, story of how that goes.

Few actors in the right role can be sweeter or more lovable than John Cusack, and he is those things almost to a fault in *Martian Child*, which is so bland and safe that it might appeal more directly to children than adults. Cusack plays another widower in his much more affecting movie *Grace Is Gone*, and you wonder why he took two fairly similar roles so closely together.

This is not to say *Martian Child* lacks good qualities. Young Bobby Coleman plays Dennis as consistent, stubborn, and suspicious, and Amanda Peet has a warm if predictable role as the woman in David's life who starts out as best friend and ends up where female best friends often do, in his arms. But it is Joan Cusack, John's real-life sister playing his movie sister, whose contribution is most welcome, because she brings a little sassiness and cynicism to a film that threatens to drown in lachrymosity.

The movie leaves no heartstring untugged. It even has a beloved old dog, and you know what happens to beloved old dogs in movies like this. Or if you don't, I don't have the heart to tell you. And there is the standard board of supervisors in control of adoptions, which without exception in this genre adopts a policy against adoptive parents who are loving and loved, or who exhibit the slightest sign of being creative or unorthodox in any way. I suspect they would rather have a kid adopted by a mercenary than a science fiction writer, especially one who hasn't already ripped off Dennis's gravity belt and left him to float up into the sky, where it is very cold and even lonelier than inside a cardboard box.

The Mechanic

(DIRECTED BY SIMON WEST; STARRING JASON STATHAM, BEN FOSTER; 2011)

The Mechanic tells a story as old as *Hamlet* in a style as new as unbaked bread. What's the point? An intriguing plot is established, a new character is brought on with a complex set of problems, and then all the groundwork disintegrates into the usual hash of preposterous action sequences. Is there an action director left who knows it isn't all about the sound and the fury?

The movie is a remake of sorts of the 1972 Charles Bronson film, which seemed fairly good at the time and might only seem better today. It follows a cool professional killer, "The Mechanic" (Jason Statham), who works for a sinister killing corporation and specializes in murders that don't seem like murders or are deliberately misleading in other ways.

My guess is that in real life such operators are lonely, brutal, and tending toward paranoia. Statham's character, Arthur Bishop, on the other hand, is a hedonist and esthete who lives alone in elegance, prizes his classic car, and apparently believes a hooker isn't a hooker if you over-pay her. For twenty bucks, you're buying sex, but for thousands you are identifying yourself as a consumer of the highest degree.

Bishop is, then, a worthless creature who prizes himself highly. It is assumed we make no moral judgment on his murders because nothing in this film has human meaning and few of its viewers will expect any. It's all an exercise in technique. George Clooney played a similar character in *The American*, an infinitely superior film that was also about an untraceable solo killer working for a murder corporation. But that film was fascinated by the Clooney character, whose attempts to deal with sex without feeling got him into trouble.

There are two human elements in *The Mechanic*. Donald Sutherland plays another killer under contract to the same company—a veteran in this line of work, who is wise and bearded and was Bishop's mentor. This would be touching if their field was science or the law, but less so since their field is killing people for money. That we are expected to be moved by what are presented as Sutherland's ethical instincts is a peculiarity best not meditated upon. The fact is that Sutherland pulls it off on the surface level, and brings more humanity than the character deserves.

The other character is Steve (Ben Foster), the son of a character I will not name. Bishop has killed this man, the son doesn't know that, and Bishop takes the kid under his arm and teaches him the theory and practice of the trade. Steve has problems with immaturity, substance abuse, and other issues that the suave, shaven Bishop is a stranger to, but Bishop works with him and has faith that the young man will grow up into a killer to make his father proud.

The film is well made by Simon West (*Tomb Raiders*), a technician in the tradition of Michael Winner, who made the Bronson film. Directors like this must be very good, regardless of whether their films are worth making in the first place. Audiences have been drilled to accept noise and movement as entertainment. It is done so well one almost forgets to ask why it has been done at all.

Mercy

(DIRECTED BY PATRICK HOELCK; STARRING SCOTT CAAN, WENDY GLENN; 2010)

I have a problem with movies about men whom women cannot resist. If a man knows that, how did he find it out? By succeeding with one woman after another? If he's thirty-five, never been married, and doesn't like to date the same woman twice, he probably has a problem, and he probably *is* a problem. Even in a town as big as Los Angeles, word would get around. You wouldn't want to be the woman watched by everyone in the room to see if you fall for the Irresistible Man.

John Ryan is apparently such a man. Played by Scott Caan as a man who is surgical in his focus, he sees, decides, and moves in. He seems to succeed. If the woman is gone when he wakes up in the morning, that was a successful date. If they go to his place, they can't even feel a kindly urge to help him clean up a messy bachelor pad. Unless there is a toothbrush in the bathroom, there seems to be nothing in his apartment that didn't come with the demonstration unit.

One night at a party his moves don't work. It must be said he uses hopelessly outdated lines. When a man says, "You are the most beautiful woman I have ever seen," a woman should reply: "I know. But why would that make me want to sleep with you?" At the party, where he has already lined up a date with a waitress, he zeroes in on Mercy Bennett (Wendy Glenn), a classy woman with a British accent. "Mercy?" he asks. "Is that a joke?" He explains that (*cough*) the party is in his honor.

He thought it might be a joke because his new novel is named *Mercy*. He chats her up, gets nowhere, and the next day is horrified to read Mercy Bennett's review of the novel. She hated, hated, hated it. He's intrigued. He calls her up and asks her to meet, not for a date, but for a talk about the book. (It doesn't occur to him, then or ever, that if she reviewed his book and was invited to the party she probably knew who he was.)

These scenes are in the half of the film titled "Before." It also establishes his married best friend (Troy Garity) and his agent (Dylan McDermott). There is his lovelorn pal Erik (John Boyd), whose own girl is manifestly trying to dump him. John tutors Erik on the theory and practice of picking up women and dumping them.

In the film's second half, titled "After," we meet a changed John Ryan. He hasn't been shaving, he's deeply depressed, for the first time in years he goes to visit his father (James Caan), an English professor. His dad says he hasn't read his books, which is probably as well; he writes "romance novels" and, as we have seen, knows nothing about romance. Father and son share the same jaundiced view of women. The apple has not fallen far from the tree.

The time shifting (in a screenplay written by Scott Caan) may leave you adrift at times. There are flash-forwards, flashbacks, and possibly imagined scenes. The point is the same. They add up to a playboy getting his comeuppance. This story arc is predictable and not very satisfying, and the film's strengths are in the performances. Scott Caan is effective as a heartless creep, Wendy Glenn is devastating as a woman so assured she can perform verbal emasculation, and James Caan relates with his (own) son in scenes that inspire speculation the screenplay might be a little autobiographical.

What's lacking is a little more depth. This is a movie that covers a lot of distance in only eighty-seven minutes. We know the basics: The pickup artist gets hurt and becomes sadder but wiser. What we'd like to know is more about the people, especially Mercy Bennett. She never has a scene without Ryan. The women in the film don't seem to talk to one another about him, or themselves. And how does a bad novelist become a good one at the age of thirty-five after one life-changing experience?

The Mist

(Directed by Frank Darabont; starring Thomas Jane, Marcia Gay Harden; 2007)
Combine (1) a mysterious threat that attacks a town and (2) a group of townspeople who take refuge together, and you have a formula apparently able to generate any number of horror movies, from *Night of the Living Dead* to *30 Days of Night*. All you have to do is choose a new threat and a new place of refuge, and use typecasting and personality traits so we can tell the characters apart.

In *The Mist*, based on a Stephen King story, a violent storm blows in a heavy mist that envelops that favorite King locale, a village in Maine. When the electric power goes out, David Drayton (Thomas Jane) and his young son, Billy (Nathan Gamble), drive slowly into town to buy emergency supplies at the supermarket. They leave Mom behind, which may turn out to be a mistake. Inside the store, we meet a mixed bag of locals and weekenders, including Brent Norton (Andre Braugher), the Draytons' litigious neighbor; Mrs. Carmody (Marcia Gay Harden), a would-be messianic leader; and the store assistant, Ollie (Toby Jones), who, like all movie characters named Ollie, is below average height and a nerd.

You may not be astonished if I tell you that there is Something Out There in the mist. It hammers on windows and doors and is mostly invisible until a shock cut that shows an insect the size of a cat, smacking into the store window. Then there are other things, too. Something with tentacles ("What do you think those tentacles are attached to?" asks David). Other things that look like a cross between a praying mantis and a dinosaur. Creatures that devour half a man in a single bite.

David and Mrs. Carmody become de facto leaders of two factions in the store: (1) the sane people, who try to work out plans to protect themselves, and (2) the doomsday apocalypse mongers, who see these events as payback for the sinful ways of mankind. Mrs. Carmody's agenda is a little shaky, but I think she wants lots of followers, and I wouldn't put the idea of human sacrifice beyond her. David advises everybody to stay inside, although of course there are hotheads who find themselves compelled to go out into the mist for one reason or another. If you were in a store and man-eating bugs were patrolling the parking lot, would you need a lot of convincing to stay inside?

David proves a little inconsistent, however, when he leads a group of volunteers to the drugstore in the same shopping center to get drugs to help a burned man. There is a moral here, and I am happy to supply it: Never shop in a supermarket that does not have its own prescription department. There is another moral, and that is that since special effects are so expensive, it is handy to have a mist so all you need is an insect here, a tentacle there, instead of the cost of entire bug-eyed monsters doing a conga line.

The movie was written and directed by Frank Darabont, whose *The Shawshank Redemption* is currently number two on IMDb's all-time best movies list, and who also made *The Green Mile*. Both were based on Stephen King's work, but I think he picked the wrong story this time. What helps, however, is that the budget is adequate to supply the cardboard characters with capable actors and to cobble together some gruesome and slimy special effects.

Everyone labors away to bring energy to the clichés, including Toby Jones, who proves that a movie Ollie may have unsuspected resources. Thomas Jane is energetic in the thankless role of the sane leader, but Marcia

Gay Harden—well, give her a break; it's not a plausible or playable role. I also grew tired of Andre Braugher's neighbor, who takes so much umbrage at imagined slights that he begins to look ominously like a plot device.

If you have seen ads or trailers suggesting that horrible things pounce on people, and they make you think you want to see this movie, you will be correct. It is a competently made Horrible Things Pouncing on People movie. If you think Frank Darabont has equaled the *Shawshank* and *Green Mile* track record, you will be sadly mistaken. If you want an explanation for the insect monsters (and this is not really giving anything away), there is speculation that they arrived through a rift in the space-time continuum. Rifts in space-time continuums are one of the handiest inventions of science fiction, so now you've got your complete formula: threat to town, group of townspeople, and rift. Be my guest.

Mister Lonely

(DIRECTED BY HARMONY KORINE; STARRING DIEGO LUNA, SAMANTHA MORTON; 2008)

I wish there were a way to write a positive two-star review. Harmony Korine's *Mister Lonely* is an odd, desperate film, lost in its own audacity, and yet there are passages of surreal beauty and preposterous invention that I have to admire. The film doesn't work, and indeed seems to have no clear idea of what its job is, and yet (sigh) there is the temptation to forgive its trespasses simply because it is utterly, if pointlessly, original.

All of the characters except for a priest played by Werner Herzog and some nuns live as celebrity impersonators. We can accept this from the Michael Jackson clone (Diego Luna), and we can even understand why when, in Paris, he meets a Marilyn Monroe impersonator (Samantha Morton), they would want to have a drink together in a sidewalk café. It's when she takes him home with her that the puzzlements begin.

She lives in a house with the pretensions of a castle in the Highlands of Scotland. It is inhabited by an extended family of celebrity impersonators, and they portray, to get this part out of the way, Charlie Chaplin (Denis Lavant), the Pope (James Fox), the Queen (Anita Pallenberg),

Shirley Temple (Esme Creed-Miles), Abraham Lincoln (Richard Strange), Buckwheat, Sammy Davis Jr., and, of course, the Three Stooges. Now consider. How much of a market is there in the remote Highlands for one, let alone a houseful of, celebrity impersonators? How many pounds and pence can the inhabitants of the small nearby village be expected to toss into their hats? How would it feel to walk down the high street and be greeted by such a receiving line? What are the living expenses?

But such are logical questions, and you can check credibility at the door. This family is not only extended but dysfunctional, starting with Marilyn and Charlie, who are a couple, although she says she thinks of Hitler when she looks at him, and he leaves her out in the sun to burn. Lincoln is foul-mouthed and critical of everyone, Buckwheat thinks of himself as foster parent of a chicken, and the Pope proposes a toast: They should all get drunk in honor of the deaths of their sheep.

Perhaps that's how they support themselves: raising sheep. However, there seem scarcely two dozen sheep, which have to be destroyed after an outbreak of one of those diseases sheep are always being destroyed for. They're shotgunned by the Three Stooges. Or maybe there are chickens around somewhere that we don't see. The chickens would probably be in the movie in homage to Werner Herzog, who famously hates chickens.

Now you are remembering that I mentioned Herzog and some nuns. No, they do not live on the estate. They apparently live in South America, where they drop sacks of rice on hungry villages from an altitude of about two thousand feet. Rinse well. When one of the nuns survives a fall from their airplane, she calls on all of the nuns to jump, to prove their faith in God. I would not dream of telling you if they do.

Herzog feels a bond with Korine, who was still a teenager when he wrote the screenplay for Larry Clark's great *Kids* (1995). Korine is visionary and surrealistic enough to generate admiration from Herzog, who also starred in his *Julien Donkey-Boy* (he plays a schizophrenic's father, who listens to bluegrass while wearing a gas mask). In addition to the chickens, *Mister Lonely* has another homage to Herzog, a shot of an airplane taking off, which you would have to be very, very familiar with the director's work to footnote.

Various melodramatic scenarios burrow to the surface. Marilyn is fraught with everything a girl can be fraught with. Lincoln has anger-management problems. The Pope insists he is not dead. Everyone works on the construction of a theater, in which they will present their show, expecting to—what? Stand in a spotlight and do tiny bits evoking their celebrities? Then fulsome music swells, and the underlying tragedy of human existence is evoked, and the movie is more fascinating than it has any right to be, especially considering how fascinating it is that it was made at all.

Monte Carlo

(DIRECTED BY THOMAS BEZUCHA; STARRING SELENA GOMEZ, KATIE CASSIDY; 2011)
Monte Carlo is a harmless, innocuous tweener fantasy that seems constructed out of bits and pieces of movies we must surely have seen before, but can't quite place because there's nothing much to remember. It's chirpy, it's bright, there are pretty locations, and lots happens. This is the kind of picture that can briefly hold the attention of a cat.

It stars Selena Gomez, a Disney discovery who is eighteen but looks fourteen and, let it be said, is cute as a button. I liked her in the movie, with her round-eyed astonishment and unaffected energy. She plays Grace, a new high school graduate who has been saving up for four years to pay for her dream, a graduation trip to Paris.

In another movie, in another universe, this would be a movie about Grace's trip to Paris. *Monte Carlo* is a movie about Grace's trip to a wheezy plot involving mistaken identities, a handsome guy who falls in love with her, and her whirlwind trip through a lifestyle of the rich and famous.

Grace has acquired a stepsister, Meg (Leighton Meester, of *Gossip Girl*), and is devastated when she finds that her mom and stepdad have arranged for Meg to join her on the trip. And Grace will bring along her BFF, Emma (Katie Cassidy, also of *Gossip Girl*). This actually may be prudent because Meg is in her twenties and will perhaps provide a chaperone for Grace and Emma.

Such a possibility is not considered by the movie, which treats the trio more as a unit, bopping through a heady series of adventures after Grace is mistaken for Cordelia Winthrop Scott, a rich little British girl who is heir to a vast fortune and is perhaps not six degrees separated from Paris Hilton. Grace is a dead ringer for Cordelia, and in playing both characters Gomez essentially has only to look like herself.

That sets up the girls for a PG-rated version of *Sex and the City*, except with no sex, one fewer girl, and different cities. Otherwise, the escapism is the same: Through the miraculous intervention of outside forces (a Middle Eastern sheik, or in this case, the mistaken identity), they are whisked off in a private jet and find themselves pampered in a luxurious hotel suite, gowned in haute couture, served thirty-pound lobsters and courted by handsome young guys. And, hey, Owen (Cory Monteith of *Glee*) likes Grace . . . for herself!

There is a puzzlement about the selection of Monte Carlo. Given any role in the decision, what girl in her right mind would want to leave Paris and go to Monte Carlo? Venice, maybe. Monte Carlo is an overbuilt condo tax shelter with bargain-basement royalty. Its sights, in this film anyway, seem to consist mostly of hotel rooms. The adventures of the girls have less to do with traveling in Europe than with conspicuous consumption. The movie gives its tweener target audience credit for little intelligence or curiosity about Europe, and dishes out the same old love-at-first-sight formulas.

I enjoyed two details. One was the budget fleabag hotel they check into. If they had only stayed there, some promising comedy might have been generated. The second was the whirlwind tour by sightseeing bus they take after arriving in Paris. As they trot through the Louvre, their guide seems to be trying to set a speed record. Then again, nothing about these characters suggests they would have ever found the Louvre on their own.

Motherhood

(DIRECTED BY KATHERINE DIECKMANN; STARRING UMA THURMAN, ANTHONY EDWARDS; 2009)

Motherhood is about a conventional family living a conventional life in a conventional way. This life isn't perfect, but whose life is? The father is absent-minded but means well, the kids are normal, the mother is trying to juggle parental duties and her plans for a career. This could be countless families. Why do we require a movie about this particular one?

The film stars Uma Thurman, doing her best with a role that may offer her less than any other in her career, even though she's constantly on-screen. She's Eliza, who takes her laptop along to the playground to work on her blog, which is just a blog. She's not cooking her way through Julia Child or anything. Her husband is played by Anthony Edwards. I didn't remember the character's name after seeing the movie, so I checked with IMDb and he doesn't seem to have one. That tells you something.

The kids are six-year-old Clara (Daisy Tahan) and two-year-old Lucas (twins David and Matthew Schallipp). The tooth-challenged Daisy is pitch-perfect at that demanding age when kids become fixated on their convictions. Watching the movie, it occurred to me that child actors are invariably terrific. Maybe we are all born as great actors, but after a certain age most of us morph into bad ones.

Some effort is made to introduce interest to the cast. Minnie Driver plays a best friend who has an unsatisfactory personal life; the two women go to a sale of women's clothing during which they have tugs-of-war with other women who want the same frocks. Did I mention the movie takes place in Manhattan? That would also explain the crotchety neighbor (Alice Drummond), who is annoyed that a movie crew is using their street as a location. It would also explain Jodie Foster's cameo as a mom being followed by paparazzi. Don't you sort of imagine that if you lived in Greenwich Village you would sometimes have a Jodie Foster sighting?

The movie suggests two directions that might fruitfully have been employed by Katherine Dieckmann, the writer and director. One is in the person of an East Indian delivery man (Arjun Gupta) who begins an intriguing conversation with Eliza. Indian-Americans are appearing in movies much more frequently—for one reason, I suspect, because we like their accents. (An Indian friend told me, "We have been speaking English longer than you have.") Could this meeting have been developed into a subplot?

The other direction might have been fundamental. Instead of jumping through hoops to make Eliza somehow seem unique, special, and besieged by her (utterly commonplace) problems, how about making her desperate with boredom and the desire to break out into the extraordinary? Maybe her blog dives off the high board and she becomes a media creature? I dunno.

The movie is billed as a comedy, but at no point will you require oxygen. There are some smiles and chuckles and a couple of actual laughs, but the overall effect is underwhelming. Meh.

Mr. Popper's Penguins
(Directed by Mark Waters; starring Jim Carrey, Carla Gugino; 2011)

Mr. Popper's Penguins is a stupefyingly dumb family movie proving that penguins have limited charisma as pets. I mean, what do they do? They sit on eggs, they waddle, they eat fish, and they squawk. Sometimes they might snap at you. The movie stars Jim Carrey, who is in his pleasant mode. It would have helped if he were in his manic mode, although it's hard to get a rise out of a penguin.

The movie is inspired by a 1938 children's book, apparently beloved by many. I haven't read it, so I'm trying to imagine why kids might like it. My best guess is that the idea of living in your home with penguins is more delightful than the experience. Penguins look cute in their little tuxedos, and kids can imagine being friends with them. The problem with a movie is that they take on an actual presence that gets old real fast.

This is, perhaps I should make clear, not an animated film. If the penguins were zooming into outer space in 3-D, that might change things. Weighted down by their apparent reality, they're more limited, although sometimes they slide down stuff on their bellies. One goes hang gliding, but not very convincingly. I assumed that all of the penguins in the movie were created with CGI, but no. I learn from IMDb: "Some are, some aren't." Since they all look and behave much the same, either the CGI is very good or the real penguins are well trained.

Jim Carrey plays Mr. Popper, a man involved in architecture and real estate, who must have great wealth because he lives in a Manhattan duplex with a spacious deck and travels in stretch limos. He is divorced from his wife, Amanda (Carla Gugino), although they seem on such good terms it is eerie. The unit of mother and two children is always available to turn up at his co-op at a moment's notice, smiling and cheerful. It's one of those cases, I guess, where the parents are apart only for the good of the children.

Mr. Popper inherits six penguins from his father. Never mind why. At first he doesn't want them in his apartment, which is modern and sleek and looks decorated by a designer with ice water in his or her veins. There is no sign of daily habitation in his living space. What with one thing and another, Mr. Popper comes to love the little creatures; guess how Stinky gets his name. You would think the spic-and-span apartment would soon be deep in penguin poop, but no, Mr. Popper squeezes them over the toilet.

There is a subplot involving Popper's employers, who also move in a unit of three like his family. Also a matter involving the sale of the historic Tavern on the Green by the rich Mrs. Van Gundy (Angela Lansbury). These need concern us no more than they will concern the kiddies in the audience. There is also some weirdly bland courtship by which Mr. Popper attempts to convince Mrs. Popper to return.

Of more interest may be the blessed event when the penguins produce three eggs, a tip-off (given penguin mating habits) that three of them are male and three female. You could have fooled me. Two eggs hatch. The third does not. That is the movie's tragic low point. Mr. Popper seems more distressed than the parents, or perhaps Carrey is the better actor.

My Life in Ruins

(DIRECTED BY DONALD PETRIE; STARRING NIA VARDALOS, RICHARD DREYFUSS; 2009)

Nia Vardalos plays most of *My Life in Ruins* with a fixed toothpaste smile, which is no wonder because her acting in the film feels uncomfortably close to her posing for a portrait. Rarely has a film centered on a character so superficial and unconvincing, played with such unrelenting sameness. I didn't hate it so much as feel sorry for it.

Vardalos plays Georgia, an American tour guide in Athens, in rivalry with Nico (Alistair McGowan), who always gets assigned the new bus with the well-behaved Canadians, while our girl gets the beater containing a group of walking human clichés who were old when *If It's Tuesday, This Must Be Belgium* was new. You got your loud Yankees, your boozy Aussies, your prowling Spanish divorcees, your ancient Brits, and, of course, your obligatory Jewish widower who is laughing on the outside and mourning on the inside.

These characters are teeth-gratingly broad and obvious, apart from Richard Dreyfuss, who brings life, maybe too much life, to Irv, who tells bad jokes even though he is old enough to have learned funnier ones. To him, I recommend the delightful Web site www.oldjewstellingjokes.com, where every single old Jew is funnier than he is. Irv, of course, eventually reveals a sentimental side and does something else that is required in the Screenplay Recycling Handbook. (Interested in reading it? Send in five dollars. I won't mail it to you, but thanks for the money. Rim shot, please.)

The central question posed by *My Life in Ruins* is, what happened to the Nia Vardalos who wrote and starred in *My Big Fat Greek Wedding*? She was lovable, earthy, sassy, plumper, more of a mess, and the movie grossed more than $300 million. Here she's thinner, blonder, better dressed, looks younger, and knows it. She's like the winner of a beauty makeover at a Hollywood studio. She has that "Don't touch my makeup!" look. And if anyone in Hollywood has whiter, straighter, more gleaming teeth, we'll never know it, because like most people they'll usually keep their lips closed.

To speculate on people's motives is risky and can be unfair. Let me gently suggest that when Nia Vardalos made *My Big Fat Greek Wedding* she was an unlikely, saucy movie star who didn't take herself seriously. She was also an incomparably better screenwriter than Mike Reiss, the autopilot sitcom veteran who cobbled together this lousy script.

Now she is rich, famous, and perhaps taking herself seriously after being worked over for one too many magazine covers. She has also made the mistake of allowing herself to be found in one of those situations that only happen in trashy romance novels. The driver of her bus is a surly Greek named Poupi (Alexis Georgoulis), who has a beard that looks inspired by the Smith Brothers. After he shaves it off, he emerges as an improbably handsome, long-locked Adonis of the sort that customarily only dates older women if he has reason to think they are rich. This romance is embarrassing.

There is, in short, nothing I liked about *My Life in Ruins,* except some of the ruins. The tourists are even allowed to consult the Oracle at Delphi. That scene reminded me of when Chaz and I visited an ancient temple at Ise in Japan. Outside the gates, monks sat on platforms inscribing scrolls. "You may ask anything you want," our guide told us. "Will there be peace in our time?" asked Chaz. The monk gave a look at our guide. Our guide said, "Ah . . . I think maybe better question be more like, 'How many monks live in temple?'"

Note: "Poupi" is pronounced "poopy." That would never get past the editor of a romance novel.

My Name Is Bruce

(DIRECTED BY BRUCE CAMPBELL; STARRING BRUCE CAMPBELL, JAMES J. PECK; 2008)
Many's the actor who has brooded in his trailer and pondered: "Maybe I could direct better than this idiot." With Bruce Campbell that is often true, with the exceptions of such directors as Sam Raimi, with whom he has worked eleven times, and the Coen brothers (four). You know you're in trouble when your top-user-rated title at IMDb is a video game, although the gameboys are such generous raters they place the game *Evil Dead: Regeneration* right above the film *Fargo.*

In that Coen brothers' film, Campbell played an uncredited soap opera actor on a TV set in the background, but that was as a favor, because he and the Coens have long been friends. They met him on *Crimewave* (1985), their first writing credit, which was directed by, no surprise, Sam Raimi. Campbell has appeared in horror and exploitation movies without number, has always provided what the role requires, has inspired fondness in the genre's fans, and has been in some movies where I've been the lonely voice protesting they are good, such as *Congo* (1995), which featured a martini-sipping gorilla, volcanoes, earthquakes, and the always economical scene in which an actor looks over his shoulder, sees something, screams, and the screen turns black.

Also please consult my review of *Bubba Ho-Tep* (2002). In that film, which is set in recent times, Elvis and JFK did not die but are roommates in an East Texas nursing home. Campbell plays Elvis. Ossie Davis plays JFK. "But you're black," Elvis observes. JFK nods: "After Lyndon Johnson faked my assassination, they dyed me."

You see that Bruce Campbell often returns value for money. And in that spirit, I welcome his first work as a director since *The Man with the Screaming Brain* (2005). He plays himself in a lampoon of his career, his movies, his genres, and everything else he stands for. Maybe it's only "one-note insider navel-gazing," writes one of its critics, but if the navel has been there, done that, and had unspeakable horrors wreaked onto it, the navel has paid its dues.

The plot involves a movie star helping to save Gold Lick, Oregon, from an ancient Chinese god named Guan-Di, played by James J. Peck, although that could be anybody inside the suit. I know Dave Prowse, who wore the Darth Vader suit, and a lot of good that did him. Guan-Di, the god of war, for reasons best known unto himself, inhabits a falling-apart shanty-board crypt in the decrepit local cemetery that looks like the set for a grade-school production of a haunted graveyard movie. His eyes are flaming coals. Hard to see the evolutionary advantage there.

Campbell depicts himself as a drunken slob behind on his alimony, a vain, egotistical monster, a phony, a poseur, and a man in flight from his most recent movie, *Cave Alien 2*. This movie would make the perfect lower half of a Bruce Campbell double feature. If you don't already know who Bruce Campbell is, it will set you searching for other Bruce Campbell films on the theory that they can't all be like this. Start with *Evil Dead II,* is my advice. Not to forget *Bubba Ho-Tep*. In fact, start with them before *My Name Is Bruce,* which is low midrange in the Master's ouvre.

The Mysteries of Pittsburgh

(DIRECTED BY RAWSON MARSHALL THURBER; STARRING JON FOSTER, PETER SARSGAARD; 2009)

After that summer, nothing would ever be the same again. Where have we seen that movie before? Most recently in *Adventureland,* another movie set in 1980s Pittsburgh. If you think about it, after every summer nothing will ever be the same again. But *The Mysteries of Pittsburgh* has an unusually busy summer, in which a hero who is a blank slate gets scrawled all over with experiences.

The movie is all the more artificial because it has been made with great, almost painful, earnestness. It takes a plot that would have been at home in a 1930s Warner Bros. social melodrama, adds sexuality and a little nudity, and Bob's your uncle. It's based on a 1988 novel by Michael Chabon, still much read and valued, but to call it "inspired by" would be a stretcher. Hardly a thing happens that doesn't seem laid on to hurry along the hero's coming of age.

That hero is Art (Jon Foster), whose voice-over narration does not shy away from the obvious. He is the son of Joe Bechstein (Nick Nolte), a mobster of such stature that he has his own FBI shadows. Joe would like Art to follow him into the family business, but Art wants nothing to do with it. He'll become a broker, which in the 1980s was an honest trade. For the summer he takes a job at a vast surplus bookstore, where the minimum wage allows him to lose himself.

Life comes racing after him. Phlox (Mena Suvari), the store manager, pages him on the intercom for sex on demand in the stock room. At a party, he meets the winsome blonde Jane (Sienna Miller), whose boyfriend, Cleveland (Peter Sarsgaard), is both friendly and disturbing. These two mess with his mind: Jane although she doesn't mean to, Cleveland because he is a sadistic emotional manipulator. The first little "joke" Cleveland plays on Art should have sent Art running as far from Cleveland as he could get. But Art is pathologically passive; the summer happens to him, but he can't be said to happen to it.

Complications from countless other movies. The fraught relationship with his father. Phlox's possessiveness. Jane's ambivalence. Cleveland's odd promotion of an emotional, if not at first sexual, ménage à trois. Then a crime-driven climax that arrives out of thin air and involves a very small world indeed. Finally a bittersweet closing narration that seems to tie up loose ends but really answers nothing about Art except whether he still lives in Pittsburgh.

Complicating this are some well-developed performances for such an underdeveloped screenplay. Peter Sarsgaard is intriguing as the seductive, profoundly screwy Cleveland. Mena Suvari is pitch-perfect in a finally thankless role. Nick Nolte, in expensive suits, hair slicked back, takes no nonsense as the hard mob boss. Sienna Miller is sweet but is never allowed to make clear why she is attracted to either man. Jon Foster, as the feckless protagonist, is the latest in a long line of manipulated male ingénues going back beyond Benjamin in *The Graduate*. This is a guy who hardly deserves the attention of the other characters in the story, with his closed-in, inarticulate, low self-esteem.

At the end, Art is supposed to have learned lessons in life from his "last summer before life begins." The melancholy likelihood is, however, that he learned nothing except the punch line to the old joke, "Don't do that no more." At summer's end he seems poised to graduate directly into the Lonely Crowd. There is an old word: nebbish. It is still a good word.

Nacho Libre

(Directed by Jared Hess; starring Jack Black, Hector Jimenez; 2006)

Jack Black is not very funny in *Nacho Libre*, and that requires some meditation. Jack Black is essentially, intrinsically, and instinctively a funny actor. He has that Christopher Walken thing going where you smile when he appears in a movie. It takes some doing to make a Jack Black comedy that doesn't work. But *Nacho Libre* does it.

The premise of the movie is just fine in theory and must have sounded great at the pitch meeting: Black plays Brother Ignacio, a monk who lives in a backwater of Mexico, cooks slop for orphans, and lusts after the beautiful Sister Encarnacion (Ana de la Reguera). Because he wants to be famous and make money and buy better food to cook for the orphans, he begins a secret career as a masked wrestler.

The sport he attempts to infiltrate actually exists in Mexico and the American Southwest. It is called *lucha libre*, and I learn from Wikipedia that it's freestyle wrestling with more freedom and less strategy than the American variety. A lucha libre wrestler is known as a *luchador*. The sport is depicted with affection in the movie. If the luchadors (especially the giant Ramses, with his golden mask) seem a little ridiculous, well, all professional wrestlers seem a little ridiculous, don't they? What can you say about a sport whose heroes include Haystacks Calhoun?

The problem with *Nacho Libre* is not its content but its style. It is curiously disjointed. Episodes meander on and off the screen without much conviction. While in training, Brother Ignacio climbs a rocky cliff to eat the yolk of an eagle's egg, and what's the payoff? He eats it and dives back into the water. Jokes do not build to climaxes, confrontations are misplaced, the professional wrestling itself is not especially well staged, and Black's tag-team partner, Esqueleto (Hector Jimenez), is not well defined; it's funny that he answers all of Ignacio's theories by saying he "believes in science," but what's the punch line? He tags along all too literally because the writers haven't carved out a role for him to play.

As for Sister Encarnacion, she is neither sexy enough nor pious enough to be funny as one or the other. She seems like an innocent not sure what she thinks about Brother Ignacio or anybody else. Nor is Brother Ignacio especially lecherous; his seduction technique is to ask her to "join me in my quarters for some toast." Again, funny, but freestanding and leading nowhere.

One of the writers on the film is Mike White (*Chuck & Buck, The School of Rock, The Good Girl, Orange County*), who usually can do no wrong. The director is Jared Hess, whose *Napoleon Dynamite* (2004) is much beloved by many moviegoers. I have been assured so often that I missed the boat on *Napoleon* that I plan to go back and have another look at it; but now here is *Nacho Libre,* which has the same incomplete and fitful comic timing I thought I found in the earlier film.

I suppose there will be those who find *Nacho Libre* offensive in one way or another, but with comedy, a little political incorrectness comes with the territory. Yes, Mexico in the movie seems to be a country where English is the language and Spanish is a hobby. Yes, Brother Ignacio is mugged by a wild child for a bag of nacho chips. And yes, Brother Ignacio's cooking is so bad that this may be the first orphanage in the history of fiction where an urchin approaches the cook and asks, "Please, sir, may I have less food?" (This doesn't actually happen in the movie, but it should have.)

I dunno. I sat there and watched scenes flex their muscles and run off in the direction of comedy and trip over something. I saw the great Jack Black occasionally at wit's end. I saw wrestling matches that were neither painful nor funny, and not well enough choreographed to make much sense. The film begins with a certain air of dejection, as if it already suspects what we're about to find out.

National Treasure: Book of Secrets

(DIRECTED BY JON TURTELTAUB; STARRING NICOLAS CAGE, JON VOIGHT; 2007)

National Treasure: Book of Secrets has without a doubt the most absurd and fevered plot since, oh, say, *National Treasure* (2004). What do I mean by fevered? What would you say if I told you that Mount Rushmore was carved only in order to erase landmarks pointing to a fabled City of Gold built inside the mountain? That the holders of this information involved John Wilkes Booth and a Confederate secret society named the Knights of the Golden Circle? And that *almost exactly the same people* who tracked down the buried treasure in the first movie are involved in this one?

Yes, even the same FBI agent and the same national archivist and Benjamin Franklin Gates (Nicolas Cage) and his father, Patrick Henry Gates (Jon Voight). They're famous now (one has written a best-seller), but they *never* discuss the coincidence that they are involved in an uncannily similar adventure. Yes, once again they are all trapped within the earth and dangling over a terrifying drop. And their search once again involves a secret document and a hidden treasure. No, this time it's not written in invisible ink on the back of the Declaration of Independence. It involves a missing page from Booth's diary, a coded message, an extinct language, and a book that each U.S. president hands over to his successor, which contains the truth about Area 51, the so-called moon landings, Nixon's missing eighteen minutes, the JFK assassination, and, let's see . . . oh, yeah, the current president would like to know what's on page 47, although if he is the only man allowed to look at the book, how does he know that he doesn't know what's on page 47?

I have only scratched the surface. The heroes of this tale have what can only be described as extraordinary good luck. Benjamin once again is an intuitive code breaker, who has only to look at a baffling conundrum to solve it. And what about their good fortune when they are on top of Mount Rushmore, looking for hidden signs, and Benjamin interprets an ancient mention of "rain from a cloudless sky" and passes out half-liter bottles of drinking water for everyone to sprinkle on the rock so the old marking will show up? It's not a real big mountain, but it's way too big for six people to sprinkle with Crystal Geyser. But, hey! After less than a minute of sprinkling, here's the mark of the spread eagle!

Compared to that, the necessity of kidnapping the president from his own birthday party and leading him into a tunnel beneath Mount Vernon is a piece of cake, even though it is never quite made clear how Benjamin knows about the tunnel. Oh, yeah: He has George Washington's original blueprints. For that matter, it's never explained why so many people over so many generations have spent so much time and money guarding the City of Gold. And why leave clues if they are designed never to be interpreted, and for that matter you don't want anyone to interpret them? And although lots of gold has been mined in South Dakota, how much would it take to build a *city*? Remember, all the gold in Fort Knox is only enough to fill Fort Knox, which is about as big as City Hall in the underground city.

Yes, I know, all of this is beside the point. That person who attends *National Treasure: Book of Secrets* expecting logic and plausibility is on a fool's mission. This is a Mouth Agape Movie, during which your mouth hangs open in astonishment at one preposterous event after another. This movie's plot plays tennis not only without a net, but also without a ball or a racket. It spins in its own blowback. And, no, I don't know what that means, but this is the kind of movie that makes you think of writing it.

I gotta say, the movie has terrific if completely unbelievable special effects. The actors had fun, I guess. You might, too, if you like goofiness like this. Look at the cast: Cage and Voight and Helen Mirren and Ed Harris and Diane Kruger and Harvey Keitel and Justin Bartha and Bruce Greenwood. You could start with a cast like that and make one of the greatest movies of all time, which is not what happened here.

New in Town

DIRECTED BY JONAS ELMER; STARRING RENEE ZELLWEGER, HARRY CONNICK JR.; 2009)
We open on a gathering of the Scrappers Club, four women around a kitchen table pasting things into scrapbooks. The moment we hear one of them talking, we're not too surprised to find her name is Blanche Gunderson. Her sister Marge, the trooper, must have been the ambitious one. Not that Blanche isn't, just that she's relentlessly nice.

So are most of the folks in the small town of New Ulm, Minnesota, which is so cold in the winter that scrapping warms you up. Old Ulm (I know you were wondering) is the town on the Danube where Einstein was born. To this frigid outpost flies Lucy Hill, a high-powered exec from Miami, whose mission is to downsize the local food products plant more or less out of existence.

Lucy is the cute-as-a-button Renee Zellweger, so we know she's only kidding when she pretends to be a heartless rhymes-with-witch who hammers around on her stiletto heels and won't smile. That doesn't scare Blanche (Siobhan Fallon Hogan), Lucy's assistant, who invites her home for dinner ("We're only havin' meat loaf"). So uncannily does her accent resemble Marge in *Fargo* that I was trying to remember where I had heard it recently, doncha know?

The extra man at Blanche's table turns out to be Ted Mitchell (Harry Connick Jr.), the widowed dad of a thirteen-year-old girl, whom Blanche obviously thinks would be a great match for Lucy. That Ted, the union guy at the plant Lucy plans to downsize, is perhaps not a perfect match never even occurs to Blanche, who like all Minnesotans and most Dakotans, is just plain nice. I mean that. I've been to Fargo. You should go sometime.

Ted doesn't seem nice at first, but then, jeez, he's originally from out of town, y'know. Ted and Lucy get in such a fight at the table that they both stalk out, which means they miss out on Blanche's famous tapioca pudding. Glossary Rule: Whenever a recipe is much discussed in the first act, it will be tasted in the third.

So firmly do we believe Lucy is visiting relatives of the *Fargo* cast that it's a surprise to learn *New in Town* was actually filmed in Winnipeg, which here looks nothing like the glittering metropolis in Guy Maddin's masterpiece. New Ulm consists of some houses, a VFW hall with a Friday fish fry, the food plant, and not a whole lot else except snow. But the people are friendly, hardworking, and proud of their plant, and soon Lucy softens, begins to like them, and reveals she was Renee Zellweger all along.

Because this is a romcom with no ambition in the direction of originality, Lucy is single, and Ted is the only eligible unmarried man in the cast, so do the math. The only remaining question is whether Lucy can save the plant, if you consider that much of a question. Am I giving too much away? This is the kind of movie that gives itself away. I've used that line before.

The real question is, do you like this sort of romcom? It's a fair example of its type, not good, but competent. The plant workers seem to function like the chorus in an opera, shutting down the line for Lucy's arias from a catwalk and moving as a unit with foreman Stu Kopenhafer (J. K. Simmons) always in the front. Simmons has grown a bushy beard and is wearing a fat suit (I hope), so you may not recognize him as Juno's dad. Let the bushy beard be a lesson: A bushy beard is the enemy of an actor's face unless he is playing Santa or attacking with a chainsaw.

The only question remaining after *New in Town* is, how come there's never a movie where a small-town girl leaves the snarly, greedy, job-ladder-climbing people behind and moves to the big city, where she is embraced by friendly folks, fed meat loaf and tapioca, and fixed up with Harry Connick Jr.?

Nick and Norah's Infinite Playlist
(DIRECTED BY PETER SOLLETT; STARRING MICHAEL CERA, KAT DENNINGS; 2008)

There is one merciful element to *Nick and Norah's Infinite Playlist*. The playlist is not infinite. The movie trudges around the Lower East Side of Manhattan in pursuit of a group of seventeen-somethings who are desperately seeking a mysterious band named Where's Fluffy. Clues are posted on the walls of toilet stalls, which are an unreliable source of information.

Nick and Norah have no relationship to the hero and heroine of *The Thin Man*, which I urgently advise you to watch instead of this film. That movie stars William Powell as a man who steadily drinks martinis and is never more than half-percolated. This one has a best friend character named Caroline (Ari Graynor) who drinks, I forget, I think it was banana daiquiris, and gets so drunk she ends up near Times Square in a toilet in the bus terminal, where she is fishing, not for Where's Fluffy clues, but for her gum, which fell into the toilet while she was vomiting. Didn't Ann Landers warn that this was one of the danger signals of alcoholism?

Nick and Norah are played by Michael Cera, best remembered as Juno's boyfriend, and Kat Dennings, best known for *The 40-Year-Old Virgin*, where she played anything but. They work well together, are appealing, and desperately require material as good as those films. Here they're not stupid; it's just that they're made to act stupidly. There's not much to recommend an all-night search through the dives of Manhattan for a lost friend who makes Britney Spears seem like a stay-at-home.

The two meet at a club, when Norah needs Nick to pose as her boyfriend to make her ex-boyfriend jealous. He is named Tal (Jay Baruchel). My first Chicago girlfriend was named Tal, which is Hebrew for "the morning dew." I don't think he knows that. So then, let's see, the plot requires an ex-girlfriend for Nick. This is Tris (Alexis Dziena), a blond vixen of the type that in most teeny movies is infinitely unattainable for nice kids like Nick.

Give Nick credit, he knows all about playlists. Tris has broken up with him as the movie opens, and he cuts many custom CDs for her in an attempt to win her back. These fall into the hands of Norah, who adores them, and What a Coincidence that Tris's ex is the very same guy she picked to play her pretend boyfriend. Ohmigosh. How Norah never previously saw Tris and Nick together is a good question since every character in this movie has built-in GPS equipment that allows them to stumble across any other character whenever the plot requires it.

I was relieved to observe that Nick doesn't drink as he pilots his battered Yugo around Manhattan. Ever notice how Yugos look like stretch Gremlins? People spot its bright yellow paint job and hail him, thinking it's a cab. This is impossible, since he doesn't have an illuminated sign for an Atlantic City casino on his roof.

Nick & Norah's Infinite Playlist lacks some of the idiocy of your average teenage romcom. But it doesn't bring much to the party. It sort of ambles along, with two nice people at the center of a human scavenger hunt. It's not much of a film, but it sort of gets you halfway there, like a Yugo.

Nick Nolte: No Exit

(DIRECTED BY THOMAS THURMAN; STARRING NICK NOLTE, JACQUELINE BISSET; 2010)

Nick Nolte is an interesting actor. Perhaps too interesting to appear in an independent documentary about himself. Perhaps too interesting to be interviewed by someone else. In *Nick Nolte: No Exit,* he interviews himself. The way he does this does what it can to assist a fairly pointless documentary.

Seated behind a silver laptop, well groomed and wearing a big white Stetson, Nolte asks questions. Seated behind a black desktop computer and looking disheveled and squinteyed (well, all right, hungover), Nolte replies to them. It would be going too far to say he "answers" them.

Here is a fine actor who has made many very good films. On the wall behind him is the poster for Paul Schrader's *Affliction* (1997), the one he and James Coburn both won Oscar nominations for (Coburn won). His credits include *Hotel Rwanda, The Thin Red Line, Who'll Stop the Rain, North Dallas Forty, Lorenzo's Oil, Q&A,* and many others.

He mentions several of these films, and others, but doesn't really discuss them. He's proud of them, and of his work, as he should be. He admires Marlon Brando, who encouraged him. He has nothing to say about his private life. He mentions "the most famous celebrity mug shot," which he posed for after a DUI arrest in 2006, but doesn't go into details.

Nolte is intercut with sound bites about him by Nick Nolte, Jacqueline Bisset, Rosanna Arquette, Barbara Hershey, Ben Stiller, Paul Mazursky, Alan Rudolph, Powers Boothe, James Gammon, F. X. Feeney, Mike Medavoy. He's worked with them all, but doesn't go into detail. Most of them he doesn't mention.

Yet despite everything, the film has a certain fascination because Nolte is such a charismatic enigma. I've interviewed him several times, including at Telluride, which he attended in a bathrobe, and at Cannes, where we did a Q&A that was light on the A's. I enjoyed his company. Can't say that he confided many secrets.

Night at the Museum: Battle of the Smithsonian
(DIRECTED BY SHAWN LEVY; STARRING BEN STILLER, AMY ADAMS; 2009)

Don't trust me on this movie. It rubbed me the wrong way. I can understand, as an abstract concept, why some people would find it entertaining. It sure sounds intriguing: *Night at the Museum: Battle of the Smithsonian.* If that sounds like fun to you, don't listen to sourpuss here.

Oh, did I dislike this film. It made me squirmy. Its premise is lame, its plot relentlessly predictable, its characters with personalities that would distinguish picture books, its cost incalculable (well, $150 million). Watching historical figures enact the clichés identified with the most simplistic versions of their images, I found myself yet once again echoing the frequent cry of Gene Siskel: Why not just give us a documentary of the same actors having lunch?

One actor surpasses the material. That would be Amy Adams, as Amelia Earhart, because she makes Amelia sweet and lovable, although from what I gather, in real life that was not necessarily the case. I found myself looking forward to the upcoming biopic about Earhart with Hilary Swank. Over the closing credits, Bonnie Koloc could sing Red River Dave McEnery's "Amelia Earhart's Last Flight":

> *Just a ship out on the ocean, a speck against the sky,*
> *Amelia Earhart flying that sad day;*
> *With her partner, Captain Noonan, on the second of July*
> *Her plane fell in the ocean far away.*

(Chorus)

> *There's a beautiful, beautiful field*
> *Far away in a land that is fair,*
> *Happy landings to you, Amelia Earhart,*
> *Farewell, first lady of the air.*

Sigh. Sort of floats you away, doesn't it? But then I crash-landed in the movie, where Amelia Earhart has to become the sidekick of Larry Daley (Ben Stiller), who has faked his résumé to get hired as a security guard and rescue his buddies from *Night at the Museum* (2006).

What has happened, see, is that the Museum of Natural History is remodeling. They're replacing their beloved old exhibits, like Teddy Roosevelt mounted on his horse, with ghastly new interactive media experiences. His friends are doomed to go into storage at the National Archives, part of the Smithsonian Institution. We see something of its sterile corridors stretching off into infinity; it looks just a little larger than Jorge Luis Borges's Library of Babel, and you remember how big *that* was.

However, Larry is able to manage one last night of freedom for them before the crates are filled with plastic popcorn. This is thanks to, I dunno, some kind of magic tablet of the villainous Pharaoh Kahmunrah (Hank Azaria). Among the resurrected are Teddy Roosevelt (Robin Williams),

General Custer (Bill Hader), Ivan the Terrible (Christopher Guest), Octavius (Steve Coogan), and Albert Einstein (Eugene Levy). Also, the stuffed monkey from our first manned (or monkeyed) satellite, on a flight where the mission controller is played, of course, by Clint Howard, who has played mission controllers in something like half a dozen movies, maybe a dozen. When he gets a job, he already knows all of the lines. I could give you the exact number of the mission controllers he has played, but looking up Clint Howard's IMDb credits for a review of *Night at the Museum: Battle of the Smithsonian* seems like dissipation.

What is the motivation for the characters? Obviously, the video game they will inspire. Wilbur Wright is here with the first airplane, and Amelia pilots the plane she went down in on that sad second of July. Rodin's Thinker (Hank Azaria) is somewhat distracted, his chin leaning on his hand, no doubt pondering such questions as: "Hey, aren't I supposed to be in the Musee Rodin in Paris?"

The reanimated figures are on three scales. Some are life-size. Some are larger-than-life-size, like the statue in the Lincoln Memorial on the National Mall. Some are the size of tiny action figures, and they're creepy, always crawling around and about to get stepped on. Nobody asks Abe Lincoln any interesting stuff like, "Hey, you were there—what did Dick Nixon really say to the hippies during his midnight visit to your memorial?"

I don't mind a good dumb action movie. I was the one who liked *The Mummy: Tomb of the Dragon Emperor.* But *Night at the Museum: Battle of the Smithsonian* is such a product. Like ectoplasm from a medium, it is the visible extrusion of a marketing campaign.

A Nightmare on Elm Street

(Directed by Samuel Bayer; starring Jackie Earle Haley, Kyle Gallner; 2010)
Forget about the plot, the actors, and the director. What you require to make a new *Nightmare on Elm Street* are these three off-the-shelf sound effects:

1. A sudden, loud clanging noise mixed with a musical chord.

2. Snicker-snack sounds, which Freddy Krueger's steel finger claws make every time they are seen.

3. A voice deepener, to drop Freddy's speaking voice to an ominous level.

On top of that, you need your sudden cuts, your lighting from below, your thump-thump-thumps, and, of course, a dog that barks at something unseen in the night, so that your teenage heroine can go out onto the lawn in bare feet and flimsy PJs and call, "Rufus! Rufus! Here, boy!" You know in your bones that Rufus is now checking into Doggie Heaven.

Oh, and actors. Lots of Dead Teenagers, seen in the last moments of their lives, when they enjoy a farewell Moment of Deceptive Safety just before there's a sudden, loud clanging noise and the snicker-snack claws disembowel them and Freddy rumbles, "You have nothing to worry about. This won't hurt one . . . little . . . bit."

The 2010 edition of *A Nightmare on Elm Street* is number 8½ in the series. I arrive at that number not out of a desperate desire to be seeing the Fellini film instead, but because *Freddy vs. Jason* (2003) should in all fairness count for half a film on this list, and half a film on the *Friday the 13th* list.

It is sad to think of all those Dead Teenagers. They were played by ambitious, talented young actors, some of them now in their forties, who survived grueling auditions for the honor of being slashed by Freddy. Some of them are now successful: Johnny Depp, for example. Robert Englund became famous playing Freddy, but where can that lead when you're always wearing a mask of makeup? Now Jackie Earle Haley plays the role. For what purpose? He might as well play Santa Claus.

It was twenty-six long years ago when Freddy first began to haunt the nightmares of the children of Elm Street in Springwood, Ohio. At least 137 victims have been claimed by Freddy in the years since then, but the shady little street is still lined with handsome homes and hasn't been leveled, covered with ashes and sprinkled with holy water. The franchise was founded by Wes Craven, the Ray Kroc of horror, who made the excellent *Wes Craven's New Nightmare* (1994), about Freddy haunting the dreams of the *makers* of the *Nightmare* movies.

Freddy is not a good argument for a supernatural existence. He can live inside wallpaper, appear anywhere, and has no need of physical existence except, arguably, when he inflicts actual physical damage. Yet he's such a bore, always growling away with his deep-voiced *hahahahaha*. If a man leads an interesting life he ought to be able to make good conversation, is what I say.

I stared at *A Nightmare on Elm Street* with weary resignation. The movie consists of a series of teenagers who are introduced, haunted by nightmares, and then slashed to death by Freddy. So what? Are we supposed to be scared? Is the sudden clanging chord supposed to evoke a fearful Pavlovian response? For Rufus, maybe, but not for me. Here, boy.

Nights in Rodanthe

(DIRECTED BY GEORGE C. WOLFE; STARRING RICHARD GERE, DIANE LANE; 2008)

Nights in Rodanthe is what *Variety* likes to call a "weeper." The term is not often intended as praise. The movie attempts to jerk tears with one clunky device after another, in a plot that is a perfect storm of cliché and contrivance. In fact, it even contains a storm—an imperfect one.

The movie stars Richard Gere and Diane Lane, back again, together again, after *Unfaithful* (2002). I have no complaints about their work here. Admiration, rather, as they stay afloat in spite of the film's plot, location, voice-overs, and not-very-special effects. They are true movie stars and have a certain immunity against infection by dreck.

He plays Paul, a surgeon. She plays Adrienne, a mother of two, separated from her snaky husband. To help out a friend, she is taking care of a rustic inn on an island of the Outer Banks of North Carolina. He is the only weekend guest. He has booked it to "be by myself," he says, and also "to find someone to talk to." To summarize: These two beautiful, unhappy people are alone in a romantic beachfront inn. If the inn is really where it seems to be, on the edge of the water in a vast stretch of deserted, high-priced beach frontage, then it is not CGI and will soon be listed as *This Week* magazine's "steal of the week."

A hurricane is approaching. Hurricane warnings are issued just hours before it arrives. A grizzled old-timer at the local grocery wisely says it's gonna be real big. Adrienne stocks up on white bread. Having spent days watching CNN as little whirling twos and threes inched across the Gulf Coast, I would say this warning was belated. Paul doesn't evacuate because of some dialogue he is made to say. Adrienne doesn't because she promised her friend to look after the inn. They put up some shutters and have a jolly game of indoor basketball while tossing spoiled canned goods into a garbage can. "Ratatouille! Spam! Lard!"

The hurricane strikes. If it has a name, they don't know it. It blows off some shutters and cuts off the power. Do they face "certain death"? They cling to each other while sitting on the floor next to a bed. Then they cling to each other after getting into the bed. Have you ever made love during a hurricane that is shaking the house? I haven't. How did it go for you?

The hurricane bangs the shutters like *The Amityville Horror.* It must have no eye, so the wind only blows once. In the morning after the storm, the sun is shining and the inn is still standing. Remarkable, really, considering the photos from Galveston. It is a three- or four-story clapboard building, taller than it is wide, standing on stilts at the veritable water's edge. We see damage: a skateboard and a bike blown up. Some trees blown over. Just the most wonderful gnarly old piece of driftwood.

Reader, they fall in love. They deal with the real reason Paul came to Rodanthe, which I will say nothing about, except that it involves a grieving man who is well played by Scott Glenn. Paul and Adrienne have found true love for the first time in their lives. Paul has an estranged son who has opened a clinic on a mountainside in Ecuador. He must go there.

They exchange letters. The mountainside has no telephones but excellent mail service. The letters serve the function of the notebook in the (much better) adaptation of Sparks's *Notebook.* These letters are read aloud in voice-overs that would not distinguish a soap opera. Does Paul find his son? Does Adrienne reunite with her snaky husband? Does her troubled and hostile teenage daughter turn into a honey bun from one scene to the next? Does the movie depend upon a deus ex machina to propel itself toward the lachrymose conclusion? Yes, no, yes, and yes.

Nine

(DIRECTED BY ROB MARSHALL; STARRING DANIEL DAY-LEWIS, MARION COTILLARD; 2009)

My problem may be that I know Fellini's *8½* too well. Your problem may be that you don't know it well enough. Both of us may be asking, who exactly was *Nine* made for? This is a big-scale version of the 1982 Broadway production, which won the Tony for best musical. It's likely that most who saw it had either seen the Fellini or made that their business.

I didn't see the musical, but I'm sure it greatly benefited from being live and right there on stage, where the energy in the performance compensated for its lack of a single great song. All the songs sound exactly like standard boilerplate Broadway show tunes, except for composer Maury Yeston's "Finale," which evokes the original Nino Rota sound track for Fellini, which is the problem.

Fellini's great films are essentially musicals. Like most Italian directors of his generation, he didn't record live dialogue and sound. He depended on dubbing. On a set, he usually had an orchestra playing and asked his actors to move, not in time with the music, but "in sympathy." Everyone in a Fellini film evokes an inner body rhythm. Then there's Rota's music itself, my favorite sound tracks. I could watch a Fellini film on the radio.

The story, recycled by Rob Marshall for *Nine*, involves aspects of Fellini's own life: his vagueness about screenplays and deadlines, his indifference to budgets, his womanizing, the guilt about sex instilled by his Catholic upbringing, his guilt about cheating on his wife and about bankrupting his producers. It was said that *8½* wasn't so much a confessional as an acting-out of the very problems he was having while making the film, including how to use a gigantic outdoor set he constructed for no clear purpose.

It's a great film; some say his best. *Nine* the musical "adapts" it, true enough, but doesn't feel it. Consider Fellini's most famous scene. The many women in the life of the hero, Guido (played by Marcello Mastroianni), assemble in a fantasy harem and greet him: the Swedish air stewardess, his wife, his mistress, his mother, Saraghina the local whore of his childhood, and above all his muse (Claudia Cardinale), a reassuringly perfect woman, encouraging, never critical. In the harem they caress him, bathe him, soothe him—and then reveal complaints and criticisms, so that he has to take up a whip and threaten them like a lion tamer.

In *Nine* this scene is, of course, reprised, but with an unclear focus. It's less like a vengeful dream, more like a reunion. There's no urgency, no passion, most of all no guilt. In fact, the subtext of Catholic guilt, which is central to Fellini, is only hinted at in *Nine*. But then *Nine* pays homage to a Broadway musical, and not Fellini at all.

In this connection, consider the odd casting of Daniel Day-Lewis in the Fellini/Mastroianni role, played on stage by Raul Julia. Of course he isn't Marcello; who could be? But he also isn't romantic, musical, comic, baffled, exasperated—and not (even though he apprenticed under a Florentine shoemaker) in the slightest degree Italian. What current movie star could play the role? I think Javier Bardem could. Gael Garcia Bernal? Maybe Alec Baldwin? You need a man who is handsome and never seems to have given it a thought. I'm crazy? Then you tell me.

Nine is just plain adrift in its own lack of necessity. It is filled wall-to-wall with stars (Marion Cotillard as the wife figure, Penelope Cruz as the mistress, Judi Dench as the worrying assistant, Nicole Kidman as the muse, the sublime Sophia Loren as the mother). But that's what they are, stars, because the movie doesn't make them characters. My closing advice is very sincere: In the life of anyone who loves movies, there must be time to see 8½. You can watch it instantly right now on Netflix or Amazon. What are you waiting for?

No Reservations

(DIRECTED BY SCOTT HICKS; STARRING CATHERINE ZETA-JONES, AARON ECKHART; 2007)

Here is a love story that ends "and they cooked happily ever after." It's the story of Kate, a master chef who rules her kitchen like a warden, and Nick, perhaps equally gifted, who comes to work for her and is seen as a rival. Since Kate is played by the beautiful Catherine Zeta-Jones and Nick by the handsome Aaron Eckhart, is there any doubt they will end up stirring the same pots and sampling the same gravies? *No Reservations* also has something to do with how a woman "should" behave. Kate's restaurant is owned by Paula (Patricia Clarkson), who hauls Kate out front to meet her "fans" but wants her to stay in the kitchen when a customer complains. This is contrary to Kate's nature. She doesn't want to waste time glad-handing, but if anyone dares to complain about her pâté or her definition of "rare," she storms out of the kitchen, and soon the customer storms out of the restaurant. We've heard about male chefs throwing tantrums (I think it's required), but for Kate to behave in an unladylike manner threatens her job.

There's a subplot. Kate finds herself caring for round-eyed little Zoe (Abigail Breslin), the orphaned child of her sister. Kate has long since vowed never to marry or have children, so this is an awkward fit. But Zoe gets along fine with Nick, who lets her chop basil in the kitchen and tempts her with spaghetti, and soon she's playing matchmaker between the two grown-ups. From meeting in the refrigerator room for shouting matches, they progress to thawing the crab legs.

The movie is focused on two kinds of chemistry: of the kitchen and of the heart. The kitchen works better, with shots of luscious-looking food, arranged like organic still lifes. But chemistry among Nick, Kate, and Zoe is curiously lacking, except when we sense some fondness—not really love—between Zoe and her potential new dad.

Kate and Nick are required by the terms of the formula to be drawn irresistibly together, despite their professional rivalry. But I didn't feel the heat. There was no apparent passion; their courtship is so laid-back it seems almost like a theoretical exercise. For that matter, Kate treats little Zoe like more of a scheduling problem than a new adoptive daughter. The actors dutifully perform the rituals of the plot requirements but don't involve us (or themselves) in an emotional bond.

The movie is a remake of *Mostly Martha* (2002), a German film very much liked by many, unseen by me. Watching its trailer, I can't decide anything about the quality of the original film, but I do recognize many of the same scenes and even similar locations. *No Reservations* doesn't seem to reinvent it so much as recycle it.

There are some nice things in the film. Zeta-Jones is convincing as a short-tempered chef, if not as a replacement mom and potential lover. Clarkson balances on the tight wire a restaurant owner must walk. Bob Balaban, as Kate's psychiatrist, has a reserve that's comically maddening. Aaron Eckhart struggles manfully with an unconvincing character (is he really afraid to run his own kitchen?). We feel Abigail Breslin has the stuff to emerge as a three-dimensional kid if she weren't employed so resolutely as a pawn.

But *No Reservations*, directed by the usually superior Scott Hicks (*Shine, Hearts in Atlantis, Snow Falling on Cedars*), has too many reservations. It goes through the motions, but the characters seem to feel more passion for food than for one another.

No Strings Attached

(Directed by Ivan Reitman; starring Natalie Portman, Ashton Kutcher; 2011)
No Strings Attached poses the question: Is it possible to regularly have sex with someone and not run a risk of falling in love? The answer is yes. Now that we have that settled, consider the case of Emma (Natalie Portman) and Adam (Ashton Kutcher), who met when they were six and now meet when they're maybe twenty-six. Busy people. He's a low-rent TV producer and she's a medical student. She doesn't have time for romance, and he's dating the sexy Vanessa (played by the well-named Ophelia Lovibond).

Still, one must do something about sex, lest the pipes run rusty, as my friend Henry Togna Sr., the London hotelier, instructed me when he was well into his seventies. Adam and Emma see each other at a party, remember each other after all those years, yet do not realize they're having a Meet Cute. Then Adam discovers Vanessa has dumped him and moved in with his father (Kevin Kline). In response, he begins to drink, which is what the Jack Lemmon character always does in these situations, and what with one thing and another he wakes up naked in Emma's apartment while she and three roommates reassure him they're all interns and it's deja vu when it comes to viewing the male netherlands on display.

Is there something a little, I dunno, *dated* about a comedy where a guy clutches a towel to his privates while girls giggle at him? And when he asks if he slept with anyone last night, why does that remind me of Doris Day in *Where Were You When the Lights Went Out?* Here is a titillating sex romp in 2011, when the very words "titillating" and "romp" have outlasted their shelf lives. The movie is rated R, but it's the most watery R I've seen. It's more of a PG-13 playing dress-up.

Anyway, finding out he hasn't slept with Emma, Adam engages in sitcom badinage that quickly leads to the old rumpy-pumpy, and they find the pipes running marvelously clear. What a discovery! They can have sex and remain just friends! This is a great convenience. They proceed to frolic like two bunnies in clover, using their cell phones and texting skills to arrange emergency trysts in roughly anything except a bed.

All of this is fun while it lasts. Then the wheels of Hollywood morality begin to grind. There was a time when the very premise of this film would have been banned, but times change, and now characters can do pretty much anything as long as they don't get away with it. Although *No Strings Attached* might have been more fun if Adam and Emma had investigated the long-term possibilities of casual sex, it is required that the specter of Romantic Love raise its ominous head. Are they . . . becoming too fond? Emma suggests they try sleeping with others so, you know, they won't get too hung up on each other. If you've ever seen a romantic comedy, you know how that works. Experience shows that *not* sleeping with others is the foolproof way of not getting too hung up, etc.

This is a strange film. Its premise is so much more transgressive than its execution. It's as if the 1970s never happened, let alone subsequent decades. Emma and Adam aren't modern characters. They're sitcom characters allowed to go all the way like grown-ups. As the wheels of the plot creak and groan, we're like kids in the backseat, asking, "Are we there yet?" Some diversion is supplied by the subplot involving Adam's dad, Alvin (Kline), an aging TV star trapped forever in his own misspent youth. Alvin is a dedicated hedonist, which Vanessa finds to her liking because

236 | The Nutcracker in 3-D

hedonists are always happy to pay, one way or another, for their hedonism, and Vanessa is happy to be paid, one way or another.

Natalie Portman won an Academy Award for *Black Swan*. Why she helped produce this I cannot say. Ambitious actors usually do dreck like this in order to afford to produce a movie like *Black Swan*. All the same, she does what she can; she has an edge, aggressive timing, and impressive enthusiasm for sex romping. Of Ashton Kutcher I have less to say. He seems to be a very nice guy, a little too large for agile romping and still too young for a Brendan Fraser role. When I saw him in *The Butterfly Effect* (2004), I registered that he could act, but in this material he's essentially just the Male Unit. There is no character there.

The Nutcracker in 3-D

(DIRECTED BY ANDREI KONCHALOVSKY; STARRING ELLE FANNING, NATHAN LANE; 2010)
From what dark night of the soul emerged the wretched idea for *The Nutcracker in 3-D*? Who considered it even remotely a plausible idea for a movie? It begins with an awkward approximation of the story behind the Tchaikovsky ballet, and then turns it into a war by the nutcracker prince against the Holocaust. Am I exaggerating? At one point, the evil Rat King (John Turturro) has his troopers snatch toys from the hands of children so they can be tossed into furnaces, and the smoke will emerge from high chimneys to blot out the sun.

Yes. And the Rats are dressed in fascistic uniforms. And against them stand our heroine, Mary (Elle Fanning), and her Christmas present, a nutcracker (voice of Shirley Henderson) that has imprisoned a handsome prince (Charlie Rowe). And two-legged helicopters swoop low over screaming children, and the city is laid waste, and the Rats dream of world domination.

You may be in disbelief. I was. This is one of those rare holiday movies that may send children screaming under their seats. Their parents, naively hoping to see a sweet version of *The Nutcracker Suite*, will be appalled or angry, take your choice. Yes, there are melodies that began with Tchaikovsky at one point, but now they have (are you sitting down?) lyrics by Tim Rice.

The Nutcracker in 3-D easily qualifies as one of the most preposterous ideas in the history of the movies. It isn't a story; it's a gag line for one of Letterman's "Top 10" lists (No. 9, It's a Horrible Life; No. 8, A Christmas Carol in Hell . . .).

Andrei Konchalovsky, who wrote and directed it, says this has been a dream project for twenty years. That is tragic. Konchalovsky made the great films Shy People and Runaway Train, and perhaps he became obsessed with this folly. But what did others think? What about Nathan Lane, who plays a character not previously associated with The Nutcracker, Albert Einstein? Yes, he gets to sing a song about the theory of relativity, but not since he played Jacqueline Susann's adoring husband in Isn't She Great has a role been more thankless.

Only one thing could have made this premise worse, and they haven't neglected it. That would be to present it in 3-D. They have. The movie was filmed in Hungary in 2007, and perhaps those screening it sensed a certain lack of enthusiasm. Maybe they thought that by retrospectively "adapting" it to 3-D, it would play better. No luck. I've seen bad retro 3-D. I have never seen 3-D as bad as this. The picture is so dim and dingy you almost wonder if the smoke from those burning toys is drifting between you and the screen.

Old Dogs

(DIRECTED BY WALT BECKER; STARRING JOHN TRAVOLTA, ROBIN WILLIAMS; 2009)

Old Dogs is stupefyingly dimwitted. What were John Travolta and Robin Williams thinking of? Apparently, their agents weren't perceptive enough to smell the screenplay in its advanced state of decomposition, but wasn't there a loyal young intern in the office to catch them at the elevator and whisper, "You've paid too many dues to get involved with such crap at this stage in your careers"?

Williams and Travolta play business partners trying to float a big deal with Japan. Meanwhile, they're saddled with baby-sitting six-year-old twins. Be sure your seat belt is visible on the outside of your blanket; you will be awakened for breakfast when this flight is about to land.

The film makes a big business meeting with Japanese investors a study in laugh-avoidance. The Japanese line up on one side of a table in a Las Vegas Japanese restaurant, and Travolta, Williams, their partner Seth Green, and a translator are on the other. Travolta tries to warm them up with the funny story of how Williams just got divorced twice in the last twenty-four hours. The Japanese sit stony-faced. So do we. Then Travolta gets to his big finish, and the Japanese break into helpless laughter. My theory: Since almost all Japanese businessmen in Vegas speak English, they've been playing a practical joke.

This film seems to have lingered in postproduction while editors struggled desperately to inject laugh cues. It obviously knows no one will find it funny without being ordered to. How else to explain reaction shots of a dog responding to laugh lines? Or the painfully obvious use of music as glaring as a yellow highlighter to point out comedy? Example: Rita Wilson gets her hand slammed by a car trunk, and the sound track breaks into "Big Girls Don't Cry."

Another clue is when characters break into bad sitcom dialogue. After the Old Dogs end up at camp with their young charges, a muscular counselor (Matt Dillon) asks them, "You girls ready to play a little Ultimate Frisbee?" Williams: "I think so, Mr. Testosterone."

Another clue: "Funny moments" repeated in case we missed them. Example: Robin Williams test-drives a buckled-on, back-mounted device that allows him to fly. It loses power and he drops into a pond. Wow, that was funny! Wait! Here it is again! Same drop, new angle! Twice as funny! Oh, no! A third drop! Ohmigod! Wait—wait—a *fourth* time? Usher, quick! Bring me oxygen!

Seth Green is not a tall man. But hell, he's only three inches shorter than Robin Williams. In this movie, you'd think he was Danny DeVito. He ends up wrapped in the arms of a gorilla. Never mind why. Doesn't matter. First Law of Movie Gorillas: Guy in a gorilla suit is never funny, unless the joke is on him.

To save himself from the enormous beast, Green sings a soothing lullaby. The gorilla dozes off peacefully. Hey, that's good! That's very good! Green gently tries to extricate himself from the gorilla's embrace. Nothing doing! Green desperately starts crooning again. Just think. If the gorilla wakes up, Green will be crushed to death! Man, oh, man!

The release of *Old Dogs* was delayed because of the death of another of its costars, Bernie Mac. I can think of another way they might have respected his memory.

Our Family Wedding

(DIRECTED BY RICK FAMUYIWA; STARRING FOREST WHITAKER, AMERICA FERRERA; 2010)
Our Family Wedding is a perfectly good idea for a comedy: A wedding between a Mexican-American woman and an African-American man leads to culture clash. The film, unfortunately, deals with the situation at the level of a middling sitcom. You almost miss the laugh track. Difficult problems are sidestepped, arguments are overacted, and there are three food fights involving wedding cakes. Well, two, actually, and the destruction of a third cake.

At the center of the wedding are Lucia Ramirez (America Ferrera), who was a law student at Columbia, and Marcus Boyd (Lance Gross), a Columbia med school graduate. The young couple plan to move to Laos, where he will work with Doctors Without Borders. They've been living together in New York, but keeping it a secret from her parents because her mom, Sonia (Diana Maria Riva), expects her to remain a virgin before marriage, and her father, Miguel (Carlos Mencia), would be crushed if he learned she had dropped out of law school. In a plot twist of startling originality, she is not pregnant.

A slimmed-down Forest Whitaker plays Marcus's father, Brad, a popular Los Angeles all-night DJ. He's doing all right and inhabits a huge house in the hills with a pool, stairs leading to a terrace, and a lawn big enough to hold a wedding party. Plus his ride is a Jaguar. Not bad for an all-night DJ.

Miguel is also well off, with the daughter at Columbia, the big luxurious house, and the passion for restoring classic cars. He owns a towing service, which is how he and Brad have a Meet Cute: All his drivers call in sick. Miguel fills in, and he and Brad meet when he tows the Jag.

The dads meet again at dinner when their children pop the big news and are immediately screaming insults and shaking each other by the throat. This scene, like all the stagy arguments between the fathers, is completely unconvincing. Their fights are drummed up for the purposes of the screenplay, and the actors hardly seem to believe them. Their families flutter their hands and beg them to calm down. Their running feud feels phony to begin with, and painfully forced by the end.

All of the family difficulties seem trumped up. Although Lucia is terrified that her mother will discover she had sex before marriage, that revelation, when it comes, is almost a throwaway. Marcus is embarrassed that his dad dates much younger women, but when he turns up at the family dinner with a girl who was Lucia's softball teammate, there's barely a mild stir. Lucia's grandmother faints when she sees Lucia's fiancé is a black man, but when she comes to, this is forgotten. (Didn't anyone tell her?) Oh, and speaking of softball, the game played between the two family teams is so badly staged, I wasn't sure which side many of the players were on, nor who won the game.

The bright spots are America Ferrera, the kind of cuddly beauty who plunges right in and kisses a guy without worrying about her makeup, and Lance Gross as the guy, who has a thankless task as the Perfect Fiancé but doesn't overplay it. Regina King steals many scenes as Brad's longtime lawyer and secret admirer; her character is smart, focused, and sympathetic, and King's costumes showcase those Michelle Obama arms.

Our Family Wedding is a pleasant but inconsequential comedy, clunky, awkward for the actors, and contrived from beginning to end. Compare it with *Nothing Like the Holidays* (2008) to see how well a movie can handle similar material.

Outlander

<small>(DIRECTED BY HOWARD MCCAIN; STARRING JIM CAVIEZEL, SOPHIA MYLES; 2009)</small>

I am tempted to describe the plot of *Outlander* as preposterous, but a movie about an alien spaceship crashing into a Viking fjord during the Iron Age is *likely* to be preposterous. Two alien life forms survive the crash: Kainan and a monster known as "the Moorwen." Kainan, played by Jim Caviezel, looks exactly like a human being. The Moorwen looks like a giant, speedy, armored hippo-beetle with a toothy front end designed in the same forges of hell that produced the alien in *Alien*.

Kainan was returning from the Moorwen's home planet, which his race had terraformed, not quite wiping out all the Moorwens. The creatures counterattacked, wiping out most of Kainan's fellow settlers; what he doesn't realize is that one Moorwen was onboard ship when he blasted off. Kainan uses a handy device to pump the local Earth language (Viking, spoken in English) into his mind through his eyeball and soon encounters the nearest Viking village.

Having seen more than a few movies, we intuit that this village will contain a venerable king (Rothgar, played by John Hurt), his bodacious daughter (Freya, played by Sophia Myles), a jealous young warrior (Wulfric, played by Jack Huston), and a menacing dissident (Gunnar, played by Ron Perlman). There are also numerous villagers who stand around in the background looking intensely interested.

The village is suspicious of this strange "outlander." Then Vikings start to disappear in the forest, and Kainan realizes he has brought along a passenger. After he saves Rothgar from the Moorwen, he wins royal favor and organizes the village in a plan to lure the beast into a deep pit with stakes at the bottom and burn it alive.

I began my study of science fiction at the age of nine, with *Tom Corbett, Space Cadet*. I grew to love the authors who incorporated as much science as possible: Clarke, Asimov, Heinlein. They would have had questions about Kainan. For example, is he as human as he appears? It seems unlikely from a Darwinian point of view that two human species should evolve independently and contemporaneously on separate worlds. Even more so that they would share common sexual feelings and be able to mate, although that is precisely what Kainan and Freya propose.

But yes, their love flowers, against a backdrop of Arthurian romance. The Moorwen is the dragon, of course. And much depends on a sword mighty enough to pierce its armor. To forge this Excalibur, Kainan dives into the fjord and retrieves scrap steel from the wreckage of his ship, thus bringing the Iron Age to a quick close—in this village, anyway. The climax involves the usual violent and incoherent special effects scenes, after which Rothgar gives Kainan the hand of his daughter, and Kainan and Freya presumably retire to discover if separate evolutionary paths have outfitted them with compatible fixtures.

Outlander is interesting as a collision of genres: The monster movie meets the Viking saga. You have to give it credit for carrying that premise to its ultimate (if not logical) conclusion. It occurs to me, however, that the Moorwen had legitimate reason to be grieved. First Kainan's race appropriated the Moorwen planet for its own purposes, then it massacred the Moorwens, now it was picking off a survivor. Do you think genocide or colonialism are concepts to be found in *Outlander*? Not a chance. That's because Kainan is so human, and the Moorwens are, well, just not our sort.

Over Her Dead Body

(Directed by Jeff Lowell; starring Eva Longoria Parker, Paul Rudd; 2008)

Why is nobody utterly in awe of ghosts in *Over Her Dead Body* and so many other ghostcoms? Here is a supernatural manifestation from another realm, and everybody treats it as a plot device. The movie even drags in a Catholic priest, who seems bewilderingly ignorant of his church's beliefs about ghosts (they don't exist) and treats the situation as an opportunity for counseling.

The setup: It's the wedding day of Henry and Kate (Paul Rudd and Eva Longoria). She's a Type A perfectionist who races manically around the reception venue, straightening place settings, adjusting decorations, and flying into a rage at the ice sculptor (Stephen Root) who has delivered an ice angel—without wings! She orders him to take it back and bring her one with wings, which, as everybody knows, all angels possess. He argues reasonably that you can't just stick wings on an ice sculpture. In a tragic accident involving the sculpture, Kate is killed.

Flash forward a decent amount of time and Henry, still in mourning, is informed by his sister, Chloe (Lindsay Sloane), that it's time for his life to begin again. He should start dating. He won't hear of it. He's still in love with Kate. She persuades him to visit Ashley (Lake Bell), a psychic she knows. He does so. Is she a real psychic? Sometimes. She begins to get vibes. So does he. Neither one needs to be psychic to realize they are falling in love with each other.

I guess it's all right for psychics (as opposed to psychiatrists) to date their clients, but Ashley seeks advice. She gets it from Dan (Jason Biggs), her partner in a catering business. Also from Father Marks (William Morgan Sheppard), who also doesn't know that his church doesn't believe in psychics. (Was he ordained by mail order? The Church teaches that consulting a psychic is a sin, although it doesn't totally rule out info from the other side, suggesting it could be disinformation from Satan.) Anyway, meanwhile . . . eek! The ghost of Kate appears, none too pleased that another woman has designs on her man. She intends to sabotage their romance.

What happens then? Kate looks completely real, although she has no material presence and can walk through walls, etc. I always wonder why walls are meaningless to such beings, but they never fall through floors. Do elevators go up without them? Never mind. The plot plays out as you would expect it to, as the amazing presence of a ghost is effortlessly absorbed into the formula plot. If it were me and a ghost, I'd put my personal agenda on hold and ask all sorts of questions about the afterlife. Wouldn't you?

Heaven, in this movie, is represented in the standard way: Everything is blindingly white, and everyone is garbed in white, even an angel (Kali Rocha) who has, by the way, no wings. Well, of course it doesn't. Being a pure spirit, it has no need to fly. Kate switches back to a conventional wardrobe for her sojourns here below. How would I depict heaven? As a featureless void with speaking voices. I haven't decided about subtitles.

Even in a movie with a ghost, the hardest thing to believe is a revelation that Dan makes to Ashley. They have worked together five years, and
yet she is astonished. I will leave the revelation for you to discover, only
adding that I believe it would be impossible for Dan to work five years in
the catering industry without his secret being obvious to everyone.

Consider for a moment how this movie might play if it took itself
seriously. Would it be better than as a comedy? I suspect so. Does the
premise "her ghost turns up and fights the new romance" make you
chuckle? Me neither. It's the kind of angle that could seem funny only at
a pitch meeting. Not only have we been there, done that, we didn't want
to go there, do that in the first place.

Paranormal Activity 2

(DIRECTED BY TOD WILLIAMS; STARRING MICAH SLOAT, KATIE FEATHERSTON; 2010)
Paranormal Activity 2 is an efficient delivery system for gotcha! moments,
of which it has about nineteen. Audiences who want to be gotchaed will
enjoy it. A gotcha! moment is a moment when something is sudden, loud,
and scary. This can be as basic as the old "it's only a cat" cliché, or as
abrupt as a character being hit by a bus. *PA2* starts slyly with pre-gotcha!
teasers, such as a door or a child's toy moving on its own. Then there are
obscure off-screen rumbles, like an uneasy stomach. Then loud bangs.
Then loud bangs with visible causes. Then all the doors in a room banging open at once. And eventually, well, you can see for yourself, because
all the activity is captured by twenty-four-hour security cameras.

The cameras, which function perfectly, never capture the Presence
on the screen. For the house is indeed haunted by a ghostlike supernatural

presence, I guess. I say "I guess" because there is a scene of a victim being dragged downstairs, and the entity doing the dragging is invisible. On the other hand, the movie ends with a strong suggestion that the malefactor was, in fact, a living human being. So would that be cheating? Hell yes. But who cares? People go to *Paranormal Activity 2* with fond memories of the original film, which was low-tech and clever in the way it teased our eyes and expectations. It scared them. They want to be scared again. They will be. When there's a loud unexpected bang, it will scare you. The structural task of the gotcha! movie is to separate the bangs so they continue to be unexpected.

Any form of separation will do. The characters include the Sloats (Micah Sloat and Katie Featherston), who are back from the first movie. But this story begins earlier in time than that one and takes place in the home of her sister, Kristi (Sprague Grayden), her husband, Daniel (Brian Boland), teenage daughter, Ali (Molly Ephraim), brand-new baby, Hunter, and his nanny, Martine (Vivis). Martine is ethnic, and we know what that means: She has an instinctive knowledge of ghosts, breaks out the magic incense at a moment's notice, and can't get anyone to listen to her.

There are six speaking roles, not counting the nonspeaking baby and the dog. Good odds, you'd think, that at least one of them would have something interesting to say, but no. The movie isn't about them. They function primarily as gotcha! separators, going through vacuous social motions between gotchas! They are not real swift. The movie numbers the days as they tick away, and along about Day No. 12 I'm thinking, "Why are these people still here?" The screening I attended was treated to a surprise appearance by three stars of that cable show about Chicago's paranormal detectives. These are real Chicago detectives. If the Sloats lived in Chicago, they'd have a SWAT team out there by Day No. 7.

The movie is presented as a documentary with no setup, unless the first movie was the setup. It begins with little Hunter being brought home, and then we get titles like "Day No. 3." Of what? One peculiar title says, "Nine days before the death of Micah Sloat." I probably have the number of days wrong, but you get the idea. What are we supposed to do with this information? I guess we should think, "Sloat, you poor bastard, you only have nine days to go." This knowledge is about as useful as the farmer who tells you to make a left turn five miles before you get to the barn. There are also titles saying things like "1:41:15 a.m.," as if we care.

The character who suffers the most is poor little Hunter. Something is always bothering him in the middle of the night. When a security camera is on the staircase, we hear his plaintive little wail. When it's focused on his bedroom, he's standing up in his wee crib and bawling. The dog is always there barking at something, because dogs, like ethnic nannies, Know About These Things. Hunter screams and screams in the movie. If you were Hunter's parents and your house was haunted, wouldn't you move the poor kid's crib into the bedroom?

My audience jumped a lot and screamed a lot, and then laughed at themselves, even after one event that wasn't really funny. Then they explained things to one another, and I could overhear useful lines like, "She got the $#!+ scared outta her!" I understand they attended in hopes of seeing gotchas! and explaining them to one another. I don't have a problem with *Paranormal Activity 2*. It delivers what it promises, and occupies its audiences. Win-win.

Paranormal Activity 3

(DIRECTED BY HENRY JOOST AND ARIEL SCHULMAN; STARRING KATIE FEATHERSTON, SPRAGUE GRAYDEN; 2011)

Paranormal Activity 3 is a prequel, revealing that the characters in *PA1* and *PA2* had already been through the all-night video-surveillance ordeal. At least in this film they are undergoing it for the first time, which is less than can be said for us. The formula for the films involves pallid characters, perfunctory dialogue, and very long waits for something to happen.

When something does, it's often a sudden shock accompanied by a startling musical chord. Sometimes there are loud bangings and other noises. Sometimes the shocks are false alarms. The audience screams, and then laughs. At my screening, it also did a lot of talking. Usually I find that obnoxious, but this time I wish they'd spoken louder; the *Mystery Science Theater* approach might enrich this film.

What we have to accept in all three films is that a house is occupied by an entity intent on being a pain in the butt and zapping us with gotcha! moments. These are cruel limitations for a supernatural being; one rather hopes the Other Side would produce more interesting company. When the origin of the manifestations is revealed or hinted at, the film closes soon after, as if the terminal scene explained the slightest thing.

This film involves the two sisters who were seen in earlier episodes as adults. Katie (Katie Featherston) and Kristi Rey (Sprague Grayden) share a two-level home with their mother, Julie (Lauren Bittner), and her boyfriend, Dennis (Chris Smith). The girls are aware of a presence in the house, perhaps an imaginary friend, although perhaps not so imaginary.

In a series of shots destined to be repeated tediously, we cut between video cameras left to run all night in the bedrooms of the girls and the adults, and a camera on an oscillating fan platform that pans back and forth between the living room and the kitchen/dining area. Long periods pass without activity. Some activity is subtle. Occasionally it's sudden and startling. Sometimes (a "ghost" in a sheet) it's like Casper the Friendly Ghost playing a practical joke. The slow deliberation of the oscillations adds implacable delays while we wait to pan back again and see what has changed. In the best shot in the film, all the tables and chairs and pots and pans in the kitchen have disappeared, and then we find out with perfect logic where they are.

Inexplicably, there are people who still haven't had enough of these movies. The first was a nifty novelty. Now the appeal has worn. Since they already know more or less what will happen, and it's lamebrained, why do audiences continue to turn out for new *Activities*? Yet you mark my words: Part 3 will gross untold millions on opening weekend. If you like horror, dread, and a twisty plot, try to find the Michael Shannon film *Take Shelter.* Let's say you like popcorn during a movie. *Paranormal Activity 3* is like eating the cardboard box.

248 | The Perfect Sleep

The Perfect Sleep

(DIRECTED BY JEREMY ALTER; STARRING ANTON PARDOE, ROSELYN SANCHEZ; 2009)

The Perfect Sleep puts me in mind of a flywheel spinning in the void. It is all burnished brass and shining steel, perfectly balanced as it hums in its orbit; yet because it occupies a void, it satisfies only itself and touches nothing else. Here is a movie that goes about its business without regard for an audience. Oh, it is well crafted, I grant you that. The cinematography contains fine compositions, looking down steeply on angled shadows and seeking down lost corridors. It has interiors that look like nineteenth-century landmarks of architecture just after the movers left with the furniture. It has grim men, a seductive woman, guns, knives, garrotes, scalpels, needles, cudgels, feet, fists, and baseball bats. It even has Patrick Bauchau, with the most insinuating voice since Orson Welles. But what in God's name is it about?

The Perfect Sleep does not lack explanation; in fact, the unnamed hero (Anton Pardoe) provides a narration that goes on and on and on, perhaps because the screenplay is by Anton Pardoe. He has returned to an unnamed city after ten years of fleeing men who would kill him, one who may be his father, a woman named Porphyria (Roselyn Sanchez), whom he loves and who has always loved him, a child he raised or fathered—or is an orphan, I'm unclear—an ambitious crime boss named The Rajah, a sinister physician named Dr. Sebastian (Tony Amendola), empty streets, wicked staircases, not many cars, and lots of streetlights.

It's all here. And after telling you so much about what's in it, wouldn't you think I could tell you the plot? I know the Narrator is back, he wants revenge, people want revenge on him, everybody is getting killed, and he personally is beaten, stabbed, kicked, thrown down stairs, skewered, hammered with karate, strangled, whipped, and shot point-blank in the head, and, what a guy, he just keeps on narrating, narrating, and narrating.

There are many unique ways of delivering mayhem in the film, some of them described in clinical detail by Dr. Sebastian while he is administering them. "Jugular . . . carotid? Carotid . . . jugular?" he debates with himself, his scalpel poised. At another point, he walks cheerfully up to two guys and stabs them in a lung apiece. Then he explains to them that they each have a collapsed lung. Dreadfully painful but not fatal.

He suggests it would be appalling for one to have two collapsed lungs. And he delivers this speech: "Our very biological structure promises us that, if it be now, 'tis not to come; if it be not to come, it will be now; if it be not now, yet it will come: Good sirs, the readiness is all." If this sounds like part of a famous speech, you are correct. I fancy the two collapsed lung guys are trying to remember where they heard it when he stabs them in the remaining two lungs. Now I know a lot about collapsed lungs, but I'm not entirely sure who Dr. Sebastian is.

Maybe it doesn't matter. Maybe if it did, the plot would give us a place to dig in our claws and hold on. The movie seems more interested in behavior. Many scenes take place in vast empty spaces like abandoned rehearsal halls or hotel function rooms. Major characters are discovered along an office corridor behind glass doors with their names stenciled on (more fun than captions). There are shadows on top of shadows. It's the film noir universe, all right. What does the title refer to? Perhaps to what you will enjoy during the film.

The Pink Panther 2

(DIRECTED BY HARALD ZWART; STARRING STEVE MARTIN, JEAN RENO; 2009)

I was smiling all the way through the opening credits of *The Pink Panther 2*. They made me miss the golden age of credits, when you actually found out who the actors were going to be and maybe saw a little cartoon in the bargain: this time, one about the misadventures of the Pink Panther, of course. And then the names in the cast!

Imagine these appearing one after another: Steve Martin, Jean Reno, Emily Mortimer, Andy Garcia, Alfred Molina, Aishwarya Rai Bachchan, John Cleese, Lily Tomlin, Jeremy Irons, Johnny Hallyday . . . wait a minute! Aishwarya Rai Bachchan! That's the Indian actress Aishwarya Rai! The most beautiful woman in the world!

As the movie began, my smile faded. The actors are let down by the screenplay and direction, which don't really pop the supporting characters out into strong comic focus. Maybe the cast is simply too star-studded?

There's sometimes the feeling they're being cycled onscreen by twos and threes, just to keep them alive.

Then there's the albatross of the Blake Edwards and Peter Sellers films. Edwards was a truly inspired director of comedies (*The Party, SOB, Victor/ Victoria*). Peter Sellers was a genius who somehow made Inspector Clouseau seem as if he really were helplessly incapable of functioning in the real world, and somehow incapable of knowing that. Steve Martin is a genius, too, but not at being Inspector Clouseau. It seems more like an exercise.

The plot: "The Tornado" has stolen the Magna Carta, the Japanese emperor's sword, and the Shroud of Turin. Next may be the Pink Panther, the pink diamond that is, for some reason, the symbol of France's greatness and not merely an example of carbon under great pressure. Clouseau is chosen, despite the apoplectic agitation of Chief Inspector Dreyfus (John Cleese), to join an international police Dream Team to thwart the possible deed.

Also onstage is Clouseau's assistant, Nicole (Emily Mortimer), a fragrant rose; she and Jacques are so in love with each other they cannot even bring themselves to admit it. The Italian team member, Vincenzo (Andy Garcia), family name Doncorleone, moves in on Nicole and tells Clouseau that Sonia (Aishwarya Rai) likes him. That creates a romcom situation that's sort of muted because of Jacques and Nicole's shyness, and because the film seems reluctant to foreground Sonia very much. Aishwarya Rai is breathtaking in Bollywood films, where they devote a great deal of expertise to admiring beauty, but here she's underutilized and too much in the background.

Molina plays Pepperidge, a Sherlockian type who claims to be a great deducer of clues. Clouseau takes one look at him and they start a deducing showdown, sort of funny. Reno is Ponton, Clouseau's associate inspector, whose considerable presence never really pays off. Yuki Matsuzaki, as the Japanese cop Kenji, seems to be projecting ideas about the character that were edited out or never written in. Tomlin is the departmental expert on P.C. behavior, whom Clouseau argues with ("But . . . blondes *are* dumb!").

Opportunities to better develop all of these characters are lost, and we're left with the sight and stunt gags, which are central to the Panther movies, of course, but feel recycled: This time, little kids are the kung fu experts, for example, instead of Cato.

Too many of the stunt gags are performed without payoffs; Buster Keaton, the master, always gave you reaction shots. When Clouseau is mistaken for the pope, for example, and seems to fall from his balcony to his death, why isn't there a crowd to contemplate the fallen Frenchman with his black moustache, maybe lurching to his feet, blessing them, and intoning *dov'e la toilette*? Or after Clouseau sets the restaurant on fire, why not make him struggle to get back inside, telling the firemen he insists on paying his check?

The first two Panther movies, *The Pink Panther* (1963) and *A Shot in the Dark* (1964), were a serendipitous coming together of Edwards and Sellers. Truth to tell, none of their others were as inspired. The moment had passed. And it still hasn't come back round again. Zut!

Pirates of the Caribbean: On Stranger Tides

(DIRECTED BY ROB MARSHALL; STARRING JOHNNY DEPP, PENELOPE CRUZ; 2011)

Before seeing *Pirates of the Caribbean: On Stranger Tides*, I had already reached my capacity for Pirates of the Caribbean movies, and with this fourth installment, my cup runneth over. Indeed, so doth Captain Jack Sparrow's, as he obtains two chalices to use while drinking from the Fountain of Youth, and seeks a mermaid's tears to invest them with magic. There's always a catch-22. You fight Spanish conquistadors and the British Navy to find the bloody fountain, and now you need a weepy mermaid.

I had fleeting hopes for this episode of the Disney franchise. An opening sequence is fun, as Captain Jack impersonates a British judge, is chased through London, and discovers his old amour Angelica (Penelope Cruz) attempting to impersonate him while raising the crew for a ship. That anyone would still want to sail under Jack's command is a tribute to the daring of British seamen. The movie is fun until they set sail.

Johnny Depp, who confesses he's rather tired of playing his

relentless hero, nevertheless does a plucky job here. He plays Jack Sparrow as an insouciant wise guy, rarely ruffled, always ready with a quip. Whether he is a competent swashbuckler is hard to say because the fight sequences here are composed in the editing room and do not seem to exist in an actual space-time continuum. We no longer see truly great sword fighting, the kind performed by Liam Neeson and Tim Roth in *Rob Roy* (1995). It's all impossible leaping and incomprehensible cutting, giving us all of the movement of action and none of the excitement.

The best way to describe the plot is by explaining that the Fountain of Youth is the MacGuffin. Angelica and Jack set sail for the New World aboard a ship commanded by Blackbeard (Ian McShane), who is said to be her father. The ship's crew includes zombies, which is a step up from previous crew members in the series, skeletons. Blackbeard is in a race to find the fountain before Captain Barbossa (Geoffrey Rush), who is being financed by King George, who needs to drink from the fountain none too soon. Rush is as always a dependable actor, but his sandpapery skin complexion is rather alarming here. Get this sailor some Lubriderm.

Also in the race is a boatload of Spanish sailors sent by their king. All three boats pitch up on the same beach and fight one another to the fountain. But wait. The mermaids. Yes, a special reflector used in an old lighthouse casts light on one of the longboats, and light attracts mermaids, and it's a nasty sight. We get to meet only one of the mermaids, the well-named Syrena (Astrid Berges-Frisbey), who is comely and doe-eyed, and has one of those official hairdos that cleverly conceals the delightful bits.

Syrena and Philip (Sam Claflin), a cleric, lock eyes and hearts, but Syrena is needed for her tears, and is held captive and transported through the jungle in a large water tank, wherein she nearly drowns because she cannot breathe, establishing at last what I have always argued, that mermaids are amphibians.

One improvement this time is the dropping of the superfluous non-pirate characters played earlier by Orlando Bloom and Keira Knightley. I was never sure what essential function they fulfilled; Depp and Cruz are so over-the-top they function as their own supporting characters.

Even in his first Pirates movie, Depp seemed to be channeling large parts of the persona of Keith Richards, not to mention all of the eyeliner. Here the Rolling Stone himself turns up again, playing Jack Sparrow's father. The hairdressers for these two characters seem to have involved themselves in some sort of a grudge bet.

Pirates of the Caribbean: On Stranger Tides is about what you'd expect. It is long, expensive, and bombastic, and the beautiful mermaid has a tantalizing way of not coming quite far enough out of the water. For me, it's too much of a muchness. The whole series was inspired by a ride at Disney World. There's a bright side to that. At least no movie has yet been inspired by "It's a Small World."

Play the Game

(DIRECTED BY MARC FIENBERG; STARRING ANDY GRIFFITH, PAUL CAMPBELL; 2009)
The Andy Griffith Show meets *Seinfeld* in the sack, in *Play the Game*, which shows Andy is not too old to star in a sex comedy. I guess. Griffith plays Grandpa Joe, who lost his beloved wife two years ago. Now his grandson Dave (Paul Campbell) thinks it's time for him to start dating again. After all, he isn't getting any younger.

Grandpa Joe is pretty much on standby in his retirement home. He'd like to get cozy with Rose (Doris Roberts). But he's unprepared for the wiles of Edna (Liz Sheridan, who played Seinfeld's mom). She supplies Joe with Viagra, and he more or less seduces her on autopilot.

Dave considers himself a babe magnet. He's a genius at fast-talking himself into relationships that, alas, have a way of ending once he's run through his prepared material. He's also a whiz at selling cars, but at least when he makes a sale the victim drives it off the lot.

The screenplay, written by first-time director Marc Fienberg, fervently stays true to an ancient sitcom tradition. We somehow suspect Grandpa Joe will end up with the adorable Rose, and whaddaya know, Dave finds genuine love with Rose's granddaughter, Julie (Marla Sokoloff).

And that's about it, except for a close-up of Andy Griffith that I could easily have lived without. I've admired Griffith ever since *No Time for*

Sergeants, but the one thing I must admit I've never wanted to do was regard his face while he's enjoying oral sex from Seinfeld's mom. I have a good friend whose own dad discovered Viagra in a retirement home and would call his son almost daily to recount his latest adventures. He called once when I was in the room with my friend, who urgently told him, "Dad, I've told you, I don't want to know!" I told him the old one about the old lady who runs naked into the TV room of her retirement village shouting, "Super sex! Super sex!" One of the guys perks up and says, "I'll have the soup, please."

Predators

(DIRECTED BY NIMROD ANTAL; STARRING ADRIEN BRODY, TOPHER GRACE; 2010)

Predators may be the first film in history to open with a deus ex machina. Yes, the entire plot and all the human characters drop into the movie from the heavens. The last thing they remember is a blinding flash of light. Now they're in free fall, tumbling toward the surface, screaming, grabbing for rip cords on the parachutes they didn't know they had.

The first to land, with a mighty thump, is Royce (Adrien Brody). The others start dropping all around him. These people are savage professional killers from all over: a mercenary, a Japanese samurai, an Israeli markswoman, a mass murderer, an African warlord, and so on. How did they get in this thick jungle, and why?

They discover they're on another world: a perfectly terraformed world, it would seem. The gravity allows them to walk normally, and they can breathe the air and drink the water. Royce notices something odd: The sun never moves. They arrive in a clear space and realize there are three or four moons in the sky, which are either very close or very huge, since their discs are many times that of our moon.

Now hold on here. As every science-fiction fan knows, if a planet always presents the same face to its sun, and is ringed by bodies apparently larger than it is, it will quickly become molten lava pulled hither and yon by vast tidal forces. But never mind. After the visitors are attacked by humongous beasts of prey, Royce figures it out: They're in a game preserve. He figures out a lot of things in the movie, which might have been more fun if he hadn't.

Who runs this game preserve, and why? If you recall the first *Predator* (1987), Arnold Schwarzenegger and other killers found themselves in the Amazon fighting an unseen predatory alien. Has that race of aliens imported humans to its solar system for a rematch? Is it a wise use of resources to transport several mammals untold light-years through space just so you can watch them getting their asses predatored?

No time to think about them. Here come some really vicious warthog-looking creatures. They weigh about half a ton apiece, move as fast as lions, and have so many horns and spikes sticking out of them that fornicating must have to be a sometime thing.

Look at an illustration of one of these fearsome beasts. Can you spot the design flaw? Its horns or fangs, whatever they are, extend too far in front of its mouth! After they kill their prey, how do they eat it? I thought, maybe they lie on their backs and shovel the food in with their feet. But no, how's that gonna work with all the spikes on their backs?

Never mind. The movie is mostly about our nasty heroes being attacked by terrifying antagonists in incomprehensible muddles of lightning-fast special effects. It lacks the quiet suspense of the first *Predator,* and please don't even mention the *Alien vs. Predator* pictures, which lacked the subtlety of *Mothra vs. Godzilla.* The resident aliens view everything in POV shots through what looks like a video monitor with a haywire color adjustment, and they appear in ways I will not go into.

There are always a few characters who get killed in attack movies like this. What confuses me is why they don't all get killed. Look at the illustration again. If that thing hit you at 20 mph and got you down on the ground and all you could do was stab it with your knife, would you expect to have dialogue later in the movie?

There is, of course, one woman in the film, Isabelle (Alice Braga). She and Royce slowly bond, and eventually at the end . . . but no, I can't tell you if they kiss. That would be a spoiler. One thing you know for sure: The alien warthogs don't spend a lot of time frenching.

Pride and Glory

(DIRECTED BY GAVIN O'CONNOR; STARRING EDWARD NORTON, COLIN FARRELL; 2008)
Pride and Glory is the kind of film where you feel like you know the words
and ought to be singing along. It follows the well-worn pathways of countless police dramas before it. We find a drug deal gone bad, corruption on
the force, brother against brother, alcoholic dad who is both their father
and their superior officer, family friend as a traitor, plus one dying wife and
another one who is fed up. There's a stroke of originality: A baby seems
about to be branded by a hot steam iron.

If you set this in New York, provide all the characters with strong ethnic identities, film under glowering skies, add a lot of dead bodies right at the
start, and have characters shout at one another, all you'd have to do is change
the names and hire different actors, and you could do this all again and again.

The setup: Four cops are killed in a drug bust gone wrong. They are
under the command of Francis Tierney Jr. (Noah Emmerich). The moment
you bring a Junior onstage, the formula requires a Senior, in this case
played by Jon Voight as a high-maintenance boozer. Senior confronts his
other son, Ray Tierney (Edward Norton), who has fled the streets for a low-
risk assignment after Something Very Bad happened a few years ago, and
persuades him to rejoin the tough guys: After all, he has to help out Junior.

Also involved is the Tierney brother-in-law, Jimmy Egan (Colin Farrell). Oh, and Junior's wife, Abby (Jennifer Ehle), is dying of cancer and has
lost her hair to chemo. And Ray's wife, Tasha (Carmen Ejogo), has split
with him and, in the tradition of all cop wives, accuses him of neglecting
his family and, on Christmas, receiving a visit from a guy who would be the
first one you would pick out of a lineup, whether or not you recognized
him, because he looks like he has just done Something Very Bad.

The plot involves how and why the four cops were killed. This may
not come as a shock to veteran filmgoers: There is a culture of corruption
in the department, and one character is guilty, one is innocent, and one is
conflicted in his loyalties. Once we know this, we know there will be a
series of angry and desperate confrontations among the three, interlaced
with violent face-downs with criminals, cops being slammed up against
walls in the basement of headquarters, and Senior drinking even more

because he is horribly confused about whether he values truth above family loyalty, and either one above loyalty to the department. Jon Voight is a fine actor, but putting him in a role like this is like hanging him out to dry. My friend McHugh used to be fond of suddenly announcing, "Clear the bar! I want to drink by myself!" Such a moment supplies the sensationally bad ending to *Pride and Glory*, when one brother enters the bar where the other brother is drinking, flashes his badge, and tells everyone to scram. Why? So he and his brother can settle everything with a brutal fistfight. As we know, under the Macho Code, this means that after two people who love each other end up beaten and bloody, they will somehow arrive at a catharsis. How that solves this tangled web of loyalty, deceit, and corruption, I can't be exactly sure.

Prince of Persia: The Sands of Time

(DIRECTED BY MIKE NEWELL; STARRING JAKE GYLLENHAAL, GEMMA ARTERTON; 2010)
Prince of Persia: The Sands of Time is a children's story beefed up to appeal to young teens. It's based on a video game, but don't make me play it, let me guess: The push-button magic dagger is used in the game to let you rewind and try something again, right? Since anything in the story (any death, for example) can be reversed, the stakes are several degrees below urgent. And there's a romance in which the boy and girl spend endless moments about to kiss for every nanosecond they actually do. If I were the Prince of Persia, I'd push the button, go back in time, and plant a wet one on Tamina's luscious lips.

The movie is set in ancient Persia, which is now named Iran. This is a land with truly astonishing landscapes: deserts, canyons, craggy monument valleys, and a mountain range that resembles the Himalayas. Fair enough, since Persia reaches "from the steppes of China to the shores of the Mediterranean," but even more impressive since it's all within a day's journey of the capital city.

That city, whose name escapes me, is ruled by the noble King Sharaman (Ronald Pickup). One day in the marketplace he sees a brave young urchin defend a boy being beaten and escape pursuit by running across rooftops. This is Dastan, who will grow up to be played by Jake Gyllenhaal. He's an orphan; his birth parents are two movies, the Douglas Fairbanks (1924) and Michael Powell (1940) versions of *The Thief of Bagdad*. Dastan is adopted by the king and raised with two brothers, Garsiv (Toby Kebbell) and Tus (Richard Coyle). The names of the movie's characters seem to have been created by a random-word generator. The king has a brother named Nizam (Ben Kingsley), first seen in a sinister close-up that could be subtitled, "I will turn out to be the villain." He has a Vandyke beard and eyes that glower smolderingly.

Dastan is good at running on rooftops. He can also leap from back to back in a herd of horses, jump across mighty distances, climb like a monkey, and spin like a top. This is all achieved with special effects, ramped up just fast enough to make them totally unbelievable. Fairbanks has a 1924 scene where he hops from one giant pot to another. He did it in real time, with little trampolines hidden in the pots, and six pots in that movie are worth the whole kitchen in this one.

Anyway, the evil Nizam insists that the Persian army invade the peaceful city of Alamut. This is a beautiful city surrounding a towering castle. King Sharaman has ordered the city not be sacked, but nooo. Nizam has secret information that Alamut is manufacturing weapons of mass destruction for Persia's enemies. Poor Dick Cheney. He can't even go to a Disney swashbuckler without running into finger wagging.

Anyway, Dastan climbs the city walls, pours flaming oil on its guards, etc., and then encounters the beautiful Princess Tamina (Gemma Arterton). She possesses the Dagger of Time, which is an honest-to-God WMD, since if it's switched on too long, all the sands of time will run out, and it's back to the Big Bang.

The plot involves portentous dialogue ("The only way to stop this Armageddon is for us to take the Dagger to the Secret Guardian Temple"), which separates tiresome CGI sequences in which clashing warriors do battle in shots so brief we can see people getting whacked, but have no conception of actual physical space. Of course, this must all lead to Tamina and Dastan fleeing from the evil Nizam, who has framed the lad for regicide.

Their flight brings them under the sway of the film's obligatory Comic Supporting Character, Sheikh Amar (Alfred Molina), a con man who runs rigged ostrich races, and those who have tried to fix an ostrich race will know that the bloody ostriches are impossible to reason with. My interest perked up with the prospect that Dastan and Tamina might try to flee by ostrich-back, but no luck. Imagine the scene! Gemma in foreground, Jake right behind her, compressed by telephoto, jerking up and down at terrific speed while sand dunes whiz past on the green screen in the background.

The irritating thing about special effects is that *anything* can happen, and often you can't tell what the hell it is. Dastan, for example, seems to fall into a vast sinkhole as the sand is sucked from beneath him at dizzying speed. Exactly how he is saved of this predicament isn't exactly clear.

Other key events are obscure. It looked to me as if Garsiv was killed on two occasions, yet is around for the end of the movie, and I don't think the Dagger of Time was involved in either of them. The workings of the Dagger are in any event somewhat murky; when you push the button in its base, it makes you light up like Sylvester the Puddy Cat sticking a paw in an electric socket, and everyone fast-reverses into their starting positions. How do people in movies always know how to do this stuff without practice?

The two leads are not inspired. Jake Gyllenhaal could make the cover of a muscle mag, but he plays Dastan as if harboring Spider-Man's doubts and insecurities. I recall Gemma Arterton as resembling a gorgeous still photo in a cosmetics ad. If the two actors had found more energy and wit in their roles (if they'd ramped up to the Alfred Molina level, say), that would have been welcome. Oh, almost forgot: Molina's ostrich racer is outraged at government taxes. If big government can't leave a man alone to race his ostriches, they're all Alamutist sympathizers.

The Promotion

(Directed by Steve Conrad; starring Seann William Scott, John C. Reilly; 2008)

The Promotion is a human comedy about two supermarket employees who are always ill at ease. It's their state of being. I felt a little ill at ease watching it because I was never quite sure whether I was supposed to be laughing at them or feeling sorry for them. It's one of those off-balance movies that seems to be searching for the right tone.

The setting: a Chicago supermarket. The central characters: Doug (Seann William Scott), thirty-three, a loyal employee, and Richard (John C. Reilly), mid-thirties, a Canadian who has immigrated to America with his Scottish wife, Laurie (Lili Taylor), and their daughter. Doug is recently married to Jen (Jenna Fischer). When their supermarket chain decides to open a new store, the two men are in line for a promotion to store manager.

They both desperately desire and need this job. Doug has convinced his wife he's a "shoo-in," and they invest all of their savings in a nonrefundable deposit on a house. Richard is a recovering alcoholic and drug addict, now in AA, trying to prove he is a trustworthy husband and father. The two men fight for the job not in a slapstick way but in an understated, underhanded way that Doug feels bad about, Richard not so much. ("We're all just out here to get some food," Richard philosophizes. "Sometimes we bump into each other.")

The movie is unusually quiet and introspective for a comedy. Doug provides a narration, and Richard gets one of his own in the form of a self-help tape he obsessively listens to. Doug decides Richard is a "nice guy" and observes, "all Canadians are nice." That's before Richard fakes an injury to lodge a dreaded "in-store complaint" that could cost Doug his job.

Richard himself is on a self-destruct mission. Consider an episode when Doug hits a young black man who has thrown a bottle of Yoo-Hoo at him in the parking lot. Doug apologizes to a "community forum," backed up by a panel including Richard and the store's board of directors. He says something about a "few bad apples." Apology accepted. Afterward, however, when they're all standing around relieved, Richard tells one of the community leaders, "You are not a black apple to me." Explaining this digs him in deeper, until he's reduced to speechlessness. He has a gift for saying the wrong things at the wrong times.

Richard actually is nice at times, however. As a member of a motorcycle gang, he once watched his fellow members roar through a toll gate without paying, and then sheepishly told the collector, "I'll pay for them all." Doug empathizes with Richard, even to the point of defending him to the board, but he feels rotten inside: Having lied to his wife that he has the job, he finds a present of long-sleeve shirts they can't afford. He's afraid he's stuck in the ranks of the short-sleeve guys.

I was interested in the fates of these two men, but mildly. I was expected to laugh, but I only smiled. Some of the race-based situations made me feel uncomfortable. All of the characters, especially the straight-arrow chairman of the board (Gil Bellows), needed to be pushed further into the realms of comedy. More could have been done with the store's other employees. At the end of *The Promotion*, I wondered what the atmosphere was like on the set every day. How does it feel to make a movie where the characters don't seem sure who they are?

The Punisher: War Zone

(Directed by Lexi Alexander; starring Ray Stevenson, Dominic West; 2008)
You used to be able to depend on a bad film being poorly made. No longer. *The Punisher: War Zone* is one of the best-made bad movies I've seen. It looks great, it hurtles through its paces, and it is well acted. The sound track is like elevator music if the elevator were in a death plunge. The special effects are state of the art. Its only flaw is that it's disgusting.

There's a big audience for disgusting, and I confidently predict the movie will "win the weekend," if not very many hearts and minds. Here you will see a man's kidney ripped out and eaten, a chair leg pushed through a head via the eyeball, a roomful of men wiped out by the Punisher revolving upside down from the chandelier and firing machine guns with both hands, a widow and her wee girl threatened with mayhem, heads sliced off, victims impaled and skewered, and the villain thrown into a machine that crushes glass bottles in much the same way concrete is mixed.

The glass-crushing machine caught my eye. Billy (Dominic West) is socked into it by the Punisher (Ray Stevenson) and revolves up to his neck in cutting edges while screaming many, many four-letter words, which, under the circumstances, are appropriate.

What confused me is that nearby in the same factory there is a conveyor belt carrying large lumps of hamburger or something. I expected Billy to emerge as ground round, but then I thought, how much ground glass can you really add to ground round? It's not often that you see meat processing and bottle crushing done in adjacent operations in the same factory. I was looking for the saltwater taffy mixer.

Billy survives his ordeal and announces to his henchmen, "From now on, my name is Jigsaw." This is after he has had operations, apparently lasting only minutes by the movie's time line, to stitch up his face with twine. He now looks like the exhibit in the entrance lobby of the Texas Chainsaw Museum, and one eye looks painfully introspective.

The movie is not heavy on plot. By my Timex Indiglo, there was no meaningful exposition at all during the first fifteen minutes, just men getting slaughtered. Then things slow down enough to reveal that the Punisher, aka Frank Castle, who avenged the murder of his family in an earlier film, has now killed a good guy who was father to little Grace (Stephanie Janusauskas) and husband to Angela (Julie Benz), who will Never Be Able to Forgive Him for What He's Done, nor should she, but she will.

The city, Montreal playing New York, has a small population, consisting only of good guys and bad guys and not much of anybody else. I'd get out, too. It's the kind of violence the president should fly over in Air Force One and regard sadly through the window. It goes without saying that the bad guys are unable to shoot the Punisher with their machine guns. That's consistent with the epidemic of malfunctioning machine guns in all recent super-violent films. Yet the Punisher kills a couple dozen hoodlums with his machine guns, while spinning upside-down under that chandelier.

Now pause to think with me. Everyone around the table is heavily armed. More armed men bust in through the door. The revolving Punisher is suspended in the center of the room. Because of the logic of the laws of physical motion, most of the time he is shooting away from any individual bad guy. How can they possibly miss hitting him? It's so hard these days, getting good help.

The Punisher: War Zone is the third in a series of Punisher movies.

It follows *The Punisher* (1989), starring Dolph Lundgren, and *The Punisher* (2004), starring Thomas Jane and John Travolta. Since the second film has the same title as the first, it's hard to tell them apart, but why would you want to? My fellow critic Bill Stamets, settling down for the screening, shared with me that he watched the 2004 movie for his homework. I did my algebra.

Push

(DIRECTED BY PAUL MCGUIGAN; STARRING CHRIS EVANS, DAKOTA FANNING; 2009)
Push has vibrant cinematography and decent acting, but I'm blasted if I know what it's about. Oh, I understand how the characters are paranormals, and how they're living in a present that was changed in the past, among enemies who are trying to change the future. I know they can read minds and use telekinesis to move things. I know they're a later generation of a Nazi experiment gone wrong, and the U.S. Army wants them for super-soldiers.

But that's all simply the usual horsefeathers to set up the situation. What are they *doing*? The answer to that involves a MacGuffin that would have Hitchcock harrumphing and telling Alma, "Oh, dear, they really have allowed themselves to get carried away." The MacGuffin is a briefcase. Yes, like in *Pulp Fiction*, but this time we know what's in it. It's a drug or serum that (is the only thing that?) kills paranormals. And the Division desperately wants it.

I'm not sure if the Division is part of the army or against it. I know that the telekinetic Nick (Chris Evans) is hiding from it in Hong Kong, and that the Pusher Cassie (Dakota Fanning) finds him there and brings along the briefcase (I think), and that she's followed there by most of the other characters, including Kira (Camilla Belle) and the Division agent Henry (Djimon Hounsou), who is another Pusher. Pushing involves not drugs but Pushing into other people's minds.

Kira is said to be the only paranormal who ever survived the deadly serum. But why did they want her dead? And who are they? And why is it so urgent to find the briefcase, which contains a syringe filled with the serum? This is an especially perplexing question for me because when the syringe was being filled to kill Kira, it looked to me like the label on the bottle of medicine clearly said "B-12," an excellent curative for anemia, which none of the characters has a problem with.

Apart from the MacGuffin, the movie is wall to wall with the Talking Killer Syndrome. Never have more people pointed more guns at more heads and said more words without anyone getting shot. Even if they are telekinetic and can point the guns without holding them.

All of these people, and others, speak very earnestly about Pushing, and they plot to outwit and outthink enemy Pushers, and clearly they are in a lot deeper than the audience is ever likely to get. It's like you're listening to shop talk in a shop that doesn't make anything you've ever seen.

Dakota Fanning's Cassie claims at one point that she's "older than twelve," but I dunno. Her mother would probably not have allowed her to fly off to Hong Kong alone, wearing a miniskirt and with purple streaks in her hair, but her mother has been killed, which is part of her problem. She does get a little drunk, which provides the movie's only laugh. Dakota's real mother probably told her, "Dakota, honey, why don't you take the role and get to see Hong Kong?" If that's what happened, she has the best reason of anybody for being in this movie.

Quantum of Solace

(Directed by Marc Forster; starring Daniel Craig, Olga Kurylenko; 2008)
OK, I'll say it. Never again. Don't ever let this happen again to James Bond. *Quantum of Solace* is his twenty-second film, and he will survive it, but for

the twenty-third it is necessary to go back to the drawing board and redesign from the ground up. Please understand: James Bond is not an action hero! He is too good for that. He is an attitude. Violence for him is an annoyance. He exists for the foreplay and the cigarette. He rarely encounters a truly evil villain. More often a comic opera buffoon with hired goons in matching jumpsuits.

Quantum of Solace has the worst title in the series save for *Never Say Never Again*, words that could have been used by Kent after King Lear utters the saddest line in all of Shakespeare: "Never! Never! Never! Never! Never!" The movie opens with Bond involved in a reckless car chase on the tollway that leads through mountain tunnels from Nice through Monte Carlo and down to Portofino in Italy, where Edward Lear lies at rest with his cat, Old Foss. I have driven that way many a time. It is a breathtaking drive.

You won't find that out here. The chase, with Bond under constant machine-gun fire, is so quickly cut and so obviously composed of incomprehensible CGI that we're essentially looking at bright colors bouncing off one another, intercut with Bond at the wheel and POV shots of approaching monster trucks. Let's all think together. When has an action hero ever, even once, been killed by machine-gun fire, no matter how many hundreds of rounds? The hit men should simply reject them and say, "No can do, Boss. They never work in this kind of movie."

The chase has no connection to the rest of the plot, which is routine for Bond, but it's about the movie's last bow to tradition. In *Quantum of Solace* he will share no cozy quality time with the Bond girl (Olga Kurylenko). We fondly remember the immortal names of Pussy Galore, Xenia Onatopp, and Plenty O'Toole, who I have always suspected was a drag queen. In this film, who do we get? Are you ready for this? Camille. That's it. Camille. Not even Camille Squeal. Or Cammy Miami. Or Miss O'Toole's friend, Cam Shaft.

Daniel Craig remains a splendid Bond, one of the best. He is handsome, agile, muscular, dangerous. Everything but talkative. I didn't count, but I think M (Judi Dench) has more dialogue than 007. Bond doesn't look like the urge to peel Camille has even entered his mind.

He blows up a hotel in the middle of a vast, barren, endless Bolivian desert. It's a luxury hotel, with angular W Hotel–style minimalist room furniture you might cut your legs on and a bartender who will stir or shake you any drink, but James has become a regular bloke who orders lager. Who are the clients at this highest of high-end hotels? Lawrence of Arabia, obviously, and millionaires who hate green growing things. Conveniently, when the hotel blows up, the filmmakers don't have to contend with adjacent buildings, traffic, pedestrians, skylines, or anything else. Talk about your blue screen. Nothing better than the azure desert sky.

Why is he in Bolivia? In pursuit of a global villain, whose name is not Goldfinger, Scaramanga, Drax, or Le Chiffre, but . . . Dominic Greene (Mathieu Amalric). What is Dominic's demented scheme to control the globe? As a start, the fiend desires to corner the water supply of . . . Bolivia. Ohooo! Nooo! This twisted design, revealed to Bond after at least an hour of death-defying action, reminds me of the famous laboratory mouse who was introduced into a labyrinth. After fighting his way for days through baffling corridors and down dead ends, finally, *finally*, parched and starving, the little creature crawled at last to the training button and hurled his tiny body against it. And what rolled down the chute as his reward? A licorice gum ball.

Dominic Greene lacks a headquarters on the moon or on the floor of the sea. He operates out of an ordinary shipping warehouse with loading docks. His evil transport is provided by forklifts and pickup trucks. Bond doesn't have to creep out to the ledge of an underground volcano to spy on him. He just walks up to the chain-link fence and peers through. Greene could get useful security tips from Wal-Mart.

There is no Q in *Quantum of Solace*, except in the title. No Miss Moneypenny at all. M now has a male secretary. That Judi Dench, what a fox. Bond doesn't even size him up. He learned his lesson with Plenty. This Bond, he doesn't bring much to the party. Daniel Craig can play suave, and he can be funny, and Brits are born doing double entendre. Craig is a fine actor. Here they lock him down. I repeat: James Bond is not an action hero! Leave the action to your Jason Bournes. This is a swampy old world. The deeper we sink in, the more we need James Bond to stand above it.

R

· · · · · · · · ·

RED

<small>(DIRECTED BY ROBERT SCHWENTKE; STARRING BRUCE WILLIS, MORGAN FREEMAN;</small>
    2010)

This would have been a hell of a cast when we were all younger. *RED* plays like a movie made for my Aunt Mary, who was always complaining, "Honey, I don't like the pictures anymore because I don't know who any of the actors are." If the name Ernest Borgnine sounds familiar, here's the movie for you.

Borgnine at ninety-three is still active and has a project "in development," I learn from IMDb, even if it's ominously titled *Death Keeps Coming*. Says here it's a supernatural Western being produced by Tarantino. Borgnine himself is a heck of a guy. I flew out of Cartagena with him one morning with a terrible hangover, and we got stranded in some forgotten Colombian airport where he fed me aspirin crushed in milk. An actor like that is a role model.

Bruce Willis stars in the title role of *RED*, which refers to his alert level ("retired: extremely dangerous") and not his hair. He's a former CIA agent who discovers bad guys want to kill him. So he summons the members of his old killing squad and they prepare a defense. The team includes Joe Matheson (Morgan Freeman), Marvin Boggs (John Malkovich), Victoria (Helen Mirren), and Ivan (Brian Cox).

(Notes: Victoria requires no second name because she is a woman in a thriller; Ivan is a Russian because the Russian in every thriller is named Ivan; Malkovich may have taken the role because he is never considered for characters named Boggs; and Freeman reveals early that he is dying of liver cancer. We know that as the black member of the team he must die first, because that's how he would have wanted it. So once again poor Morgan

Freeman is hung out to dry. He'd rather play the villain. As he once explained to me: The villain is usually the most interesting character in the movie, and one thing you *know* is, he'll still be around for the last scene.)

In addition to his old comrades, Frank Moses takes along Sarah Ross (Mary-Louise Parker), a telephone operator, for his retirement plan. He's fallen in love with her voice. He explains she has to go on the run with him because her life is in danger. Like any federal employee, she finds this reasonable. Her life will be much safer with a man who is the target of thousands of rounds of automatic weapon fire. The villains in thrillers are such bad shots they'd suck at video games.

The bad guys are in the upper reaches of the CIA, and the conspiracy reaches all the way to a vice president with connections to a huge private defense contractor. This man is played by Richard Dreyfuss, who subtly signals to us, "You only *think* this is my Dick Cheney imitation, but if the studio let me loose, I could nail this role." Are sinister Dick Cheney roles growing uncommonly frequent? Hollywood is always fearful of running out of villains and, having run through Russians, Chinese, Nazis, and Mongols, seems to have fallen upon poor Cheney with relief.

RED is neither a good movie nor a bad one. It features actors we like doing things we wish were more interesting. I guess the movie's moral is, these old people are still tougher than the young ones. You want tough? I'll show you tough. In one scene, Helen Mirren is gut-shot and a blood stain spreads on her white dress. In a closing scene not a day later, she's perfectly chipper, and has had time to send the dress out to the cleaners.

Red Riding Hood

(DIRECTED BY CATHERINE HARDWICKE; STARRING AMANDA SEYFRIED, GARY OLDMAN; 2011)

Of the classics of world literature crying out to be adapted as a sexual fantasy for teenage girls, surely *Red Hiding Hood* is far down on the list. Here's a movie that cross-pollinates the *Twilight* formula with a werewolf, and adds a girl who always wears a hooded red cape, although I don't recall her doing any riding. It's easy to imagine a story conference in which they said: "Hey! Let's switch the vampires with a werewolf and recycle the theme of a virgin attracted to a handsome but dangerous hunk, only let's get two hunks!"

What this inspiration fails to consider is that while a young woman might toy with the notion of a vampire boyfriend, she might not want to mate with a wolf. And although she might think it was, like, cool to live in the woods in Oregon, she might not want to live in the Black Forest hundreds of years ago because, like, can you text from there?

Red Riding Hood has the added inconvenience of being dreadfully serious about a plot so preposterous it demands to be filmed by Monty Python. The only scene that amused me was a dream sequence where Grandma says, "The better to eat you with." I'm asking myself, "How can Red Riding Hood dream about dialogue in her own fairy tale when she hasn't even gone over the hill and through the dale to Grandmother's house yet?"

The movie was directed by Catherine Hardwicke, who made *Twilight*. It opens with aerial shots of hundreds of square miles of forests, dotted here and there by stubby, grim castles. Then we meet the narrator, Valerie, who always wears a red cape. She is but a lass when she steals away with her prepubescent boyfriend, Peter, so they can trap a bunny rabbit and possibly slit its throat, although the camera moves away from the bunny at the crucial moment to focus upon their faces as the young actors think, "OK, this is where they flash forward and we are replaced by Amanda Seyfried and Shiloh Fernandez."

They live in a village which is one of the most peculiar nonplaces in the history of production design. Because the original fairy tale was by the Brothers Grimm, I suppose there's a chance the village is in Germany, but it exists outside time and space and seems to have been inspired by little plastic souvenir villages in airport gift shops. You know, populated mit Hansel und Gretel.

Valerie (Seyfried) wants to marry Peter (Fernandez), who is a woodchopper, but her parents have promised her to a rich kid named

Henry (Max Irons). The village since time immemorial has been terrorized by a werewolf, who turns up when the moon is full and must be pacified by a pathetic little piggie left chained to a stump, lest it develop an appetite for villagers. Alarmingly, Valerie's sister is found dead, amid distracting cone-shaped haystacks dotted with blue flowers, which is not the sort of detail you want to be noticing when a young girl has been killed but (spoiler) not eaten by a werewolf.

The villagers send off for Father Solomon (Gary Oldman), a famed werewolf fighter, and he arrives with his band of warriors and a very large metal elephant. Solomon, an expert, knows that werewolves are not werewolves all the time, and in between full moons take the form of men. Therefore, one of the villagers must be a werewolf. This has enormous implications for Valerie's possible future love life.

But I know you, my readers. Right now you aren't thinking about Valerie's romance. You're thinking, "Did I just read that Father Solomon arrived with a very large metal elephant?" Yes, he did. A very large metal elephant. I thought the same thing. That must have been a *hell* of a lot of trouble. Even harder than Herzog dragging the boat over the mountain. Showing Father Solomon's men dragging a metal elephant through the woods—there's your movie right there.

Repo Men

(Directed by Miguel Sapochnik; starring Jude Law, Forest Whitaker; 2010)
Repo Men makes sci-fi's strongest possible case for universal health care. In a world of the near future, where they still drive current cars, a giant corporation named the Union will provide you with a human heart, kidney, liver, or other organ. Let's say a pancreas costs you, oh, $312,000. No, it's not covered by insurance, but the sales guy says, "You owe it to yourself and your family." For a guy in need of a pancreas, this is an eloquent argument. Interest rates are around 19 percent.

Now let's say you can't make the payments. If you fall behind more than three months, they send around a repo man who shoots you with a stun gun, slices open your body, reaches in, and repossesses the organ. To be sure, he puts on latex gloves first. I don't believe the gun kills you, but after they leave you on the floor with an organ missing, your prognosis is poor. Let's say you were conscious during such a procedure. Would it hurt? You bet it would. At one point in the film, our heroes Remy and Beth (Jude Law and Alice Braga) decide the only way to outwit the company's computer is to repossess themselves. He has a donor heart, and as for Beth, her heart is her own, but it is surrounded by guest organs. They don't actually carve themselves open and *remove* the organs. No, that would be fatal. But they have to reach inside each other with a bar-code scanner and scan them in. As Remy carves into his chest with a big old knife, you oughta see the way his fist clenches and he grits his teeth. He's thinking, I wish I had the public option.

I don't know if the makers of this film intended it as a comedy. A preview audience regarded it with polite silence, and left the theater in an orderly fashion. There are chases and shootouts, of course, and a standard overwrought thriller sound track, with the percussion guy hammering on cymbals and a big bass drum. Even then, you wonder.

Remy and Beth find themselves locked in a corridor with a dozen guys from the evil corporation who are well armed. They dodge the bullets and wham some guys with karate, and then Remy pauses, strips off his shirt, reveals his bare (pre-repo) chest, and is wearing kinky leather pants with buckles. From scabbards in the back, he withdraws two long knives that help explain why he wasn't seated earlier in the scene. He slices some other guys. Then he shouts "Hacksaw!" to Beth, and she slides it to him on the floor, and he whirls around and *decapitates* three guys, it looked like, although it happened real fast.

What are people supposed to think? Is this an action scene, or satire? Does it make any difference? I dunno. I know the actors play everything with deep, earnest seriousness. The head of the Union corporation is Frank (Liev Schreiber), who demands complete dedication from his repo men and is humorously not humorous. Maybe he's not the head of the whole Union, but only their immediate boss. The Union's headquarters building is maybe one hundred stories high, and Remy stumbles into a room with guys in white suits working at tables that stretch farther than a football field. There are enough props in this movie to clean out the organ department at Moo & Oink's. When I say they're up to their elbows in blood, I mean it. This work takes its toll. Remy's friend at work is a repo man named Jake, played by Forest Whitaker. Like most Forest Whitaker characters and Whitaker himself, he is a warm, nice man. I noticed for the second time in a week (after *Our Family Wedding*) that Whitaker has lost a lot of weight and looks great. I hope the extra pounds weren't repo'ed.

Reprise

(DIRECTED BY JOACHIM TRIER; STARRING ESPEN KLOUMAN HOINER, ANDERS DANIELSEN; 2008)

If there was ever a movie that seems written and directed by its characters, that movie is Joachim Trier's *Reprise*. Here is an ambitious and romantic portrait of two young would-be writers that seems made by ambitious and romantic would-be filmmakers. In the movie, the young heroes idolize Norway's greatest living writer, who tells one of them his novel is good and shows promise, except for the ending, where he shouldn't have been so poetic. The movie itself is good and shows promise, except for the ending, when Trier shouldn't have been so poetic. Not only does *Reprise* generate itself, it contains its own review.

The twenty-three-year-old heroes are Erik and Phillip. They seem to be awfully nice boys who have some growing-up to do. It opens with the two of them simultaneously dropping the manuscripts of their first novels into a post box. Then an anonymous narrator takes over and describes some possible futures of the characters and their novels. We will be hearing a lot from that narrator, and he, along with Erik and Phillip and Phillip's girlfriend, Kari, remind us inescapably of Francois Truffaut's *Jules and Jim*.

The movie is set in Oslo, with a visit to Paris. I have been to Oslo, and it's nowhere near the gray arrangement of apartment blocks and perfunctory landscaping that we see in the movie. (Nor is it Paris.) I have met Norwegians, who are nowhere near the bland, narcissistic Erik and

Phillip. The big problem with the movie is our difficulty in working up much real interest in the characters. They're not compelling. Even when Phillip becomes so obsessed with Kari that he has to be accommodated in a mental institution, and even after (back on the streets) he takes her to Paris on the exact anniversary of their first trip there, it's impossible to see him as passionate. His emotions never seem to be at full volume.

The high point, passion-wise, comes during their Paris trip. His mother has confiscated his photos of Kari, fearing they will trigger a relapse. So in Paris he poses her to take them again, Kari even helpfully hitching up her skirt to more closely match the original. They visit the same café (I think). Then they check into the same hotel and make love in (one assumes) much the same way.

The movie finds it necessary to do something I'm growing weary of: It depicts their love-making at greater length than depth. They're seen in profile, in dim lighting, with a sound track that reminded me of the Hondells ("First gear—it's all right. Second gear—hold on tight").

After their breathing reaches overdrive, they disengage and she soon enough says, "You don't still love me." That word *love* is such a troublemaker. For characters like those in the movie, it represents an attainment like feeling patriotic or missing your dog. It's a state not consuming, not transcendent, but obligatory.

I also wearied of Phillip's countdowns. At a party, he bets himself Kari will turn and look at him at "zero" when he counts down from "ten." He tempts fate on his bicycle, in traffic, by closing his eyes while counting down. It's the kind of numerology that was charming in *Me and You and Everyone We Know,* when the heroine imagines that the sidewalk stretching ahead of her represents the life span of herself and the guy she likes, and they're halfway to the corner. It was fanciful and fetching in that film, but disposable in this one—indeed, bordering on idiotic, because Phillip isn't that kind of person. For him the counting down not only seems to represent (a) something meaningful, but also (b) age-appropriate. If I were Kari, I'd jump ship at "seven," and actually she does tell Phillip, "I can't take it any more." Bonus points for taking it as long as she does.

Erik has a girlfriend, too, the seldom-seen (by his friends) Lillian, whom he pulls apart from because he fears she might not fit in with his friends, who therefore seldom see her. The characters meet in cafés, restaurants, one another's apartments, lakesides, and punk concerts. They take music very seriously, or say they do, but with fans like these, punk audiences would applaud politely.

Then there is the matter of their novels and the title of one of them, *Prosopopeia*. Well, Norway's greatest living writer thinks it's a good title, just as the book is a "good" book. You get the impression that, at his age, "great" would trigger a seizure. I never got any clear idea of what the novels were about, not even during a torturous television chat show that later triggers the greatest living writer's observation that TV is not the ideal medium for discussing literature. The cinema is an ideal medium for considering characters like those in *Reprise*, but you'd have to see *Jules and Jim* to find out why.

Revolver

(DIRECTED BY GUY RITCHIE; STARRING JASON STATHAM, RAY LIOTTA; 2007)

Guy Ritchie's *Revolver* is a frothing mad film that thrashes against its very sprocket holes in an attempt to bash its brains out against the projector. It seems designed to punish the audience for buying tickets. It is a "thriller" without thrills, constructed in a meaningless jumble of flashbacks and flash-forwards and subtitles and mottos and messages and scenes that are deconstructed, reconstructed, and self-destructed. I wanted to signal the projectionist to put a gun to it.

The plot. What is the plot? Jason Statham has spent seven years in jail between a con man in the cell on one side and a chess master on the other. Back on the street, he walks into a casino run by his old enemy Ray Liotta and wins a fortune at the table. Did he cheat or what? I dunno. Liotta sics some hit men on him. Then two mysterious strangers (Vincent Pastore and Andre Benjamin) materialize in Statham's life at just such moments when they are in a position to save it. Who, oh who, could these two men, one of whom plays chess, possibly be?

The movie begins with a bunch of sayings that will be repeated end-lessly like mantras throughout the film. Chris Cabin at filmcritic.com thinks these have some connection with the Kabbalah beliefs of Ritchie and his wife, Madonna. I know zilch about the Kabbalah, but if he's right, and if Ritchie follows them, I would urgently warn other directors to stay clear of the Kabbalah. Judging by this film, it encourages you to mistake hopeless confusion for pure reason.

Oh, this film angered me. It kept turning back on itself, biting its own tail, doubling back through scenes with less and less meaning and purpose, chanting those sayings as if to hammer us down into accepting them. It employed three editors. Skeleton crew. Some of the acting is better than the film deserves. Make that all of the acting. Actually, the film stock itself is better than the film deserves. You know when sometimes a film catches fire inside a projector? If it happened with this one, I suspect the audience might cheer.

Ricky

(DIRECTED BY FRANÇOIS OZON; STARRING ALEXANDRA LAMY, SERGI LOPEZ; 2010)

Parables are stories about other people that help us live our own lives. The problem with *Ricky* is that the lesson of the parable is far from clear, and nobody is likely to encounter this situation in their own life. That would be pretty much impossible. The story begins in gritty realism, ends in pure fantasy, and leaves out most of the alphabet as it makes its way from A to Z.

The story begins with Katie (Alexandra Lamy), a morose French factory worker who has been abandoned, she thinks, by the man she lives with. It's hard to pay the rent. We flash back to the beginning, see her living with her peppy seven-year-old daughter, Lisa (Melusine Mayance), and working in a French chemical factory. There she meets a Spanish worker named Paco (Sergi Lopez). He's warm and attracted, they smile, they live together and have a baby.

These events take place in a series of time jumps that are momentarily jolting, but easy enough to follow. Not so easy is what happens to their son, Ricky (Arthur Peyret), as he grows up. In appearance he seems at first like an outtake from *Babies,* but then when Paco cares for him at home alone, Katie discovers bruises on his shoulders. Paco is enraged to be accused of child beating and stalks out, explaining Katie's opening scene.

These scenes are absorbingly created and well acted, and we settle in for a French slice of life. I can hardly deal with any more of the film without revealing details. Here goes, after a spoiler warning.

Those aren't bruises, they're the beginning of wings. Yes. Little wings, which at first look so much like poultry parts that Katie tape-measures a turkey wing at the supermarket, just to get an idea. One night, in slow-mo, the wings begin to sprout tiny feathers, which in close-up look like one of those life forms you don't want to make friends with. Soon the little lad has flapped his way to the top of an armoire.

No, he isn't an angel. Maybe more likely the result of his parents working at the chemical factory, although the movie doesn't make that a point. It doesn't much make anything a point. Katie and Lisa are about as amazed as if the child had a lot of hair on its head. You'd think babies with wings were born every day. Later, after Paco rejoins the family, baby Ricky gets a little injury, and the family doctor seems, to me, insufficiently amazed. Surely this is an OMG case?

Because the film is directed by the esteemed Francois Ozun (*Swimming Pool, Under the Sand, See the Sea*), I waited to see where it would take me. At the end, I wasn't sure. The ending has the form of a statement, but not the content of one. Its last half seems to be building to a life lesson, and perhaps the lesson is: "Parents! If you have a baby with wings, don't be this calm about it!"

I couldn't help myself. All during the film I was distracted by questions of aeronautics. In early scenes, those wings are way too small to allow a healthy baby to fly. Even later, the ratio of wingspan to baby weight seems way off. A scene where Ricky breaks free and flies around a supermarket seems designed for comedy, but doesn't play that way. And what kind of a cockamamie idea is it to hold a press conference and let Ricky fly with only Katie holding a string around his ankle? This is worse than the hot air balloon kid, if there had been one.

The film is bewildering. I don't know what its terms are, and it doesn't match any of mine. I found myself regarding it more and more as an inexplicable curiosity. It's so curiously flat in tone that when a baby grows wings and flies (think about that!), people in the film and in the audience seem to watch with no more than mild interest. *Ricky* makes a good case for lurid melodrama.

Robin Hood

(DIRECTED BY RIDLEY SCOTT; STARRING RUSSELL CROWE, CATE BLANCHETT; 2010)

Little by little, title by title, innocence and joy is being drained out of the movies. What do you think of when you hear the name of Robin Hood? I think of Errol Flynn, Sean Connery, and the Walt Disney character. I see Robin lurking in Sherwood Forest, in love with Maid Marian (Olivia de Havilland or Audrey Hepburn), and roistering with Friar Tuck and the Merry Men. I see a dashing swashbuckler.

That Robin Hood is nowhere to be found in Ridley Scott's new *Robin Hood*, starring Russell Crowe as a warrior just back from fighting in the Third Crusade. Now Richard is dead, and Robin is essentially an unemployed mercenary. This story is a prequel. It takes place entirely *before* Robin got to be a folk hero. The idea of taking from the rich and giving to the poor was still in storyboard form. Grieving Richard the Lionheart and now faced with the tyrant King John, he leads an uprising.

This war broadens until, in the words of the movie's synopsis, "it will forever alter the balance of world power." That's not all: "Robin will become an eternal symbol of freedom for his people." Not bad for a man who, by general agreement, did not exist. Although various obscure bandits and ne'er-do-wells inspired ancient ballads about such a figure, our image of him is largely a fiction from the nineteenth century.

But so what? In for a penny, in for a pound. After the death of Richard, Robin Hood raises, arms, and fields an army to repel a French army as it lands on an English beach in wooden craft that look uncannily like World War II troop carriers at Normandy. His men, wielding broadswords, backed by archers, protected from enemy arrows by their shields, engage the enemy in a last act devoted almost entirely to nonstop CGI and stunt carnage in which a welter of warriors clashes in confused alarms and excursions, and Russell Crowe frequently appears in the foreground to whack somebody.

Subsequently, apparently, Robin pensioned his militia and retired to Sherwood Forest to play tag with Friar Tuck. That's my best guess; at the end the film informs us, "and so the legend begins," leaving us with the impression we walked in early.

Ah, you say, but what of Maid Marian? In this telling, Marion (Cate Blanchett) is not a maid but a widow, and not a merry one. At one point she threatens to unman Robin with her dagger, which is unlike the Maid Marians I've known and loved. Blanchett plays the role with great class and breeding, which is all wrong, I think. She's the kind of woman who would always be asking Robin, "Why do you let that smelly so-called friar hang around you like a fanboy?"

If you listen closely to the commercials, you may hear of a royal edict being issued against "Robin of the Hood." A hood, in medieval English, was, of course, a wood, or forest—a point that may be lost on many of the commercial's viewers.

Robin Hood is a high-tech and well-made violent action picture using the name of Robin Hood for no better reason than that it's an established brand not protected by copyright. I cannot discover any sincere interest on the part of Scott, Crowe, or the writer Brian Helgeland in any previous version of Robin Hood. Their Robin is another weary retread of the muscular macho slaughterers who with interchangeable names stand at the center of one overwrought bloodbath after another.

Have we grown weary of the delightful aspects of the Robin Hood legend? Is witty dialogue no longer permitted? Are Robin and Marion no longer allowed to engage in a spirited flirtation? Must their relationship seem like high-level sexual negotiations? How many people need to be covered in boiling oil for Robin Hood's story to be told these days? How many parents will be misled by the PG-13 rating? Must children go directly from animated dragons to skewering and decapitation, with no interval of cheerful storytelling?

The photography is, however, remarkable, and Crowe and the others are filled with fierce energy. Ridley Scott is a fine director for work like this, although in another world Hollywood would let him make smarter films. God, he must be tired of enormous battle scenes.

Note: The film was the opening night attraction at the 2010 Cannes Film Festival. There must be a reason for that.

Rush Hour 3

(DIRECTED BY BRETT RATNER; STARRING CHRIS TUCKER, JACKIE CHAN; 2007)
I like this movie about as much as it's possible to like a movie with a two-star rating. Given its materials, it couldn't have been much better, but it's every bit as good as it is, if you see what I mean. Once you realize it's only going to be so good, you settle back and enjoy that modest degree of goodness, which is at least not badness, and besides, if you're watching *Rush Hour 3*, you obviously didn't have anything better to do anyway.

The filmmakers didn't either, I guess. It has been six years since *Rush Hour 2*, and unless you believe that director Brett Ratner and his stars, Chris Tucker and Jackie Chan, spent all that time turning down offers for a sequel, it seems fairly likely that this is a case of returning once more with a bucket before the well runs dry. Tucker is again Carter, the motormouth LAPD cop who's always in trouble, and Chan is again Lee, the ace Hong Kong cop called in to partner with him. This is, you realize, a formula. A friend of mine (I think it is me) calls these Wunza Movies. You know, wunza L.A. cop and wunza cop from China, and neither wunza guy you want to mess with.

Curious how Carter is always being hauled in from a punishment gig like traffic cop and being assigned to super-important cases that will require him to investigate backstage at the Folies Bergere in Paris, etc. This time one of Lee's old pals, Ambassador Han, has been shot in L.A., probably by a Chinese Triad gang, who are getting to be as handy as the Mafia for movie plots. Lee, in town as the ambassador's bodyguard, runs after the shooter in one of those impossible Jackie Chan chase scenes; it used to be we were amazed by his stunts, but these days I find myself even more amazed that he can still run that far.

Lee partners with his old friend Carter, and they go to the hospital to question the ambassador's beautiful daughter, Soo Yung (Jingchu Zhang). This produces the movie's funniest line, by Carter: "Let's go to the gift shop and get her a little teddy bear." Soo Yung had possession of an envelope with key evidence her father was going to use in testimony before the World Court. The envelope is, of course, this movie's MacGuffin, and was stolen from Soo Yung at her karate academy.

The cops go there and have a battle with the world's tallest man (Sun Ming Ming). I think he's the same man who got married recently and was about twice as tall as his bride. Or maybe he's another tall guy—naw, it has to be the same guy. Yao Ming, the basketball player, is only seven feet six inches, and Sun Ming Ming is seven feet nine inches. When Jackie Chan engages him in kung fu, he has to call on some of his wall-climbing skills.

Anyway, the chase leads to Paris, where the fragrant Genevieve (Noemie Lenoir) appears. Her function in the film, apart from certain plot details, is—to appear, which she does to great effect. And soon Carter is backstage at the Folies Bergere, and all the time we know, just *know*, that the Eiffel Tower is in the background of so many shots for a reason.

Yes, there is a pursuit up and down the tower, with Jackie Chan doing the usual impossible things, although at fifty-three, he doesn't do all of his own stunts. What difference does it make? In these days of special effects, who can tell anyway? For years, I suspected that the only reason Jackie did the stunts himself was to provide footage for the shots during the closing credits, showing him waving cheerfully as he was taken to the hospital.

All of these events take place efficiently and I was amused, even in a dialogue sequence involving a "Mr. Yu" and a "Mr. Mee," in which "He's Mee" and "I'm Yu," and who's on first? If you are trapped in a rainstorm in front of a theater playing this picture, by all means go right in. You won't have a bad time, will feel affectionate toward Lee and Carter, and stay dry.

S

• • • • • • • • • •

Saint John of Las Vegas

(DIRECTED BY HUE RHODES; STARRING STEVE BUSCEMI, ROMANY MALCO; 2010)

If you were to view the trailer of *Saint John of Las Vegas,* it would probably look like a good time. It seems to have so much great stuff. Promise me a movie with Steve Buscemi, Sarah Silverman, Peter Dinklage, and Tim Blake Nelson, and I'm there. But this movie is all elbows. Nothing fits. It doesn't add up. It has some terrific free-standing scenes, but they need more to lean on.

Consider the burning man. This is a sideshow performer who wears a suit designed to burst into flames. Unfortunately, the suit has malfunctioned and he can't take it off until the fuel is exhausted. He waits it out on a folding chair behind the carnival midway, consumed in flames every thirty seconds. That's funny, especially when he's dying for a cigarette. But . . . what? He exists only to be existing.

Well, not quite. The flaming also seems to fit into the movie's overall symbolism. The screenplay, we learn, was written by the director Hue Rhodes, based on the story by Dante Alighieri. That name may not ring a bell with a lot of moviegoers and had better not be a question on the Tea Baggers' literacy test. We all recall that Dante's *Inferno* told the story of a journey into hell, with the poet Virgil as the tour guide.

In the movie, Steve Buscemi plays John Alighieri, an insurance claims adjuster who is assigned a partner named Virgil (Romany Malco) and sets off on a journey through the desert to Las Vegas (hell).

Let's have some fun. Dante's First Circle of Hell was Limbo. In the movie, that would be the main office of the insurance company. People in Limbo have trouble controlling their weaknesses. John's weakness is compulsive gambling. Second Circle is Lust. He lusts for Jill (Silverman), a chirpy coworker who labors in the next cubicle. Later, in a lap-dance bar, he undergoes but resists temptation from a stripper (Emmanuelle Chriqui), who sprained her neck in a car crash but tries to give him a lap dance from her wheelchair. It's her crash the insurance company doesn't want to pay the claim on.

Third Circle, Gluttony. In this circle are rain and hail, which the two drive through. Fourth Circle, Avarice. John dreams of winning the lottery and spends every dollar on scratch cards. Virgil also has greed, revealed later. Fifth Circle, Anger. They argue with a cop and arrive at a senseless flaming gateway in the desert, guarded by Tim Blake Nelson and other naked men with guns. Sixth Circle, Heresy. Virgil seems not to take the insurance company seriously.

Seventh Circle, Violence. In a used car lot, they are led into a trap and John, knocked senseless, barely escapes with his life. The lot is guarded by a savage dog, no doubt based on Cerberus, the watchdog of Hell. Eighth Circle, Fraud. John discovers the nature of a scheme to defraud the insurance company. Ninth and last Circle, Treason against God—or, in this case, Mr. Townsend (Dinklage), who is their boss at the insurance company.

If you recall Dante very well, or jot some reminders on your palm with a ballpoint, you can possibly follow the movie in this way. But if like most people your command of the *Inferno* is shaky, the film may seem disjointed and pointless. There is also this inescapable storytelling dilemma: Once you arrive in the Ninth Circle of Hell, what do you do for an encore?

The acting is first-rate. Buscemi is an apologetic loser who fled Vegas after losing his net worth, and now unwisely returns. Malco's Virgil, now that we think of it, is a guide who seems to have been this way before. Silverman's Jill is part temptress, part saint. It must have taken all of Rhodes's willpower to avoid naming her character "Beatrice," although of course Beatrice was Dante's guide into heaven. That would be the sequel.

And who is Saint John of Las Vegas? That would be John the Baptist or "John of the desert," divine messenger, not to be confused with the brother of Jesus. Why is he "of Las Vegas"? I think the answer must relate to John's gambling history. When Anna Dudak, my landlady on Burling Street, would take a trip to Las Vegas, her husband, Paul, would tell me she had gone to Lost Wages.

Sanctum

(DIRECTED BY ALISTER GRIERSON; STARRING RICHARD ROXBURGH, RHYS WAKEFIELD; 2011)

Sanctum tells the story of a terrifying adventure in an incompetent way. Some of it is exciting, the ending is involving, and all of it is a poster child for the horrors of 3-D used wrongly. The film is being heavily marketed as a "James Cameron Production," but if this were a "James Cameron Film," I suspect it would have fewer flaws and the use of 3-D would be much improved.

The movie, based on a true story, involves a scuba-diving expedition into the Esa-ala Caves of New Guinea, said to be the largest cave system in the world. The plan is to retrace an already explored route to reach a "base camp" somewhere far beneath the surface, and then to press on, perhaps to find how the surface water draining into the caves finds its way to the sea. There's no *need* to discover this, you understand, but after some loss of life, Frank (Richard Roxburgh), the leader of the expedition, tells his son, Josh (Rhys Wakefield), that only in a cave does he feel fully alive; the humdrum surface world is not for him and "human eyes have never seen this before."

After awkward opening scenes of almost startling inanity, we find ourselves deep inside the cave system, and our heroes deep in trouble. They are combining dangerous climbing with risky diving, and it's a good question why an inexperienced girlfriend was allowed to come along. Still, tactical errors are not what concerned me. I only wanted to figure out what was happening, and where, and why.

This movie should be studied in film classes as an example of inadequate film continuity. At no point are we oriented on our location in the cave as a whole or have a clear idea of what the current cave space looks like. If you recall Cameron's *Titanic*, its helpful early animation briefed us on the entire story of how the great ship sank. That was a great help in comprehending the events of its final hour. In *Sanctum*, there's a computer animation showing the known parts of the cave, but as the POV whizzes through caverns and tunnels, it achieves only a demonstration of computer animation itself. We learn damn little about the cave. The animated map even flips on its horizontal axis, apparently to show off. Hey, I can do stuff like that on my Mac, and then my hair is parted on the other side!

The movie is a case study of how not to use 3-D. *Sanctum* takes place in claustrophobic spaces with very low lighting, which are the last places you want to make look dimmer than they already are. The lighting apparently comes from battery-powered headlamps, and the characters are half in darkness and half in gloom. Now why put on a pair of glasses and turn down the lights?

One purpose of 3-D is to create the illusion of depth. One way to do this is to avoid violating the fourth wall by seeming to touch it. Let me give a famous example from *Jaws 3-D*. The problem with that movie is that when the shark attacked, it was so big its body touched the sides of the screen, and the 3-D illusion was lost. (The movie has a scene of an eel attack, and *that's* scary.)

Alas, the cinematographer of *Sanctum*, Jules O'Loughlin, consistently touches the side of the screen. He even has the curious practice of framing middle action with large, indistinct blocks of foreground stones and stuff. These are out of focus so that the midrange can look sharp, and 3-D only makes us wonder why the closer objects are less distinct. In close quarters he has to use many close-ups, and those, too, get old in a hurry in 3-D. The Brendan Fraser 3-D movie *Journey to the Center of the Earth* (2008) did a much better job of placing its actors in its spaces. Of course, the spaces were mostly f/x, but there you are.

In its editing continuity, *Sanctum* doesn't make clear how the actions of one character relate to another's. There is great spatial disorientation in the use of the close shots. There is a scene where a character gets in trouble underwater, and I invite anyone to explain exactly what happens. The movie has a tactic to distract from this visual confusion. Three team members follow many of the events from above on a large computer monitor. Alas, we don't see what they see. We only get reaction shots of them seeing it. Where does their screen image come from? Head-mounted webcams? A cam in that submersible lighting device? I dunno. How is the image transmitted? I doubt the cell phone service is great in a cave in the jungles of New Guinea. Maybe they set up a LAN?

How is it powered? They even complain about the batteries on their headlamp.

There are a few closing scenes that involve the ruthless reality of who survives in a cave and who doesn't. One of these involves Frank and Josh. We've had a long wait, but the scene works. It has absolutely no need for 3-D. I wonder if people will go to *Sanctum* thinking the James Cameron name is a guarantee of high-quality 3-D. Here is a movie that can only harm the reputations of Cameron and 3-D itself.

Scre4m

(DIRECTED BY WES CRAVEN; STARRING NEVE CAMPBELL, COURTENEY COX; 2011)

The great pleasure in the *Scream* movies is that the characters have seen other horror films. At times they talk as if they're in the chat room of a horror site. Wes Craven's *Scre4m*, the typographically skewed fourth movie in the series, opens with a clever series of horror scenes that emerge one from another like nested Russian dolls, and Kevin Williamson's dialogue is smart and knowing. All through the movie, *Scre4m* lets us know that it knows exactly what it's up to—and then goes right ahead and gets up to it.

The premise is that a psychopath has returned to the town of Woodsboro, which has already seen so many fatal slashings you question why anyone still lives there, let alone watches horror movies. This killer seems at times to be supernormal, is able to appear simultaneously at the front and back doors of a house, and predict precisely where victims will be, and when. As a result, the body count in *Scre4m* mounts relentlessly until you wonder whether everyone in the cast is going to be killed, with the movie ending on an empty room (with the phone ringing—heh, heh).

There is a dark nihilism here that seems to appeal to *Scream* fans. No one deserves to die, but so many do, and horribly, with geysers of blood spurting from their wounds. Why must they die? Why is the killer, "Ghost Face," so driven? The motive is eventually revealed, but I wouldn't go so far as to say it's explained.

Neve Campbell returns as Sidney Prescott, a hometown girl who has written a best-seller and has returned to Woodsboro to promote it. My own inclination would be to stay the hell away from the location of the killings in the original *Scream*, but hey, that's just me. Also back are David Arquette as the local sheriff, and Courteney Cox, the newscaster who is now his wife.

Sidney's cousin Jill (Emma Roberts) has a posse of fellow teenagers who spend most of the time picking up the phone and answering the door when they absolutely shouldn't. They're sophisticated; they know that in a horror movie when you walk past a dark doorway, something is likely to jump out at you. But when they get a call from someone saying, "My face will be the last sight you see," and then the doorbell rings—do they answer it? Of course they do. Survival of the fittest needs another million years to take effect in Woodsboro.

Karl Malden once said the hardest thing he ever had to do as an actor was act as if he didn't know he was about to be hit in the head with a beer can. He could have taken lessons from these girls, who go through the whole movie acting as if they're not about to be stabbed to death.

Wes Craven is a good director, and the film is done with some wit and style. The actors do what they can in a film that doesn't care about human insights. The characters are almost preternatural in their detachment; if you were embedded in events like these, wouldn't you be paralyzed with panic? Let's say you were the sheriff. Would you act so competent when you were obviously powerless? What about the film's many ambulance drivers? In *Bringing Out the Dead*, Nicolas Cage was in a constant frenzy, and that was supposedly a realistic story. In *Scre4m*, the locals are almost catatonic in their ability to carry on dialogue. How can you dissect a plot when you know you're next on the dissection table?

Maybe that's the point. Perhaps Craven and Williamson are making an ironic and cynical comment on the bloody tradition of the genre. Are they counting on their knowing fans to pick up all their self-aware nods? Could be. Does anyone—*anyone*—watch a movie like this as if it's in any way depicting reality? I dunno. *Scre4m* provides exactly what its audience will expect: one victim after another being slashed, skewered, stabbed, gutted, and sliced, with everyone in on the joke. Maybe that's your idea of a good time.

Season of the Witch

(DIRECTED BY DOMINIC SENA; STARRING NICOLAS CAGE, RON PERLMAN; 2011)

I lost track of the sieges and battles. *Season of the Witch* opens with a series of helpfully labeled sequences in which desert battles are fought, cites are sacked, buttresses stormed, redoubts doubted, enclosures enclosed, and so on. I didn't take notes, but an example might be "The Siege of Synecdoche, April 1, AD 1239."

Anyway, there's a slew of them. Crusaders in armor do battle with fierce desert tribesmen under the blazing sun. Heads are lopped off and roll across the plain. Horses whinny, women scream, children flee, warriors are disemboweled, limbs are severed, dogs would bark if there were dogs. The horror!

After about a dozen years of this, we pause for a discussion between the two hero Crusaders, Behmen (Nicolas Cage) and Felson (Ron Perlman). Yes, Cage and Perlman, so you suspect *Season of the Witch* will not be an exercise in understatement. "The killing of the women and children must stop!" they agree. Having arrived at this conclusion after twelve years of rape and pillage, they do not qualify as quick studies. The comrades abandon the armies of the Crusades, hit the road, and happen across a town somewhere in the vastness.

They have an excellent reason for ending up here, of all places: Why, this is the very same town of the pretitle sequence! Where three women were forced to confess to witchcraft, thrown backward off a bridge with nooses around their necks, hanged dead, and then prudently drowned in the river below! We liberals are earnestly deploring the superstition that forced them to confess Salem-style, until they spring back up from the dark waters and, hey, they *were* witches. Sometimes Glenn Beck is right.

Time has passed since that day (whether the full twelve years, I cannot say), and Behmen and Felson are quickly assigned to convey a surviving (if technically dead) witch (Claire Foy) to a distant monastery where there is a crumbling ancient tome containing the only known incantation that can exorcise her and bring an end to the Black Plague— so hey, we're back in medieval Europe now, specifically Hungary. A possible clue to this film's mind-set as a guy flick is that the Claire Foy character has no name and is known only as The Girl. Not even The Witch.

I am about out of Astonishments for you, but buckle your seat belt for this one: The director, Dominic Sena, has been inspired by Ingmar Bergman's *The Seventh Seal* (1957), that classic tale of a knight who returns from the Crusades and encounters Death on the road. Audiences for *Season of the Witch* may not be thickly larded with students of *The Seventh Seal*, but those few will be rewarded by sundry parallels and allusions. Ever since Bergman's *The Virgin Spring* was remade as *The Last House on the Left*, his work has suggested a rich mine for homage.

You know I am a fan of Nic Cage and Ron Perlman (whose very existence made *Hellboy* possible). Here, like cows, they eat the scenery, regurgitate it to a second stomach found only in actors, and chew it as cud. It is a noble effort, but I prefer them in their straight-through *Human Centipede* mode.

September Dawn

(DIRECTED BY CHRISTOPHER CAIN; STARRING JON VOIGHT, TRENT FORD; 2007)

On September 11, 1857, at the Mountain Meadows Massacre, a group of fanatic Mormons attacked and slaughtered a wagon train of about 120 settlers passing through Utah on their way to California. Can we all agree that the date has no significance? No, we cannot, because *September Dawn* is at pains to point out that on another September 11, another massacre took place, again spawned by religion.

But hold on. Where did I get that word "fanatic"? In my opinion, when anybody believes their religion gives them the right to kill other people, they are fanatics. Aren't there enough secular reasons for war? But there is no shortage of such religions, or such people. The innocent, open-faced Christians on the wagon train were able to consider settling California, after all, because some of their co-religionists participated in or benefited from the enslavement of Africans and the genocide of Native Americans.

Were there fanatics among those who ran the Salem Witch Trials or the Inquisition or the Crusades? Or the Holocaust? No shortage of them. Organized religion has been used to justify most of the organized killing in our human history. It's an inescapable fact, especially if you consider the Nazis and communists as cults led by secular gods. When your god inspires you to murder someone who worships god in a different way or under another name, you're barking up the wrong god. Football teams praying before a game reduce the same process to absurdity: What god worthy of the name cares which team wins?

The vast majority of the members of all religions, I believe and would argue, don't want to kill anybody. They want to love and care for their families, find decent work that sustains life and comfort, live in peace, and get along with their neighbors. It is a deviant streak in some humans, I suspect, that drives them toward self-righteous violence and uses religion as a convenient alibi.

That is true, wouldn't you agree, about Mormons, Christians, Muslims, Jews, Hindus, Buddhists, and so on? No, not all of you would agree, because every time I let slip the opinion that most Muslims are peaceful and nonviolent, for example, I receive the most extraordinary hate mail from those assuring me they are not. And in a Muslim land, let a newspaper express the opinion that most Christians and Jews are peaceful and nonviolent, and that newspaper office is likely to be burned down. The worst among us speak for the best.

Which brings us back to September 11, 1857, when a crazy Mormon zealot named Bishop Jacob Samuelson (Jon Voight) ordered the massacre of the visiting wagon train after first sending his spokesman, John D. Lee (Jon Gries), to lie that if they disarmed, they would be granted safe passage. Whether the leader of his church, Brigham Young (Terence Stamp), approved of this action is a matter of much controversy, denied by the church, claimed by *September Dawn*.

What a strange, confused, unpleasant movie this is. Two theories have clustered around it: (1) It is anti-Mormon propaganda in order to muddy the waters around the presidential campaign of Mitt Romney, or (2) it is not about Mormons at all, but an allegory about the 9/11/01 terrorists. Take your choice. The problem with allegories is that you can plug them in anywhere. No doubt the film would have great impact in Darfur.

My opinion is that there isn't anything to be gained in telling this

290 | Seven Days in Utopia

story in this way. It generates bad feelings on all sides, and at a time when Mormons are at pains to explain they are Christians, it underlines the way that these Mormons consider all Christians to be "gentiles." The Mormons are presented in no better light than Nazis and Japanese were in Hollywood's World War II films. Wasn't there a more thoughtful and insightful way to consider this historical event? Or how about a different event altogether? What about the Donner Party? They may have been cannibals, but at least they were nondenominational.

If there is a concealed blessing, it is that the film is so bad. Jon Voight, that gifted and versatile actor, is here given the most ludicrous and unplayable role of his career, and a goofy beard to go along with it. Terence Stamp, as Brigham Young, comes across as the kind of man you'd find at the back of a cave in a Cormac McCarthy novel. The Christians are so scrubbed and sunny they could have been teleported in time from the Lawrence Welk program.

And isn't it sickening that the plot stirs in some sugar by giving us what can only be described as a horse whisperer? This movie needs human whisperers. And giving us a romance between the bishop's son and a pretty gentile girl? And another son of the bishop who dresses up like an Indian and goes batty at the scent of blood? And real Native Americans who assist the Mormons in their killing, no doubt thinking, well, we can get around to the Mormons later? I am trying as hard as I can to imagine the audience for this movie. Every time I make any progress, it scares me.

Seven Days in Utopia

(DIRECTED BY MATT RUSSELL; STARRING LUCAS BLACK, ROBERT DUVALL; 2011)
I would rather eat a golf ball than see this movie again. It tells the dreadful parable of a pro golfer who was abused by his dad, melts down in the Texas Open, and stumbles into the clutches of an insufferable geezer in the town of Utopia (pop. 375) who promises him that after seven days in Utopia he will be playing great golf. He will also find Jesus, but for that you don't have to play golf, although it might help.

The geezer is named Johnny Crawford. He is played by Robert Duvall. Only a great actor could give such a bad performance. Duvall takes the arts and skills he has perfected for decades and puts them at the service of a flim-flam man who embodies all the worst qualities of the personal-motivation movement. That is the movement that teaches us that if we buy a book, view some DVDs, or sit for hours in the "Conference Center" of some crappy motel, we won't be losers anymore.

How do we know we were losers? Because we were suckers for the fraud. How will we know we are winners? When we rent our own motel rooms and fleece the innocent. The formula of the movement can be seen at work in this classified ad: "Send 25 cents for the secret of how to receive lots of quarters in your mail."

The movie stars Lucas Black as Luke Chisholm, whose father (Joseph Lyle Taylor) browbeat him sadistically since childhood to force him to become a pro golfer. When Luke's game blows up on the final hole of the Texas Open, the old man turns his back on him and stalks away in full view of the TV cameras. Devastated, Luke drives blindly into the night and stumbles across the town of Utopia, where he has a Meet Cute with Johnny Crawford. Johnny runs a nearby golf resort, and, wouldn't you know, it will take exactly seven days to repair Luke's truck, which is how long Johnny needs to work his spells on the young man.

Robert Duvall can play crafty con men as well as anyone. I was looking for a twinkle in his eye as he inflicts young Luke with his bull$#!t, but unfortunately I'm afraid the character is intended to be real. Only exposing him as a boring fraud could possibly redeem him. The three great secrets of golf, we learn, are to "See it. Feel it. Trust it."

Johnny Crawford's approach is a variation on the methods always used in the movies by wise old gurus to redeem clueless young men. To make Luke a better golfer, he makes him paint landscapes, go fly fishing, and attend church with him on Sunday. He forgets to train him to capture flying golf balls with a pair of chopsticks. Johnny has a wife (Melissa Leo) who nurtures the forlorn youth. There is a pretty waitress (Deborah Ann Woll) who has been kept on hold for a lifetime waiting for Luke's putt shot. The landscape is majestic, and Luke spends much time regarding its vistas from horseback from high plateaus while the sound track swells devoutly.

Utopia is another one of those movie towns where every single citizen, without exception, knows all the others and can always be found in the local restaurant. There is a TV on the wall where they all watch nothing but golf, and know exactly who poor Luke is. One of the local men has his eye on the comely waitress, but when the slicker turns up, does he get mean and possessive? Not a chance. The good people of Utopia have such charity that they give up their homes, families, horses, cows, waitresses, and dogs to the wayfaring stranger.

Let me give you an idea what good people these are. Many things go wrong during the week. Many, many things. All this in the land beyond San Antonio. Do we hear the f-word? Do we hear the s-word? Do we even hear the d-word or the h-word? No, dear reader. This is the first general-audience movie in quite some time that is rated G. Robert Duvall must seldom have had a greater challenge to overcome.

Sex and the City

(DIRECTED BY MICHAEL PATRICK KING; STARRING SARAH JESSICA PARKER, KIM CATTRALL; 2008)

I am not the person to review this movie. Perhaps you will enjoy a review from someone who disqualifies himself at the outset, doesn't much like most of the characters, and is bored by their bubble-brained conversations. Here is a 145-minute movie containing one (1) line of truly witty dialogue: "Her forties is the greatest age at which a bride can be photographed without the unintended Diane Arbus subtext."

That line might not reverberate with audience members who don't know who Diane Arbus was. But what about me, who doesn't reverberate with the names on designer labels? There's a montage of wedding dresses by world-famous designers. I was lucky I knew who Vivienne Westwood was, and that's because she used to be the girlfriend of the Sex Pistols' manager.

The movie continues the stories of the four heroines of the popular HBO series, which would occasionally cause me to pause in my channel surfing. They are older but no wiser, and all facing some kind of a romantic crossroads. New Line has begged critics not to reveal plot secrets, which is all right with me, because I would rather have fun with plot details. I guess I can safely say: Carrie (Sarah Jessica Parker) is in the tenth year of her relationship with Mr. Big (Chris Noth) when they sort of decide to buy a penthouse they name "Heaven on Fifth Avenue." Publicist Samantha (Kim Cattrall) has moved to Los Angeles, where her client Smith (Jason Lewis) has become a daytime TV star. Charlotte (Kristin Davis) and her husband, Harry (Evan Handler), have adopted a Chinese daughter. And Miranda (Cynthia Nixon) is in a crisis with her husband, Steve (David Eigenberg).

What with one thing and another, dramatic developments cause the four women to join each other at a luxurious Mexican resort, where two scenes take place that left me polishing my pencils to write this review. The girls go sunbathing in crotch-hugging swimsuits, and Miranda is ridiculed for the luxuriant growth of her pubic hair. How luxuriant? One of her pals describes it as *the National Forest,* and there's a shot of the offending proliferation that popped the Smith Brothers right into my head.

A little later, Charlotte develops a tragic case of *turista* and has a noisy accident right there in her pants. This is a key moment, because Carrie has been so depressed she has wondered if she will ever laugh again. Her friends say that will happen when something really, really funny happens. When Charlotte overflows, Carrie and the others burst into helpless laughter. Something really, really funny has finally happened! How about you? Would you think that was really, really funny?

Sex and the City was famous for its frankness, and we expect similar frankness in the movie. We get it, but each *frank* moment comes wrapped in its own package and seems to stand alone from the story. That includes (1) a side shot of a penis, (2) sex in positions other than the missionary, and (3) Samantha's dog, which is a compulsive masturbator. I would be reminded of the immortal canine punch line ("because he can"), but Samantha's dog is a female. "She's been fixed," says the pet lady, "but she hasn't lost the urge." Samantha can identify with that. The dog gets friendly with every pillow, stuffed animal, ottoman, and towel, and here's the funny thing, she ravishes them male-doggy-style. I went to AskJeeves.com and typed in "How do female dogs masturbate?" and did not get a satisfactory answer, although it would seem to be: "Just like all dogs do, but not how male dogs also do."

On to Mr. Big, the wealthy tycoon and victim of two unhappy marriages, who has been blissfully living in sin with Carrie for ten years. I will supply no progress report on their bliss. But what about Mr. Big himself? As played by Chris Noth, he's so unreal he verges on the surreal. He's handsome in the Rock Hudson and Victor Mature tradition, and has a low, preternaturally calm voice that delivers stock reassurances and banal clichés right on time. He's so . . . passive. He stands there (or lies there) as if consciously posing as The Ideal Lover. But he's . . . kinda slow. Square. Colorless. Notice how, when an old friend shouts rude things about him at an important dinner, he hardly seems to hear them, or to know he's having dinner.

The warmest and most human character in the movie is Louise (Jennifer Hudson), who is still in her twenties and hasn't learned to be a jaded consumerist caricature. She still believes in True Love, is hired as Carrie's assistant, and pays her own salary on the first day by telling her about a Netflix of designer labels (I guess after you wear the shoes, you send them back). Louise is warm and vulnerable and womanly, which does not describe any of the others.

All of this goes on for nearly two and a half hours, through New Year's Eve, Valentine's Day, and other bonding holidays. The movie needs a Thanksgiving bailout opportunity. But this is probably the exact *Sex and the City* film that fans of the TV series are lusting for. I know some nurses who are going to smuggle flasks of cosmopolitans into the theater on opening night and have a Gal Party. "Do you think that's a good idea?" one of them asked me. "Two flasks," I said.

Sex and the City 2

(DIRECTED BY MICHAEL PATRICK KING; STARRING SARAH JESSICA PARKER, KIM CATTRALL; 2010)

Some of these people make my skin crawl. The characters of *Sex and the City* 2 are flyweight bubbleheads living in a world that rarely requires three sentences in a row. Their defining quality is consuming things. They gobble food, fashion, houses, husbands, children, vitamins, and freebies. They must plan their wardrobes on the phone, so often do they appear in different basic colors, like the plugs of a Playskool workbench. As we return to the trivialities of their lives for a sequel, marriage is the issue. The institution is affirmed in an opening sequence at a gay wedding in Connecticut that looks like a Fred Astaire production number gone horribly overbudget. There's a sixteen-man chorus in white formal wear, a pond with swans, and Liza Minnelli to perform the ceremony. Her religious or legal qualifications are unexplained; perhaps she is present merely as the patron saint of gay men. After the ceremony, she changes to a Vegas lounge outfit and is joined by two look-alike backups for a song-and-dance routine possibly frowned upon in some denominations.

Then it's back to the humdrum married life of our gal Carrie Bradshaw (Sarah Jessica Parker) and the loathsome Mr. Big (Chris Noth). Carrie, honey, how can you endure life with this purring, narcissistic, soft-velvet idiot? He speaks loudly enough to be heard mostly by himself, his most appreciative audience. And he never wants to leave the house at night, preferring to watch classic black-and-white movies on TV. This leads to a marital crisis. Carrie thinks they should talk more. But sweetheart, Mr. Big has nothing to say. At least he's provided you with a Manhattan apartment that looks like an *Architectural Digest* wet dream.

Brief updates. Miranda Hobbes (Cynthia Nixon) is a high-powered lawyer who is dissed by her male chauvinist pig boss. Samantha Jones (Kim Cattrall) is still a sexaholic. Charlotte York (Kristin Davis) has the two little girls she thought she wanted, but now discovers that they actually expect to be raised. Mothers, if you are reading this, run this through your head. One little girl dips her hands in strawberry topping and plants two big handprints on your butt. You are on the cell to a girlfriend. How do you report this? You moan and wail out: "My vintage Valentino!" Any mother who wears her vintage Valentino while making muffin topping with her kids should be hauled up before the Department of Children and Family Services.

All of this is pretty thin gruel. The movie shows enterprise and flies the entire cast away to the emirate of Abu Dhabi, where the girls are given a $22,000-a-night suite and matching Maybachs and butlers, courtesy of a sheikh who wants to have a meeting with Samantha and talk about publicity for his hotel.

This sequence is an exercise in obscenely conspicuous consumption, which the girls perform in so many different outfits they must have been followed to the Middle East by a luggage plane. I don't know a whole lot about fashion, but I know something about taste, and these women spend much of the movie dressed in tacky, vulgar clothing. Carrie and Samantha also display the maximum possible boobage, oblivious to Arab ideas about women's modesty. There's more cleavage in this film than at a pro wrestling wedding.

And crotches, have we got crotches for you. Big close-ups of the girls themselves and some of the bulgers they meet. And they meet some. They meet the Australian World Cup team, for example, which seems to have left its cups at home. And then there's the intriguing stranger Samantha meets at the hotel, whose zipper-straining arousal provokes the fury of an offended Arab guest and his wife. This prodigy's name is Rikard Spirt. Think about it.

Samantha is arrested for kissing on the beach, and there's an uncomfortable scene in which the girls are menaced by outraged men in a public market, where all they've done is dress in a way more appropriate for a sales reception at Victoria's Secret. They're rescued by Arab women so well covered only their eyes are visible, and in private these women reveal that underneath the burka they're wearing Dior gowns and so forth. Must get hot.

I wondered briefly whether Abu Dhabi had underwritten all this product placement, but I learn that *SATC2* was filmed in Morocco, which must be Morocco's little joke. That nation supplies magnificent desert scenes, achieved with CGI, I assume, during which two of the girls fall off a camel. I haven't seen such hilarity since *Abbott and Costello in the Foreign Legion*.

The movie's visual style is arthritic. Director Michael Patrick King covers the sitcom by dutifully cutting back and forth to whoever is speaking. A sample of Carrie's realistic dialogue in a marital argument: "You knew when I married you I was more Coco Chanel than coq au vin." Carrie also narrates the film, providing useful guidelines for those challenged by its intricacies. Sample: "Later that day, Big and I arrived home."

Truth in reviewing: I am obliged to report that this film will no doubt be deliriously enjoyed by its fans, for the reasons described above. Male couch potatoes dragged to the film against their will may find some consolation. Reader, I must confess that while attending the sneak preview with its overwhelmingly female audience, I was gob-smacked by the delightful cleavage on display. Do women wear their lowest-cut frocks for one another?

Note: From my understanding of the guidelines of the MPAA Classification and Rating Administration, Samantha and Mr. Spirt have one scene that far, far surpasses the traditional MPAA limits for pumping and thrusting.

Sex Drive

(DIRECTED BY SEAN ANDERS; STARRING JOSH ZUCKERMAN, CLARK DUKE; 2008)

Sex Drive is an exercise in versatile vulgarity. The actors seem to be performing a public reading of the film's mastery of the subject. Not only are all the usual human reproductive and excretory functions evoked, but new (and I think probably impossible) ones are included. This movie doesn't contain "offensive language." The offensive language contains the movie.

Was I offended? I'm way over that. I was startled. The MPAA ratings board must have been scribbling furiously in the dark, to come up with: "Rated R, for strong crude and sexual content, nudity, language, some drug and alcohol use, all involving teens." What did they forget? Violence. Nothing much blows up real good, and there is a lack of vivisection and disembowelment.

The plot involves Ian (Josh Zuckerman), who is that tragic creature, a virgin eighteen-year-old boy, deeply fascinated by an online girlfriend who calls herself Ms. Tasty (Katrina Bowden). This suggests several topics: (1) Since when is an eighteen-year-old's virginal status *automatically* assumed to be tragic? Never mind. Forget about it. I was going to dig up some statistics proving many eighteen-year-olds are virgins, but when I Googled the topic, the top hits involved eighteen-year-olds complaining about it. (2) Most of the people you meet in chat rooms are much older than they claim, of a different gender, a cop, or your so-called buddy who is goofing on you, ha ha. (3) Every female named Ms. Tasty is either a hooker or take your choice from (2).

Ian has a best buddy suitably named Lance (Clark Duke), who is pudgy, has zits, and only has to smile at a girl to have her offer herself. This is not unrealistic. The unrealistic part is that Ian himself is not pudgy and does not have zits. The two friends live in Wisconsin, and Ms. Tasty, who lives in Tennessee, wants Ian to drive down for guaranteed sex. Personal to Ian: When having sex with anyone named Ms. Tasty, in addition to a nice block of smoked cheddar, take along protection. Ian is in love with a hometown girl named Felicia (Amanda Crew), who is in love with Lance, as all females are. She comes along for the ride, essentially because she is needed to allow the in-car triangle to function.

Ian steals his brother's most prized possession, a perfectly restored 1969 GTO, to impress Ms. Tasty. Ian, Ian, Ian! Anyone calling herself Ms. Tasty who promises you sex doesn't *have* to be impressed. As they motor south, they pass through Amish country. Luckily it's the day of the annual Amish sex orgy, and Ian meets sexy Mary (Alice Greczyn), who falls in love with him, flashes her boobs, etc. The director, Sean Anders, should be ashamed of himself. Lucky the Amish don't go to movies, or he'd be facing a big lawsuit. Better be nice to the Amish. In a year we'll be trading gold bars for their food, ha ha.

What happens in Tennessee, stays in Tennessee. The movie has some laughs, to be sure, even a few big ones, but is so raunchy and driven by its formula that you want to cringe. Let's see. What else . . . Oh, I just noticed the pun in the title, ha ha.

Shuttle

(DIRECTED BY EDWARD ANDERSON; STARRING PEYTON LIST, CAMERON GOODMAN; 2009) Why do I have to watch this movie? Why does anyone? What was the impulse behind this sad, cruel story? Is there, as they say, "an audience for it"? I guess so. The critic *Tex Massacre* at bloody-disgusting.com rates it four skulls out of five and says, "While gorehounds might not be doing backflips over the blood loss, they should appreciate that director Edward Anderson makes the kills relatively painful and wholly grounded in reality."

I'm not sure if the gorehounds will think there is too much blood loss or too little. Never mind. At least the killings are relatively painful. There's that to be said for it. But I think it's a cop-out to review this movie only as an entry in the horror/slasher genre and not pull back for a larger context. Do images have no qualities other than their technical competence?

Shuttle opens with two young women arriving at an almost empty airport at 2 a.m. It's raining. They can't get a cab. A guy in a van says he'll take them downtown for fifteen dollars. He already has one passenger. Now two young guys also want a ride. Guy says, nothing doing. One girl says, they're with us. Two guys get on board.

Under the driver's window is painted, "No more than three stops." That's strange. Looks like there's room for sixteen, twenty people in the van. The driver takes them on a strange route into no-man's land, pulls a gun, takes all five passengers hostage. OK, so far we're in standard horror territory.

It's what comes next that grows disturbing. The women, played by Peyton List and Cameron Goodman, are resourceful and try to fight back. The young guys help but are neutralized. The other passenger is a crybaby. The film seems set up to empower women. I won't say more about the plot except to say that it leads to utter hopelessness and evil.

That things happen as they do in *Shuttle* I suppose is true, however rarely. But a film can have an opinion about them. This one simply serves them up in hard, merciless detail. There is no release for the audience, no "entertainment," not even much action excitement. Just a remorseless march into the dark.

There is good work here. Peyton List, now twenty-two, working on TV since 2000, is effective as Mel, the more resourceful of the girls. She has a Neve Campbell quality. Tony Curran, as the driver, isn't your usual menacing monster but has more of a workaday attitude inflicting suffering. And the writer-director, Edward Anderson, is reasonably skilled at filmmaking, although it becomes a major distraction when he has the van drive through miles of empty streets when, as the plot reveals, there is little reason.

Last week I reviewed the latest version of *The Last House on the Left*. It had qualities, too, including more developed characters and more ingenious action sequences. But *Shuttle* is uninterested in visual style; it wants to appear nuts-and-bolts, unsentimental, pushing our faces in it. I know the horror genre is a traditional port of entry for first-time directors on low budgets, and I suppose that is Anderson's purpose. All right, he has proven himself. Now let him be less passionately infatuated with despair.

Note: The R *rating proves once again that it is impossible for a film to be rated* NC-17 *on violence alone.*

Silk

(DIRECTED BY FRANÇOIS GIRARD; STARRING KEIRA KNIGHTLEY, MICHAEL PITT; 2007)

Silk is a languid, too languid, story of romantic regrets, mostly ours, because romance is expected to carry the film without explaining it. It is told as a mournful flashback, narrated by a man who has been in love with two women, or maybe it was one all the time. He is a young Frenchman as his story begins circa 1860, who falls in love with a local girl, marries her, and then is sent to Japan and falls in love again.

The Frenchman is named Herve, played by Michael Pitt as the passive, soft-spoken plaything of every circumstance he falls into. His complaint seems to be that his life has happened to him. His wife is Helene (Keira Knightley), whom he truly loves, and who truly loves him, but cannot give him a child, although this plays less like a tragedy than just one of those things.

His father is a rich businessman, perhaps the mayor (I could not be sure), who takes the counsel of an entrepreneur, or maybe his employee (I could not be sure), named Baldabiou (Alfred Molina) that they revive the local silk mills. All goes well until disease attacks the silkworms. Then Baldabiou decides to send Herve to Japan to obtain uncontaminated silkworm eggs.

This journey, by carriage, train, ship, caravan, and horseback, takes him to a small Japanese village where the fearsome man in charge (Koji

Yakusho) sizes him up, agrees to sell him eggs, and introduces him, in a way, to his beautiful mistress (Sei Ashina). Their eyes meet, and something happens between them, or Herve is sure it does. He returns to France and his wife with the eggs, which make them all rich. But he is obsessed by thoughts of the woman, and that inspires two more trips to Japan and certain undercurrents in his marriage to the wife he still loves.

There are some mysteries in the storytelling, a central one being the night he is told by a Dutch trader that the mistress "is not what she seems." How so? "She is not Japanese." Then what is she? The IMDb has no doubts, reporting that she is "European," which she is certainly not. My guess is Korean or Chinese, but since the question remains unanswered, one wonders why it was introduced. (Find out on the IMDb, which will correct this error the moment they learn about it.)

Another mystery is how long silkworm eggs can survive during a journey back to France, since their fortunes seem to have no relationship to the nature of the journeys. But never mind. Herve's problem is, when he's not with the one he loves, he loves the one he's with, and is sincere about that at all times.

Our problem, on the other hand, is that we don't care. Michael Pitt almost whispers his way through the film, reveals not passion but damp-eyed self-pity, and (given the language barrier) has no reason to be in love with the Japanese woman except for the movie's blatant exoticism, which argues: Why would you be satisfied with a high-spirited, beautiful wife like Helene, who shares jolly tumbles in the sack, when you could have a Japanese woman who kneels submissively before you, takes forever to serve you tea, looks soulfully into your eyes, speaks not a word, and touches you only once (although we know that, not Herve, who is blindfolded at the time).

There are additional unforgivable plot elements that I dare not reveal, meant to be much more stirring than, under the circumstances, they can possibly be. And a piano score that weeps under many a scene. And a lot of beautiful photography. And then everything is brought together at the end in a flash of revelation that is spectacularly underwhelming.

Something Borrowed

(Directed by Luke Greenfield; starring Kate Hudson, Ginnifer Goodwin; 2011)

One of the curious problems with *Something Borrowed* is that Kate Hudson's performance is too effective. She plays Darcy, the lifelong best friend of the heroine, Rachel (Ginnifer Goodwin). Blond, rich, and headstrong, Darcy always gets her way in their relationship. And as the film opens she's about to be married to Dex (Colin Egglesfield), whom Rachel has had a crush on since law school. No good can come of this.

The plot mechanics are more or less inevitable. Thrown together again as the ceremony approaches, Rachel and Dex realize they have always been in love. But what to do? Rachel doesn't want to hurt her best friend. And Dex has a mother who struggles with depression; only the marriage seems capable of cheering her up.

To be married as an aid to someone else's mental health calls, I think, your own into question. This is especially true because the depressed mother (Jill Eikenberry) doesn't have a single line in the movie, and is seen only looking sad sometimes and happy sometimes. I believe, but cannot be sure, that a surprise decision made late in the film is triggered by her single ambivalent expression.

Now as to Kate Hudson. She plays an alcoholic. This is as clear as day, although I'll bet you won't see her described that way in many other reviews. Among the danger signals of alcoholism must certainly be playing badminton on the beach with a glass of wine in your hand, sitting down in a bar and ordering six shots of tequila, and drinking in every scene where she is not literally being fitted for a wedding dress. If you are marrying an alcoholic and are not one yourself, you shouldn't do it to cheer up your mom.

Kate Hudson plays Darcy so well that she almost forces the film apart at the seams; her character is too strong for it. Dex and Rachel, on the other hand, are sweet, inoffensive, beautiful people, who let others determine key decisions in their lives. As played by Ginnifer Goodwin and Colin Egglesfield, they are also extraordinarily attractive, and I almost held that against them until the story developed some of their depths. Goodwin has one of those faces of which you can think no bad things.

The movie supplies two other male characters, Ethan (John Krasinski) and party animal Marcus (Steve Howey). Ethan is Rachel's confidant during their lunch hours together. He figures out the whole story and pleads with Rachel to express her own feelings for once and not always let Darcy be the winner. It was even Rachel who introduced Darcy to Dex, for criminy sakes, and all but gave him away. Ethan avoids the clutches of their lustful friend Claire (Ashley Williams), a woman whose appearance can only be explained by the need for someone clutchy.

If Dex's mother says nothing, his father (Geoff Pierson) has a speech that is succinct and powerful, essentially ordering his son to go ahead with the wedding. The problem with that is that few fathers order their sons to marry ditzy drunks, but then again, maybe he doesn't know about Darcy's style at badminton.

Something Borrowed gathers an undeniable narrative momentum in its last half because all of the characters are treated sincerely and played in a straightforward style. It's just that we don't love them enough. Dex is too weak, Rachel is too sweet, Ethan has the same problem he accused Rachel of, and only Marcus finally seems to get what he deserves.

Southland Tales

(DIRECTED BY RICHARD KELLY; STARRING DWAYNE JOHNSON, SEANN WILLIAM SCOTT; 2007)

After I saw the first cut of Richard Kelly's *Donnie Darko* (2002), I was left dazed and confused but somehow convinced that I might have seen *something*. After I saw the director's cut (2004), which was twenty minutes longer, I began to comprehend some of what I had seen, and it became more interesting, even though I still didn't entirely understand it. It even nudged itself up into a favorable review.

After I saw the first cut of Kelly's *Southland Tales* at Cannes 2006, I was dazed, confused, bewildered, bored, affronted, and deafened by the boos all around me at the most disastrous Cannes press screening since, yes, *The Brown Bunny*. But now here is the director's cut, which is twenty minutes shorter, lops off a couple of characters and a few of the infinite subplots, and is even more of a mess. I recommend that Kelly keep right on cutting until he whittles it down to a ukulele pick.

Yes, I admire Kelly's free spirit. In theory. He is a cinematic anarchist, but the problem is, he's throwing bombs at his own work. He apparently has no sympathy at all for an audience unable to understand his plot, and every scene plays like something that was dreamed up with little concern for what went before or would follow after. It's like the third day of a pitch session on speed. What does he imagine an audience feels like while watching this movie? Did his editor ever suggest that he might emerge with a more coherent product if he fed the footage through a revolving fan and spliced it together at random?

The time is the Future: one year from now. By the time the DVD comes out, the time will be the Present. Two Texas towns have been nuked, including Abilene, the prettiest town that I've ever seen. America is in a state of emergency. A left-wing revolution is being masterminded from Venice Beach and the Santa Monica Pier against the oppressive right-wing government. A Schwarzeneggerian actor, related to a political dynasty, has been kidnapped, replaced with a double, and—I give up. A plot synopsis would require that the movie have a plot.

The dialogue consists largely of statements that are incomprehensible, often delivered with timing that is apparently intended to indicate they are witty. All of the actors seem to have generated back stories for their characters that have nothing to do with one another. Only Wallace Shawn emerges intact, because he so easily can talk like that, but a spit curl does not become him. Justin Timberlake is the narrator, providing what are possibly quasi-rational explanations for movies in other time dimensions.

The population of America consists entirely of character actors with funny names. I'm not sure that by the end of the movie they have all met one another, even the ones in the same scenes together. I haven't committed all of *Ebert's Little Movie Glossary* to memory, but I'm pretty sure it contains a Law of Funny Names, which instructs us that funny names are rarely funny in the movies, especially if they are not borne by Groucho Marx or W. C. Fields.

When I tell you I am helpless to describe the plot, perhaps you will have pity on me if I tell you it involves characters named Boxer Santaros;

Krysta Kapowski, aka the porn star Krysta Now; Dr. Soberin Exx; Starla Von Luft; Inga Von Westphalen, aka Marion; Dion Warner, aka Dion Element; Nana Mae Frost; Baron Von Westphalen; and Simon Theory. Boxer Santaros is played by Dwayne Johnson, who used to be billed as the Rock and should have led a movement among characters to change their names.

These people mostly seem to have dressed themselves earlier in the day at a used-costume store, although from the Cannes version I particularly miss a character played by Janeane Garofalo, who apparently used the Army surplus store. She was some kind of guerrilla general operating out of what I vaguely recall as a Venice Beach head shop, or maybe it was a bookstore. What a comedown from her great performance in nearby Santa Monica in *The Truth About Cats and Dogs*.

Note to readers planning to write me messages informing me that this review was no more than a fevered rant: You are correct.

Spider-Man 3

(DIRECTED BY SAM RAIMI; STARRING TOBEY MAGUIRE, KIRSTEN DUNST; 2007)

The great failing of *Spider-Man 3* is that it failed to distract me from what a sap Peter Parker is. It lingers so long over the dopey romance between Peter and the long-suffering Mary Jane that I found myself asking the question: Could a whole movie about the relationship between these two twenty-somethings be made? And my answer was: No, because today's audiences would never accept a hero so clueless and a heroine so docile. And isn't it a little unusual to propose marriage after sharing only one kiss, and that one in the previous movie, and upside-down?

Faithful readers will recall that I found *Spider-Man 2* (2004) the best superhero movie since *Superman* (1978). But I made the mistake of declaring that was because "the movie demonstrates what's wrong with a lot of other superhero epics: They focus on the superpowers, and short-change the humans behind them." This time, I desperately wanted Peter Parker to be short-changed. If I argued earlier that Bruce Wayne and Clark Kent were boring human beings, I had no idea how Peter would begin to wear on my nerves.

And what's with Mary Jane? Here's a beautiful, (somewhat) talented actress good enough to star in a Broadway musical, and she has to put up with being trapped in a taxi suspended eighty stories in the air by alien spiderwebs. The unique quality of the classic comic books was that their teenagers had ordinary adolescent angst and insecurity. But if you are still dangling in taxicabs at age twenty, you're a slow learner. If there is a *Spider-Man 4* (and there will be), how about giving Peter and Mary Jane at least the emotional complexity of soap opera characters?

Superhero movies and James Bond movies live and die by their villains. Spidey number two had the superb Doc Ock (Alfred Molina), who is right up there with Goldfinger and the Joker in the Supervillain Hall of Infamy. He had a *personality*. In Spidey number three we have too many villains, too little infamy. Take the Sandman (Thomas Haden Church). As an escaped con and the murderer of Uncle Ben, he has marginal interest at best. As the Sandman, he is absurd. Recall Doc Ock climbing buildings with his fearsome mechanical tentacles, and now look at this dust storm. He forms from heaps of sand into a creature that looks like a snowman left standing too late in the season. He can have holes blown into him with handguns but then somehow regains the bodily integrity to hammer buildings. And how does he *feel* in there? Molina always let you know precisely how Doc Ock felt, with a vengeance.

Then there is the black microorganism from outer space, which is not a villain but plays one in the movie. It arrives on Earth in a meteorite that lands, oh, maybe twenty yards from Peter and Mary Jane, but this impact somehow escapes notice by the fabled Spidey-sense. Then it produces little black beasties that look like squids crossed with licorice rope. They not only coat people with a way-cool black, glossy second skin, but specialize in spray-painting Spidey and Spidey wannabes. No ups, no extras.

We know that Spider-Man's powers do not reside in his red suit, which lives in a suitcase under his bed. So how do fake Spideys like Venom gain their powers when they are covered with the black substance? And how does a microorganism from outer space know how to replicate the intricate pattern-work of the Spidey costume, right down to the chest decoration? And to what purpose from an evolutionary point of view? And what good luck that the microorganism gets Peter's rival photographer, Eddie Grace, to infect, so that he becomes Venom! And how does Eddie know who he has become?

Another villain is Harry Osborn, aka the New Green Goblin (James Franco), son of the interesting original (Willem Dafoe), but not a drip off the old gob. While the first GG had the usual supervillain motivations (malevolence, envy, twisted abilities), his son is merely very angry and under the misapprehension that Peter/Spidey murdered his old dad. And *then* Peter and Harry have a *fist fight* when they should be doing Spidey and Goblin stuff.

Yes, there are some nice special effects in the movie. I liked the collapsing construction crane sequence. But the damsel in distress that time was not Mary Jane but Gwen Stacy (Bryce Dallas Howard), the sexy blond lab partner Peter has somehow neglected to mention to Mary Jane, causing her heartbreak because at a civic ceremony he kisses her with "our kiss," i.e., the upside-down one. While Peter goes through a period of microorganism infection, he combs his hair forward, struts the streets, attracts admiring glances from every pretty girl on the street, and feels like hot stuff. Wait until he discovers sex.

Spider-Man 3 is, in short, a mess. Too many villains, too many pale plot strands, too many romantic misunderstandings, too many conversations, too many street crowds looking high into the air and shouting "oooh!" this way, then swiveling and shouting "aaah!" that way. And saints deliver us from another dinner date like the one where Peter plans to propose to Mary Jane. You know a movie is in trouble when the climactic romantic scene of the entire series is stolen by the waiter (Bruce Campbell). And poor Aunt May (Rosemary Harris). An actress of Harris's ability, asked to deliver a one-note performance, and that single note is fretting.

How could Sam Raimi, having gone so right with *Spider-Man 2,* have gone so wrong with *Spider-Man 3*? Did the $250 million budget paralyze him? Has the series grown too heavy on its feet? How many times can we see essentially the same romantic scenario repeated between Peter and Mary Jane? How much dangling in the air can one girl do? And how does Spidey keep his identity a secret anyway, when there are more arrivals and departures through his apartment's window than on a busy day at LaGuardia?

The Spirit

(DIRECTED BY FRANK MILLER; STARRING GABRIEL MACHT, SAMUEL L. JACKSON; 2008)
The Spirit is mannered to the point of madness. There is not a trace of human emotion in it. To call the characters cardboard is to insult a useful packing material. The movie is all style—style without substance, style whirling in a senseless void. The film's hero is an ex-cop reincarnated as an immortal enforcer; for all the personality he exhibits, we would welcome Elmer Fudd.

The movie was written, directed, and fabricated largely on computers by Frank Miller, whose *300* and *Sin City* showed a similar elevation of the graphic novel into fantastical style shows. But they had characters, stories, a sense of fun. *The Spirit* is all setups and posing, muscles and cleavage, hats and ruby lips, nasty wounds and snarly dialogue, and males and females who relate to one another like participants in a blood oath.

The Spirit (Gabriel Macht) narrates his own story with all the introspection of a pro wrestler describing his packaging. The Octopus (Samuel L. Jackson) heroically overacts, devouring the scenery as if following instructions from Gladstone, the British prime minister who attributed his success to chewing each bite thirty-two times. The Spirit encounters a childhood girlfriend, Sand Saref (Eva Mendes), pronounced like the typographical attribute, who made good on her vow of blowing off Central City and making diamonds her best friend. The Octopus has an enigmatic collaborator named Silken Floss (Scarlett Johansson), pronounced like your dentist.

These people come and go in a dank, desolate city, where always it's winter and no one's in love and their duty is to engage in impossible combat with no outcome, because The Octopus and The Spirit apparently cannot slay each other, for reasons we know (in a certainty approaching dread) will be explained with melodramatic, insane flashback. In one battle in a muddy pond, they pound each other with porcelain commodes and rusty anchors, and The Spirit hits The Octopus in the face as hard as he can twenty-one times. Then they get on with the movie.

The Octopus later finds it necessary to bind The Spirit to a chair so that his body can be sliced into butcher's cuts and mailed to far-off zip codes. To supervise this task, he stands in front of a swastika attired in full Nazi fetishwear, whether because he is a Nazi or just likes to dress up, I am not sure. A monocle appears in his eye. Since he doesn't wear it in any other scene, I assume it is homage to Erich von Stroheim, who wasn't a Nazi but played one in the movies.

The objective of Sand Saref is to obtain a precious vial containing the blood of Heracles or Hercules; she alternates freely between the Greek and Roman names. This blood will confer immortality. Fat lot of good it did for Heracles or Hercules. Still, maybe there's something to it. At one point, The Spirit takes three bullets in the forehead, leans forward, and shakes them out. At another, he is skewered by a broadsword. "Why, oh why, do I never die?" he asks himself. And we ask it of him.

I know I will be pilloried if I dare end this review without mentioning the name of the artist who created the original comic books. I would hate for that to happen. Will Eisner.

The Spy Next Door

(DIRECTED BY BRIAN LEVANT; STARRING JACKIE CHAN, AMBER VALLETTA; 2010)

Let's see. Jackie Chan is a spy working for China and the CIA, who falls in love with a widow with three kids. He retires to be with them, but his job follows him home. Mom goes to be with her sick dad. Evil Russians have a plot to control the world's oil supply, and this requires them to chase Jackie and the kids through shopping malls, large empty factories, and so on. Jackie's character is named Bob Ho, which reminds me of someone.

Truth in reviewing requires me to report that *The Spy Next Door* is precisely what you would expect from a PG-rated Jackie Chan comedy with that plot. If that's what you're looking for, you won't be disappointed. It's not what I was looking for.

There are things you learn from movies like this. (1) All kids know how to use weapons better than Russian mobsters. (2) A villainess in a spy movie always dresses like a dominatrix. (3) Hummers are no help. (4) Kids always hate the guy their mom is dating until they survive in battle with him, and then they love him. (5) Whenever an adult turns away, a small child will instantly disappear. The smaller the child, the more agile.

(6) Even in New Mexico, Russian gangsters wear heavy long black leather coats, which they just bought in customs at Heathrow. These, added to their six-foot-five-inch heights and goatees, help them blend in. (7) The mole in the CIA is always the white boss, never the Latino.

What else? Oh, (8) if you put a cell phone under a rock with iron in it, it cannot be traced. Only such a rock miles into the desert will work. No good putting it in the stove. (9) Little girls would rather dress in a pink princess outfit than wear a Hulk mask. (10) Spies always have fiery kitchen disasters the first time they cook for kids, and the second time produce perfect French toast with powdered sugar on it. Oh, and (11) no spy has the slightest idea of a reasonable ratio of oatmeal to water.

Such sights made a young Saturday morning audience happy. Nothing to a kid is quite as funny as a food fight. A cat trapped on a roof is a suspense builder. They don't like the guy dating their mom until they save him with their well-timed action moves. And all young audiences find it perfectly reasonable that when a kid runs away from a residential neighborhood on a bike, that kid will, of course, pedal into the large empty factory where Jackie Chan is facing the Russian mob giants.

Jackie Chan is fifty-five. Just sayin'. He no longer runs up walls by using the leverage of a perpendicular surface. Back in the days before CGI, he used to really do that. OK, maybe some wires were involved, but you try running up a two-story wall with wires. I wouldn't even want to be winched up.

Chan was famous for doing his own stunts. He had so many accidents it's a wonder he can walk. Everybody knew to wait for the outtakes during the closing credits because you'd see him miss a fire escape or land wrong in the truck going under the bridge. Now the outtakes involve his use of the English language. What's that? Your name *isn't* Bob Hope?

Star Wars: The Clone Wars

(DIRECTED BY DAVE FILONI; STARRING MATT LANTER, JAMES ARNOLD TAYLOR; 2008)
Has it come to this? Has the magical impact of George Lucas's original vision of *Star Wars* been reduced to the level of Saturday morning anima-

tion? *Star Wars: The Clone Wars,* which is a continuation of an earlier animated TV series, is basically just a ninety-eight-minute trailer for the autumn launch of a new series on the Cartoon Network.

The familiar *Star Wars* logo and the pulse-pounding John Williams score now lift the curtain on a deadening film that cuts corners on its animation and slumbers through a plot that (a) makes us feel like we've seen it all before, and (b) makes us wish we hadn't. The action takes place between the events in the "real" movies *Episode II: Attack of the Clones* and *Episode III: Revenge of the Sith.* The Republic is still at war with the Separatists, its access to the Galactic Rim is threatened, and much depends on pleasing the odious Jabba the Hutt, whose child has been kidnapped— by the Jedi, he is told.

It's up to Anakin Skywalker and his new Padawan pupil, Ahsoka Tano, to find the infant, as meanwhile Obi-Wan Kenobi and Yoda lead the resistance to a Separatist onslaught. And if all of this means little to you, you might as well stop reading now. It won't get any better.

This is the first feature-length animated *Star Wars* movie, but instead of pushing the state of the art, it's retro. You'd think the great animated films of recent years had never been made. The characters have hair that looks molded from Play-Doh, bodies that seem arthritic, and moving lips on half-frozen faces—all signs that shortcuts were taken in the animation work.

The dialogue in the original *Star Wars* movies had a certain grace, but here the characters speak to each other in simplistic declamation, and Yoda gets particularly tiresome with his once-charming speech pattern. To quote a famous line by Wolcott Gibbs, *Backward ran sentences until reeled the mind.*

The battle scenes are interminable, especially once we realize that although the air is filled with bullets, shells, and explosive rockets, no one we like is going to be killed. The two armies attack each other, for some reason, only on a wide street in a towering city. First one army advances, then the other. Why not a more fluid battle plan? To save money on backgrounds, I assume. The trick that Anakin and his Padawan learner use to get behind the enemy force field (essentially, they hide under a box) wouldn't even have fooled anybody in a Hopalong Cassidy movie—especially when they stand up and run with their legs visible but can't see where they're going.

Ahsoka Tano, by the way, is annoying. She bats her grapefruit-sized eyes at Anakin and offers suggestions that invariably prove her right and her teacher wrong. At least when we first met Yoda, he was offering useful advice. Which reminds me, I'm probably wrong, but I don't think anyone in this movie ever refers to the Force.

You know you're in trouble when the most interesting new character is Jabba the Hutt's uncle. The big revelation is that Jabba has an infant to be kidnapped. The big discovery is that Hutts look like that when born, only smaller. The question is, who is Jabba's wife? The puzzle is, how do Hutts copulate? Like snails, I speculate. If you don't know how snails do it, let's not even go there. The last thing this movie needs is a Jabba the Hutt sex scene.

Step Brothers

(DIRECTED BY ADAM MCKAY; STARRING WILL FERRELL, JOHN C. REILLY; 2008)

When did comedies get so mean? *Step Brothers* has a premise that might have produced a good time at the movies, but when I left I felt a little unclean. The plot: Will Ferrell and John C. Reilly play Brennan and Dale, two never-employed fortyish sons who still live at home, eating melted cheese nachos and watching TV. When their parents (Mary Steenburgen and Richard Jenkins) get married, they become stepbrothers and have to share the same room. This causes them to inflict agonizing pain upon each other and use language that would seem excessive in the men's room of a truck stop.

Is this funny? Anything can be funny. Let me provide an example. I am thinking of a particular anatomical act. It is described in explicit detail in two 2008 movies, *Step Brothers* and *Tropic Thunder.* In *Step Brothers* it sounds dirty and disgusting. In *Tropic Thunder,* described by Jack Black while he is tied to a tree and undergoing heroin withdrawal, it's funny.

Same act, similar descriptions. What's the difference? It involves the mechanism of comedy, I think. The Jack Black character is desperately motivated. He will offer to do *anything* to be released. In *Step Brothers,* the language is simply showing off by talking dirty. It serves no comic function and just sort of sits there in the air, making me cringe.

I know, I know, four-letter language is the currency of a movie like this and many of the other films Judd Apatow produces. I would be lying if I said I was shocked. I would also be lying if I said I had no taste or judgment of comic strategy. I'm sure I've seen movies with more extreme language than *Step Brothers,* but here it seems to serve no purpose other than simply to exist. In its own tiny way, it lowers the civility of our civilization.

Now what about the violence? These two adult children do horrible things to each other. The movie must be particularly proud of one scene because they show part of it in the trailer. Dale thinks he has killed Brennan by slamming him with the cymbal of his drum set. He rolls him in a rug and prepares to bury him in the lawn. Brennan comes to, bangs Dale with the shovel, and starts to bury him alive.

I dunno. Maybe it sounds funny when you read it. Coming at the end of a series of similar cruelties, it was one living burial too many. There is also an attempted drowning. And—never mind.

Mary Steenburgen and Richard Jenkins, two gifted actors, do what they can. They despair of their grown-up, unemployed brats. They lay down the law. They realize their sons are destroying their marriage. But they exist in another dimension than Brennan and Dale—almost in another movie. Their reaction shots are almost always curious because the only sane reaction would be sheer horror, followed by calls to the men with the butterfly nets.

Sometimes I think I am living in a nightmare. All about me, standards are collapsing, manners are evaporating, people show no respect for themselves. I am not a moralistic nut. I'm proud of the x-rated movie I wrote. I like vulgarity if it's funny or serves a purpose. But what is going on here?

Back to the movie. I suppose it will be a success. Will Ferrell and John C. Reilly have proven how talented they are in far better movies. If it makes millions, will they want to wade into this genre again? I hope not.

Ferrell actually cowrote the movie with Adam McKay, the director. Maybe he will. But why not a comedy with more invention, with more motivation than hate at first sight? There is one genuinely funny moment in the movie: The blind man who lives next door has a guide dog that misbehaves, snarls, and bites people. Bad taste, yes. But . . . I'm desperate here. Do you see why the dog doing it is funny, but Will Ferrell doing it to John C. Reilly is not funny?

The Strangers

(DIRECTED BY BRYAN BERTINO; STARRING LIV TYLER, SCOTT SPEEDMAN; 2008)

My mistake was to read the interview with the director. At the beginning of my review of *The Strangers,* I typed my star rating instinctively: "One star." I was outraged. I wrote: "What a waste of a perfectly good first act! And what a maddening, nihilistic, infuriating ending!" I was just getting warmed up.

And then, I dunno, I looked up the movie on IMDb, and there was a link to an interview with Bryan Bertino, the writer and director, and I went there, read it, and looked at his photo. He looked to be in his twenties. This was his first film. Bertino had been working as a grip on a peanuts-budget movie when he pitched this screenplay to Rogue Pictures and was asked to direct it. He gave a friend his grip tools and thought: "Cool, I'm never going to need this anymore! I'm never using a hammer again." Then he tells the interviewer: "I still had to buy books on how to direct."

So I thought, Bryan Bertino is a kid, this is his first movie, and as much as I hate it, it's a competent movie that shows he has the chops to be a director. So I gave it 1½ stars instead of one. Still harsh, yes. I think a lot of audience members will walk out really angry at the ending, although it has a certain truthfulness and doesn't cheat on the situation that has been building up. The movie deserves more stars for its bottom-line craft, but all the craft in the world can't redeem its story.

Yes, Bertino can direct. He opens on a dark night in a neighborhood of deserted summer homes with two people in a car. These are Kristen (Liv Tyler) and James (Scott Speedman). They are coming from a wedding reception. They go inside James's summer home. We learn that he proposed to her, but she "isn't ready." The camera focuses on a 33 rpm turntable that, along with their Volvo, are the easiest two props I can imagine to create a 1970s period look.

I am intrigued by these people. Will they talk all night? Will they do things they'll regret forever? Will they . . . *there is a knock on the door!* Not the sound of a human hand hitting wood. The sound of something hard hitting wood. It is very loud, and it echoes. To evoke an infinitely superior film, it creates the same sense of alarm and danger as the planks do, banging against each other in *Le Fils* (*The Son*), by the Dardenne brothers.

They open the door and find a young girl. They tell her she has the wrong house. She goes and stands in the yard. And then, all night long, their sense of security is undercut by more knocks, breaking glass, scraping, smashing. The sound track is the third protagonist. After a time, Bertino creates an empty space in one of his compositions, and it attracts a . . . figure . . . that casually fills it, wearing a mournful, shroudlike mask. We will see the mask again. Also two figures wearing little-doll masks that are not sweet, but ominous. We recall the opening credits telling us, "This film is inspired by true events." Never a good sign.

Is *The Strangers* inspired by other movies? Asked by Moviesonline.ca if he was influenced "by the film" (never named), Bertino answers, as only someone young and innocent could answer: "I don't *necessarily* think that I looked at it, you know." The *necessarily* is a masterstroke. He adds: "I'm definitely influenced by, like, '70s genre stuff in general, structure wise. . . . I read *Helter Skelter* when I was, like, eleven. That was where I first started getting interested in the idea of people just walking into a house that you didn't know. I lived in a house in the middle of nowhere in Texas on this road where you could call out in the middle of the night and nobody would hear you."

There have been great movies about home invasion, like *In Cold Blood,* that made more of it than gruesome events. *The Strangers* is a well-shot film (the cinematographer is the veteran Peter Sova). It does what it sets out to do. I'm not sure that it earns the right to do it. I will say that Bertino shows the instincts and choices of a good director; I hope he gets his hands on worthier material. It's a melancholy fact that he probably couldn't have found financing if his first act had lived up to its promise. There's a market for the kind of movie that inspires the kinds of commercials and trailers that *The Strangers* inspires, ending with a chilling dialogue exchange:

"Why are you doing this to us?"

"Because you were home."

Sunshine Cleaning

(DIRECTED BY CHRISTINE JEFFS; STARRING AMY ADAMS, EMILY BLUNT; 2009)

Sunshine Cleaning is a little too sunny for its material. Its heroine, Rose, is a single mom in desperate need of income, trapped in a one-way affair with her high school boyfriend, who fathered her son but married someone else. Her son is always in trouble at school. Her sister, Norah, is a hard-living goofball. Rose starts a new business cleaning up messy crime scenes.

Does this sound sunny to you? The material might have promise as a black comedy, but its attempt to put on a smiling face is unconvincing. That despite the work by Amy Adams as Rose and Emily Blunt as Norah, two effortless charmers who would be terrific playing these characters in a different movie. And Alan Arkin is back, and engaging, in what is coming dangerously close to "the Alan Arkin role." He's their father, Joe, forever hatching new get-poor-quick schemes.

Rose is a good mom. She understands her seven-year-old son, Oscar (Jason Spevack), who is not really troubled but simply high-spirited. I wonder how many little boys are accused of misbehaving simply because they are boys. Why does she still sleep with Mac, the faithless high school quarterback (Steve Zahn) who seduced and abandoned her? She asks herself the same question.

It's Mac, at least, who tips her off on a possible business. He's a cop and notices that people get paid well for mopping up after gruesome murders. So is born Rose and Norah's Sunshine Cleaning, which will clean up the rugs and scrape the brains off the wall, etc. This job by its nature allows them to witness the aftermath of lives unexpectedly interrupted; an ID in a dead woman's purse leads them to make an awkward new acquaintance.

This is promising material. Gene Siskel loved movies about what people actually do all day long. There is even a documentary subject here. But not this film that compromises on everything it implies, because it wants to be cheerful about people who don't have much to be cheerful about. How can you make a feel-good movie about murder-scene cleanups? "Life's a messy business," the poster says. Yes, and death is messier.

There are times when the movie works, but those are the times it (and even we) forget what it's really about. If you could plot it on a curve, it might look like a cross-section of a roller-coaster. The poster also evokes *Little Miss Sunshine,* by the same producers, also with Alan Arkin, and the presence of Amy Adams evokes the sublime *Junebug*. Those were both movies with more consistent tones and, although based on contrivance, felt more natural.

There's one element in the film that does work, and it's sort of off to the side, apart from the rest of the plot. It involves Winston (Clifton Collins Jr.), a one-armed hardware store owner, who babysits Oscar in an emergency and provides an oasis of warmth and common sense. You may remember him as Perry, one of the killers Truman wrote the book about in *Capote* (2005). An actor like this works a lot but doesn't always get ideal roles. Now he's beginning to emerge, with seven more films in postproduction.

You won't have a bad time seeing *Sunshine Cleaning*. You may get a little frustrated waiting for it to take off. It keeps heading down different runways. There's a movie here somewhere. Not this one.

Super

(DIRECTED BY JAMES GUNN; STARRING RAINN WILSON, ELLEN PAGE; 2011)
Super is being sold as a comedy, but I doubt it will play that way. It begins as the portrait of a lovable loser named Frank, and as it ends we're pretty

sure he's an insane, ruthless killer. That's not a joke. Maybe the filmmaker, James Gunn, intended it as a joke, but after the camera lingers on the young heroine with a third of her face blown off, it's hard to laugh.

I quite understand that this could all be seen as an ironic commentary on audience expectations; when Ellen Page of *Juno* stars in a movie, we don't much expect to see her brains dripping. But let's face it: Most audiences have little appetite for irony about themselves. One possible way to like the movie might be to observe how unenjoyable it is for people expecting something funny and upbeat, but that would be unkind.

Rainn Wilson stars as Frank, a short-order cook who is married to the lithesome Sarah (Liv Tyler). He's a loser who is content to be a loser. He is also palpably stupid and clueless, a pawn in the hands of the slickster Jacques (Kevin Bacon). Sarah is a recovering addict, a paragon of sweetness until she falls in among low companions, including Jacques, a big-time drug dealer involved with a strip club.

When Jacques comes to Frank's house looking for Sarah, so clueless is Frank that he cooks eggs for his rival. It must be said that Kevin Bacon plays the scene (and praises the eggs) with such wicked comic timing that you can imagine the whole film centering on that scene and flowering in other directions.

It was not to be. Jacques steals Sarah, hooks her on drugs, and requires her for ominous obscure purposes. Frank dissolves into self-pity. While watching a Christian cable channel, he sees a half-witted drama about a superhero and is inspired to imitate it. He goes to a comic book store seeking instructional reading, and meets a clerk named Libby (Ellen Page), who claims she is twenty-two, but has the savvy of a credible eight-year-old.

Frank identifies Jacques with evil in general and reinvents himself as the Crimson Bolt, a masked superhero wearing a tight-fitting red suit he ran up himself on his wife's sewing machine. He then (this is kind of funny) hides behind Dumpsters, hoping to spot crimes being committed, and later, after getting beaten senseless, arms himself with a big wrench and starts pounding drug dealers. The Crimson Bolt becomes a big local news item; Libby figures out who he is and recruits herself as his junior sidekick, Boltie.

This isn't necessarily funny. It approaches humor, however, with the work by Rainn Wilson and Ellen Page, and with the cool, mocking detachment of the Kevin Bacon character, who visits as if an ambassador from another, better movie. There's something I like very much about Wilson, who plays an unaffected klutz with about as much grace and humor as possible. He never seems to be trying to be funny, and that's a strength. But what can he do with this screenplay?

Setting aside the details of the plot mechanics (Jacques, his gated mansion, his henchmen, his drugs, his evil), what we're left with are scenes of Frank the madman appointing himself as the wrath of God and smashing people senseless. When one of the Three Stooges gets beaned with a wrench, it's funny. When presumably actual characters are maimed and possibly killed, not so much.

The movie plunges into nihilistic despair in its third act. This isn't a black comedy because it isn't a comedy. It's a trick played on our expectations, I concede, but to what end? Is there any requirement that a film develop organically from beginning to end? No. There's no rule book. But audiences feel uneasy when they feel toyed with. I'm all for movies that create unease, but I prefer them to appear to know why they're doing that. *Super* is a film ending in narrative anarchy, exercising a destructive impulse to no greater purpose than to mess with us.

Survival of the Dead

(DIRECTED BY GEORGE A. ROMERO; STARRING ALAN VAN SPRANG, KENNETH WELSH; 2010)
For the purposes of watching *Survival of the Dead*, I'm perfectly willing to believe in zombies. It's a stretch, however, to believe in an island off the coast of Delaware where life looks like outtakes from *Ryan's Daughter,* everyone speaks with an Irish accent, and there's a bitter feud between those who believe in capital punishment for zombies, and those who call for their rehabilitation and cure.

How can you kill *or* rehabilitate a zombie, since by definition it is dead? Here's my reasoning: If it can attack you and dine on your throbbing flesh, it isn't dead enough. George A. Romero is our leading researcher in this area, having reinvented zombies for modern times with *Night of the Living Dead* (1968), and returned to them from time to time, most successfully in the excellent *Dawn of the Dead* (1978).

Zombies, as I have noted before (and before, and before), make excellent movie creatures because they are smart enough to be dangerous, slow enough to kill, and dead enough we need not feel grief. Romero has not even begun to run out of ways to kill them. My favorite shot in this film shows a zombie having its head blown apart, with the skullcap bouncing into the air and falling down to fit neatly over the neck. If that doesn't appeal to you, nothing will.

I've seen a whole lot of zombies killed. I've been cordial over the years with Romero, who in addition to reinventing zombies demonstrated how horror movies were a low-cost point of entry for independent filmmakers. To him we possibly owe such directors as David Cronenberg and John Carpenter. *Dawn of the Dead* was a biting indictment of the culture of the shopping mall, with most of its action in a landscape of modern retailing and merchandising. It was also funny.

All true. But after you've seen, oh, I dunno, twenty or thirty zombie movies, you sort of stop caring very much, unless something new is going on, as in *Zombieland*. At this point, I find myself watching primarily to spot and appreciate entertaining new ways to slaughter zombies. That's why the skullcap moment appealed to me. It was new.

Not much else is new in *Survival of the Dead*. After a vaguely explained plague of zombies has broken out, America has descended into post-apocalyptic warfare. The zombie disease is spreading. If one bites you, you become a zombie. That ability to infect others was once the special gift of vampires, and I suspect it has now been bestowed on zombies by gene-splicing at the genetic level. All zombies share one characteristic: They take a lickin' and keep on tickin'.

On the island off Delaware, we meet the O'Flynns and Muldoons, who are in the dependable tradition of the Hatfields and McCoys. The O'Flynns believe zombies exist to be destroyed. The Muldoons, more humane, want to chain them up and keep them around until a cure is discovered. How do you vote? How would you feel if the Muldoon scheme worked, and you were a cured zombie? Would your flesh still look a little decomposed? Would you mention it in your entry on Match.com?

The leader of the O'Flynns is exiled to the mainland via rowboat, and in Philadelphia we encounter paramilitaries who are fighting off zombies and considering going to . . . the island off the Delaware coast. I was unable to stir up the slightest interest in the O'Flynns and Muldoons, the military types reminded me of the better *28 Days Later,* and finally, all that kept my attention were the ingenious ways Romero killed the zombies. The man is a fount of imagination. Scarcely a zombie dies in a boring way. So there's that.

T

● ● ● ● ● ● ● ● ●

Take

(DIRECTED BY CHARLES OLIVER; STARRING MINNIE DRIVER, JEREMY RENNER; 2008)

Well, you can't fault the actors. That must mean it's the fault of the writer and director. *Take* is a monotonous slog through dirge land, telling a story that seems strung out beyond all reason, with flashbacks upon flashbacks delaying interminably the underwhelming climax.

Minnie Driver and Jeremy Renner star, and both of their performances would distinguish a better screenplay. She is Ana, a house cleaner, the wife of an elementary schoolteacher, the mother of a hyperactive little boy named Jesse (Bobby Coleman). Renner plays Saul, a loser at a very low level, who owes two thousand dollars to a lowlife and works for a storage company. He gets fired by stealing possessions from one locker and planting them in a locker where the contents will be auctioned. He pockets the extra cash. Neat, right? I don't know how the boss finds out about it. Just Saul's rotten luck.

It's one of those days for him. After getting fired, he splits his knuckles while breaking the window of his car, which won't start. Then he begs a pal for the two thousand dollars, and is lent a car and assigned to steal a Range Rover. Then the owner of the Range Rover beats him to a pulp. He finds a gun in the loaner car, slips it in his pocket, and goes to a drugstore to get his ailing dad's prescription filled. Seeing the cashier's window, he decides on the spot to rob the store, and in the process shoots the cashier and takes little Jesse as hostage. If only he hadn't been fired, a lot of people would have been saved a lot of trouble.

These events are doled out parsimoniously by Charles Oliver, who wrote and directed, intercutting with Ana driving her own broken-down car and towing a trailer. She is driving to the prison where Saul is scheduled to be executed, and wants to talk to him before he dies. Although there is an enigmatic phone call over the opening credits that may explain this, I am not at all sure how by this point she seems to have misplaced her husband.

Meanwhile (the whole movie takes place meanwhile), we see Saul sitting chained to a chair, being walked down corridors, being prepared for death, and then having a long theological chat with the prison chaplain. The chaplain is certainly a good sport, trying to convince the murderer that everything is part of God's plan. Saul is not too bright, but he cannot quite see how what he has done and what is being done to him represent good planning.

Ana and Saul do indeed meet and talk, but if you're hoping for a conversation along the lines of *Dead Man Walking*, you'll be disappointed. I spent more time wondering how long it takes to try to execute a prisoner in whatever state this is, since Saul still has a not-quite healed scar from the Range Rover beating, and a Band-Aid from the window smashing.

One critic of the movie accuses it of having a sneaky ending that suggests it might all have been a dream. I guess that would explain the emphasis placed on close-ups showing Ana and Saul staring at each other's ID patches on their uniforms. Maybe they imagined each other's lives? But then why would they meet? The backseat shot that may have misled the critic is obviously only in Ana's imagination. Little Jesse can't really be there. After all that's happened, do you think she would walk off and leave her son unattended in a prison parking lot?

Take Me Home Tonight
(DIRECTED BY MICHAEL DOWSE; STARRING TOPHER GRACE, ANNA FARIS; 2011)

I follow the Darwin Awards carefully. Those are the mentions given out on the Internet every year of people whose deaths may have improved the species by removing them from the gene pool. Many of the characters in *Take Me Home Tonight* might make a contribution in that way.

Let me run this past you. Your name is Matt (Topher Grace). You are maybe ten years out of high school. You work at a Los Angeles video store. You want to impress a girl named Tori (Teresa Palmer) you lusted after in school. She walks into the video store. You lie and tell her you are a trader with Goldman Sachs. You end up at a party, and she's there. It turns out she's also in banking, and happens to know that Goldman Sachs doesn't have a Los Angeles office.

Everybody then gets drunk and exchanges inane dialogue during the longest scene set at a party since the forty-five-minute formal ball in Visconti's *The Leopard* (1963). Your most hated rival is throwing the party. Your high school class had some kind of cockamamie ritual test involving the Ball (I may have the name wrong, but I'm close). This is a large metal sphere, apparently hammered together out of old junkyard parts. It's in the bed of your rival's dump truck.

You decide one way to regain your self-respect and win esteem in Tori's eyes is to risk the challenge of the Ball. The idea is, you climb inside the Ball, he tilts the truck bed, and the Ball rolls out of control downhill on a canyon road above Los Angeles. To get into the Ball is to qualify yourself as a finalist for the Darwin Award. To aid and abet anyone involved in this process is to act as an accessory to murder.

Now let me get back to that party scene. It is unendurably long. There are endless camera setups to define various groupings of characters who perform badly written dialogue. Among these characters are Matt's twin sister, Wendy (Anna Faris), and her boyfriend, Kyle (Chris Pratt). Wendy got all the brains in the family. Matt got to be Topher Grace. In that family, a trade-off. Wendy is holding an envelope that will tell her if she has been accepted to "Oxford University." Kyle thinks they should get married. He doesn't know where Oxford is. This gives you a notion of the depth of his interest in her.

I put the words "Oxford University" in quotes to mislead you into thinking nobody calls Oxford by that name. Actually, that's its official name, but it is uncool to say "Oxford University." Most people say "Oxford" and people know what you're talking about. You know, like "Berkeley." Anybody tells you they're going to the "University of California at Berkeley," they must think you just got off the train.

Take Me Home Tonight must have been made with people who had a great deal of nostalgia for the 1980s, a relatively underprivileged decade. More power to them. The movie unfortunately gives them no dialogue expanding them into recognizable human beings. They speak entirely in plot points and punch lines, and seem to be motivated only by lust, greed, and ego. Well, we all are, but few bring to this motivation so little intelligence and wit.

Besides, I have news for Tori, who works in banking and thinks she's so smart. If she thinks Goldman Sachs doesn't have a Los Angeles office, she should pay a visit to Suite 2600 in Fox Plaza at 2121 Avenue of the Stars.

Terminator: Salvation

(DIRECTED BY MCG; STARRING CHRISTIAN BALE, SAM WORTHINGTON; 2009)
One of Hollywood's oldest axioms teaches us: The story comes first. Watching *Terminator Salvation,* it occurred to me that in the new Hollywood, the story board comes first. After scrutinizing the film, I offer you my summary of the story: Guy dies, finds himself resurrected, meets others, fights. That lasts for almost two hours.

The action scenes, which is to say, 90 percent of the movie, involve Armageddon between men and machines ten years in the future. The most cheerful element of the film is that they've perfected Artificial Intelligence so quickly. Yes, Skynet is self-aware and determines to wipe out humankind for reasons it doesn't explain. A last-ditch resistance is being led by John Connor, or "J.C." for you Faulkner fans.

Christian Bale plays the role of Connor, in a movie that raises many questions about the lines between man and machine. Raises them and leaves them levitating. However, it has many fights between a humanoid cyborg and robotic Skynet men made of steel. How do these antagonists fight? Why, with their fists, of course, which remains a wonderfully cinematic device. They also shoot at each other, to little effect. In fact, one metal man is covered in molten ore and then flash-frozen, and keeps on tickin'. And listen, Skynet buddies, what Bale thought about that cameraman is only the tip of the iceberg compared to what he thinks about you.

There is nothing visible in this world but a barren wasteland. No towns, no houses, no food, no farms, no nothing. Maybe they live on Spam. The Resistance is run from a submarine commanded by General Ashdown (Michael Ironside), who wants to destroy Skynet and all of its human POWs. Connor, who is not even human, vows to save them. Wait. That's Marcus Wright (Sam Worthington), the guy from the past, who looks so much like Connor that maybe he only thinks he's Wright. Marcus is a convicted murderer from the past, awakened from cryogenic sleep.

I know with a certainty approaching dread that all of my questions will be explained to me in long, detailed messages from *Terminator* experts. They will also charge me with not seeing the movie before I reviewed it. Believe me, I would have enjoyed traveling forward through time for two hours, starting just before I saw the movie. But in regard to the answers to my questions: You know what? I *don't care.*

I regret (I suppose) that I did not see the first *Terminator* movie. *Terminator 2: Judgment Day* (1991) was a fairly terrific movie, set in the (then) future, to prevent the nuclear holocaust of 1997. You remember that. It was *about something.* In it, Edward Furlong was infinitely more human as John Connor than Christian Bale is in this film. Think about that.

Schwarzenegger, indeed, reappears in this fourth film, thanks to a body double and a special effects face, which makes him, I think, a cyborg of a cyborg. His famous line "I'll be back" is uttered by one John Connor or another, and I hope it draws more chuckles than it did at the screening I attended. Why, those immortal words are chiseled into granite, or at least into the lobby floor at the AMC River East theaters.

If there is one wholly sympathetic character in this film, that would be Blair Williams, played by the fragrant Moon Bloodgood. She murmurs some tender words at the forty-five-minute mark, representing the most complex dialogue up to that point. Dr. Serena Kogan (Helena Bonham Carter) has a longer speech, but you can't be sure it's really her, and she may have been lying.

Anyway, most of the running time is occupied by action sequences, chase sequences, motorcycle sequences, plow truck sequences, helicopter sequences, fighter plane sequences, towering android sequences, and fistfights. It gives you all the pleasure of a video game without the bother of having to play it.

Thor

(DIRECTED BY KENNETH BRANAGH; STARRING CHRIS HEMSWORTH, NATALIE PORTMAN; 2011)

I didn't attend the critics' screening for *Thor* because it was at the same time Ebertfest was showing *A Small Act*, about an eighty-eight-year-old woman named Hilde Back. She'd flown from Sweden, and I wanted to be onstage to present her with the Golden Thumb. Missing *Thor* 3-D was not an inconsolable loss, because I was able to see it in Chicago in nice, bright 2-D. The house was surprisingly well populated for an 8:50 p.m. screening on a Monday, suggesting that some people, at least, will make an effort to avoid 3-D.

Thor is a failure as a movie, but a success as marketing, an illustration of the ancient carnival tactic of telling the rubes anything to get them into the tent. "You won't believe what these girls take off!" a carny barker promised me and my horny pals one steamy night at the Champaign County Fair. He was close. We didn't believe what they left on.

The failure of *Thor* begins at the story level, with a screenplay that essentially links special effects. Some of the dialogue is mock heroic ("You are unworthy of your title, and I'll take from you your power!") and some of it winks ironically ("You know, for a crazy homeless person, he's pretty cute"). It adapts the original Stan Lee strategy for Marvel, where characters sometimes spoke out of character.

The story might perhaps be adequate for an animated film for children, with Thor, Odin, and the others played by piglets. In the arena of movies about comic book superheroes, it is a desolate vastation. Nothing exciting happens, nothing of interest is said, and the special effects evoke not a place or a time but simply special effects.

Thor, to begin with, is not an interesting character. The gods of Greek, Roman, and Norse mythology share the same problem, which is that what you see is what you get. They're defined by their attributes, not their personalities. Odin is Odin and acts as Odin and cannot act as other than Odin, and so on. Thor is a particularly limited case. What does he do? He wields a hammer. That is what he does. You don't have to be especially intelligent to wield a hammer, which is just as well, because in the film, Thor (Chris Hemsworth) doesn't seem to be the brightest bulb in Asgard.

The land (sphere? state of mind? heaven?) known as Asgard is described in Norse mythology as being near Troy, or perhaps in Asia Minor. In the movie, as nearly as I can gather, it is not of this earth and must be elsewhere in the universe. It consists of towering spires and skyscrapers linked by bridges and buttresses and betraying no sign of a population, except when untold thousands of Asgardians are required to line up at attention like robotic Nazis to receive dictates from the throne of Odin (Anthony Hopkins).

Asgard's ancient enemies are the Frost Giants, whose home is Jotunheim. I believe, but cannot promise you, that Jotunheim and Asgard are linked by a bridge, although this bridge also seems to be the way Thor reaches Earth, so perhaps it's more of a gateway through time and space, which would explain why Asgardians hurtle across intergalactic light-years and land in New Mexico without a hair out of place.

Thor is the first to arrive, and encounters three human scientists. Whether he is human himself is a question the film sidesteps. We know from mythology that gods sometimes mated with humans, which is a hopeful sign. The humans are astrophysicist Jane Foster (Natalie Portman), her friend Darcy (Kat Dennings), and the distinguished Dr. Erik Selvig (Stellan Skarsgard). I mention she's an astrophysicist because she behaves more like a storm chaser, cruising the desert in a van and peering into the skies, which won't get you far in astrophysics. The van hits Thor after he unluckily lands in front of it. This is not a Meet Cute for the gods. Later there's a meteoric event in which Thor's hammer hurtles to Earth and becomes embedded so firmly that it can't be pulled loose by a pickup truck or even the federal government.

So now Thor is on Earth, his hammer is stuck, and I am underwhelmed. Thor luckily speaks English, and Jane and her friends take him to the local diner, where he eats lots of Pop Tarts and, when he finishes his coffee, smashes the empty cup to the ground. "We don't do that," Jane explains as if to a child, and advises him to simply order another cup, after which he apparently absorbs human behavior and the movie drops the Taming of the Thor angle.

The three scientists are thin soup. Jane flirts demurely with Thor, Darcy stands next to her and does nothing very important, and Dr. Selvig regards them gravely and looms slightly above a low-angle camera while looking on with wise concern. There is also a government agent (Clark Gregg), whose every action is the remedy to an immediate requirement of the plot.

Superhero movies live and die on the quality of their villains. *Thor* has a shabby crew. The Frost Giants spend most of their time being frosty in their subzero sphere of Jotunheim and occasionally freezing their enemies. Thor's brother Loki (Tom Hiddleston) is dark-haired, skinny, shifty-eyed, and sadly lacking in charisma. He might as well be wearing a name tag: "Hi! I can't be trusted!" These villains lack adequate interest to supply a climactic battle, so the movie fabricates a Metal Giant, sends him to the New Mexico town, and has him blast fiery rays that blow up gas stations real good but always miss his targets. He is apparently killed by a sword through his spine, but why does he need a spine, since when his mask lifts we can see his head is an empty cavern?

And what about that town? It seems to be partly a set with two interiors (the diner and Jane's office) and partly CGI. It seems to go for a few blocks and then end abruptly in barren desert. Not even any suburbs or strip malls. I know aliens from other worlds are required to arrive in New Mexico, but why stay there? Why can't the Metal Giant attack the Golden Gate Bridge or scale a Trump Tower somewhere? Who cares if he turns a 7-Eleven into a fireball?

Here is a film that is scoring 79 percent on Rotten Tomatoes. For what? The standards for comic book superhero movies have been established by *Superman*, *The Dark Knight*, *Spider-Man 2*, and *Iron Man*. In that company *Thor* is pitiful. Consider even the comparable villains (Lex Luthor, the Joker, Doc Ock, and Obadiah Stane). Memories of all four come instantly to mind. Will you be thinking of Loki six minutes after this movie is over?

The director given this project, Kenneth Branagh, once obtained funding for a magnificent 70 mm version of *Hamlet*. Now he makes *Thor*. I wonder with a dread fear if someone in Hollywood, stuck with a movie about a Norse god, said, "Get Branagh. He deals with that Shakespeare crap."

Tooth Fairy

(DIRECTED BY MICHAEL LEMBACK; STARRING DWAYNE JOHNSON, ASHLEY JUDD; 2010)

In the pantheon of such legends as Santa Claus and the Bogeyman, the Tooth Fairy ranks down in the minor leagues, I'd say, with Jack Frost and the Easter Bunny. There is a scene in *Tooth Fairy* when the hero is screamed at by his girlfriend for even *beginning* to suggest to her six-year-old that there isn't a Tooth Fairy, but surely this is a trauma a child can survive. Don't kids simply humor their parents to get the dollar?

The film reveals that there's not one Tooth Fairy anyway, but a whole workforce, tightly scheduled and supervised by the strict head fairy (Julie Andrews). This comes as rather an astonishment to a rugged hockey player named Derek, played by Dwayne (The Rock) Johnson, who is sentenced to a term in Fairy Land for almost spoiling the young girl's faith. It happens so abruptly that he finds himself wearing a pink tutu. Oddly, a still photo of this sight is not included in the movie's press materials.

Derek's nickname in pro hockey is "The Tooth Fairy" because he is a specialist in body-slamming opponents so hard that you can fill in the rest. He hasn't scored a goal in ages. The coach puts him in just so he can take someone out. He spends so much time in the penalty box he has his own recliner installed.

The Rock plays this role straight, which is basically the way he plays every role. He's a pleasant, relaxed screen presence, but a Method Actor he's not. His idea of a tone for the Tooth Fairy is sincerity.

The movie's best scenes involve Fairy Land, where a brisk but very tall fairy social worker named Tracy (Stephen Merchant) adds some quirkiness. Merchant is a six-foot-seven British comedian, inheritor of the possibly genetic trait that populated Monty Python. His great regret in life is that he was never issued wings. Also in Fairy Land is Jerry (Billy Crystal), in charge of magic weapons, who issues Derek visibility sprays and suchlike.

Look, I hate to say this, but Billy Crystal has put on a few pounds. I say it not as a criticism but as an observation. Good for him. He seems more avuncular now, more confiding. Maybe he could start looking for dramatic roles as your favorite wise-guy uncle. Anyway, I've noticed in a lot of movies lately that the stars I've grown old with have, good lord, also grown old with me. There's a kind of fascination in how film so accurately records the passage of time. Julie Andrews, by still looking like Julie Andrews, seems to be swimming upstream.

Derek's girlfriend, mentioned above, is played by the divine Ashley Judd, thanklessly. I guess as an actor you know that in a movie named *Tooth Fairy* you're going to have a lot of scenes where you're tucking someone in. Fair enough, but where can you go with them dramatically?

The film is rated PG. I wondered why it didn't make Derek a husband instead of a boyfriend, but parents can relax: He seems to sleep on the couch. Uh, huh. The chemistry between the two suggests that they're together primarily because they work so well together at tucking time.

There's no way I can recommend this movie to anyone much beyond the Tooth Fairy Believement Age, but I must testify it's pleasant and inoffensive, although the violence in the hockey games seems out of place. It must be said in closing that given his nickname and reputation, it's a miracle the Tooth Fairy has been allowed to survive with such a dazzling row of pearlies.

The Tourist

(DIRECTED BY FLORIAN HENCKEL VON DONNERSMARCK; STARRING ANGELINA JOLIE, JOHNNY DEPP; 2010)

There's a way to make a movie like *The Tourist*, but Florian Henckel von Donnersmarck doesn't find that way. Here is a romantic comedy crossed with a crime thriller, shot in Paris and Venice, involving a glamorous mystery woman and a math teacher from Wisconsin. The plot is preposterous. So what you need is a movie that floats with bemusement above the cockamamie, and actors who tease one another.

Angelina Jolie does her darnedest. She gets the joke. Here is a movie in which she begins in a Paris cafe, eludes cops by dashing into the Metro, takes an overnight train to Venice, picks up a strange man (Johnny Depp), and checks them both into the Royal Danieli without one wrinkle on her dress or one hair out of place. And is sexy as hell. This is the Audrey Hepburn or Grace Kelly role, and she knows it.

Depp is in the Cary Grant role, of the obliging, love-struck straight man who falls in love and finds himself neck deep in somebody else's troubles. In theory these two should engage in witty flirtation and droll understatement. In practice, no one seems to have alerted Depp that the movie is a farce. I refer to "farce" in the dictionary sense, of course: *A comic dramatic work using buffoonery and horseplay and typically including crude characterization and ludicrously improbable situations*. Depp plays his math teacher seriously and with a touch of the morose.

The plot involves—oh, hell, you know, the usual mystery man who has stolen millions from a gangster and gone into hiding while meanwhile smuggling instructions to Jolie, his lover, instructing her to take the train to Venice, etc. And the cops from Scotland Yard who are tailing her in hopes of nailing the guy. And the gangster and his hit men who are also on the thief's trail. And chases over the rooftops of Venice, and dinner on a train, and a scene in a casino, and designer gowns, and a chase through the canals with Jolie at the controls of a motor taxi, and . . .

Well, there was really only one cliché left, and I was grateful when it arrived. You know how a man in a high place will look down and see a canvas awning that might break his fall, and he jumps into it? Yep. And it's shielding a fruit cart at the open-air market and he lands on the oranges and runs off leaving the cart owner shaking his fist. This is a rare example of the Vertical Fruit Cart Scene, in which the cart is struck not from the side but from the top.

The supporting roles are filled by excellent actors, and it's a sign of the movie's haplessness that none of them make a mark. You have Paul Bettany and Timothy Dalton as cops, Steven Berkoff as the gangster and Rufus Sewell as "The Englishman," who must be important because he hangs around without any apparent purpose. Once in London I saw Steven Berkoff play a cockroach in his adaptation of Kafka's *Metamorphosis*. It might have helped this role if he'd tried the cockroach again.

A depressing element is how much talent *The Tourist* has behind the camera. Florian Henckel von Donnersmarck, the director, made *The Lives of Others*, winner of the Oscar for best foreign film in 2007. The screenplay is by Henckel von Donnersmarck, Christopher McQuarrie (an Oscar for *The Usual Suspects*), and Julian Fellowes (an Oscar for *Gosford Park*). It's based on a French film written by Jerome Salle, which was nominated for a Cesar. All three winners seem to have used their awards as doorstops.

It doesn't matter that the plot is absurd. That goes with the territory. But if it's not going to be nonstop idiotic action, then the acting and dialog need a little style and grace and kidding around. Jolie plays her femme fatale with flat-out, drop-dead sexuality. Depp plays his Wisconsin math teacher as a man waiting for the school bell to ring so he can go bowling. The other actors are concealed in the shadows of their archetypes. Cary Grant would have known how to treat a lady.

Towelhead

(DIRECTED BY ALAN BALL; STARRING AARON ECKHART, TONI COLLETTE; 2008)

Towelhead presents material that cries out to be handled with quiet empathy, and hammers us with it. I understand what the film is trying to do, but not why it does it with such crude melodrama. The tone is all wrong for a story of child sexuality and had me cringing in my seat. It either has to be a tragedy or some kind of dark comedy like Kubrick's brilliant Lolita, but here it is simply awkward, embarrassing, and painful.

It tells the story of Jasira, a thirteen-year-old Lebanese-American girl with an obsession about her emerging sexuality. Well, all thirteen-year-olds feel such things. That's why so many of them stop talking to us. They don't know how to feel about themselves. Jasira thinks she does. She's turned on by taxi ads for showgirls, by sexy photos, by her own body. She discovers masturbating more or less by accident, likes it, precociously discusses orgasms.

Her American mother (Maria Bello) lives in Syracuse. Her Lebanese father (Peter Macdissi, of Six Feet Under) works for NASA in Houston. Neither is the parent of the year in any conceivable year. Her mother discovers her own boyfriend carefully shaving Jasira's pubic hair and is angry with the girl, not the boyfriend. She ships Jasira off to her father in Houston. He can seem cheerful and ingratiating, but slaps her for wearing a T-shirt to the table, forbids her to wear tampons ("only whores and married ladies wear them"), and is boiling with rage—partly because some of his neighbors think he is an Arab, and he is a Lebanese Christian who hates Saddam even more than they do.

Jasira starts babysitting the younger kid next door, who turns her on to his dad's porno magazines. His dad, known only as Mr. Vuoso, is played by Aaron Eckhart, who was brave enough to take on this slimy role. He actually begins with a variation on the ancient theme "come sit over here on the bed next to me," and escalates to rape. That Jasira is fascinated and to some degree encourages him is meaningless; she knows little about what she is encouraging, and apparently thinks of having sex with an adult as merely the sort of thing her reactionary dad would slap her for.

The progress of her journey involves bloody tampons and other details that could be relevant if handled with more sensitivity. She has sex with an African-American fellow student, who seems polite and nice but is experienced enough to know he is doing wrong. Her dad forbids her to see him because he is black. Meanwhile, Mr. Vuoso's son calls her a towelhead, a camel jockey, and worse. Racism is everywhere here.

The movie was written and directed by Alan Ball, who also wrote *American Beauty*. Two movies, two suburban men obsessed with underage beauties. Is there a pattern here? Ball also created and has directed *Six Feet Under*, which specializes in acute embarrassment and spectacular misbehavior. So does the director Todd Solondz, whose *Welcome to the Dollhouse* (1995) also dealt with a troubled adolescent girl. But Solondz knew how to do it, what his intentions were, how to challenge us and yet involve our sympathy. Ball seems to be merely thrashing about in a plot too transgressive for his skills.

The actors were courageous. Another key role is played by Toni Collette, as a pregnant neighbor who suspects what's going on and tries to help Jasira and offer her refuge from both her father and Mr. Vuoso. Trouble is, Jasira thinks she doesn't want to be rescued and has come to love orgasms, as is not uncommon. She's played by an appealing young actress named Summer Bishil, who certainly looks as if she were thirteen, but was eighteen when the film was made. Without showing nudity, Ball plays tricks with lighting and camera angles that sometimes regard her like a cheesecake model. I didn't enjoy that feeling. When Billy Wilder's lighting gives Marilyn Monroe a teasingly low neckline in *Some Like It Hot*, that's one thing. When Ball's framing provides one for a child, that's another.

Yes, the sexual abuse of children is a tragedy. Yes, there are adults who need to be educated, enlightened, warned, or thrashed and locked up. This is not the film to assist that process. The actors labor to be true to their characters and sincere in their work, and they succeed. The movie lets them down. It is more clueless than its heroine.

Trade

(DIRECTED BY MARCO KREUZPAINTNER; STARRING KEVIN KLINE, CESAR RAMOS; 2007)
Trade is a movie about trade in human beings, in this case, a thirteen-year-old Mexican girl who is kidnapped and brought to New Jersey, where her virginity will be auctioned on the Internet for an expected $50,000. Chill-

ingly, the movie is based on fact, on an article by Peter Landesman in the *New York Times Magazine*. And it's not an isolated case.

The girl, named Adriana (Paulina Gaitan), is handed off in a smooth cross-country operation. She finds only one friend along the way, a kidnapped older Polish woman named Veronica (Alicja Bachleda-Curus). Their transportation is handled by Manuelo (Marco Perez), a cruel man with a deeply buried streak of morality that begins to trouble him along the road.

The trip from Mexico to New Jersey turns into a chase, although Manuelo and his captives don't know it. Adriana's seventeen-year-old brother, Jorge (Cesar Ramos), sees her (against all odds) kidnapped in Mexico City and follows Manuelo's car all the way to the border by one means or another (against even greater odds). At a crucial moment near the border, he meets a Texas Ranger named Ray (Kevin Kline), and after some verbal scuffles, they join forces to follow Manuelo, rescue his captives, and penetrate to the heart of the slave-smuggling operation.

A nasty, vile business made more slimy because the director, Marco Kreuzpaintner, doesn't trust the intrinsic interest of his story and pumps it up with chase details, close calls, manufactured crises, and so many scenes of the captives being frightened and abused that they begin to seem gratuitous, even suspect. Yes, it is evil that these heartless gangsters, connected with the Russian Mafia, terrorize young women and sell them as objects. But is it not also evil that the film lingers on their plights with almost as much relish as the camera loved the perils of Pauline tied to the railroad tracks?

My description makes the film sound more urgent than it is. The German director seems to have fallen in love with the American genre of the road picture, and there are altogether too many shots of the trip itself, the land it covers, the roadside civilization, the open spaces.

What is fascinating, in a scary way, are the details of the Internet auction business and how it works and the money made in it. When I watch those TV shows where pedophiles are pounced on by cops, I think "entrapment," but you know what? Some people are asking to be entrapped. How about that Florida federal prosecutor who flew to Michigan hoping to meet a five-year-old girl? Your rights to do what you want in your sex life run into a dead end, I believe, when they involve others doing what they don't want.

All obvious, although not to some deranged creeps. But what is the purpose of this movie? Does it manipulate its subject matter a little too much in its quest to be "entertaining"? Why *should* this material be entertaining? Anything that holds our interest can be entertaining, in a way, but the movie seems to have an unwholesome determination to show us the victims being terrified and threatened. When I left the screening, I just didn't feel right.

Transformers: Dark of the Moon

(DIRECTED BY MICHAEL BAY; STARRING SHIA LABEOUF, MARKISS MCFADDEN; 2011)

Michael Bay's *Transformers: Dark of the Moon* is a visually ugly film with an incoherent plot, wooden characters, and inane dialogue. It provided me with one of the more unpleasant experiences I've had at the movies.

The series exists to show gigantic and hideous robots hammering one another. So it does. The last hour involves a battle for the universe that for some reason is held at the corner of Michigan Avenue and Wacker Drive in Chicago. This battle is protracted mercilessly beyond all reason, at an ear-shattering sound level, with incomprehensible Autobots and Decepticons sliced up into spurts of action with no sense of the space they occupy.

There is more of a plot in this third *Transformers*. It is a plot that cannot be described in terms of structure, more in terms of duration. When it stops, it's over. We learn that mankind's first mission to the moon was intended to investigate an alien spacecraft that crashed on the dark side. This ship, "the Arc," carried the robots to this solar system from their own, so that the good bots could continue their struggle for "freedom" against the bad bots. It is a bad omen when Lincoln's statue on the National Mall is decapitated.

Humans get involved. These include Sam Witwicky (Shia LaBeouf), who earlier saved the world but now has a job in a mail room, and Carly (Rosie Huntington-Whiteley), who is his sexy girlfriend because the movie requires a sexy girlfriend. There are also such characters as Mearing (Frances

McDormand), a government official; Bruce Brazos (John Malkovich), Sam's anal-retentive boss; Carly's former boyfriend Dylan (Patrick Dempsey), whose classic-car collection upstages every robot in the movie; the FBI manipulator Simmons (John Turturro); the peculiar Jerry Wang (Ken Jeong); and the expert warriors Lennox (Josh Duhamel) and Epps (Tyrese Gibson). If you pause to consider for a second, not one of these characters is actually required in the conflict, which is, after all, pretty much between the bots.

Oh, but the humans are needed for us. They are required because bots have no personalities and little intrinsic interest apart from the banging noises they make. They speak in dubbed English that sounds oddly separate from the other voices in the film. And they are so many times larger than the humans that I was reminded of the scale used in *The Incredible Shrinking Man*. We also need people because I, for one, will never care for Optimus Prime any more than for an engine block.

There is no style or wit in the dialogue, except when Malkovich adds his own spin. This is one of those annoying pictures where disembodied voices are heard during chaotic action: "Class dismissed!" "Decepticon punk!" "We've got a Mexican standoff here!" "What do you think you're doing?" "Return what belongs to me!"

Shia LaBeouf is scarcely heroic, and his girlfriend has no particular function except to be in constant peril and (in two hilarious shots) stare thoughtfully into space as if realizing something. The only considerable dramatic scene LaBeouf has is when his mother (Julie White) brings the manic plot to a standstill long enough to urge a self-help book upon her son.

I hesitate to mention another problem with the film because in all fairness it may not be Bay's fault. The framing looks wrong. When you look at enough movies, you develop a sixth sense for what feels correct within the frame. This film seemed too close to its compositions. There was a paucity of headroom, feet were nearly cut off, the sides seemed to squeeze. This wasn't dramatic, but I could feel it.

Of course, I could be mistaken. If I'm correct, here's what may have happened. In the multiplex theater originally set for the screening, it was explained, technicians spent three hours programming the 3-D projector—and then their programming didn't "take." The multiplex resourcefully moved the film to another screen already configured for 3-D. I suspect, however, that the aspect ratio in that room was not quite correct.

Nothing, however, would have repaired the film's lack of narrative coherence. I have a quaint notion that one of the purposes of editing is to make it clear why one shot follows another, or why several shots occur in the order that they do. *Transformers 3* has long stretches involving careless and illogical assemblies of inelegant shots. One special effect happens, and then another special effect happens, and we are expected to be grateful that we have seen two special effects.

Note: Bay is said to have tried to improve the characteristic light level of 3-D. In my screening, it was as dim as usual.

Transformers: Revenge of the Fallen
(DIRECTED BY MICHAEL BAY; STARRING SHIA LABEOUF, MEGAN FOX; 2009)

Transformers: Revenge of the Fallen is a horrible experience of unbearable length, briefly punctuated by three or four amusing moments. One of these involves a doglike robot humping the leg of the heroine. Such are the meager joys. If you want to save yourself the ticket price, go into the kitchen, cue up a male choir singing the music of hell, and get a kid to start banging pots and pans together. Then close your eyes and use your imagination.

The plot is incomprehensible. The dialogue of the Autobots, Deceptibots, and Otherbots is meaningless word flap. Their accents are Brooklynese, British, and hip-hop, as befits a race from the distant stars. Their appearance looks like junkyard throw-up. They are dumb as rocks. They share the film with human characters who are much more interesting, and that is very faint praise indeed.

The movie has been signed by Michael Bay. This is the same man who directed *The Rock* in 1996. Now he has made *Transformers: Revenge of the Fallen*. Faust made a better deal. This isn't a film so much as a toy tie-in. Children holding a Transformer toy in their hand can invest it with wonder and magic, imagining it doing brave deeds and remaining always their friend. I knew a little boy once who lost his blue toy truck at the movies and cried as if his heart would break. Such a child might regard *Transformers: Revenge of the Fallen* with fear and dismay.

The human actors are in a witless sitcom part of the time, and a lot of the rest of their time is spent running in slo-mo away from explosions, although—hello!—you can't outrun an explosion. They also make speeches like this one by John Turturro: "Oh, no! The machine is buried in the pyramid! If they turn it on, it will destroy the sun!" "Not on my watch!" The humans, including lots of U.S. troops, shoot at the Transformers a lot, although never in the history of science fiction has an alien been harmed by gunfire.

There are many great-looking babes in the film, who are made up to a flawless perfection and look just like real women, if you are a junior fanboy whose experience of the gender is limited to lad magazines. The two most inexplicable characters are Ron and Judy Witwicky (Kevin Dunn and Julie White), who are the parents of Shia LaBeouf, whom Mephistopheles threw in to sweeten the deal. They take their son away to Princeton, apparently a party school, where Judy eats some pot and goes berserk. Later they swoop down out of the sky on Egypt, for reasons the movie doesn't make crystal clear, so they also can run in slo-mo from explosions.

The battle scenes are bewildering. A Bot makes no visual sense anyway, but two or three tangled up together create an incomprehensible confusion. I find it amusing that creatures that can unfold out of a Camaro and stand four stories high do most of their fighting with fists. Like I said, dumber than a box of staples. They have tiny little heads, except for Starscream, who is so ancient he has an aluminum beard.

Aware that this movie opened in England seven hours before Chicago time, and the morning papers would be on the streets, after writing the above I looked up the first reviews as a reality check. I was reassured: "Like watching paint dry while getting hit over the head with a frying pan!" (Bradshaw, *Guardian*); "Sums up everything that is most tedious, crass and despicable about modern Hollywood!" (Tookey, *Daily Mail*); "A giant, lumbering idiot of a movie!" (Edwards, *Daily Mirror*). The first American review, however, reported that it feels "destined to be the biggest movie of all time" (Todd Gilchrist, Cinematical). It's certainly the biggest something of all time.

Tru Loved

(Directed by Stewart Wade; starring Najarra Townsend, Jake Abel; 2008)

Tru Loved as a movie is on about the same level as a not especially good high school play. Student directors could learn from it. I'm sure its heart is in the right place, but it fails at fundamentals we take for granted when we go to the movies. By lacking them, it illustrates what the minimum requirements are for a competent film. Yes, you can clearly see and hear them, especially when they're missing.

1. Line readings. That's what they sound like, readings. Classroom readings. The actors lack the knack of making their dialogue sound spontaneous and realistic. They sound like bright English students who have memorized their lines but find themselves onstage without having had much experience or training.

2. Body language. One of the first things an actor learns is not to gesture to emphasize lines unless the lines really call for it. Insecure actors often seem to punch up dialogue physically as a sort of insurance policy.

3. Framing. When you have five characters at a picnic table, you don't (necessarily) want to block those on the other side with the bodies of those on this side. There are ways to do that or fudge it. Or forget it. But don't have those on side A separated so we can see those on side B centered between persons 1 and 2, and 2 and 3, and then in the reverse shot separate those on side B so we can see those on side A.

4. Don't let the dialogue scream, "I paid attention in Gay Lit class!" When a kid comes home from Walt Whitman High School, don't make a point of establishing a lesbian connection to a name.

> Grandmother: *Tru? What kind of a name is that?*
> Lodell: *Short for Gertrude. As in Stein. She's a writer.*
> Grandma: *I know who Gertrude Stein was. "A rose is a rose is a rose."*
> Lodell: *Yeah. Whatever.*

After bringing up the sainted Gertrude, why does Lodell immediately reject her? "Whatever," when used by a teenager to an adult, is a way of dismissing what has been said. Lodell is a bright kid. Since he has *just now come* from a class studying *Romeo and Juliet, maybe* he might have replied, "And by any other name it smells as sweet as sweet as sweet." Grandma seems as if she'd like that.

5. Daydreams. Can be annoying, especially when absurdly stagy. Even more especially when the daydreams are in soft focus and then we cut frequently to the heroine in sharp focus, looking at scenes in her own daydreams and nodding and smiling.

6. Speech patterns. It's my impression most gay men do not "sound like gay men." But we all know exactly what I mean by sounding like gay men. The other side of the rule is, many men who sound gay are gay, and in many cases intend to sound gay. Don't get all homophilic on me. You know I'm right.

7. Cameo appearances. Their use must be carefully controlled to avoid breaking a film's mood with the "Hey! There's Donald Trump!" Syndrome. That is doubly true when the cameo star is famous and appears in a double role, as does Bruce Vilanch, from *Hollywood Squares*. Here he plays "Daniel" and "the Minister." Senator, I know Bruce Vilanch, and he's no Minister.

8. Music. Not necessary to blast in with literal and urgent punch lines and transitions.

The movie is about how Tru moves from idyllic San Francisco to conservative suburbia with her lesbian mothers. This just in: Except for some jocks and those who doth protest too much, today's suburban teens are mostly cool with people who are gay, except in the Palin Belt.

Full disclosure: I lifted the words "San Francisco to conservative suburbia with her lesbian mothers" straight from the plot summary on IMDb.com, because I stopped watching the movie at the 00.08.05 point. IMDb is also where I found out about Bruce Vilanch's dual role. I never did see the lesbian mothers or my friend Bruce. For *Tru Loved*, the handwriting was on the wall. The returns were in. The case was closed. You know I'm right. Or tell me I'm wrong.

Q: How can you give a one-star rating to a movie you didn't sit through?

A: The rating only applies to the first eight minutes. After that you're on your own.

21 and a Wakeup

(DIRECTED BY CHRIS MCINTYRE; STARRING AMY ACKER, FAYE DUNAWAY; 2009)

I learn that Chris McIntyre served in Vietnam and that *21 and a Wakeup*, set in an army hospital in the waning days of the war, is based on events he experienced and heard about. I'm sure his motivations were heartfelt, but his film is awkward and disjointed, and outstays its welcome.

It stars Amy Acker as a dedicated young army nurse named Caitlin Murphy, assigned to an army combat field hospital. She considers her profession a vocation, as indeed it is. Vocations and an army career don't always go hand in hand, and bureaucracy often wins out. Enforcing the Army Way is the uptight and unfortunately named Major Rose Thorn (Faye Dunaway), who seems opposed to innovation, improvisation, inspiration, and any other inclinations Caitlin might have in mind.

Her character is emblematic of the film's problems. I suspect McIntyre was so happy to enlist a star like Dunaway that it never occurred to him she's inappropriate for the role. God help me if I mention the age of an actress, but let me observe that Dunaway is about my age, and I consider myself beyond the age for optimum combat service.

Even more unfortunately, McIntyre hasn't written a believable character. I doubt Major Thorn as a nurse and as an officer. Her primary function seems to be materializing in a self-contained shot while issuing stiff formal announcements somewhat in the tone of a judge at a debutante charity function. She's stiffly poised in many shots; we can almost hear, "Ready for your close-up, Miss Dunaway."

But let's stop right there. Faye Dunaway is a fine actress and has been miscast in a badly written role. Amy Acker and other leading characters have been well cast in equally badly written roles. In contrast to the energy and life Robert Altman brought to his combat hospital in *M*A*S*H*, this film plays like a series of fond anecdotes trundled onstage without much relationship to one another.

Some of them strain credulity. McIntyre may indeed know about a nurse who went AWOL with a civilian war correspondent (Todd Cahoon) on an unauthorized visit to Cambodia. Such a trip may even have happened. But I didn't believe it.

I also didn't believe the punctuality with which critically wounded soldiers were rushed onscreen at crucial moments in the action in order to punctuate dialogue. These emergencies are tended to by medical personnel who seem like nothing so much as actors impersonating characters they've seen on TV.

McIntyre has enlisted an experienced cast, including Ed Begley Jr., Wes Studi, and Ben Vereen, and while Vereen creates a convincing human, none of them create convincing characters. How can they? They're pawns on a storyboard. The film lacks a sense of time and place. I discover on IMDb that it was actually filmed on location in Vietnam, but its Southeast Asia looks nowhere near as convincing as the locations of Coppola's *Apocalypse Now* and Stone's *Platoon* (shot in the Philippines) or Herzog's *Rescue Dawn* (Thailand).

Maybe I'm being too cynical. Perhaps I'll hear from nurses who served in Vietnam and inform me it was just like this. Even if it was, it plays like an assortment of stories that someone might tell you, "You ought to make a movie about that someday."

The Twilight Saga: Eclipse

(DIRECTED BY DAVID SLADE; STARRING KRISTEN STEWART, ROBERT PATTINSON; 2010)
The price for surrendering your virginity is so high in *The Twilight Saga: Eclipse* that even Edward Cullen, the proposed tool of surrender, balks at it. Like him, you would become one of the undead. This is a price that Bella Swan, the virtuous heroine, must be willing to pay. Apparently, when you marry a vampire, even such a well behaved one as Edward, he's required to bite you.

This romantic dilemma is developed in *Eclipse*, the third installment in this inexhaustible series, by adding a complication that has been building ever since the first. Jacob Black, the shape-shifting werewolf, is also in love with Bella (Kristin Stewart), and she perhaps with him. Jacob (Taylor Lautner) and his tribe are hot-blooded and never wear shirts, inspiring little coos and ripples of delight in the audience. Here is a fantasy to out-steam any romance novel: A sweet young girl is forced to choose between two improbably tall, dark, and handsome men who brood and smolder and yearn for her.

Nothing is perfect. There is a problem. The flame-tressed vampire Victoria (Bryce Dallas Howard) has been active in Seattle initiating new vampires, or Newbies, who in their youth are ravenous for blood and would have superhuman strength, if they were human. Victoria wants to destroy Bella in revenge for the murder of her boyfriend, James. Edward and Jacob both vow to protect the girl they love, and their fellow vampires and werewolves of course are prepared to fight to the death in this cause. This is true buddy love.

The movie contains violence and death, but not really very much. For most of its languorous running time, it listens to conversations between Bella and Edward, Bella and Jacob, Edward and Jacob, and Edward and Bella and Jacob. This would play better if any of them were clever conversationalists, but their ideas are limited to simplistic renderings of their desires. To be sure, there is a valedictory address, reminding us that these kids have skipped school for three movies now. And Edward has a noble speech when he tells Bella he doesn't want to have sex with her until after they're married. This is self-denial indeed for a 109-year-old vampire, who adds a piquant flavor to the category "confirmed bachelor."

Of Taylor Lautner's musculature, and particularly his abs, much has been written. Yes, he has a great build, but I remind you that an abdominal six-pack must be five seconds' work for a shape-shifter. More impressive is the ability of both Edward and Jacob to regard Bella with penetrating gazes from 'neath really heavy eyebrows. When my eyebrows get like Edward's, the barber trims them and never even asks me first.

There is a problem with the special effects. Many of the mountain ranges, which disappear into the far distance as increasingly pale peaks, look suspiciously like landscapes painted by that guy on TV who shows you how to paint stuff like that. The mountain forests and lakes are so pristine we should see Lewis and Clark just arriving. And the werewolves are inexplicable. They look snarly enough, have vicious fangs, and are larger than healthy ponies, but when they fall upon Newbies, they never quite seem to get the job done. One werewolf is nearly squeezed to death, and another, whose identity I will conceal, hears "he has broken bones on one whole side." Luckily, repairing the damage is only a night's work for Dr. Carlisle Cullen (Peter Facinelli). The problem with the effects is that the wolves don't seem to have physical weight and presence.

Much leads up to a scene in a tent on a mountaintop in the midst of a howling blizzard, when Bella's teeth start chattering. Obviously a job for the hot-blooded Jacob and not the cold-blooded Edward, and as Jacob embraces and warms her, he and Edward have a cloying cringe fest in which Edward admits that if Jacob were not a werewolf, he would probably like him, and then Jacob admits that if Edward were not a vampire—well, no, no, he couldn't. Come on, big guy. The two of you are making eye contact. Edward's been a confirmed bachelor for 109 years. Get in the brokeback spirit.

The audience watched this film with rapt attention. They obviously had a deep understanding of the story, which is just as well, because anyone not intimately familiar with the earlier installments could not make heads or tails of the opening scenes. The *Twilight* movies are chaste eroticism to fuel adolescent dreams, and are really about Bella being attracted and titillated and aroused and tempted up to the . . . very . . . BRINK! . . . of surrender, and then, well, no, no, she shouldn't.

The Twilight Saga: New Moon

(DIRECTED BY CHRIS WEITZ; STARRING KRISTEN STEWART, ROBERT PATTINSON; 2009)
The characters in this movie should be arrested for loitering with intent to moan. Never have teenagers been in greater need of a jump-start. Granted, some of them are more than one hundred years old, but still: Their charisma is by Madame Tussaud.

The Twilight Saga: New Moon takes the tepid achievement of *Twilight* (2008), guts it, and leaves it for undead. You know you're in trouble with a sequel when the word of mouth advises you to see the first movie twice instead. Obviously the characters all have. Long opening stretches of this film make utterly no sense unless you walk in knowing the first film, and hopefully both Stephenie Meyer novels, by heart. Edward and Bella spend murky moments glowering at each other and thinking, "So, here we are again."

Bella (Kristen Stewart) is still living at home with her divorced dad (Billy Burke), a cop whose disciplinary policy involves declaring her grounded for the rest of her life and then disappearing so she can jump from cliffs, haunt menacing forests, and fly to Italy so the movie can evoke the sad final death scene from—why, hold on, it's *Romeo and Juliet!* The very play Edward was reciting narcissistically and contemptuously in an opening scene.

Yes, Edward (Robert Pattinson) is back in school, repeating the twelfth grade for the eighty-fourth time. Bella sees him in the school parking lot, walking toward her in slow-motion, wearing one of those Edwardian Beatles jackets with a velvet collar, pregnant with his beauty. How white his skin, how red his lips. The decay of middle age may transform him into the Joker.

Edward and the other members of the Cullen vampire clan stand around a lot with glowering skulks. Long pauses interrupt longer ones. Listen up, lads! You may be immortal, but we've got a train to catch.

Edward leaves because Bella was not meant to be with him. Although he's a vegetarian vampire, when she gets a paper cut at her birthday party, one of his pals leaps on her like a shark on a tuna fish.

In his absence she's befriended by Jake (Taylor Lautner), that nice American Indian boy. "You've gotten all buff!" she tells him. Yeah, real buff, and soon he's never wearing a shirt and standing outside in the winter rain as if he were—why, nothing more than a wild animal. They don't need coats like ours, remember, because God gave them theirs.

SPOILER WARNING: Those not among that 5 percent of the movie's target audience that doesn't already know this will be surprised that Jake is a werewolf.

Bella: "So . . . you're a werewolf?"
Jake: "Last time I checked."
Bella: "Can't you find a way to . . . just stop?"
Jake (patiently): "It's not a lifestyle choice, Bella."

Jake is influenced, or controlled, or something, by Sam, another member of the tribe. He's like the alpha wolf. Sam and his three friends are mostly seen in long shot, shirtless in the rain, hanging around the edges of the clearing as if hoping to dash in and pick off some fresh meat.

Bella writes long letters to her absent vampire friend Alice (Ashley Greene), in which she does nothing to explain why she is helplessly attracted to these sinister, humorless, and vain men. It can't be the sex. As I've already explained in my review of the first film, *The Twilight Saga* is an extended metaphor for teen chastity, in which the punishment for being deflowered I will leave to your imagination.

The movie includes beauteous fields filled with potted flowers obviously buried hours before by the grounds crew, and nobody not clued in on the plot. Since they know it all and we know it all, sitting through this experience is like driving a pickup in low gear through a sullen sea of Brylcreem.

U

• • • • • • • • •

The Ugly Truth

(DIRECTED BY ROBERT LUKETIC; STARRING KATHERINE HEIGL, GERARD BUTLER; 2009)

Katherine Heigl and Gerard Butler are so pleasant in *The Ugly Truth* that it's a shame to spoil their party. But toil and try as they do, the comedy bogs down in relentless predictability and the puzzling overuse of naughty words. Once, the movies were forbidden to drop the f-word at all, but in this one, it's only an opening salvo in a potty-mouth bombing run.

Heigl plays Abby, producer of the Sacramento early morning news on a station that is operated like no other station in the history of television. Anchored by a bickering married couple, the broadcast is tanking in the ratings, and so she's forced to bring in Mike Chadway (Gerard Butler), a macho local cable personality whose ideas about the battle of the sexes date back to about *Alley Oop*.

On his first appearance, he departs from his script, diagnoses the anchor as the victim of his control-freak wife, and suggests they've probably stopped sleeping together. "This is great!" the station manager enthuses, despite that the segment runs so long it steps on the first five minutes of the network morning slot.

Abby is a raving beauty who, of course, can't find a man, maybe because her standards are so perfectionist. A handsome young orthopedic surgeon (Eric Winter) comes within her sights, after she twists an ankle falling from a tree outside his bedroom window watching him dry off after a shower while she was trying to rescue her cat. That's the sort of thing, wouldn't you agree, that happens all too rarely in life? Mike, the rugged sex-talk guru, tells her she's making all the wrong moves if she ever wants to catch this guy, and starts coaching her.

So which guy does she end up with? Guess. The movie leaves not a stone unturned, including the semi-obligatory Beauty Makeover Montage, during which Mike advises her on the requirements of a push-up bra and tells her to acquire longer hair. Uh, huh. And when the doc takes her to a ball game, Mike broadcasts instructions to her earphone, just as a producer might speak in an anchor's ear.

There's one scene with real comic possibilities, but it doesn't pay off. Mike gives her a pair of remote-controlled battery-powered vibrating panties. (Yes, they actually manufacture such items. Isn't the Web a useful resource?) Abby, the silly girl, foolishly decides to wear these to a business dinner, and takes along the remote controller for reasons it is hard to explain. A kid at a nearby table grabs the vibrator. We all know what's coming, and Heigl makes a real effort, but I'm afraid Meg Ryan's restaurant orgasm in *When Harry Met Sally* remains the gold standard in this rare but never boring genre.

The TV news as portrayed in the film makes *Anchorman: The Legend of Ron Burgundy* look like a documentary. Every segment can run as long as necessary. Macho Mike ad libs everything. Yes, he's good for ratings, but if after a few days he's really pulling in a twelve in the 5 a.m. hour, in prime time he would outscore the Oscars. And TV cameras do not usually follow newsmen out of the studio and into the street and watch whatever they do then—although if it were funnier, we might not mind.

Katherine Heigl and Gerard Butler are awfully nice here. The movie does them in. Amazing that this raunchy screenplay was written by three women. At its conclusion, I am forced to report, it provides abundant evidence of my belief that a good movie has rarely featured a hot-air balloon.

Unknown

(DIRECTED BY JAUME COLLET-SERRA; STARRING LIAM NEESON, DIANE KRUGER; 2010)

Is there a term for the paradox of intended accidental consequences? That's when a movie shows something that must be an accident, and it turns out to be part of a plan. Since *Unknown* opens with examples of such events, it won't be a spoiler for me to discuss them. I'll bail out before the tricky stuff.

As the movie opens, we meet Dr. Martin Harris (Liam Neeson) and his wife, Elizabeth (January Jones), who are on a flight to a biotechnology conference in Berlin. I'm thinking all we need to know about biotechnology in a thriller is that it probably involves either genetically altered crops or dangerous plagues. Anyway, at the airport Dr. Harris lets a guy load his luggage and as the taxi leaves, we get a big shot of his briefcase, still on the luggage trolley.

So OK. Was this an accident? If I'm carrying a briefcase that contains a cure for world hunger or a formula of mass destruction, I'm not gonna leave it on the curb. That's like leaving a laptop sitting on the sink when you go into a stall at a public toilet. Anyway, Dr. Harris and his wife get to the hotel, she starts to check in, he realizes his briefcase was left behind, and *without telling her* he grabs another taxi to the airport. He tries to call her but can't get a signal. Ever had that happen to you in Berlin?

A container falls off the truck in front of them, the taxi swerves and plunges through a bridge rail. Dr. Harris is knocked unconscious, but his life is saved by the quick actions of the driver, Gina (Diane Kruger). He's in a coma for four days. He pulls himself together and races to the hotel, only to find that his wife says she has never seen him before and is happily married to the "real" Dr. Martin Harris (Aidan Quinn). Now his ordeal begins: How can he prove his real identity and understand the conspiracy that has taken control of his life?

As a veteran thriller watcher, you can think of several possibilities here. It was all a dream. He has been brainwashed. He only thinks he's Martin Harris. He only imagined he was on a plane with the real Mrs. Elizabeth Harris. The second taxi was waiting to pick him up. And on and on. Or possibly none of the above.

But let's do an instant rewind. Was it an accident he left the briefcase behind? If he hadn't, there would have been no need to return to the airport. Was the falling container an accident? Was it an accident that he got a (beautiful) undocumented Bosnian refugee taxi driver who performed a heroic rescue in icy winter waters? Was it planned that he would be able to walk into the biotechnology conference and find the (real or fake) Dr. Martin Harris?

I'm thinking, if I'm an operative for some sinister secret organization and I want that briefcase and the MacGuffin it contains, here's what I'll do: I'll knock off Liam Neeson, whoever he is, and steal the briefcase. Or break into his hotel room. Or drug him. Anything. Because, think: If he isn't the real Martin Harris, why does he possess the briefcase containing the MacGuffin in the first place? But if he's a fake Martin Harris, who is the real one?

The movie has answers of a sort to some, but not all, of these questions. All the same, it left me rerunning events in my mind and thinking, Wait! Are we dealing with the Paradox of the Intended Accidental Consequences here, or what? *Unknown* is a skillfully photographed and acted film, and few actors are better than Liam Neeson at playing a man who has had the rug pulled out from under him. I was reminded of Roman Polanski's *Frantic* (1988), in which Harrison Ford played a doctor attending a convention in Paris with his wife. In that movie, the wrong briefcase was picked up at the airport, Ford stepped into the hotel shower, and when he stepped out, he found his wife had vanished.

Frantic wasn't watertight, either. The basic situation (an innocent man trapped in a conspiracy he doesn't understand) was a favorite of Hitchcock's, but in his films every consequence is intended. I confess I felt involved in *Unknown* until it pulled one too many rabbits out of its hat. At some point a thriller has to play fair. We're not satisfied when characters find it necessary to come out of nowhere and explain to the hero the underlying reality of his situation. Why does he need to know? Just bump him off. Whenever I hear one of those underlying reality speeches, I think there should be a crawl across the bottom of the screen: "This is actually the voice of the screenwriter desperately trying to explain the plot to himself."

Anyway, maybe this is all just me talking. Maybe I've seen too many movies. *Unknown* isn't really a bad movie, just an absurd one. It has its qualities from moment to moment. It left me with this thought: It's a damn good thing Dr. Martin Harris got that blond Bosnian taxi driver. A lot of taxi drivers, you don't get service like that.

Valentine's Day

(Directed by Garry Marshall; starring Jessica Alba, Kathy Bates; 2010)

I've heard of all-star casts, but *Valentine's Day* has a *complete* star cast. What did other movies do for talent when this one was filming? It has twenty-one actors who can be considered stars, and some are very big stars indeed. It's like the famous poster for *It's a Mad Mad Mad Mad World*, with a traffic jam of famous faces.

That's the movie's problem. Gridlock. It needs somebody like that tough traffic warden who stands under the L at Wabash and Randolph and fiercely wags her finger at drivers who don't shape up. The actors in this movie could populate six romantic comedies with reasonable plots, and a couple of sitcoms. Of course you'd need scripts. *Valentine's Day* is so desperate to keep all the characters alive, it's like those Russian jugglers who run around trying to keep all their plates spinning on poles.

I won't even attempt to describe the plot. Nor will I tell you who the characters are and who plays them. Just the names would come to sixty-three words, and if I described each character in twenty words, I'd run out of space way before I got to Captain Kate Hazeltine (Julia Roberts). I will mention it was nice to see Shirley MacLaine and Hector Elizondo as an old married couple, and of interest that two Taylors (Swift and Lautner) had scenes together.

For the rest, words fail me. The structure of the film involves a large number of couples and additional characters who are not in couples. We wake up with them on the morning of February 14, and all of their stories are completed by midnight, and as Ricky told Lucy, there's a lot of 'splainin to do. Several ancient formulas are employed. (1) Best friends who don't realize they're really in love. (2) Guy who thinks she loves him but she doesn't. (3) Girl who thinks he loves her but he's married. (4) People sitting next to each other on an airplane strike up a conversation. (5) Guy misunderstands phone call, draws wrong conclusion. (6) Fifth-grader's first crush.

The most important characters are a florist named Reed (Ashton Kutcher) and his best friend, Julia (Jennifer Garner). They don't have enough screen time to create three-dimensional characters, but at least they get up to two, leaving everyone else stuck at one or below. They're both attractive, but then all twenty-one stars are attractive, especially if, like me, you think George Lopez is handsome, especially when he smiles.

There's one peculiarity. Usually in formula pictures with this huge a cast, maybe one couple will be African-American, one Latino, and one Asian. No such luck. There are no Asians at all. The black characters include a goofy TV sports reporter (Jamie Foxx) and a wise agent (Queen Latifah). Lopez, a Mexican-American, is relegated to the role of Kutcher's sidekick (i.e., the Tonto role). There are a lot of Indians in the movie, at the next table in an Indian restaurant, revealing that when Indians are out to dinner, they act just like Indians in a movie comedy.

The form of the movie may remind you wistfully of a much better one, *Love, Actually,* which created characters we cared a great deal about. None of the characters here ever get beyond the Look—There's (Name of Star) Threshold. You know, when your mind says, Look—There's Patrick Dempsey! Look—There's Anne Hathaway! Look—There's Topher Grace! Wow—That's Jessica Biel!

Valentine's Day is being marketed as a Date Movie. I think it's more of a First Date Movie. If your date likes it, do not date that person again. If you like it, there may not be a second date.

Waiting for Dublin

(Directed by Roger Tucker; starring Andrew Keegan, Jade Yourell; 2009)

As nearly as I can tell, *Waiting for Dublin* is having its world premiere on March 13 in (can you guess?) Chicago, Boston, and New York. The timing could not be better. The St. Patrick's Day parades will be over in time for an afternoon matinee. And if you are the kind of person who marches in or attends the parade, you may enjoy this film. Other kinds of people, not so much.

Waiting for Dublin is like a time capsule, a film that, in every detail, could have been made in the 1940s and starred Bing Crosby, Pat O'Brien, Maureen O'Hara, and Edmund Gwenn as dear old Father Quinlan, who has the narcolepsy something fierce. It takes place in an Irish hamlet that has one telephone, in the post office that is also the pub. A horse and cart is the favored mode of transport, especially because there is no petrol in wartime.

The time is 1945. The hero is Mike (Andrew Keegan), an American pilot. He and his copilot, Twickers (Hugh O'Conor), run out of fuel and make an emergency landing in Ireland, where they are taken in, given lodging, and welcomed at the pub. The village has another guest, the German pilot Kluge (Guido De Craene). Ireland is officially neutral, and so such visitors are welcome, so long as they are not English, of course.

The town is inhabited, as the old movie rules required, by only colorful eccentrics, who spend all of their time in the pub waiting to be entertained by strangers. They move as a unit, decide as a unit, observe as a unit, and go to Sunday Mass as a unit to see whether Father Quinlan can get as far as *"Introibo ad altare Dei"* before falling asleep.

They quickly grow sympathetic to Mike's plight. Back home in Chicago, he made a $10,000 bet that he would shoot down at least five German fighter planes in the war. He needs one more, the war is about to end, and there is another problem: He made the bet with Al Capone's nephew, who in the movie is named Vito but in real life was named Ralph (Risky) Capone Jr. The movie was wise to change his name; in Chicago, you probably wouldn't make a bet you couldn't cover with a man named Risky Capone.

Mike is desperate—to make a fifth kill and to have sex with the lovely local lass Maggie (Jade Yourell), who says nothing doing unless he proposes marriage and means it. He comes up with a plan to get his fifth kill, and how he does that and with which weapons, I will leave for you to discover, pausing only to wonder how petrol was obtained. His solution and how it plays out is of course utterly preposterous, beginning from the moment Twickers begs off because he has a "cold."

Look, this is a perfectly sweet and harmless film, and if it were in black and white on TCM on St. Paddy's Day, you might watch it. It's so old-fashioned it's almost charming. It is constructed entirely with clichés and stereotypes, right down to the brotherhood of pilots, which was not original when Jean Renoir used it in *The Grand Illusion* (1937). The actors are pleasant, the locations (County Galway) are beautiful, but the movie is a wheeze.

What Just Happened?

(DIRECTED BY BARRY LEVINSON; STARRING ROBERT DE NIRO, CATHERINE KEENER; 2008)
Julia Phillips's famous autobiography was titled *You'll Never Eat Lunch in This Town Again.* Barry Levinson and Art Linson will. At this point, if you're going to make a film about Hollywood greed, hypocrisy, and lust, you have to be willing to burn your bridges. There's not a whole lot in *What Just Happened?* that would be out of place in a good *SNL* skit.

Linson is an A-list producer (*Fight Club, Into the Wild*) who wrote this screenplay based on his memoir, subtitled *Bitter Hollywood Tales from the Front Line.* He knows where the bodies are buried and who buried them, but he doesn't dig anybody up or turn anybody in. If you want to see a movie that Rips the Lid Off Tinseltown, just go ahead and watch Robert Altman's *The Player* (1992). Altman took no hostages. He didn't give a damn. And the book and screenplay he started with were by Michael Tolkin, who was closer to the front line and a lot more bitter. He didn't give a damn, either.

What Just Happened? stars Robert De Niro as a powerful Hollywood producer who has two troubled projects on his hands and a messy private life. De Niro warmed up for this film in *The Last Tycoon* (1976), in a role inspired by Irving Thalberg. That screenplay was by Harold Pinter, based on the novel by F. Scott Fitzgerald. Levinson himself directed the brilliant *Wag the Dog* (1998), where De Niro played a political spin doctor assigned to fabricate reasons for a war.

Mamet wrote that screenplay, which was astonishingly prescient. The movie, which premiered on December 17, 1997, gave us a U.S. president accused of luring a "Firefly Girl" into a room near the Oval Office and presenting her with unique opportunities to salute her commander in chief. The first hints of the Monica Lewinsky scandal became public in January 1998. For the White House methods used to invent reasons for a phony war, Mamet was six years ahead of Iraq.

So what am I saying? Should Mamet have written *What Just Happened?* Why not? For Mamet's *Heist,* produced by Linson, he gave Danny DeVito one of the funniest lines ever written: "Everybody loves money! That's why they call it money!" For that matter, *Variety*'s Todd

McCarthy thinks some of the characters in this film are inspired by the making of Linson's *The Edge,* also written by Mamet. A pattern emerges. But everything I think of is luring me farther away from *What Just Happened?*

Anyway, Ben, the De Niro character, has just had a disastrous preview of his new Sean Penn picture, *Fiercely.* The audience recoils at the end, when a dog is shot. The problem with the footage of *Fiercely* we see is that it doesn't remotely look like a real movie. Meantime, Ben is trying to get his next project off the ground. It will star Bruce Willis as an action hero, but inconveniently Willis has put on a lot of weight and grown a beard worthy of the Smith Brothers.

Ben is still in love with Kelly, his ex-wife number two (Robin Wright Penn), but they just haven't been able to make it work and are now immersed in something I think is called Break-Up Therapy. And their daughter Zoe (Kristen Stewart) is having anguish of her own, which goes with the territory for a rich kid from a shattered home in 90210. And Lou Tarnow (Catherine Keener), Ben's studio chief, is scared to death that *Fiercely* will tank. And the film's mad-dog British director (Michael Wincott) defends the dog's death as artistically indispensable. And the writer of the Bruce Willis thriller (Stanley Tucci) is having an affair with Ben's ex-wife number two.

This isn't a Hollywood satire—it's a sitcom. The flywheels of the plot machine keep it churning around, but it chugs off onto the back lot and doesn't hit anybody in management. Only Penn and Willis are really funny, poking fun not at themselves but at stars they no doubt hate to work with. Wincott is great as the Brit director who wants to end with the dead dog; one wonders if Linson was inspired by Lee Tamahori, the fiery New Zealand director of *The Edge,* who stepped on the astonishing implications of Mamet's brilliant last scene by fading to black and immediately popping up a big credit for Bart the Bear.

X Games 3D: The Movie

(DIRECTED BY STEVE LAWRENCE; STARRING SHAUN WHITE, DANNY WAY; 2009)

Well, it's awesome all right, what these X Games stars achieve. It's also awesome how little there is to be said about it. If you're a fan of extreme skateboarding, motorcycling, and motocross, this is the movie for you. If not, not. And even if you are, what's in the film other than what you might have seen on TV? Yes, it's in 3-D, which adds nothing and dims the picture.

Although *X Games 3D: The Movie* is billed as a documentary, let me mention two things that struck me as peculiar. During the final Mega Ramp extreme skateboarding competition in the Staples Center in Los Angeles, we learn almost accidentally that this is a sport that is scored on a point system, like diving or gymnastics. This is referred to only indirectly by the narrator, Emile Hirsch, who lavishes time on such inanities as "He treats gravity like some people do evolution, as only a theory," and "The present is past; only the future has currency." The flaw in this time theory is that when the future becomes the present it is the past. And gravity is more than a theory when you fall fifty feet onto a hard surface, as one X Gamer does.

We start to notice the competitors glancing up at what must be a scoreboard, but we're never shown it or informed of anybody's score. Why not? The film also has an annoying way of frequently not showing the beginning, middle, and end of a shot in one unbroken take. What's the point? During a two-car motocross "race," it's peculiar that the two cars are only seen together in one brief shot, as one flies off a dirt ramp and over the other, crossing below. Are they on different tracks? The narrator doesn't ever say.

What the athletes do is dangerous and risky. For example, hurtling down an almost perpendicular incline on a skateboard, using your speed to climb another terrifying ramp, and then launching into midair to perform "360s" and even "540s" before landing again on another ramp. Or, flying straight up from a ramp, doing a flip and/or a rotation, and landing again on the same ramp.

On motorcycles, they fly off earthen ramps, twist in the air, and land on another ramp. Or they do a high jump—flying almost straight up in the air to clear a bar at thirty-two or thirty-three feet. Often they fail, fall hard, and there's a tense silence while medics rush to the rescue. One competitor, Danny Way, apparently breaks something at Staples and returns to jump two more times. Earlier, he breaks his ankle in a practice jump and returns the next day to attempt to go over the Great Wall of China on a skateboard.

Athletes are asked why they take such risks and play with such pains (all of them have had broken bones and concussions). Their answers are the usual sports clichés about challenges and "taking the sport to a new level." Their cars and clothing are plastered with commercial endorsements, and at the X Games there are big ads for Pizza Hut, the navy, and so on. I guess they get paid. A lot, I hope.

"Who wants an A in history when you can get an X?" we're asked. Here's my theory about time. Yesterday is history, tomorrow's a mystery—so why get killed today?

X-Men Origins: Wolverine

(DIRECTED BY GAVIN HOOD; STARRING HUGH JACKMAN, LIEV SCHREIBER; 2009)

X-Men Origins: Wolverine finally answers the burning question, left hanging after all three previous Wolverine movies, of the origins of Logan, whose knuckles conceal long and wicked blades. He is about 175 years old, he apparently stopped changing when he reached Hugh Jackman's age, and neither he, nor we, find out how he developed such an interesting mutation.

His half brother was Victor (Liev Schreiber). Their story starts in "1840—the Northwest Territories of Canada," a neat trick, since Canada was formed in 1867, and its Northwest Territories in 1870. But you didn't come here for a history lesson. Or maybe you did, if you need to know that Logan and Victor became Americans (still before they could be Canadians) and fought side by side in the Civil War, World War I, World War II, and Vietnam. Why they did this, I have no idea. Maybe they just enjoyed themselves.

Booted out of the army in Vietnam, Logan/Wolverine joined a secret black ops unit under General Stryker (Danny Huston), until finally, in Nigeria, he got fed up with atrocities. Nevertheless, he was recruited by Stryker for a *super* secret plan to create a mutant of mutants, who would incorporate all available mutant powers, including those of the kid whose eyes are like laser beams. He wears sunglasses. Lotta good they'll do him.

Am I being disrespectful to this material? You bet. It is Hugh Jackman's misfortune that when they were handing around superheroes, he got Wolverine, who is, for my money, low on the charisma list. He never says anything witty, insightful, or very intelligent; his utterances are limited to the vocalization of primitive forces: anger, hurt, vengeance, love, hate, determination. There isn't a speck of ambiguity. That Wolverine has been voted the number one comic book hero of all time must be the result of a stuffed ballot box.

At least, you hope, he has an interesting vulnerability? I'm sure X-Men scholars can tell you what it is, although since he has the gift of instant healing, it's hard to pinpoint. When a man can leap from an exploding truck in midair, cling to an attacking helicopter, slice the rotor blades, ride it to the ground, leap free, and walk away (in that ancient cliché where there's a fiery explosion behind him but he doesn't seem to notice it), here's what I think: Why should I care about this guy? He feels no pain, and nothing can kill him, so therefore he's essentially a story device for action sequences.

Oh, the film is well made. Gavin Hood, the director, made the great film *Tsotsi* (2005) and the damned good film *Rendition* (2007) before signing on here. Fat chance *Wolverine* fans will seek out those two. Why does a gifted director make a film none of his earlier admirers would much want to see? That's how you get to be a success in Hollywood. When you make a big box-office hit for mostly fanboys, you've hit the big time. Look at Justin Lin with *The Fast and the Furious*.

Such films are assemblies of events. There is little dialogue, except for the snarling of threats, vows, and laments, and the recitation of essential plot points. Nothing here about human nature. No personalities beyond those hauled in via typecasting. No lessons to learn. No joy to be experienced. Just mayhem, noise, and pretty pictures. I have been powerfully impressed by film versions of Batman, Spider-Man, Superman, Iron Man, and the Iron Giant. I wouldn't walk across the street to meet Wolverine.

But wait! you say. Doesn't the film at least provide a learning experience for Logan about his origins for Wolverine? Hollow laugh. Because we know that the modern Wolverine has a form of amnesia, it cannot be a spoiler for me to reveal that at the end of *X-Men Origins: Wolverine,* he forgets everything that has happened in the film. Lucky man.

Year One

(DIRECTED BY HAROLD RAMIS; STARRING JACK BLACK, MICHAEL CERA; 2009)

Harold Ramis is one of the nicest people I've met in the movie business, and I'm so sorry *Year One* happened to him. I'm sure he had the best intentions. In trying to explain why the movie was produced, I have a theory. Ramis is the top-billed of three writers, and he is so funny that when he read some of these lines, they sounded hilarious. Pity he didn't play one of the leads in his own film.

As always, I carefully avoided any of the movie's trailers, but I couldn't avoid the posters or the ads. "Meet Your Ancestors," they said, with big photos of Jack Black and Michael Cera. I assumed it was about Adam and Eve. Cera has smooth, delicate features, and with curly locks falling to below his shoulders, I thought: "Michael Cera in drag. I wonder where Harold will take that?"

But no, even though Cera is sometimes mistaken for a woman, he's all primitive man, banging women on the head. Then he and Black eat of the forbidden apple and make a leap from tribal "hunter-gatherers" (a term they enjoy) to royal security guards. Everyone throughout the film talks like anyone else in a Judd Apatow comedy, somewhere between stoned and crafty.

It must be said that Jack Black and Michael Cera were not born to be costars. Black was fresh and funny once, a reason then to welcome him in a movie, but here he forgets to act and simply announces his lines. Cera plays shy and uncertain, but then he always does, and responds to Black as if Jack were Juno and a source of intimidating wit.

Another leading role is taken by Oliver Platt, as an extremely hairy high priest, who orders Cera to massage his chest with oil. The close-up of Cera kneading his matted chest foliage is singularly unappetizing. There are several good-looking babes in the city (did I mention it is Sodom?), who, as required in such films, all find the heroes inexplicably attractive. Cera and Juno Temple have a good exchange. She plays a slave. "When do you get off?" he asks. "Never."

That and several other of the film's better moments are in the trailer, of which it can be said, if they were removed from the film, it would be nearly bereft of better moments. The movie takes place in the land now known as Israel (then too, I think), although no one does much with that. The Sodomites include in their number Abraham, Cain, and Abel; it's surprising to find them still in action in the Year One, since Genesis places them—well, before the time of the Year One. Sodomy is not very evident in Sodom, perhaps as a result of the movie being shaved down from an R to a PG-13.

The film has shaggy crowds that mill about like outtakes from *Monty Python and the Holy Grail,* and human sacrifice in which virgins are pitched into the blazing mouth of a stone ox, and a cheerful turn when the gods more appreciate a high priest than a virgin. But *Year One* is a dreary experience, and all the ending accomplishes is to bring it to a close. Even in the credit cookies, you don't sense the actors having much fun.

Yes Man

(DIRECTED BY PEYTON REED; STARRING JIM CARREY, ZOOEY DESCHANEL; 2008)

Jim Carrey made a movie in 1997 titled *Liar Liar* in which his character is a lawyer who suddenly finds he cannot tell a lie. Now here is *Yes Man*, with Carrey playing a bank loan executive who cannot say no. If the movie had been made just a little later to take advantage of the mortgage crisis, it could have been a docudrama.

Carrey begins as a recluse mired in depression, a man named Carl who has been avoiding his friends and not returning his messages for three years, all because his great love walked out on him. His negative stance makes it easy to do his job, which amounts to denying loan applications. He's so indifferent to this work that he isn't even nice to his boss, who desperately wants to make friends. For Carl, it's just up in the morning and no, no, no all day.

Saying no all the way, he's dragged to a meeting of Say Yes!, which is one of those con games that convince large numbers of people to fill hotel convention centers and enrich those who have reduced the secrets of life to a PowerPoint presentation. The Guru of Yes is named Terrence Bundley, and is played by Terence Stamp, whose agent didn't wonder about the extra R. Stamp's message is: Turn your life around by saying yes to everything. This could be dangerous. Anyone who could word the questions cleverly could get you to do anything. For example, "Will you give me all of your money?"—an example used in the film.

The problem with the premise is that the results are clearly telegraphed by the plot. When Carl meets a beautiful girl named Allison (Zooey Deschanel), for example, he is clearly destined to fall in love with her. And when he encounters his sex-mad, toothless, elderly neighbor (Fionnula Flanagan), he is fated to—I wish the movie hadn't gone there. I get uncomfortable seeing reenactments of the dirty jokes we told when we were twelve.

Carrey performs some zany physical humor in the movie, including a drunken bar fight with a fearsome jealous boyfriend who, like all fearsome jealous boyfriends in the movies, stands tall and has a shaved skull. Remember when baldness was a sign of the milquetoast and not the bruiser? I like that phrase "stands tall." Makes me think of John Wayne, who was bald enough, but came along before Mr. Clean.

Every time there's a setup in *Yes Man* we know what must happen. If a homeless guy comes along and asks for a midnight ride to a forest preserve, of course Carl must say yes. We can also foresee what will happen when Allison doubts his love because maybe he only said yes because of his vow. Allison's doubts come perfectly timed to supply the movie's third act crisis. In fact, the whole story plays as if written by a devout student of the screenplay guru Robert McKee, who also fills rented ballrooms but has the advantage of being smarter and more entertaining than the Guru of Yes. Also, I think you will make more money by saying yes to *Casablanca* than to everything else.

Jim Carrey works the premise for all it's worth, but it doesn't allow him to bust loose and fly. When a lawyer *must* tell the truth and wants desperately not to (even pounding himself over the head with a toilet seat to stop himself), it's funny. When a loan officer must say yes and *wants* to, where is the tension? The premise removes all opportunity for frustration, at which Carrey is a master, and reduces Carl to a programmed creature who, as long as he follows instructions, lacks free will.

As I watched *Yes Man,* I observed two things: (1) Jim Carrey is heroic at trying to keep the movie alive, and succeeds when he is free to be goofy and not locked into yes-and-consequences. (2) It is no news that Zooey Deschanel is a splendid actress and a great beauty, but this is her first movie after which two of my fellow critics proposed marriage to the screen. And I thought they only sat in the front row to better appreciate the film stock.

You Again

(Directed by Andy Fickman; starring Kristen Bell, Jamie Lee Curtis; 2010)
If only *You Again* understood that its story was suited for screwball comedy. It labors under the delusion that this assembly of half-baked ideas is destined for a higher comic calling, for example, in the warmhearted romantic weeper category. The movie is so laboriously contrived in every atom of its being that the only interest is in seeing if the characters can avoid the destinies decreed for them by ancient formulas.

No luck. Those who hate each other at the beginning will forgive each other at the end. Those who try to deceive will have their deceptions unmasked. Those destined for love will find it, but not without an obligatory setback at the 66 percent point. If there is a party, it will go wrong. If there is a tree house, it will fall out of the tree. If it is necessary to improvise a wedding at a hospital, a ward will be cleared to make space for a wedding so elaborate it would look unlikely in a church. I hope they save pieces of the wedding cake for the patients whose beds have been wheeled out into the hallway.

The actors are plucky. They're stuck in a movie that gives their characters not even a chance at a human characteristic. Benevolence, jealousy, resentment, charity, wisdom, disappointment, and love are turned on and off like water faucets, often with only a few lines of motivation. Occupations are like name tags: Wise old dad is revealed as a "doctor," mom runs a "bakery," daughter is "vice president of a national public relations firm" in her twenties, brother is a "lawyer," his fiancée is "working with the sick and underprivileged," the fiancée's mother "owns fourteen hotels" and a private jet. None of these jobs figures in any way in the plot, except that the hotelier knows how to say three words in each of six languages (she is played by Sigourney Weaver with such latent energy that I'm sure she would know more words if this movie were not rated PG).

The heroine is Marni (Kristen Bell). In high school she wore braces and glasses, was pimply, and was called "Moo" because her initials were M.O.O. (hint: Don't use your middle name). She is a blonde, of course, and was bullied by a brunette, of course. This was Joanna (Odette Yustman), who has now morphed into Florence Nightingale. Marni's mother is Gail (Jamie Lee Curtis), and wouldn't you know Gail went to high school with Joanna's Aunt Ramona (Sigourney Weaver), and they . . . oh, never mind.

Marni's grandmother Bunny is played by Betty White, whom I urgently advise to start playing against type, because the standard eighty-eight-year-old Betty White, although one hell of a woman, has grown a tad overfamiliar.

There were two parts of the movie I liked. The beginning, with a voice-over by the then unpopular high school sophomore version of

Marni, starts out funny before the plot settles in. And there is a moment when Aunt Ramona and mother Gail find out they were on the same cheerleader squad, and do an awesomely physical cheer together, and that is flat-out funny. Aside from that, the movie's pleasures are scant, apart from its observance of Gene Siskel's Rule of Swimming Pool Adjacency, which states that when well-dressed people are near a swimming pool, they will . . . yeah, you got it.

Your Highness

(DIRECTED BY DAVID GORDON GREEN; STARRING DANNY MCBRIDE, JAMES FRANCO; 2011)
Your Highness is a juvenile excrescence that feels like the work of eleven-year-old boys in love with dungeons, dragons, warrior women, pot, boobs, and four-letter words. That this is the work of David Gordon Green beggars the imagination. One of its heroes wears the penis of a Minotaur on a string around his neck. I hate it when that happens.

This is the kind of farce Mel Brooks did ever so much better in *Robin Hood: Men in Tights*, and that was far from a good movie. It takes place in medieval days on a planet that looks like Earth except it has two moons—or maybe it only looks like two moons when the characters smoke that funny-looking pipe. I don't know how much money it cost, but I hope the money all went into sets, costumes, and special effects, because the screenplay cowritten by Danny McBride is so hopeless he doesn't even write himself a good role, and he plays the lead.

Can you believe the film also stars Natalie Portman, James Franco, Zooey Deschanel, Justin Theroux, and Charles Dance? Why did they do it? Maybe because David Gordon Green's previous film was a nice stoner comedy named *Pineapple Express* and they figured he could do it again? McBride, Green, and Deschanel worked before on a good movie named *All the Real Girls*, but that film came from a different time and a different David Gordon Green.

What calamity has befallen him? He carried my hopes. His first three features were *George Washington* (2000), *All the Real Girls* (2003), and *Undertow* (2004), and I gave all three four stars. I was in the hospital when he released *Snow Angels*, but it got good reviews. Then came *Pineapple Express*, produced by Judd Apatow, which was a pretty good Apatow-style movie, and I figured, all right, David wanted to see how it would feel to have a real budget and work with actors such as Seth Rogen, James Franco, Kevin Corrigan, Rosie Perez, and McBride (his buddy from college days). That was fair enough.

Now comes *Your Highness*. The movie is a perplexing collapse of judgment. Assume for the sake of argument that David thought the time had come for him to direct a farce. Fair enough. One with a severed cyclops head, an emasculated Minotaur, damsels in distress, crowds of witless extras, a castle, hydras, and . . . a mechanical bird? OK, they come with the territory. Not so much the bird. But why this screenplay? What did they think would be funny? They're satirizing a genre that nobody goes to see when it's played straight. It's sad when good actors dress funny and go through material more suitable for a campfire skit on the closing night of summer camp.

One strange thing about the movie is the relentless obscenity in the dialogue. I don't have the slightest difficulty with the f-word or most other words, as themselves. What I don't understand is why almost every single sentence has to be filled with them. Why is that funny? Was I supposed to be "shocked"? Was it intended as daring? It's puerile.

I mentioned boobs. Yes, there are a lot of boobs in this movie. But not much interest in women. Zooey Deschanel plays the intended bride of Franco, the son of the king. She's brought onstage, quickly kidnapped by an evil sorcerer, spends a good deal of time as a captive in his lair, is rescued, and lives happily ever after. She might as well be a mannequin, for all she's given to say and do. This intelligent, nuanced actress, standing there baffled. Used as a placeholder.

Natalie Portman is the Xena clone, a fierce warrior, laid on for anime fans who seem to regard such characters as masturbatory fantasies. She, too, has no personality, although she has more dialogue, all of it expressing clichés of steely determination.

Franco is likable. Likable? That's not good enough for a hero.

McBride's character is pathetic, not in a good way. Rasmus Hardiker plays Courtney, the king's aide, who comes along on the quest so he can basically stand there and look at stuff. Oh, what a sad movie this is. David Gordon Green has made great films. He should remind himself of that.

Youth Without Youth

(DIRECTED BY FRANCIS FORD COPPOLA; STARRING TIM ROTH, ALEXANDRA MARIA LARA; 2007)

Youth Without Youth proves that Francis Ford Coppola can still make a movie, but not that he still knows how to choose his projects. The film is a sharp disappointment to those who have been waiting for ten years since the master's last film. The best that can be hoped is that, having made a film, Coppola has the taste again and will go on to make many more, nothing like this.

His story involves Dominic (Tim Roth), a seventy-year-old Romanian linguist who fears he will die alone and with his life's work unfinished, so he decides to kill himself. Before he can do that, he is struck by a bolt of lightning that should have turned him into a steaming puddle, but instead lands him in a hospital, burned to a crisp. Then a peculiar process begins. He starts to grow younger. His hair thickens and loses its gray. His rotten teeth are pushed out by new ones. His skin heals. His health returns.

It is the eve of World War II, and Dominic becomes of intense interest to the scientists of the Third Reich. Perhaps Hitler thinks his wounded soldiers can be made whole, or that he himself can turn back the march of time. Dominic, now hale and hearty, finds himself in Switzerland being seduced by a sexy German spy, when one day he sees, or thinks he sees, a woman on a mountain hike who resembles Laura, the lost love of his youth. This is Veronica (Alexandra Maria Lara), who is, wouldn't you know, struck by lightning and starts to grow older. In the process, she regresses backward in linguistic time and begins speaking Sanskrit, Babylonian, and perhaps even the Ur language from which all others descended.

This is exciting beyond all measure to Dominic, who has researched the origins of language, but it is also heartbreaking, because he seems to have had his lost love restored to him, only to be taken away by the implacable advance of age. Coppola found this story in a novella by the Romanian Mircea Eliade, for many years a professor of history of religions at the University of Chicago. It is possible to see how it might have been simplified and clarified into an entertainment along the lines of *Time After Time,* but Coppola seems to positively embrace the obscurity and impenetrability of the material.

There is such a thing as a complex film that rewards additional viewing and study, but *Youth Without Youth,* I am afraid, is no more than it seems: a confusing slog through metaphysical murkiness. That it is so handsomely photographed and mounted, and acted with conviction, only underlines the narrative confusion. We know from interviews that the story means a great deal to Coppola, at the same age as his protagonist. But his job is to make it mean a great deal to us. He is a great filmmaker, and I am sure this film is only a deep, shuddering breath before he makes another masterpiece.

index
• • • • • • • • •

U

V

W

X

Y